Mozambique's Cabo Delgado Conflict

This book uses a multidisciplinary approach to examine the ongoing conflict in Mozambique's Cabo Delgado province, which has killed thousands and displaced a million people since 2017.

The book investigates how the conflict developed, the regional and international responses and its wider implications. From a broad range of African perspectives, the book addresses issues related to the conflict including international humanitarian law, regional security and terrorism. Part I assesses the regional security concerns of the conflict, the success of cross-border counter-terrorism operations and their implications for the southern African region. Part II focuses on the conflict in relation to international humanitarian law. It discusses the Islamic State's presence in the region, the trajectory and issues pertaining to sexual and gender-based violence and the relationship between the conflict and the environment. Finally, Part III examines regional and continental responses to the conflict, from the military intervention by the Southern African Development Community and Rwanda, to the perceived inaction of the African Union.

The first comprehensive analysis of the conflict in Cabo Delgado, this book will be of interest to scholars and practitioners of international humanitarian law, security, African politics, war and conflict studies, terrorism and human rights.

Marko Svicevic is Lecturer and Researcher at the Centre for International Humanitarian and Operational Law at Palacký University in Olomouc, Czech Republic, and Post-doctoral Research Fellow with the South African Research Chair in International Law at the University of Johannesburg, South Africa.

Martha M. Bradley is Associate Professor in the Department of Public Law at the University of Johannesburg, South Africa, and External Expert at the Centre for International Humanitarian and Operational Law at Palacký University in Olomouc, Czech Republic.

Routledge Studies in Peace, Conflict and Security in Africa
Edited by Cyril Obi
Social Science Research Council, New York, USA

4. **Human Security and Sustainable Development in East Africa**
   Edited by Jeremiah O. Asaka and Alice A. Oluoko-Odingo

5. **Living through Crisis by Lake Chad**
   Violence, Labor and Resources
   Alessio Iocchi

6. **Youth-Led Social Movements and Peacebuilding in Africa**
   Ibrahim Bangura

7. **Rural Violence in Contemporary Nigeria**
   The State, Criminality and National Security
   Edited by Usman A. Tar and Bashir Bala

8. **Disarmament, Demobilisation and Reintegration of Ex-Combatants in Africa**
   Edited by Ibrahim Bangura

9. **Conflict Management and Resolution in South Sudan**
   Edited by Nelson Alusala, Emmaculate Asige Liaga and Martin Revai Rupiya

10. **Banditry and the Security Crisis in Nigeria**
    Edited by Al Chukwuma Okoli and Saliou Ngom

11. **Traditional Authority and Security in Contemporary Nigeria**
    Edited by David Ehrhardt, David Oladimeji Alao and M. Sani Umar

12. **Mozambique's Cabo Delgado Conflict**
    International Humanitarian Law and Regional Security
    Edited by Marko Svicevic and Martha M. Bradley

For more information about this series, please visit: www.routledge.com/Routledge-Studies-in-Peace-Conflict-and-Security-in-Africa/book-series/RSPCSA

Mozambique's Cabo Delgado Conflict

International Humanitarian Law and Regional Security

Edited by Marko Svicevic and Martha M. Bradley

Routledge
Taylor & Francis Group
LONDON AND NEW YORK

First published 2024
by Routledge
4 Park Square, Milton Park, Abingdon, Oxon OX14 4RN

and by Routledge
605 Third Avenue, New York, NY 10158

Routledge is an imprint of the Taylor & Francis Group, an informa business

British Library Cataloguing-in-Publication Data
A catalogue record for this book is available from the British Library

ISBN: 978-1-032-32989-5 (hbk)
ISBN: 978-1-032-32990-1 (pbk)
ISBN: 978-1-003-31764-7 (ebk)

DOI: 10.4324/9781003317647

Typeset in Times New Roman
by Apex CoVantage, LLC

Contents

Acknowledgements

As with any project such as this one, successful completion is rarely achieved alone. The editors are grateful to everyone who was involved in the production and completion of this edited volume. In no specific order, the editors wish to acknowledge the following persons and institutions. The editors are grateful to all the authors for their timely contributions and without whom this book would not have succeeded: Professor Elmarie Fourie, Head of the Department of Public Law at the University of Johannesburg, who accommodated the necessary time needed to complete this book; Ms Tamalin Bolus of the International Committee of the Red Cross and Professor Stuart Maslen from the University of Pretoria, who were indispensable in providing advice and meticulously reviewing multiple versions of this work; Professor Sandesh Sivakumaran, DHET Future Professors Program Mentor, for his continued guidance and willingness to answer every late-night email received; Ms Jessie Phyffer, who proved invaluable to the editors in finalising the book; the peer reviewers, who took time to review chapters and ensure quality output; and Professor Erika de Wet at the Institute for International Law and International Relations (Faculty of Law, University of Graz) and the Land Steiermark Senior Fellowship, where the manuscript was written to its completion.

The editors wish to especially thank Professor Hennie Strydom, holder of the South African Research Chair in International Law (SARCIL), who supported and contributed to this project through mentorship and financial support from its very inception, and Dr Martin Faix, Dr Petr Stejskal and the team at the Centre for International Humanitarian and Operational Law of the Faculty of Law of Palacký University, for all their advice, support and mentorship. The completion of this book is owed to the generous financial support of these institutions.

The editors are also thankful to the language editors, Dr Walter McKay and Ms Isabeau de Meyer, for their meticulous and thorough reviews, and to Mr Freddy Mukodzeri, SARCIL financial officer who oversaw the handling of finances related to the project. The editors would also like to thank Danielle Crafford for her meticulous review of the final text.

Finally, the editors are grateful to Helena Hurd, Alexandra de Brauw, Rosie Anderson, Katie Stokes and the Series Editor, Cyril Obi, for their dedication to see this project to fruition.

International board of reviewers

Contributors

Editors

Martha M. Bradley Associate Professor, Department of Public Law, University of Johannesburg, Johannesburg, South Africa; External Expert, Centre for International Humanitarian and Operational Law, Faculty of Law, Palacký University in Olomouc, Olomouc, Czech Republic.

Marko Svicevic Lecturer and researcher, Centre for International Humanitarian and Operational Law, Faculty of Law, Palacký University in Olomouc, Olomouc, Czech Republic; Post-Doctoral Research Fellow, South African Research Chair in International Law, University of Johannesburg, Johannesburg, South Africa.

Authors

Brenda Akia Member, United Nations Committee on the Elimination of Discrimination against Women

Najimdeen Bakare Centre for International Peace and Stability, NUST, Islamabad

Aniel de Beer Research Associate, South African Research Chair in International Law, University of Johannesburg

Ntombizozuko Dyani-Mhango Professor and Head of the Department of Public Law, Faculty of Law, University of Pretoria

Chazanne Grobler Senior Lecturer, School of Law, University of the Witwatersrand

Erick Kabendera Freelance journalist; doctoral candidate, King's College London

Josephat M. Kilonzo Lecturer, Strathmore Law School, Nairobi, Kenya; Doctoral candidate, University of Pretoria

Emma Charlene Lubaale School of Law and Criminology, University of Greenwich; Research Associate, Faculty of Law, Rhodes University

Annelize McKay Professor and Head: Division of Law, School of Business, Law and Social Science, Abertay University

Ayodele Ojedokun Doctoral candidate, Department of Public Law, University of Pretoria

Jessie Phyffer LLD candidate, University of Pretoria.

Jeanique Serradinho Disaster Law Coordinator for Southern Africa, International Federation of Red Cross and Red Crescent Societies.

Egna Sidumo Doctoral researcher and Ph.D. student, Christian Michelsen Institute, University of Bergen.

André Smit Former State Law Advisor (International Law), Government of the Republic of South Africa

Hennie Strydom South African Research Chair in International Law, University of Johannesburg; Professor of International Law, Faculty of Law, University of Johannesburg

Dire Tladi South African Research Chair in International Constitutional Law, University of Pretoria; Future Africa Chair in Global Equity and Professor of International Law, University of Pretoria

Quillene M. Vertue Doctoral candidate, South African Research Chair in International Constitutional Law, University of Pretoria

Gus Waschefort Associate Professor, Essex Law School and Human Rights Centre; Barrister, Guernica 37 Chambers, London

Foreword

The violent Islamic insurgency by Ansar al-Sunna between 2017 and 2021 in northern Mozambique has claimed the lives of more than 3000 civilians and has caused the displacement of close to a million people. The implications for domestic and regional security increased in nature and scope with the insurgents' deadly attack on Palma in March 2021, which also impacted significantly on the region's economic development potential in the wake of the discovery of and foreign investment in the biggest gas reserves in Africa. While this development in the conflict raised regional and international concerns about the spread of and capabilities of militant Islamic groups in the southeastern parts of Africa, it also laid bare the many and varied roots of the conflict, which, in no small measure, were nourished by a long-standing discontent among the inhabitants of the region about the political and economic marginalisation they were subjected to. Like in so many other conflicts in Africa, the situation in northern Mozambique is made worse and more difficult to resolve by a thriving cross-border illicit economy which thrives on the back of weak and corrupt state institutions and poor law enforcement.

This well-researched and commendable volume will further enlighten the reader about the historical context of the conflict, and, more importantly, its national, regional, legal and security ramifications. These aspects and more are covered in 16 chapters, which focus on contemporary and topical issues relating to conflicts of this kind and which have a specific relevance for the continent and the region. In summary, the contributions cover cross-border cooperation in combating insurgencies; security concerns of neighbouring countries; Mozambique's double jeopardy: armed conflict and natural disasters; the relationship between the insurgents and the Islamic State; the classification of the conflict in terms of the law of armed conflict; the labelling of the insurgents – terrorists or armed group; sexual and gender-based violence during the conflict; the protection of the environment in the context of the armed conflict; the relationship between international disaster response law and international humanitarian law; the COVID-19 pandemic and its implications for the law of non-international armed conflicts; third-generation disarmament, demobilisation and reintegration programmes in Cabo Delgado; the use of private military companies to counter the insurgency; the Southern African Development Community mission in Mozambique and its legality; and the African Union's right to intervene.

While there are signs that Ansar al-Sunna's capacity to undertake large-scale and high-profile attacks has been destroyed, at least for the moment, the threat is far from over. The group's capacity to launch guerrilla-type attacks still exists, and attacks on villages and the killing of civilians have not come to an end. According to the 2023 Human Rights Watch World Report, the humanitarian situation has also worsened, making the ongoing displacement of people inevitable. It therefore seems that post-Palma developments further underscore the importance of this volume, and the editors and contributing authors must be commended for this initiative.

Hennie Strydom
Professor of International Law and incumbent
of the South African Research Chair in
International Law, University of Johannesburg

1 Introduction

The evolving conflict in northern Mozambique and the rise of Ansar al-Sunna

Egna Sidumo, Marko Svicevic and Martha M. Bradley

1.1 Introduction

Salafi-jihadi insurgencies, led by groups affiliated with Al-Qaeda and the Islamic State (IS) (both two major brands of jihadism), are growing across much of Africa.[1] From North Africa to the East, an increasing number of countries are fighting against IS and Al-Qaeda insurgencies, with Mozambique and the Democratic Republic of the Congo being those that have non-state groups active on its territory with direct links to IS in the region.[2] After its fall in the Middle East, IS has moved much of its attention to Africa, where it has been able to build a network of official and non-official provinces and supporters that conduct attacks and control territory.[3] Mozambique now seems to be a part of this network.

The development of the violence in Mozambique has over time gained international interest in part due to alleged links with IS and the threat of such violence spilling across borders.[4] The consolidation of Islamic State Mozambique (ISIS-M), more commonly known as *Ansar al-Sunna*, as a province of the Islamic State Central Africa Province (ISCAP), aims to establish a base for future attacks inside and beyond Mozambique, threatening the stability of both the country and the region. Although in general Ansar al-Sunna acts autonomously as a subordinate that benefits from its affiliation with ISIS to obtain branding,[5] a greater involvement with the transnational network of IS through other affiliates in Africa is possible,[6] which could worsen the situation of violence not only in Mozambique but in the wider region.

According to the United Nations (UN) Population Fund, in 2022, Mozambique had a population of approximately 33.1 million people.[7] The country's population consists of a range of ethnic and linguistic groups,[8] of which the major ethnic groups include that of the Makua, the Makonde, the Sena and the Shona.[9] Mozambique's official language is Portuguese, which is spoken by the majority of the population.[10] With approximately 62 per cent of its population living and working in rural areas,[11] Mozambique is characterised as a predominantly rural country[12] and with high levels of poverty.[13] Although Mozambique has ample natural resources, including arable land, sufficient water, mineral resources, energy and natural offshore gas, as well as deep seaports, the country battles a multitude of challenges, including political instability, frequent and severe natural disasters and

DOI: 10.4324/9781003317647-1

ongoing violence in some of its regions.[14] Nevertheless, despite these many challenges, Mozambique has made advances in a number of important areas, such as increasing its population's access to education and healthcare services, reducing child mortality rates and expanding economic opportunities.[15]

In October 2017, the first acts of organised violence were registered in the province of Cabo Delgado. An unknown group reportedly consisting of some 30 individuals attacked a string of police stations in Mocímboa da Praia, a port town within proximity of Tanzania.[16] Following this incident, Mozambican authorities closed a number of mosques and detained more than 300 people including religious leaders and foreigners, mostly Tanzanians.[17] The suspects were accused of being linked to the violent attacks.[18] However, these actions did little to prevent the rise of Ansar al-Sunna. Since then, attacks have spread across the region to the south of Cabo Delgado and in the neighbouring provinces of Nampula and Niassa, threatening economic investments and the safety of entire populations.[19]

1.2 The causes of violence

Initially, the Mozambican government portrayed the violence as acts committed by disgruntled youths who may have been exploited by foreign groups to commit violence and destabilise Mozambique.[20] However, by 2021, the group, referred to locally as Al-Shabaab ('the youth'), or Ansar al-Sunnah, had been able to deal significant blows to the military forces of Mozambique.[21] Motivated by a brand of fundamentalist Islam, the group developed ties over the years with the Al-Shabaab (Somalia) and the ISCAP, further enabling it to expand in geographical scope, strategic coordination, and sophistication.[22] As a result, Mozambique sought international assistance to fight against the group. The Mozambican government requested military assistance from the government of Rwanda, as well as accepted troops offered by the Southern African Development Community (SADC).[23] Mozambique has also received military and humanitarian aid from the European Union (EU),[24] the United States,[25] and several other countries and organisations.[26]

In 2019 Mozambique's President Filipe Nyusi for the first time used the term 'terrorism' to classify the nature of the violence which had spread across Cabo Delgado. However, the official recognition of the presence of terrorists in Mozambique took place only in April the following year, when the National Defence and Security Council stated that Mozambique was facing an 'external aggression perpetrated by terrorists'.[27] Prior to this, the approach of the Mozambican government was somewhat confusing, characterised by the extensive use of force and aggression, with the support of private military companies, such as the Russian Wagner Group and the South African Dyck Advisory Group (DAG). Its reliance particularly on these private military companies resulted in the Mozambican government being accused of a lack of transparency in hiring these companies, and DAG abandoned its operations in Mozambique with serious accusations of human rights violations. Amnesty International, through a report published in March 2021,[28] accused DAG of committing war crimes and violating international humanitarian law by firing machine guns from helicopters and throwing hand grenades indiscriminately at crowds and civilian infrastructure, including homes and hospitals.[29]

Over the years, terrorist tactics have allowed Ansar al-Sunna to gain control over the headquarters of the districts of Quissanga (March 2020), Macomia (May 2020), Mocímboa da Praia (August 2020)[30] and Palma (March 2021), causing an unprecedented humanitarian crisis. The Palma attack of 2021 was a turning point in the conflict in so far as its international visibility concerns: first, because it took place a few kilometres from the area of the security belt for massive investments in the gas sector and, second, because it forced the immediate suspension of total investments in the region.[31] These developments finally prompted a regional response. First was the deployment of Rwandan troops, which was then followed swiftly by the deployment of the SADC Mission in Mozambique (SAMIM).[32]

Scholars argue that the outburst of violent extremism in Cabo Delgado is due largely to a cocktail of interconnected internal factors: from socio-economic and socio-political factors to cultural and religious factors and factors related to the lack of public security that allowed illicit activities to flourish.[33] In addition, recent reports point out that except for natural conservation areas in Cabo Delgado, almost all land in the province has been given on concession to prospectors, investors, and mining companies, reinforcing the arguments according to which the main cause of the conflict in Cabo Delgado was the interest of global powers, allied with national political elites.[34] Giving away control of these resources in Cabo Delgado[35] has led to widespread dissatisfaction among hundreds of illegal foreign miners, mostly Tanzanians, who operated in the Rubi areas in Montepuez.[36] With the increasing control and fight against illegal mining by the Mozambican authorities between 2017 and 2018, some are of the opinion that these groups took advantage of economic, social, and even religious weaknesses to promote and equip the group of insurgents that grew and gained new contours over time in Cabo Delgado.[37]

Another relevant perspective put forward is that Mozambique's decision to explore natural resources in Cabo Delgado was taken without proper consideration. These considerations include the prevailing poverty situation of the communities in Cabo Delgado and previous tensions in the area related to the 2005 riots when members of Frente de Libertação de Moçambique (FRELIMO) – the ruling party in Mozambique and Resistência Nacional Moçambicana (RENAMO) – the largest opposition party, clashed after holding an early election that was won by FRELIMO.[38] The Mozambican government had further mishandled the issue of illegal miners, mostly foreigners, who operated in the vicinity of the ruby mines in Montepuez,[39] and warnings from local clerics in Mocímboa da Praia about the emergence of new forms and versions of the Islamic religion were not taken seriously by the government.[40]

Bonate[41] argues that the conflict has emerged out of a local Mozambican intra-Islamic and inter-generational fight between two factions sharing the same religious outlook but with a different political orientation rather than due to the influence of an outside radical jihadi force with the purpose of imposing Shari'a law.[42] Other scholars such as Bekoe and others point to external causes linked to the migration of radicalised people from Kenya and Somalia who promoted a brand of Islamist extremism popularised by the late Kenyan cleric Aboud Rogo Mohammed.[43]

Finally, it is worth noting that violence in Mozambique is not a new phenomenon, and the rise today of Ansar al-Sunna exploiting marginalised communities can be directly traced back to Mozambique's War of Independence. From 1964, Mozambique was involved in a bitter war against its Portuguese coloniser. That war only came to an end some 10 years later in 1974. It will be recalled that the beginning of FRELIMO's attacks against Portuguese positions took place in Cabo Delgado from Tanzania. Despite its formal independence in 1975, a decade of war had torn the country apart. What followed only two years post-independence was Mozambique's civil war, with estimates of some one million people killed and millions more displaced. These conflicts no doubt left already-marginalised populations vulnerable, and despite numerous reconstruction programmes, the country and Cabo Delgado in particular remain ravaged by poverty and unemployment.

1.3 The impact of violence

The result of nearly six years of violence in northern Mozambique has been staggering. Violence in Mozambique has had a significant impact on the lives of Mozambicans and displaced populations that face restrictions on freedom of movement and a lack of documents and employment, increasing their vulnerabilities and propensity to join criminal and radical groups. Mozambique currently has approximately one million internally displaced persons (IDPs), mainly in Cabo Delgado and Nampula. Until the latest attacks that affected the districts of Ancuabe,[44] Montepuez[45] and Chiure[46] in Cabo Delgado, and Erati[47] and Memba[48] in Nampula for the first time, the southern districts of Cabo Delgado and the Nampula province were considered the safest, and thousands of people have moved into these areas during the last five years of the conflict. However, in recent times the situation has been changing with reports of attacks coming from almost all districts of the province of Cabo Delgado as well as neighbouring provinces.[49] While there is a considerable spread of violence across the southern districts of Cabo Delgado, the Mozambican authorities and the International Organisation for Migration[50] have reported in recent months the return to Macomia of displaced populations that were scattered mainly in the Ancuabe and Chiure districts.

IDPs that faced violence in their origin communities or discrimination in the displaced centres are returning to areas previously controlled by the insurgency.[51] There are reports that Ansar al-Sunna has been changing their violent strategy from murder and pillage of villages to a strategy of less violent means, to gain greater sympathy from these communities.[52] This in turn may further entrench the insurgency and could cause greater retaliatory violence against vulnerable IDP populations by military forces if they agree to collaborate and join rebel groups and by insurgent groups if they refuse.[53]

There is a widespread idea that the repression of terrorism should encompass both hard and soft measures.[54] With the arrival of foreign troops in Mozambique, the repression against organised violence gained new proportions. New areas have been attacked, and there are difficulties in assisting displaced people who are distributed in various centres. These problems are exacerbated by the decision of the World Food Programme to cut food aid that has assisted almost a million people.[55] Moreover, there remains a significant void in Mozambique's strategy to deal with the violence.

1.4 Combating violent extremism

Countering violent extremism or preventing violent extremism refers to the 'soft' side of counterterrorism[56] strategies that tackle the drivers that lead people to engage in politically or ideologically motivated violence and aims to engage with the individual causes at the micro level.[57] Officially, Mozambique does not yet seem to be implementing a sufficiently prepared strategy to prevent and contain violent extremism.[58] However, the government and civil society organisations (CSOs) have implemented isolated initiatives in an attempt to adjust their actions to *prevent and contain* violent extremism strategy.[59] Such actions take place in the context of disarticulation, leaving some level of distrust and lack of clarity between the government and CSOs. According to Sidumo,[60] the new initiatives approved at the legal and political levels, despite being ambitious, do not seem to be sufficient to contain violence for several reasons. These include not paying enough attention to poverty, unemployment, and exclusion as the main causes of the violence. In addition, initiatives taken because of international pressure appear to be uncoordinated, and there are no effective mechanisms capable of guaranteeing that the objectives for which they were created will be met. There is also a significant lack of international funding for the number of projects that Mozambique needs to implement to address multiple challenges related to the violence.

What remains far clearer is that Mozambique has adopted a military-first strategy to combat violent extremism in Cabo Delgado. This has been particularly evident with the arrival of Rwandan troops, which, in addition to countering Ansar al-Sunna, have also become involved in rebuilding efforts. This has allowed the Rwandan government to present their deployment as the dominant protagonist. Additionally, Rwanda has benefited from support from the European Peace Facility to increase the continued deployment of Rwandan military personnel to combat armed violence and contracts to implement resettlement projects for displaced persons in Cabo Delgado. Whether these efforts will prove to be a long-term solution remains to be seen.

1.5 Structure of book and its core issues

The contributions to this edited volume address a variety of aspects from an international humanitarian law perspective and a regional security dimension. Part I examines regional security issues, many of which are neither unique nor limited to Cabo Delgado but represent a growing concern across Southern Africa. Kabendera departs with an assessment of the ongoing cooperation between Mozambique and Tanzania and their joint efforts in stemming the insurgency in Cabo Delgado. Smit then examines the security concerns that have arisen for the regional powerhouse, South Africa, as a direct result of events in northern Mozambique. In Chapter 4 Phyffer explores the intersection between armed conflict and climate change. Specifically, she discusses the consequences of climate change aggravating already dire circumstances of a state in the middle of an armed conflict. Thereafter, de Beer considers the link between IS and Ansar al-Sunna from an international law perspective, given the latter's recent pledge of allegiance to IS.

Part II then delves into issues of IHL. IHL has been selected as the appropriate focus corresponding to operational demands and the reality of the situation in Cabo Delgado.[61] The themes that have been addressed are in response to issues raised by the International Committee of the Red Cross (ICRC) as needing legal interrogation.[62] As a point of departure, it is noted that for the application of IHL an armed conflict must exist, but no international body is officially tasked with making that classification. The hesitancy by governments to publicly admit that they are involved in a non-international armed conflict delays the debate around classification. To our knowledge, by the end of June 2023, the Mozambican government has not publicly deemed the situation in Cabo Delgado an armed conflict and employs labels such as 'insurrection', 'sporadic violence', 'extremism' and 'terrorism'.

The current situation in Cabo Delgado is identified as constituting a non-international armed conflict. The parties to the conflict are the Mozambican armed forces and Ansar al-Sunna. The *Tadić* formulation, which defines the notion 'non-international armed conflict', requires that minimum thresholds inherent in the notions of organisation[63] and intensity are met.[64] The notion of organisation requires the military wing of a non-state actor party to the conflict to meet a minimum degree of organisation, and the notion of intensity asserts that the severity of the fighting between parties to the conflict equates to protracted armed violence.[65] Only when the *Tadić* thresholds are met does a situation cross over from a domestic law enforcement paradigm to the realm of the law of non-international armed conflict.[66]

The complex religious and political situation in Mozambique, as well as the anonymity of the leaders of Ansar al-Sunna, has proved a challenge in determining the structure of the group.[67] Additionally, the relationship between the group and IS is not clear.[68] On these points, the analysis of the organisational structure of the *Walendu-Bindi Collectivité* by Trial Chamber II in the *Katanga* case is of assistance and indicates that, at a minimum, a non-state fighting unit must be able to organise itself to the extent that it can execute a military attack.[69] The continuing attacks on the Mozambican armed forces compelled the Mozambican government to request neighbouring countries, including Tanzania, Rwanda and South Africa, and private security contractors for assistance in fighting Ansar al-Sunna.[70] Clearly, Ansar al-Sunna is sufficiently organised to engage in military attacks. It should be mentioned that the nationality of fighters does not impact the classification of the conflict. The assessment is solely made on the organisational indicators. It is therefore irrelevant for IHL whether or not Ansar al-Sunna fighters are Mozambican nationals or not.

A second question relates to establishing whether the nature of violence in Cabo Delgado between parties to the conflict equates to protracted armed violence.[71] Case law has developed various indicators to facilitate the assessment of whether a situation is sufficiently intense to equate to a level of protracted armed violence.[72] In the *Haradinaj* case,[73] the Trial Chamber considered how, in practice, the criterion of 'protracted violence' was established by examining case law.[74] The Trial Chamber concluded that to determine whether violence was protracted in nature, the following indicative factors need to be considered: the number, duration and intensity of individual confrontations; the type of weapons and other military equipment used; the number and calibre of munitions fired; the number of persons and type of forces partaking in the fighting; the number of casualties; the extent of material destruction; and the number of civilians fleeing combat zones. The involvement of the UN Security Council may also be a reflection of the intensity of a conflict.[75] The involvement of SADC and outside military forces on the invitation of the Mozambican government is indeed an indicator of protracted armed violence – yet does not impact the classification of the situation and the conflict remains non-international in nature.

Ansar al-Sunna has been able to launch coordinated military attacks, the most notable example being the attack on the town of Palma in March 2021.[76] Further, the group has deployed relatively large fighting units. For example, hundreds of fighters were involved in the battle in the town of Mocímboa da Praia in August 2020.[77] The group's battlefield tactics have developed since 2017 and more sophisticated weaponry than AK 47 rifles and occasional PKM machine guns are employed than initially in 2017.[78] Reportedly, Ansar al-Sunna's arsenal now includes racks of RPG-7 rocket launchers and multiple 60- and 82-millimetre mortar firing systems.[79] Ansar al-Sunna has been so successful that the Mozambican government has enlisted assistance from the Wagner and Dyck private security groups,[80] as well as the armed forces of neighbouring states.[81] Regional organisations such as SADC and the AU have become involved.[82]

It is estimated that by May 2021 more than 800 000 people were internally displaced as a consequence of the fighting in the Cabo Delgado region.[83] Clearly, the situation meets the protracted armed violence requirement; at the time of writing, there is an ongoing armed conflict in Cabo Delgado, Mozambique.

In Chapter 6, Bakare and Ojedokun examine the possibility of whether the situation in Cabo Delgado constitutes an Additional Protocol II-type non-international armed conflict. The editors of this volume agree with the interpretation that establishing the requirements demanded by article 1(1) of Additional Protocol II is a functional assessment in that the factual determination of the existence of certain requirements infers territorial control. In theory, even if Additional Protocol II is not triggered, the discussion is a valid interpretation of the situation as many norms in this instrument reflect or have achieved customary status under IHL.[84]

Chapter 7, 'Ansar al-Sunna (IS-affiliates) engaging in a mosaic of violence in Mozambique: terrorists, rebels or both – legal implications and challenges' by Waschefort, Phyffer and Bradley, explores complex legal issues in cases where a group traditionally considered a terrorist organisation can also be considered an organised armed group in an armed conflict as defined under IHL.

Chapter 8 by Lubaale and Akia tackles the serious and pertinent issue of sexual and gender-based violence (SGBV) during armed conflict and specifically examines the situation in Cabo Delgado. According to Human Rights Watch, at least 600 women and girls have been kidnapped and enslaved between 2018 and 2021.[85] Women and girls are the victims of forced marriage at the hands of Ansar al-Sunna.[86] Reports suggest that SGBV crimes have been committed by government forces and by Ansar al-Sunna.[87]

Chapters 9, 10 and 11 of this contribution then reflect on the protection of the environment in Cabo Delgado as well as on the relationship between conflict and the impact of climate change and COVID-19 in Mozambique. Environmental damage is serious collateral of the violence generated in a non-international armed conflict.[88] The damage arises, for example, from the burning of huts, fields and, at times, entire villages.[89] In Cabo Delgado, Ansar al-Sunna has not refrained from destroying civilian infrastructure.[90] Despite limited reporting of the damage to the environment in Cabo Delgado, where fighting has been ongoing since 2017, it is reasonable to assume a deterioration in the natural environment. The ICRC's *Twelve Issues for 2022* draws attention to the fact that the consequence of conflict-related environmental damage is compounded by an intensifying climate crisis.[91]

Natural disasters inherently are destructive to the natural environment. Mozambique, specifically the Cabo Delgado region, was struck by cyclones Idai and Kenneth. These natural disasters occurred at the same time as the ongoing non-international armed conflict. Chapter 9, titled 'Towards protecting the environment in Cabo Delgado: Looking beyond the existing legal framework and engaging Ansar al-Sunna' by Vertue is a response highlighting the obligation of both parties to the conflict to protect the environment in Cabo Delgado.

Chapter 10 by Serradinho titled 'The conflict in Cabo Delgado and the relationship between international disaster response law and international humanitarian law treaties' examines how IHL, IDL and IDRL relate to one another as different bodies of law in mixed and parallel situations of disaster and armed conflict.

Chapter 11, authored by McKay, Grobler and Bradley, considers the implications of COVID-19 on the conflict in Cabo Delgado. The COVID-19 pandemic exacerbated existing humanitarian needs, including heightening the difficulty in aiding those affected by the conflict. The internal conflict between the Mozambican government and Ansar al-Sunna is governed by the law of non-international armed conflict that provides protective measures for the affected population. However, the COVID-19 pandemic raises a question of whether the current rules are sufficient to protect the rights of those affected during a public health crisis. The final chapter of Part II of this edited volume explores this overall question.

Part III of this book specifically examines the involvement of the AU and SADC as an element of the regional and continental responses to the conflict. Kilonzo begins with an examination of the potential of rights-based third-generation disarmament, demobilisation and reintegration's suitability in Mozambique. Strydom subsequently tackles the issue of private military company (PMSCs) use in Cabo Delgado. The use of PMSCs continues to be an evolving challenge to international law and their increased use, particularly by the Russian Federation, represents a new wave of influence in Africa. Svicevic then examines the intervention in Cabo Delgado by SAMIM under the guise of international law and undertakes a comparative analysis of earlier SADC operations. In this same context, Tladi evaluates the use of military force by SADC and Rwanda against non-state actors in international law. Finally, Dyani-Mhango considers the role and right of the AU to intervene in the ongoing conflict.

Notes

1 Emily Estelle Perez and Jessica Trisko Darden, 'Combating the Islamic State's Spread in Africa: Assessment and Recommendations for Mozambique' *American Enterprise Institute* (24 February 2021) 3–4.
2 See UN Doc. S/2023/95 (13 February 2023) 6–8.
3 Jason Warner and others, *The Islamic State in Africa. The Emergence, Evolution and Future of the Next Jihadist Battlefront* (Hurts Publishing 2021) 14–16.
4 The conflict in Mozambique gained international attention after the widely publicised attacks on Palma. See Christina Goldbaum, 'Insurgents Seize Mozambique Town, Killing Several People; Fate of Hundreds Unknown' *The New York Times* (27 March 2021).
5 Warner and others (n 3) 19.
6 Austin Doctor, 'After Palma: Assessing the Islamic State's Position in Northern Mozambique' *George Washington Program on Extremisms* (August 2022) 19.
7 UNFPA, 'World Population Dashboard – Mozambique' (2023).
8 WHO, 'Data – Mozambique'; UN, UNDATA Statistics-Mozambique (2023).
9 Ibid.
10 Ibid.
11 The World Bank, 'The World Bank in Mozambique'.
12 WHO (n 8).
13 UNFPA (n 7).
14 Ibid.
15 Ibid.
16 'Armed Men Attack Police Stations in Mocímboa da Praia – AIM Report' *Club of Mozambique* (5 October 2017).
17 'Mozambique Cracks Down on Tanzanians Accused of Terrorism' *Business Day* (28 December 2017); Gregory Pirio, Robert Pittelli and Yussuf Adam, 'The Emergence of Violent Extremism in Northern Mozambique' *Africa Centre for Strategic Studies* (25 March 2018); Nadia Issufo, 'Encerramento de mesquitas em Moçambique: Justa ou exagerada?' *DW* (22 November 2017).
18 David Matsinhe and Estacio Valoi, 'The Genesis of Insurgency in Northern Mozambique' *Institute for Security Studies* (31 October 2019).
19 'Mozambique, Events of 2022' *Human Rights Watch World Report 2023* <https://www.hrw.org/world-report/2023/country-chapters/mozambique>.
20 '189 Islamist Suspects Stand Trial in Mozambique' *France24* (3 October 2018).
21 Daveed Gartenstein-Ross, Emelie Chace-Donhue and Colin P Clarke, 'The Evolution and Escalation of the Islamic State Threat to Mozambique' *Foreign Policy Research Institute* (13 April 2021).
22 See, broadly, Austin Doctor, 'After Palma: Assessing the Islamic State's Position in Northern Mozambique' *The George Washington University Program on Extremism* (August 2022).
23 Pedro Seabra, 'O Conflito em Cabo Delgado em perspectiva' *Institutoda Defesa Nacional* (2021) 4.
24 'Moçambique pede apoio logístico à União Europeia para combater terrorismo' *RFI* (23 September 2020). See also EU, 'European Union Training Mission in Mozambique'.
25 U.S. Department of State, 'US Relations with Mozambique' (31 October 2022).
26 ICRC, 'Mozambique'; 'Japan Pledges to Help Mozambique Fight "Terrorism"' *Africa News* (5 May 2023).

27 Republic of Mozambique, *National Defence and Security Council Press Release* (2020) <https://www.presidencia.gov.mz/por/layout/set/print/content/download/8757/62236/version/1/file/COMUNICADO+DE+IMPRENSA+23.04.2020+-CNDS+%3D.pdf>.
28 For more details, see Amnesty International, 'Mozambique: "What I Saw Is Death": War Crimes in Mozambique's Forgotten Cape' (2 March 2021).
29 Ibid, 37, 39.
30 U.S. Department of State, 'Country Reports on Terrorism 2020: Mozambique' (2020).
31 Joesph Cotterill and David Keohane, '"Some Hid in the Sea": Islamist Attack on Mozambique Town a Turning Point in Africa's Ignored War' *Financial Times* (6 April 2021).
32 The deployment of Rwandan troops prior to SAMIM seemed to have displeased SADC at the time. See Peter Fabricius, 'Rwanda's Deployment of Forces into Mozambique Irks SADC' *Daily Maverick* (11 July 2021).
33 Saide Habibe, Salvador Forquilha and João Pereira, 'Islamic Radicalisation in Northern Mozambique: The Case of Mocímboa da Praia' *Cadernos IESE* (2019).
34 Luís Nhachote, 'Humanising Security in Cabo Delgado: A CSO Report on the Drivers of Conflict and Its Impact on Civilians' *The Investigative Journalism Centre* (2021).
35 See Padil Salimo, Lars Buur and Jose Macuane, 'The Politics of Domestic Gas: The Sasol Natural Gas Deals in Mozambique' (2020) 7 *The Extractive Industries and Society*.
36 For more details about this argument, see Julia Stanyard and others, 'Insurgency, Illicit Markets and Corruption: The Cabo Delgado Conflict and Its Regional Implications' *Global Initiatives* (23 February 2022) 10–15.
37 Ibid.
38 Ana Margarida Sousa Santos, 'Violence, Rumour, and Elusive Trust in Mocímboa da Praia' (2021) 65 *The International Journal of Anthropology*.
39 Joseph Hanlon, 'Cabo Delgado's History of Violence' *Club of Mozambique* (14 August 2020).
40 International Crisis Group, 'Stemming the Insurrection in Mozambique's Cabo Delgado' (11 June 2021) 6.
41 Liazzat JK Bonate, 'Why the Mozambican Government's Alliance with the Islamic Council of Mozambique Might Not End the Insurgency in Cabo Delgado' *Zitamar News* (2019).
42 Ibid.
43 Aboud Rogo Mohammed was a Kenyan cleric who seems to have contributed to the U.S. embassy bombings in Kenya and Tanzania in 1998. He allegedly provided support to Al-Shabaab in Somalia. His radical teachings condemn the enrichment of elites and corporations at the expense of local populations and, given the economic and political situation in northern Mozambique, this sermon gained traction among aggrieved groups.
44 'Mozambique: Terrorists Attack Village in Ancuabe' *allAfrica* (6 June 2017).
45 'Mozambique: Militants Attack Ruby Mine in Cabo Delgado Province' *Crisis24* (20 October 2022).
46 'Insurgents Threaten Nampula as Attacks Sweep Through Chiure' *Zitamar* (27 October 2022).
47 'Mozambique: Armed Men Attack in Nampula Province – AIM Report' *Club of Mozambique* (5 September 2022).
48 'Mozambique: Terrorist Attack Village in Memba' *allAfrica* (7 September 2022).
49 Egna Sidumo, 'Resilience Factors and Prevention of Radicalisation and Violent Extremism in Mozambique' *USAID* (2022).
50 IOM, 'Displacement Tracking Matrix – Mozambique' (28 December 2022).
51 UN Office for the Coordination of Humanitarian Affairs, '2023 Mozambique Humanitarian Response Plan' (24 February 2023).
52 'Mocímboa da Praia: Relato sugere 'namoro' de insurgentes à população local' *Voz de Cabo Delgado* (27 January 2023).
53 Emily Estelle and Jessica Darden, 'Combating the Islamic State's Spread in Africa' *American Enterprise Institute* (2021).

54 Owen Frazer and Christian Nünlist, 'The Concept of Countering Violent Extremism' *CSS Analyses in Security Policy* (2015).
55 'Mozambique: WFP Suspends Food Aid in February – AIM Report' *Club of Mozambique* (30 January 2023).
56 On disarmament, demobilisation and reintegration, see Chapter 12.
57 Frazer and Nünlist (n 54).
58 Also referred to as PCVE.
59 On Mozambique's Resilience and Development Strategy for the North, see Borges Nhamirre, 'Mozambique Shifts Gear with Its New Strategy for the North' *Institute for Security Studies* (8 February 2022).
60 Sidumo (n 49).
61 This volume concerns itself specifically with the ongoing (at the time of publication) non-international armed conflict between Ansar al-Sunna and the government of Mozambique.
62 These include the application of the law of non-international armed conflict; the relationship between climate change and a situation of armed conflict and determining the applicable legal framework; and the protection of the natural environment against the type of consequences that result from fighting between the parties to the conflicts and are expected to cause long-term, widespread, and severe damage to the natural environment. See also ICRC, *International Humanitarian Law and the Challenges of Contemporary Armed Conflicts* (ICRC 2019) (2019 Challenges Report).
63 For a discussion concerning the minimum threshold of organisation demanded by the *Tadić* criterion, see Tilman Rodenhäuser, *Organizing Rebellion: Non-State Armed Groups Under International Humanitarian Law, Human Rights Law, and International Criminal Law* (OUP 2018), 61–96; Noam Zamir, *Classification of Conflicts in International Humanitarian Law: The Legal Impact of Foreign Intervention in Civil Wars* (Edward Elgar Publishing 2017) 63–69.
64 *Prosecutor v Dusko Tadic a/k/a 'Dule'* (IT-94–1-T) Opinion and Judgment (7 May 1997), para 561; *Prosecutor v Dusko Tadic aka 'Dule'* (IT-94–1-A) Decision on the Defence Motion for Interlocutory Appeal on Jurisdiction (19 July 1998) para 70.
65 For an introduction to the notion of intensity, see Martha M Bradley, 'Additional Protocol II: Elevating the Minimum Threshold of Intensity?' (2020) 102 *ICRC* 1125–1152.
66 *Tadić* (Opinion and Judgment) (n 64) 561; *Tadić* (Decision on Defence Motion) (n 64) para 70.
67 Dorina A Bekoe, Stephanie M Burchard and Sarah A Daly, 'Extremism in Mozambique: Interpreting Group Tactics and the Role of the Government's Response in the Crisis in Cabo Delgado' *Institute for Defence Analysis* (March 2020) 12.
68 Ibid, 8, 12.
69 *Prosecutor v Katanga* (ICC-01/04–01/07) Judgment (7 March 2014) para 681.
70 RULAC, 'Mozambique' *RULAC* (18 May 2023).
71 Ibid.
72 To offer a few examples: *Prosecutor v Zejnil Delalic Zdravko Mucic, also Known as 'Pavo', Hazim Delic Esad Landzo, also Known as 'Zenga'* (IT – 96–21 – T) Judgment, Trial Chamber (16 November 1998), paras 183–192; *Prosecutor v Jean – Paul Akayesu* (ICTR 96–4 – T) Judgment, Trial Chamber I (2 September 1998), para 627. *Prosecutor v Ramush Haradinaj Idriz Balaj Lahi Brahimaj* (IT – 04–84 – T) Judgment, Trial Chamber (3 April 2008) para 49.
73 *Haradinaj* (n 72) para 49.
74 In the *Boškoski* case, the ICTY consideration of cases included *Tadić* (*Tadić* (Decision on the Defence Motion for Interlocutory Appeal on Jurisdiction) (n 65) para 70), *Slobodan Milosevic (Milosevic* (n 73); *Prosecutor v. Kordić and Čerkez* (IT-95–14/2-A) Appeals Chamber Judgment (17 December 2004), Halilovic Indictment (*Prosecutor v Sefer Halilovic* (IT 01–48 – T), Trial Chamber (16 November 2005)); *The Prosecutor v Enver Hadzihasanovic Amir Kubara* (IT – 01–47 – T) Judgment, Trial Chamber (15

March 2006); and *Mrksic & Others* (*Prosecutor v Mile Mrksic, Miroslav Radic, Veselin Sljivancanin* (IT – 95–13/1 – T) Trial Chamber Judgment (27 September 2007)).
75 *Haradinaj* (n 72) para 49.
76 Tim Lister, 'The March 2021 Palma Attack and the Evolving Terror Threat to Mozambique' *Combating Terrorism Center at West Point* (April/May 2021); '40 000 Displaced in North Mozambique After Assault in Palma' *Africanews* (20 April 2021); Stemming the Insurrection in Mozambique (n 40) 18.
77 International Crisis Group (n 40) 18.
78 Ibid.
79 Ibid.
80 Ibid, 1; see also RULAC (n 70).
81 International Crisis Group (above n 40) 1; see also RULAC (n 70).
82 International Crisis Group, 'Winning Peace in Mozambique's Embattled North' (10 February 2022).
83 Save the Children, 'Cabo Delgado: Displaced Children Tell of Lost Parents, Lack of Schooling, Diseases, but Also of Hope in New Report' (19 May 2021).
84 Should intelligence surface that Ansar al-Sunna did not exercise stable military control over territory in Cabo Delgado as required under Additional Protocol II, there is value in the legal analysis grounded in a discussion of Additional Protocol II as most norms inherent in this provision, according to the ICRC's customary study, reflect rules of customary IHL.
85 OCHA, 'Mozambique Gender Based Violence AoR – Rapid GBV Safety Assessment Cyclone Freddy, Nicoadala, Namacura – Zambézia (April 2023)' *Reliefweb* (3 May 2023).
86 Neha Wadekar and Ed Ram, '"Kidnapped, Raped and Trafficked": Women and Girls Exposed to Sexual Violence in War-Torn Mozambique' *Pulitzer Centre* (3 January 2023).
87 Ibid; see also Amnesty International (n 28).
88 ICRC, *International Humanitarian Law and the Challenges of Contemporary Armed Conflicts* (ICRC 2019) 66.
89 Ibid.
90 See generally UNDP, 'Infrastructure Damage Assessment Cabo Delgado – Mozambique August 2022' (2022).
91 ICRC, 'Twelve Issues for 2022: What States Can Do to Improve Respect for International Humanitarian Law' (2022).

Bibliography

'189 Islamist Suspects Stand Trial in Mozambique' *France24* (3 October 2018).
'40 000 Displaced in North Mozambique After Assault in Palma' *Africanews* (20 April 2021).
Amnesty International, 'Mozambique: "What I Saw Is Death": War Crimes in Mozambique's Forgotten Cape' (2 March 2021).
Ana Margarida Sousa Santos, 'Violence, Rumour, and Elusive Trust in Mocímboa da Praia' (2021) 65 *The International Journal of Anthropology*.
'Armed Men Attack Police Stations in Mocímboa da Praia – AIM Report' *Club of Mozambique* (5 October 2017).
Austin Doctor, 'After Palma: Assessing the Islamic State's Position in Northern Mozambique' *The George Washington University Program on Extremism* (August 2022) <https://extremism.gwu.edu/sites/g/files/zaxdzs5746/files/Islamic-State-in-Northern-Mozambique_Doctor_August-2022.pdf>.
Borges Nhamirre, 'Mozambique Shifts Gear with Its New Strategy for the North' *Institute for Security Studies* (8 February 2022).

Christina Goldbaum, 'Insurgents Seize Mozambique Town, Killing Several People; Fate of Hundreds Unknown' *The New York Times* (27 March 2021).
Crisis Group, 'Stemming the Insurrection in Mozambique's Cabo Delgado' (2021) 6.
Daveed Gartenstein-Ross, Emelie Chace-Donhue and Colin P Clarke, 'The Evolution and Escalation of the Islamic State Threat to Mozambique' *Foreign Policy Research Institute* (13 April 2021).
David Fisher, 'Domestic Regulation of International Humanitarian Relief in Disasters and Armed Conflict: A Comparative Analysis' (2007) 89 *International Review of the Red Cross*.
David Matsinhe and Estacio Valoi, 'The Genesis of Insurgency in Northern Mozambique, Southern Africa Report' *Institute for Security Studies* (31 October 2019).
Dorina A Bekoe, Stephanie M Burchard and Sarah A Daly, 'Extremism in Mozambique: Interpreting Group Tactics and the Role of the Government's Response in the Crisis in Cabo Delgado' *Institute for Defense Analyses* (March 2020).
Egna Sidumo, 'Resilience Factors and Prevention of Radicalisation and Violent Extremism in Mozambique' *USAID* (2022).
Emily Estelle and Jessica Trisko Darden, 'Combating the Islamic State's Spread in Africa: Assessment and Recommendations for Mozambique' *American Enterprise Institute* (24 February 2021).
EU, 'European Union Training Mission in Mozambique' <www.eeas.europa.eu/eutm-mozambique_en?s=4411>.
Gregory Pirio, Robert Pittelli and Yussuf Adam, 'The Emergence of Violent Extremism in Northern Mozambique' *Africa Centre for Strategic Studies* (25 March 2018).
ICRC, 'Guidelines on Protection of Natural Environment in Armed Conflict' (2020).
ICRC, 'International Humanitarian Law and the Challenges of Contemporary Armed Conflicts' (2019).
ICRC, 'Islamic Law and International Humanitarian Law: Common Principles of the Two Legal Systems' *ICRC* (25 November 2020) <www.icrc.org/en/document/islamic-law-international-humanitarian-law>.
ICRC, 'Mozambique' <www.icrc.org/en/where-we-work/africa/mozambique>.
ICRC, 'Q&A: Sexual Violence in Armed Conflict' *ICRC* (19 August 2019) <www.icrc.org/en/document/sexual-violence-armed-conflict-questions-and-answers>.
ICRC, 'Rule 45: Causing Serious Damage to the Natural Environment' (ICRC) <https://ihl-databases.icrc.org/en/customary-ihl/v1/rule45>.
ICRC, 'Twelve Issues: What States Can Do to Improve Respect for IHL in 2022' (March 2022).
ICRC, 'What Is the Humanitarian Impact of the COVID-19 Pandemic?' (15 September 2020) <www.icrc.org/en/document/what-humanitarian-impact-covid-19-pandemic#:~:text=%22It%20will%20have%20a%20devastating,devastation%20brought%20about%20by%20conflict>.
IFRC, 'Law and Legal Issues in International Disaster Response: A Desk Study' (2007).
ILC, 'Protection of the Environment in Relation to Armed Conflicts' <https://legal.un.org/ilc/guide/8_7.shtml>.
'Insurgents Threaten Nampula as Attacks Sweep Through Chiure' *Zitamar* (27 October 2022).
International Crisis Group, 'Stemming the Insurrection in Mozambique's Cabo Delgado' (11 June 2021) 18 <www.crisisgroup.org/africa/southern-africa/mozambique/303-stemming-insurrection-mozambiques-cabo-delgado>.
International Crisis Group, 'Winning Peace in Mozambique's Embattled North' (10 February 2022) <www.crisisgroup.org/africa/southern-africa/mozambique/winning-peace-mozambiques-embattled-north>.
International Organisation for Migration, 'Displacement Tracking Matrix – Mozambique' (28 December 2022).
Jann Kleffner, 'Collective Accountability' in Harmen van der Wilt and Andre Nollkaemper (eds), *System Criminality in International Law* (CUP 2009).

'Japan Pledges to Help Mozambique Fight "Terrorism"' *AfricaNews* (5 May 2023).
Jason Warner and others, *The Islamic State in Africa. The Emergence, Evolution and Future of the Next Jihadist Battlefront* (Hurts Publishing 2021).
Joseph Cotterill and David Keohane, '"Some Hid in the Sea": Islamist Attack on Mozambique Town a Turning Point in Africa's Ignored War' *Financial Times* (6 April 2021).
Joseph Hanlon, 'Cabo Delgado's History of Violence' *Club of Mozambique* (14 August 2020).
Julia Stanyard and others, 'Insurgency, Illicit Markets and Corruption: The Cabo Delgado Conflict and Its Regional Implications' *Global Initiatives* (February 2022).
Liazzat JK Bonate, 'Why the Mozambican Government's Alliance with the Islamic Council of Mozambique Might Not End the Insurgency in Cabo Delgado' *Zitamar News* (2019).
Luís Nhachote, 'Humanising Security in Cabo Delgado: A CSO Report on the Drivers of Conflict and Its Impact on Civilians' *The Investigative Journalism Centre* (2021).
Marco Sassòli, *International Humanitarian Law: Rules, Controversies, and Solutions to Problems Arising in Warfare* (Edward Elgar 2019).
Martha M. Bradley, 'Additional Protocol II: Elevating the Minimum Threshold of Intensity?' (2020) 102 *International Review of the Red Cross.*
Martha M. Bradley, 'A Delightful Review of Overlooked Topics' *International Law Agendas* (7 July 2023) <http://ila-brasil.org.br/blog/a-delightful-review-of-overlooked-topics/>.
Martha M. Bradley and Aniel de Beer, 'The Collective Responsibility of Organised Armed Groups for Sexual and Gender-Based Violence During a Non-International Armed Conflict' (2021) 32 (1) *Stellenbosch Law Review.*
'Moçambique pede apoio logístico à União Europeia para combater terrorismo' *RFI* (23 September 2020) <www.rfi.fr/pt/mo%C3%A7ambique/20200923-uni%C3%A3o-europeia-apoia-mo%C3%A7ambique-no-combate-ao-terrorismo>.
'Mocímboa da Praia: Relato sugere 'namoro' de insurgentes à população local' *Voz de Cabo Delgado* (27 January 2023).
'Mozambique: Armed Men Attack in Nampula Province – AIM Report' *Club of Mozambique* (5 September 2022).
'Mozambique Cracks Down on Tanzanians Accused of Terrorism' *Business Day* (28 December 2017).
'Mozambique, Events of 2022' *Human Rights Watch World Report* (2023) <https://www.hrw.org/world-report/2023/country-chapters/mozambique>.
'Mozambique: Militants Attack Ruby Mine in Cabo Delgado Province' *Crisis24* (20 October 2022).
'Mozambique: Terrorist Attack Village in Memba' *allAfrica* (7 September 2022).
'Mozambique: Terrorists Attack Village in Ancuabe' *allAfrica* (6 June 2017).
'Mozambique: WFP Suspends Food Aid in February – AIM Report' *Club of Mozambique* (30 January 2023).
Mrksic & Others (Prosecutor v Mile Mrksic, Miroslav Radic, Veselin Sljivancanin (IT – 95–13/1 – T) Trial Chamber Judgment (27 September 2007).
Nadia Issufo, 'Encerramento de mesquitas em Moçambique: Justa ou exagerada?' *DW* (22 November 2017).
Neha Wadekar and Ed Ram, '"Kidnapped, Raped and Trafficked": Women and Girls Exposed to Sexual Violence in War-Torn Mozambique' *Pulitzer Centre* (3 January 2023) <https://pulitzercenter.org/stories/kidnapped-raped-and-trafficked-women-and-girls-exposed-sexual-violence-war-torn-mozambique>.
Noam Zamir, *Classification of Conflicts in International Humanitarian Law: The Legal Impact of Foreign Intervention in Civil Wars* (Edward Elgar Publishing 2017).
OCHA, 'Mozambique Gender Based Violence AoR – Rapid GBV Safety Assessment Cyclone Freddy, Nicoadala, Namacura – Zambézia (April 2023)' *Reliefweb* (3 May 2023) <https://reliefweb.int/report/mozambique/mozambique-gender-based-violence-aor-rapid-gbv-safety-assessment-cyclone-freddy-nicoadala-namacura-zambezia-april-2023>.

Owen Frazer and Christian Nünlist, 'The Concept of Countering Violent Extremism' *CSS Analyses in Security Policy* (December 2015).

Padil Salimo, Lars Buur and Jose Macuane, 'The Politics of Domestic Gas: The Sasol Natural Gas Deals in Mozambique' (2020) 7 *The Extractive Industries and Society*.

Pedro Seabra, 'O Conflito em Cabo Delgado em perspectiva' *Instituto de Defesa Nacional* (2021).

Peter Fabricius, 'Rwanda's Deployment of Forces into Mozambique Irks SADC' *Daily Maverick* (11 July 2021).

Prosecutor v Akayesu (ICTR-96–4-T) Judgment (2 September 1998).

Prosecutor v. Bagosora (ICTR-98–41-T), Judgment and Sentence (18 December 2008).

Prosecutor v Dusko Tadic aka 'Dule' (IT-94–1-A) Decision on the Defence Motion for Interlocutory Appeal on Jurisdiction (19 July 1998).

Prosecutor v Dusko Tadic a/k/a 'Dule' (IT-94–1-T) Opinion and Judgment (7 May 1997).

The Prosecutor v Enver Hadzihasanovic Amir Kubara (IT – 01–47 – T) Judgment, Trial Chamber (15 March 2006).

Prosecutor v Jean – Paul Akayesu (ICTR 96–4 – T) Judgment, Trial Chamber I (2 September 1998).

Prosecutor v Katanga (ICC-01/04–01/07) Judgment (7 March 2014).

Prosecutor v. Kordić and Čerkez (IT-95–14/2-A) Appeals Chamber Judgment (17 December 2004).

Prosecutor v Ramush Haradinaj Idriz Balaj Lahi Brahimaj (IT – 04–84 – T) Judgment, Trial Chamber (3 April 2008).

Prosecutor v Sefer Halilovic (IT 01–48 – T), Trial Chamber (16 November 2005).

Prosecutor v Zejnil Delalic Zdravko Mucic, also known as 'Pavo', Hazim Delic Esad Landzo, also known as 'Zenga' (IT – 96–21 – T) Judgment, Trial Chamber (16 November 1998).

Republic of Mozambique, *National Defence and Security Council Press Release* (2020) <https://www.presidencia.gov.mz/por/layout/set/print/content/download/8757/62236/version/1/file/COMUNICADO+DE+IMPRENSA+23.04.2020+-CNDS+%3D.pdf>.

Rome Statute of the International Criminal Court (1998) <https://treaties.un.org/Pages/showDetails.aspx?objid=0800000280025774&clang=_en>.

RULAC, 'Mozambique' *RULAC* (18 May 2023) <www.rulac.org/browse/conflicts/non-international-aarmed-conflicts-in-mozambique>.

Saide Habibe, Salvador Forquilha and João Pereira, 'Islamic Radicalisation in Northern Mozambique: The Case of Mocímboa da Praia' *Cadernos IESE* (2019).

Sarah Jean Mabeza and Tamalin Bolus, 'Changing the Narrative: A Tool on African Traditions and the Preservation of Humanity during War' *ICRC* (November 2022) <https://international-review.icrc.org/articles/changing-the-narrative-african-traditions-preservation-of-humanity-during-war-920>.

Save the Children, 'Cabo Delgado: Displaced Children Tell of Lost Parents, Lack of Schooling, Diseases, But Also of Hope in New Report' <www.savethechildren.org/us/about-us/media-and-news/2021-press-releases/cabo-delgado-displaced-children-report#:~:text=At%20least%20800%2C000%20people%20are%20now%20displaced%20in,result%20of%20violence%20and%20insecurity%20in%20Cabo%20Delgado>.

Tilman Rodenhäuser, *Organizing Rebellion: Non-State Armed Groups Under International Humanitarian Law, Human Rights Law, and International Criminal Law* (OUP 2018).

Tim Lister, 'The March 2021 Palma Attack and the Evolving Terror Threat to Mozambique' *Combating Terrorism Center at West Point* (April/May 2021) <https://ctc.westpoint.edu/the-march-2021-palma-attack-and-the-evolving-jihadi-terror-threat-to-mozambique/>.

UN Doc. S/2023/95 (13 February 2023).

UN Office for the Coordination of Humanitarian Affairs, '2023 Mozambique Humanitarian Response Plan' (24 February 2023).

UN, 'UNDATA Statistics-Mozambique' (2023) <http://data.un.org/Data.aspx?q=Mozambique&d=PopDiv&f=variableID%3a12%3bcrID%3a508>.

UNDP, 'Infrastructure Damage Assessment Cabo Delgado – Mozambique August 2022' (2022) <https://www.undp.org/sites/g/files/zskgke326/files/2022-09/UNDP_220906_ENG-IDA%20Report_0.pdf>.

UNFPA, 'World Population Dashboard – Mozambique' (2023) <www.unfpa.org/data/world-population/MZ>.

UNHCR, 'Gender Based Violence Response Factsheet' *UNHCR* (18 June 2022) <https://reliefweb.int/report/mozambique/unhcr-mozambique-cabo-delgado-gender-based-violence-response-factsheet-april-2022>.

UNRCO and OCHA, '2018–2019 Humanitarian Response Plan, Revised Following Cyclones Idai and Kenneth' (May 2019).

U.S. Department of State, 'US Relations with Mozambique' (31 October 2022).

U.S. State Department, 'Country Reports on Terrorism 2020: Mozambique' (2020).

WHO, 'Data – Mozambique' <https://data.who.int/countries/508>.

WHO, 'Ebola Virus Disease – Democratic Republic of the Congo' (29 September 2022) <www.who.int/emergencies/disease-outbreak-news/item/2022-DON411>.

The World Bank, 'The World Bank in Mozambique' <www.worldbank.org/en/country/mozambique/overview>.

Part I

Regional security dimensions

2 Tanzania and Mozambique

Cooperation to counteract a cross-border Islamist insurgency

Erick Kabendera

2.1 Introduction

The issue of a cross-border conflict affecting Southern Tanzania and Northern Mozambique which became increasingly prominent due to the violent attacks that began in 2013 and peaked in 2017.[1] The prominence given to these attacks at the time disguises a reality that for decades the insurgents have operated through a network of radical mosques established in the early 1980s. They have taken advantage of the historical marginalisation of the area to present themselves as the sole provider of a solution to problems among the population.[2]

The preachers used their influence to recruit and supply fighters to international terrorist groups active in Pakistan, Afghanistan and Somalia, which were also a major source of their revenues.[3] The fighters, under the guise of being preachers, returned with the goal of founding terrorist groups that pledge their loyalty to international terrorist organisations. Once established, the network of groups expanded their activities across East and Central Africa, making it easier to recruit fighters through these mosques and to set up clandestine training camps.[4]

In Tanzania these groups gained influence in provinces bordering Kigoma, which shares a border with the eastern Democratic Republic of the Congo (DRC).[5] They also gained influence in four regions in Southern Tanzania (Lindi, Mtwara, Ruvuma and Pwani) that share a border with Northern Mozambique, as well as in the north-western province of Kagera which borders Southwestern Uganda.[6] By the early 1990s the port city of Tanga, which is on the border with Eastern Kenya, was also under their influence. Since 2014, except for Kigoma and Kagera, the provinces have experienced major violent attacks.[7]

Of particular interest to the groups is Southern Tanzania. For more than 50 years the region, as is the case with the provinces of Northern Mozambique, has physically and economically been isolated from the rest of Tanzania due to poor roads and the lack of a telecommunications infrastructure, which makes the region inaccessible, especially during the rainy season.[8] Endemic poverty and a lack of government interest in bringing development to the region triggered a movement among politicians from Southern Tanzania to consider seceding and founding an independent country.[9]

DOI: 10.4324/9781003317647-3

The focus among radical preachers is to radicalise children in madrassa schools to recruit them to fight and establish an Islamic caliphate.[10] The envisioned caliphate would stretch from the Kibiti area along Tanzania's southern coastal line into Northern Mozambique. Tanzania and Mozambique share an 860-kilometre-long border, part of which is the Ruvuma basin (400 kilometres long and 160 kilometres wide) along the southern Tanzanian border with Mozambique.[11] Tanzania exhibits over 40 informal entry points along the border with Mozambique, mainly used for illicit trade, especially in timber from Northern Mozambique.[12] The province of Cabo Delgado is separated from the capital, Maputo, by 1,672 kilometres of coastline. Its political economy has been shaped by the war of independence and its aftermath, and Tanzania is the closest source of supplies for most Cabo Delgado communities, especially Mocímboa da Praia, Mueda, Nangade, Mountepuez and Palma.[13] The insurgents took advantage of the presence of trans-border ethnic groups living in Northern Mozambique and Southern Tanzania, especially the Yao, Makonde and Makua, to operate between the two regions.[14] The insurgents exploited centuries of informal cross-border links between mutual ethnic groups to establish themselves and to preach an extremist ideology.[15]

Subsequently, the groups evolved to provide security to criminal cross-border activities, especially the smuggling of rubies and timber.[16] To be effective, the extremist networks operating in Southern Tanzania and Northern Mozambique needed powerful weapons.[17] An easy target was poorly guarded police stations across Dar es Salaam and elsewhere, where they would kill police officers and steal their weapons.[18] Although maintaining close ties across Tanzania, the insurgents operate in pockets and without strategic coordination.[19]

The chief goal is to fund training and recruitment and to establish a caliphate in Southern Tanzania, Northern Mozambique, Eastern DRC and Uganda, before pledging allegiance to ISIS.[20] The group planned to launch their mission in 2030, but the killing of police officers and attacks on the village leadership in Rufiji led to Tanzania intervening in 2014 with a special military operation that targeted extremists in Tanga,[21] Morogoro,[22] Mtwara and Lindi, disrupting the plan.[23] The attacks forced members of the network to flee to Mocímboa da Praia from where they organised retaliatory attacks.[24]

2.2 Link with the Mozambican insurgency

The historical marginalisation that characterises the situation in Northern Mozambique and Southern Tanzania makes the regions vulnerable to the emergence of radical elements, even before the development of a full-scale Islamist insurgency. As mentioned earlier, populations in Southern Tanzania and Northern Mozambique share ethnic ties and centuries of interaction and, in addition, the colonial experience was similar. In Northern Mozambique Muslims were considered a threat to colonial rule; the Portuguese colonial government co-opted the Makua, a non-Muslim ethnic group, creating religious and ethnic divisions that were not addressed after independence.[25] Portuguese colonial efforts to restrain the rise of Islam did not deter the spread of Sufi Islam. The arrival of Wahhabism in Mozambique in the 1960s, brought from Tanzania, Egypt and Saudi Arabia, where the Salafists had gained prominence, gave Islamic religious leaders influence and power.[26] Portugal changed its initial stance and backed local Sufi leaders during the war for independence from 1964 to 1974 to prevent them from supporting the independence movement, but this move failed.[27]

The expansion of conservative Islam in Northern Mozambique triggered an increase in the numbers of Mozambicans travelling to Saudi Arabia and attendance at conservative Islamic schools in Zanzibar, Somalia, Mombasa and Saudi Arabia.[28] These developments changed the character and the appearance of Islamic communities in Mozambique with increasing tension between conservative and liberal Muslims, especially in Northern Mozambique.[29] In the 2010s there were reports of Muslim youth groups storming mosques with shoes and weapons in violation of Islamic custom of sanctity to protest state-sanctioned Islamic institutions.[30] Despite this trend, cases of actual violence did not emerge until 2014 in Cabo Delgado and particularly in Macomia district in 2017.[31]

Morier-Genoud concurs that the group responsible for the attacks in Cabo Delgado emerged long before October 2017.[32] He notes: '[This group] is old and started in 2007 as an Islamist sect that wanted to have a Muslim government. When that did not work, from 2015, they switched to an armed "jihad" movement'.[33] As is the case in Tanzania, the group targeted those it accused of collaborating with the police and government security forces or who resisted the attacks. Additionally, in February, March and May 2019 the group killed teachers in three attacks.[34] The attack on the education system sought to change the fabric of society and the lives of future generations.

The rise in radicalisation and insurgency in their communities created concerns among local Islamic leaders who reported the cases to the local and central governments.[35] Mainstream Islamic religious leaders categorised the group as 'risky' and sought the involvement of the security agencies.[36] Between 2017 and 2018 the insurgency conducted violent attacks, which included stabbings, shootings, the beating of victims and the destruction of villages and state security structures.[37] The insurgency used firearms in carrying out most of the attacks, but the group also uses machetes in most of its attacks as these are inexpensive and are widely available.[38]

The national Muslim leaders' conference in 2016 asserted that the Islamist sectarian group had spread to four districts in Cabo Delgado, namely, Montepuez, Palma, Nangade, and Mocímboa da Praia.[39] Mainstream Muslim organisations increased their opposition, which prompted the group to change strategy from an Islamist sectarian group that advocates Shari'a law to armed jihadism.[40] For years security agencies have rejected calls to intervene against the group and argued that they were concerned that it was the wrong approach for a secular government to intervene in an intra-Muslim conflict.[41] However, increased tension among mainstream religious leaders prompted the government to intervene militarily and forced the group to change tactics.[42]

The Islamic Council of Mozambique (CISLAMO) propelled the growth of Salafi influence in Mozambique as a result of the monetary support provided by foreign charities in the 1990s.[43] This influence prompted the building of new mosques and *madrasahs* in Cabo Delgado and among the broader Muslim-majority north, which challenged the decades-long dominance of Sufism.[44] The youthful fighters who returned from being trained abroad built on this influence across the Swahili coast to establish commercial ties which they used to smuggle illicit goods and minerals from Tanzania, Kenya and Somalia out of the port town of Mocímboa da Praia.[45]

A number of known Mozambican leaders of Al-Shabaab, eyewitnesses and Mozambican officials report that Tanzanian Islamists who fled to Mozambique after a security crackdown in their home country in recent years represent an important section of the group's leadership.[46] While Ansar al-Sunna predominantly is composed of locals from Cabo Delgado, it is believed that several members are from other countries in the region, including Tanzania and Somalia.[47] This opinion supports the view that radical Islam is not bounded by international borders and spreads with ease, especially in areas where its development is underpinned by cultural ties. Foreign fighters come from countries with established terrorist organisations such as Al-Shabaab in Somalia, to fight in the cross-border conflict in Northern Mozambique and Southern Tanzania.[48]

It is well known that fighters from Tanzania constitute a significant part of the insurgency leadership, having fled to Mozambique following a security crackdown in Tanzania.[49] The Tanzanian fighters are believed to be part of the Islamist group that dominated the Swahili Coast in East Africa.[50] Despite the involvement of Al-Shabaab and ISIS in the conflict being unclear, there is mounting concern about the possibility of the insurgency drawing foreign fighters into the conflict.[51] Security forces have cracked down on Islamist youth in Kibiti district south of the capital, Dar es Salaam, most of whom fled to Northern Mozambique in 2017.[52] Many of them are connected to trafficking rings operating between Mozambique and Tanzania and previously were involved in trafficking rings run by fighters from Tanzania to Somalia.[53]

In July 2019 Tanzanian police reported that five insurgents linked to the Ntole attack in Mozambique had been arrested, which was followed by the arrest of a number of people attempting to cross from the Southern Tanzanian region of Mtwara into Cabo Delgado in Mozambique.[54] This example is strong evidence of the crossover of insurgents between the two countries and underscores the inevitability that they will form strong cross-border security cooperation.[55] Tanzania clearly is a key recruiting ground and a transit route for terrorists going to Mozambique, the DRC and Burundi.[56]

Insurgents mostly target Cabo Delgado province in Northern Mozambique.[57] The link between insurgents operating in Mozambique and Tanzania is based largely on the shared use of the Swahili language there and beyond.[58] This link illustrates the significance of cultural associations in the sustainability of an insurgency; youths in Cabo Delgado listen to extremist views taped and distributed in Swahili.[59] Additionally, the population of Cabo Delgado enjoys strong cultural, linguistic, social and economic ties with Southern Tanzania that date back centuries.[60] Although Portuguese is the most commonly spoken language in Mozambique and is used for official purposes by the government, many in Cabo Delgado speak Swahili and other local dialects.[61]

2.3 Cooperation between Tanzania and Mozambique

Cooperation between the two countries played a crucial part in helping Mozambique attain its independence from colonial rule in 1975 and to end the Mozambican civil war in 1992.[62] After independence bilateral defence agreements have resulted in the deployment of over 40 000 troops in support of Mozambique. Mozambique reciprocated by providing troops to Tanzania during the Kagera war fought between Tanzania and Uganda from 1978 to 1979.[63] Mozambique had benefited from the Tanzanian government adopting an activist foreign policy to aid liberation movements in Southern Africa.[64] Tanzania's founding President Nyerere, handing over to his successor in 1985, left a memorandum which stated that '[w]e have blood relationship with Mozambique so we [Tanzania] are like Mozambique's big brother and any future president should prioritise the relationship between the two countries'.[65]

Tanzania and Mozambique had bilateral defence agreements during the liberation struggle, but Tanzania deployed troops to aid Mozambique and provided training, first, during the civil war against RENAMO in 1978 as part of its support for FRELIMO.[66] As part of the agreement, Tanzania deployed 3 000 troops to Mozambique between 1986 and 1988 although other countries turned down Mozambique's request to provide troops.[67]

Before the insurgents launched attacks in Northern Mozambique, there had been attacks in Southern Tanzania.[68] The Tanzanian security agency cautioned the Mozambican government that Islamist fighters fleeing military operations in Tanzania had triggered an exodus to Mozambique.[69] Tanzania deployed troops to protect its border to deal with a spill-over in the conflict, but the killing of citizens in the border town of Kitaya in October 2020 demonstrates the risk Tanzania faces in not fully engaging in the conflict.[70] Clearly, a solution to the problem involves bilateral and international cooperation to prevent the further recruitment of terrorist fighters and the export of conflict between countries.

Tanzania deployed troops to protect its southern border. Mozambique hired the Dyck Advisory Group (DAG), a South African private military company, to support its military from being overwhelmed by the insurgency.[71] In addition, the two countries signed comprehensive security agreements in 2018 to exchange intelligence and conduct joint operations against the insurgents, paving the way for a military response to the insurgency.[72]

Following an escalation of the attacks on civilians, in April 2021 the Southern African Development Community (SADC) passed a resolution in favour of a military response.[73] For all intents and purposes, it is an attempt to restore peace and security and sends the message that terrorism will not be tolerated in the region. Also, it indicates a preference for bilateral and non-state support to counter the insurgency.[74] Tanzania and Mozambique have chaired the SADC regional bloc between 2018 and 2019, but there is scant evidence that they used the position to chart a concrete route to find a solution.

The terrorist attacks have escalated in violence, and the jihadist-linked insurgents are growing in confidence. In March 2021 hundreds of well-armed fighters overran the town of Palma in the province of Cabo Delgado, targeting shops, banks and the military barracks and killing dozens of civilians.[75] At least 300 insurgents crossed the Tanzania–Mozambique border to conduct an attack on Kitaya village in Southern Tanzania, killing an unknown number of people. This attack prompted a military operation in which some Islamists (who claimed to have killed security officers) were captured and ammunition and weapons confiscated.[76]

Despite a deep and shared history, the two countries have not been able to effectively join forces to counter Ansar al-Sunna and, in contrast to previous situations, the insurgency has strained the Tanzania–Mozambique relationship. Prior to signing a security agreement in 2018, there were accusations and counter-accusations that the insurgents originated from each other's territory.[77] The Tanzanian military were accused of crossing the border without consent and of transferring radicalised individuals from Tanzania to Mozambique.[78] International humanitarian organisations accused Tanzania of rejecting over 1 000 displaced people seeking asylum to escape violence in Northern Mozambique due to a concern that the insurgents might be disguised as refugees and enter the country to plot further attacks.[79] During interrogation almost all the refugees claimed that they had family members in Tanzania.[80]

2.4 Reasons behind cooperation issues

Tanzania provided support during the Mozambican War of Independence by allowing FRELIMO fighters to establish military camps in Tanzania and providing financial support.[81] Mozambique contributed troops to Tanzania during the Uganda–Tanzania war in 1978.[82] When FRELIMO waged war against RENAMO in 1978, Tanzania contributed over 3 000 troops to fight and to provide training to the ruling party. In addition to Tanzania's support in the liberation struggle, there was a close personal friendship between the leaders, and an understanding of the history between their countries demonstrates that it has played an important role in fostering the relationship.[83]

After the deaths of Mozambique's founding president, Samora Machel, in 1986 and Tanzania's founding president, Julius Nyerere, considered to be the architects of cooperation, political leaders in both countries have continued the tradition of cooperation.[84] There were strong ties when Presidents Joaquim Chissano of Mozambique (1985–2005) and Benjamin Mkapa of Tanzania (1995–2005) were in power. They had been friends for 30 years before becoming presidents, which made it easier to facilitate frequent meetings between the countries to discuss bilateral security issues.[85]

The relationship between the two became weaker after John Magufuli of Tanzania and Phillipe Nyusi of Mozambique became presidents.[86] In Tanzanian political circles, Magufuli was considered as lacking an understanding of the historical relationship between the two countries.[87] In this era of a weakened relationship, the shared border was the only issue of common interest.[88] There was a strong belief among the top leadership in the Tanzanian governing party, Chama Cha Mapinduzi, that Mozambique's first female prime minister, Luisa Diogo (2004–2015) would become President of Mozambique instead of Nyusi.[89] Both had participated in the liberation struggle, but there was consensus that she embodied the spirit of the relationship between the two countries in the way Samora Machel and the founder of the FRELIMO party, Eduardo Chivambo Mondlane, had done.[90]

Nyusi turned to Tanzania for assistance immediately after the security situation in Northern Mozambique had become serious. At least three times Nyusi requested a state visit to Tanzania, but President Magufuli behaved coldly.[91] President Nyusi eventually travelled to Tanzania for his first state visit on 4 December 2017.[92] President Magufuli shared Nyusi's concern that the insurgents were moving between the two countries, but said that Tanzania had single-handedly dealt with the instances of Islamist insurgents in Southern Tanzania without seeking support from other countries and advised the Mozambicans to deal with the problem themselves.[93] This response sets out the problem in a nutshell: Tanzania and Mozambique need to tackle cross-border problems *together* to mitigate the threat of terrorism.

By 2020 the Tanzania People's Defence Force's Southern Brigade declared that it had deployed along the border with Mozambique to deal with insurgents spilling over and, subsequently, declared the area a military zone.[94] The deployment further sought to protect the formal and informal borders with Mozambique.[95] The focus was stopping the spill-over from the conflict, but little was done to encourage cooperation. The two countries are talking, but prevailing circumstances suggest that there is a lack of political will to reach an agreement and to carry out the implementation of cooperation.[96]

The countries are engaged with a common enemy but have different strategies. Mozambique is involved in a full-blown war, but Tanzania is focused on protecting its border against a spill-over of the conflict despite evidence that the insurgents use Tanzania as a rear base.[97] Tanzania remains a source of supplies for the insurgents. In Kilambo village in the Mtwara district, where there is a border post on the Ruvuma River, insurgents from Mozambique have since 2018 crossed on foot from Mozambique to Tanzania during the dry seasons to buy goods.[98] These differences and a lack of a coherent and mutual strategy make it more difficult to police the porous border.[99]

Tanzania has been reluctant to cooperate with Mozambique due to differences in approach to fighting the insurgency.[100] Tanzania's approach has been to avoid attracting international attention not to make the conflict permanent, whereas Mozambique has invited the attention of international media and players.[101] International attention could attract terrorist groups in Somalia and Nigeria to intervene on the side of the insurgents, escalating the conflict.[102] Another concern has been a lack of professionalism on the part of the factionalised Mozambican military.[103] This lack of cooperation has resulted in an absence of transparency with regard to the way in which they are dealing with the insurgency, raising questions as to whether they have developed a joint mechanism to deal with arrested cross-border insurgents in line with international humanitarian law.[104]

The increase in incidents of cross-border attacks by Islamist insurgents bouncing back and forth between the two countries[105] forced Mozambique and Tanzania to sign a counter-terrorism joint operation agreement in July 2020, which involved the extradition of 500 suspected insurgents.[106]

Mozambican President Filipe Nyusi travelled to Tanzania in January 2021 for the signing of a security agreement between the two countries to facilitate the extradition of alleged terrorists as part of their bilateral relations.[107] The outcome of the meeting is that the Mozambican and Tanzanian police forces signed a memorandum of understanding aimed at 'revamping collaborations' between the security agencies and sharing information regarding cross-border crime.[108] The International Crisis Group (ICG) described relations as 'cordial but at times strained'.[109]

Despite the agreements signed between the two countries and the meetings between their heads of states, tensions persist. The agreement is a positive step forward in creating a cooperative relationship to deal with the real threat of terrorism. Mozambican officials remain concerned that Tanzanian security forces 'were tolerant of the smugglers and traffickers, who are in turn connected to the Mozambican al-Shabab and who allegedly receive protection from the powerful political and security figures in Tanzania'.[110]

In July 2021 the SADC decided to deploy a standby force to Cabo Delgado as part of the regional effort to fight the insurgency.[111] Before the SADC could deploy the force, Rwanda entered into an agreement with Mozambique to deploy troops despite not being a member of the SADC.[112] The SADC Secretary-General, Stergomena Tax, stated that Mozambique had not disclosed to the SADC that Rwanda would be deploying troops.[113] However, SADC involvement raises concerns due to its lack of experience in fighting an insurgency and in mobilising a regional military deployment.[114] The SADC should have focused on supporting Tanzania and Mozambique in disrupting the networks of businesses linked to the insurgents rather than engaging in military intervention which will take longer and consume greater resources.[115]

The ICG argues that, despite SADC seeking international support in the deployment of troops to Mozambique on the grounds that the conflict endangers the security of SADC member states, the deployment of foreign troops without knowledge of the local terrain will not be a great help and may be unnecessary in defeating the insurgents.[116] Instead, future regional joint intervention should focus on preventing individuals from providing financial support and training to Islamists. Such interventions work only if Tanzania and Mozambique are willing to share information with regional partners about the cross-border network that is in operation. This observation further strengthens the argument for increased international cooperation in the prevention of terrorism.[117] The ICG links the criminal networks operating across the border of Mozambique and Tanzania with the network of business people and senior FRELIMO generals from the Makonde ethnic group, who were key to the success of the liberation war but have continued to dominate Cabo Delgado's politics and the economy.[118]

Despite the renewed cooperation under Magufuli's presidency, the Tanzanian government continued to raise concerns that President Nyusi intended to politicise the conflict. The involvement of Rwanda, despite its not being impacted by the conflict and not being a member of the SADC, intensified that suspicion.[119] It is clear that Tanzania's military, conventionally trained to protect the border, has struggled to deal with an insurgency-related threat. The border community continues to host insurgents in their homes, offering them food, and encouraging their children to join the fight.

After a visit by French President Emmanuel Macron to Rwanda,[120] Rwanda announced that it was deploying troops to Northern Mozambique to assist in fighting the insurgency.[121] This decision, it was said, had been made without Mozambique sharing information with SADC which already had adopted a resolution to deploy to Mozambique.[122] Around the same time, Nyusi travelled to meet President Paul Kagame in Rwanda.[123] These developments created concerns in Tanzanian security and diplomatic circles that the leaders of France, Mozambique and Rwanda had reached an agreement to deploy in Mozambique because Mozambique did not value Tanzania's support in the same way it valued that of Rwanda.[124]

The two countries have faced problems in coordinating border security and communication and in developing a joint military strategy, but nevertheless have conducted covert joint military operations for which they take no credit.[125] President Magufuli's government approached all the issues affecting the SADC countries as national issues.[126] His position created mistrust when it comes to sharing intelligence and Tanzania considers the rise of the insurgency as a border security challenge and not as a regional security issue.[127]

2.5 Cooperation under President Samia Suluhu

Under the leadership of President Samia, Tanzania's approach to countering the insurgency has changed from the use of force to addressing root problems, such as a lack of employment, which result in the youth joining Ansar al-Sunna. Security agencies in Tanzania have also re-introduced *ulinzi shirikishi* (community participatory policing) in most areas and the military is training these communities on how to spot insurgents and report them to the local leadership. She also has shown a greater willingness to cooperate internationally on security issues after signing an additional bilateral defence agreement with Mozambique on 21 September 2022.

To renew their bilateral ties under Samia's presidency, the two countries opened a direct line of communication which is likely to revive strong security cooperation. It will take deliberate efforts by the two countries to build trust and resume discussions in the military and security agencies, even if these discussions do not lead to joint military operations.

The then Tanzanian Foreign Affairs Minister, Liberata Mulamula, stated that Tanzania would not deploy troops to Mozambique because Tanzania did not believe in military intervention, and recommended that Tanzania and Mozambique recognise the 'need for talks [with the insurgents] as a means of promoting peace and tranquility in Mozambique, calling on the international community to help the country [Mozambique] by sending development aid'.[128] With that said however, Tanzania and Mozambique have to establish robust intelligence and law enforcement cooperation to curb transnational jihadists providing propaganda and financial support to the insurgents operating in the two countries.[129]

2.6 Conclusion

President Samia of Tanzania has argued against the use of force to fight the Islamists and proposed Western governments increase the amount of aid they provide to address the socio-economic factors that triggered the rise of extremism and led to the insurgency.[130] The argument is based on the failure of the military option to have an effect. However, the lesson of past attempts shows her approach to be ineffective in preventing radicalisation. For example, the flow of aid from developed countries to poor countries increased in the aftermath of 9/11 as a result of a perceived increase in the number of incidents of terrorism.[131] Yet, despite high levels of reported cases of terrorism, Pakistan, Iraq and Afghanistan were not the chief recipients of aid between 1993 and 1994. The approach fails to recognise the fact that radical Islamists exploit other than socio-economic grievances.[132]

To counteract terrorism effectively, it is important first to understand the causes. Bird recommends the most effective counter-terror approach to be 'based on *ex ante* prevention, rather than *ex post* detection . . . [which] requires quiet, covert, intelligence-based operations, given the internationalization of terrorism'.[133] In theory, Bird is correct, but the reality is that there often is a response only after an attack.

It is recommended that, to address the problem of endemic poverty, governments should consider establishing a free-trade zone in Mozambique and Tanzania to allow cross-border trade free of duties. There are cultural ties between the ethnic groups on the Tanzanian and Mozambican sides of the border, the populations are related, they speak the same languages and share customs, all of which will facilitate the adoption of the policy.

In addition, the two countries should cooperate on security issues and to protect investment at the border. The governments should enlist the assistance of private enterprises in the development of skills building to incorporate the population into the value chain. The conflict has been militarised. However, it can be only a temporary intervention with the aim of neutralising the immediate insurgency.

Notes

1 'Police Seize 38 Terror Suspects in Three Regions' *The Citizen* (20 April 2021). The article quotes the then Dar es Salaam Special Zone Police Commander, Suleiman Kova, as saying that persistent bank robberies and attacks on police stations in Tanzania's largest city, Dar es Salaam, were linked to terrorist groups stealing money and collecting guns to finance terrorist activities, particularly in Southern Tanzania.
2 Author's interview with retired senior police investigator, Dar es Salaam, July 2021. The officer revealed that most of the counter-terrorism operations until the early 1990s focused primarily on tracing radical preachers.
3 Author's interview with Islamic religious scholar, May 2016.

4 Ibid.
5 Author's interview with former police commander, February 2017.
6 Ibid.
7 Author's interview (n 3).
8 Pekka Seppala and Bertha Koda, 'The Making of a Periphery: Economic Development and Cultural Encounters in Southern Tanzania' (1998) *Nordic Africa Institute* 45; author's interview with former Tanzanian diplomat, May 2021.
9 Seppala and Koda (n 8) 61. The book quotes a statement by the MP for Tandahimba, Steven Salum Nandonde, who in a parliamentary debate in 1993 said that Mtwara would 'pull out' of Tanzania due to underdevelopment. The statement has since been interpreted as suggesting that Mtwara wanted to form a new country with Northern Mozambique.
10 Author's interview (n 2). See also 'Tanzania Hit by Recent ISIS Attack Near Mozambique Border' *News 24* (23 October 2020). The article confirms the view that the aim of the insurgents is to establish a caliphate encompassing the natural gas-rich areas of Southern Tanzania and Northern Mozambique.
11 Seppala and Koda (n 8) 11–40.
12 Emmanuel Sulle, 'A Rapid Assessment of the Illegal Timber Trade Across the Ruvumba River on the Tanzania and Mozambique Border' (December 2024) *World-wide Fund* 1–4.
13 Ibid.
14 Edward A. Alpers, 'Ethnicity, Politics, and History in Mozambique' (January 2011) *Africa Today* 39–52.
15 Author's interview, researcher on Southern Tanzania, January 2011.
16 Author's interview with former senior police criminal investigator in Mtwara, May 2022.
17 Ibid.
18 Ibid.
19 Ibid.
20 Author's interview with retired MP and member of Parliamentary Committee for Security Affairs, June 2016.
21 'Soldier Killed in Raid Against Al-Shabaab Linked Gang' *The Citizen* (15 February 2015).
22 'Police Confirm Terror Suspects Arrested' *Dar Post* (15 April 2015).
23 Mtulya Athuman, 'Send Army to Curb Coast Killings, Opposition Says' *The Citizen* (17 May 2017).
24 Erick Kabendera, 'Militants in Mozambique Could Be Tanzanian' *The East African* (11 August 2018).
25 Dorina A Bekoe, Stephanie M Burchard and Sarah A Daly, 'Extremism in Mozambique: Interpreting Group Tactics and the Role of the Government's Response in the Crisis in Cabo Delgado' *Institute for Defense Analyses* (1 March 2020) 2–10.
26 Ibid.
27 Ibid.
28 Ibid, 4.
29 Ibid.
30 Eric Morier-Genoud, 'The Jihad Insurgency in Mozambique: Origin, Nature and Beginning' (2020) 14 (3) *Journal of Eastern African Studies* 1.
31 Ibid.
32 Ibid.
33 'Mozambique Attacks: Armed Group Was Born 10 Years Before the First Attack – Researcher' *Club of Mozambique* (22 June 2020).
34 Erin Kearns, 'When to Take Credit for Terrorism? A Cross-National Examination of Claims and Attributions' (2021) 33 (1) *Terrorism and Political Violence* 164.
35 David M Matsinhe and Estacio Valoi, 'The Genesis of Insurgency in Northern Mozambique' *Institute for Security Studies* (1 October 2019) 8.

36 Morier-Genoud (n 30) 8.
37 Bekoe and others (n 25).
38 Ibid.
39 Ibid.
40 Ibid.
41 Ibid.
42 Ibid.
43 International Crisis Group, 'Stemming the Insurrection in Mozambique's Cabo Delgado' (11 June 2021).
44 Ibid, 10.
45 Ibid.
46 Ibid, 12.
47 Bekoe and others (n 25).
48 Ibid.
49 Ibid, 12.
50 Ibid, 20.
51 Ibid, 27.
52 Ibid.
53 Ibid, 28.
54 Ibid.
55 Ibid.
56 Ibid.
57 Matsinhe and Valoi (n 35) 10.
58 Author' interview, MP from Southern Tanzania, August 2021.
59 Bekoe and others (n 25) 13.
60 Ibid, 8.
61 Ibid, 8–9.
62 Alan Cowel, 'Tanzania Military Advisers Will Be Sent to Mozambique' *The New York Times* (23 February 1982).
63 Ibid.
64 Author's interview with former Tanzanian government minister, August 2021.
65 Author's interview with senior Tanzanian diplomat, August 2021.
66 Gilbert Khadiagala, *Allies in Adversity: The Frontline States in Southern African Security, 1975–1993* (Ohio University Press, 1994) 198.
67 Lucy Shule, 'From Southern Africa to the Great Lakes Region: Challenges to Tanzanian Foreign Policy and Conflict Resolution in Sub-Saharan Africa' (doctoral thesis; University of Newcastle, 2014).
68 Erick Kabendera, 'Militants in Mozambique Could Be Tanzanians' *The East African* (11 August 2018).
69 Ibid.
70 Chris Alden and Sérgio Chichiva, 'Cabo Delgado: 'Al shabab/ISIS and the Crisis of Southern Africa' *Policy Centre for the New South* (May 2021).
71 Ibid.
72 'Mozambique, Tanzania to Launch Joint Operations Against Insurgents' *Reuters* (23 November 2020).
73 Marko Svicevic and Timothy Walker, 'Limited Legal Options for SADC Military Action in Cabo Delgado' *Institute for Security Studies* (22 April 2021).
74 Ibid.
75 Emilia Columbo and Austin. C. Doctor, 'Foreign Fighters and the Trajectory of Violence in Northern Mozambique' *War on the Rocks* (13 April 2021).
76 George Obulutsa, 'Militants from Mozambique Staged Deadly Attack in Tanzania, Police Say' *Reuters* (2020).
77 Interview with security source who attended a joint meeting between Mozambique police commander, Bernardino Rafael, and the Tanzanian Inspector-General of Police,

Simon Sirro, to discuss joint operations against cross-border insurgents on 23 November 2020.

78 'Tanzania yakanusha madai kuwa linahusika na mzozo wa msumbiji' *BBC Swahili* (7 September 2020).
79 UNHCR, 'UNHCR Appeals for Mozambicans Fleeing Violence to be Given Access to Asylum in Tanzania' (18 May 2021).
80 Interview with senior military official from Mozambique, June 2022.
81 Author's interview with FRELIMO senior official, May 2017.
82 Author's interview with former US diplomat to Mozambique.
83 Interview with senior Tanzanian government official, August 2021.
84 Ibid.
85 Ibid.
86 Magufuli was elected President in October 2015; Nyusi was inaugurated as President in January 2015.
87 Author's interview with former Tanzanian diplomat, October 2022.
88 Author's interview with former Mozambican senior government official.
89 Ibid.
90 Ibid.
91 Author's interview with Mozambican ruling party Frelimo official.
92 'President Nyusi Leaves Tanzania After Short Visit to Hold Talks with Magufuli' *Club of Mozambique* (10 December 2017). Further details about the discussions of the two leaders were provided by two Mozambican ruling party officials.
93 Author's interview with retired military official from Tanzania, August 2021.
94 'TPDF to Launch Manhunt Along the Border with Mozambique' *The Citizen Tanzania* (11 August 2020).
95 Author's interview with retired military official from Tanzania, August 2021.
96 Author's interview with retired South African diplomat, August 2021.
97 Author's interview with United Nations counter-terrorism official, August 2021.
98 Author's interview with senior Mozambique government official, August 2021.
99 Author's interview (n 95).
100 Author's interview (n 91).
101 Ibid.
102 Isaac Olawale Albert, 'Rethinking the Functionality of Multinational Joint Task Force in Managing the Boko Haram Crisis in the Lake Chad Basin' (2017) 42 (3) *Africa Development* 119–135.
103 Ibid.
104 Author's interview with former European diplomat, 2021.
105 George Obulutsa, 'Militants from Mozambique Staged Deadly Attack in Tanzania, Police Say' *Reuters* (23 October 2020).
106 'Mozambique, Tanzania to Launch Joint Operations Against Insurgents' *Reuters* (23 November 2020).
107 Mozambique High Commission, 'President Nyusi to Discuss Terrorism with Tanzanian Counterpart, High Commission of the United Republic of Mozambique' (11 January 2021).
108 James Kandoya, 'Tanzania, Mozambique to Fight Terrorism, Drug Trafficking' *IPP Media* (16 January 2018).
109 Ibid, 31.
110 International Crisis Group (n 43) 32.
111 Ibid.
112 Borges Nhamirre, 'Rwanda Expands Its Protection of Mozambique's Natural Resources' *Institute for Security Studies* (1 February 2023).
113 Ibid.
114 Ibid, 43.
115 Ibid, 56.

116 International Crisis Group (n 43) ii.
117 Ibid.
118 Ibid, 9.
119 Interview with senior military official from South Africa, August 2021.
120 Saul Butera and Ania Nussbaum, 'Macron Acknowledges French Responsibility in Rwanda Genocide' *Bloomberg* (27 May 2021).
121 Clement Uwiringiyimana and Manuel Mucari, 'Rwanda Deploys Troops to Mozambique to Help Fight Insurgency' *Reuters* (9 July 2021).
122 Marko Svicevic, 'Concurrent Military Deployment in Mozambique and Their Permissibility under SADC Treaty Law' *AfricLaw* (28 July 2021).
123 'Mozambique: Nyusi Flew to Rwanda for Talks with Kagame; Fighting Against Terrorism at the Top of Agenda' *Club of Mozambique* (29 April 2021).
124 Interview with retired military general from Mozambique, August 2021.
125 Interview with European senior diplomat, August 2021.
126 Ibid.
127 Ibid.
128 Bethsheba Wambura, 'Tanzania Will Not Send Troops to Mozambique' *allAfrica* (27 May 2021).
129 See also the recommendations of International Crisis Group (n 43) 37.
130 Wambura (n 128).
131 Graham Bird et al, 'International Terrorism: Causes, Consequences and Cures' (2008) 31 (2) *The World Economy* 255–274.
132 Victor H Mlambo and Mfundo Mandla Masuku, 'Terror at the Front Gate: Insurgency in Mozambique and Its Implications for the SADC and South Africa' (2022) 22 (1) *Journal of Public Affairs*.
133 Bird et al (n 131) 270.

Bibliography

Alan Cowel, 'Tanzania Military Advisers Will Be Sent to Mozambique' *The New York Times* (23 February 1982).

Bethsheba Wambura, 'Tanzania Will Not Send Troops to Mozambique' *allAfrica* (27 May 2021).

Borges Nhamirre, 'Rwanda Expands Its Protection of Mozambique's Natural Resources' *Institute for Security Studies* (1 February 2023).

Chris Alden and Sérgio Chichiva, 'Cabo Delgado: "Al shabab/ISIS and the Crisis of Southern Africa"' *Policy Centre for the New South* (May 2021) <www.iese.ac.mz/wp-content/uploads/2021/06/PB_14-21_Alden_Chichava.pdf>.

Clement Uwiringiyimana and Manuel Mucari, 'Rwanda Deploys Troops to Mozambique to Help Fight Insurgency' *Reuters* (9 July 2021).

David M Matsinhe and Estacio Valoi, 'The Genesis of Insurgency in Northern Mozambique' *Institute for Security Studies* (1 October 2019).

Dorina A Bekoe, Stephanie M Burchard and Sarah A Daly, 'Extremism in Mozambique: Interpreting Group Tactics and the Role of the Government's Response in the Crisis in Cabo Delgado' *Institute for Defense Analyses* (1 March 2020).

Edward A Alpers, 'Ethnicity, Politics, and History in Mozambique' *Africa Today* (January 2011).

Emilia Columbo and Austin C Doctor, 'Foreign Fighters and the Trajectory of Violence in Northern Mozambique' *War on the Rocks* (13 April 2021).

Emmanuel Sulle, 'A Rapid Assessment of the Illegal Timber Trade Across the Ruvumba River on the Tanzania and Mozambique Border' *Worldwide Fund* (December 2024).

Eric Morier-Genoud, 'The Jihad Insurgency in Mozambique: Origin, Nature and Beginning' (2020) 14(3) *Journal of Eastern African Studies*.

Erick Kabendera, 'Militants in Mozambique Could Be Tanzanians' *The East African* (11 August 2018).

Erin Kearns, 'When to Take Credit for Terrorism? A Cross-National Examination of Claims and Attributions' (2021) 33 (1) *Terrorism and Political Violence.*

George Obulutsa, 'Militants from Mozambique Staged Deadly Attack in Tanzania, Police Say' *Reuters* (23 October 2020).

Gilbert Khadiagala, *Allies in Adversity: The Frontline States in Southern African Security, 1975–1993* (Ohio University Press, 1994).

Graham Bird et al, 'International Terrorism: Causes, Consequences and Cures' (2008) 31(2) *The World Economy.*

Institute for Economics and Peace, 'Global Terrorism Index 2019: Measuring the Impact of Terrorism' <https://www.economicsandpeace.org/wp-content/uploads/2020/08/GTI-2019web.pdf>.

International Crisis Group, 'Stemming the Insurrection in Mozambique's Cabo Delgado' (11 June 2021).

Isaac Olawale Albert, 'Rethinking the Functionality of Multinational Joint Task Force in Managing the Boko Haram Crisis in the Lake Chad Basin' (2017) 42(3) *Africa Development.*

James Kandoya, 'Tanzania, Mozambique to Fight Terrorism, Drug Trafficking' *IPP Media* (16 January 2018) <www.ippmedia.com/en/news/tanzania-mozambique-fight-terrorism-drug-trafficking>.

Lucy Shule, 'From Southern Africa to the Great Lakes Region: Challenges to Tanzanian Foreign Policy and Conflict Resolution in Sub-Sahkaran Africa' (Doctoral thesis, University of Newcastle, 2014).

Marko Svicevic, 'Concurrent Military Deployments in Mozambique and their Permissibility Under SADC Treaty Law' *AfricLaw* (28 July 2021).

Marko Svicevic and Timothy Walker, 'Limited Legal Options for SADC Military Action in Cabo Delgado' *Institute for Security Studies* (22 April 2021).

'Mozambique Attacks: Armed Group Was Born 10 Years Before the First Attack – Researcher' *Club of Mozambique* (22 June 2020).

'Mozambique: Nyusi Flew to Rwanda for Talks with Kagame; Fighting Against Terrorism at the Top of Agenda' *Club of Mozambique* (29 April 2021).

'Mozambique, Tanzania to Launch Joint Operations Against Insurgents' *Reuters* (23 November 2020).

Mtulya Athuman, 'Send Army to Curb Coast Killings, Opposition Says' *The Citizen* (17 May 2017).

Pekka Seppala and Bertha Koda, 'The Making of a Periphery: Economic Development and Cultural Encounters in Southern Tanzania' (1998) *Nordic Africa Institute.*

'Police Confirm Terror Suspects Arrested' *Dar Post* (15 April 2015).

'Police Seize 38 Terror Suspects in Three Regions' *The Citizen* (20 April 2021).

'President Nyusi Leaves Tanzania After Short Visit to Hold Talks with Magufuli' *Club of Mozambique* (10 December 2017).

'President Nyusi to Discuss Terrorism with Tanzanian Counterpart, High Commission of the United Republic of Mozambique' *Mozambique High Commission* (11 January 2021) <www.mozambiquehighcommission.org.uk/president-nyusi-to-discuss-terrorism-with-tanzanian-counterpart.html>.

Saul Butera and Ania Nussbaum, 'Macron Acknowledges French Responsibility in Rwanda Genocide' *Bloomberg* (27 May 2021).

'Soldier Killed in Raid Against Al-Shabaab Linked Gang' *The Citizen* (15 February 2015).

'Tanzania Hit by Recent ISIS Attack Near Mozambique Border' *News 24* (23 October 2020).

'Tanzania yakanusha madai kuwa linahusika na mzozo wa msumbiji' *BBC Swahili* (7 September 2020).

'TPDF to Launch Manhunt Along the Border with Mozambique' *The Citizen Tanzania* (11 August 2020).

UNHCR, 'UNHCR Appeals for Mozambicans Fleeing Violence to be Given Access to Asylum in Tanzania' (18 May 2021) <https://www.unhcr.org/news/briefing-notes/unhcr-appeals-mozambicans-fleeing-violence-be-given-access-asylum-tanzania>.
Victor H Mlambo and Mfundo Mandla Masuku, 'Terror at the Front Gate: Insurgency in Mozambique and Its Implications for the SADC and South Africa' (2022) 22(1) *Journal of Public Affairs*.

3 South Africa's security concerns in Mozambique and the growing threat of domestic terrorism

André Smit

3.1 Introduction

On 1 March 2022, the United States (US) Department of the Treasury's Office of Foreign Assets Control (OFAC) designated four 'Islamic State of Iraq and Syria (ISIS) and ISIS-Mozambique (ISIS-M)' financial facilitators based in South Africa as targets of the US domestic counter-terror sanctions regime.[1] Later in the year, on 26 October 2022, the US embassy in Pretoria[2] announced that the US government had received information that terrorists may be planning to conduct an attack targeting large gatherings of people at an unspecified location in the greater Sandton area of Johannesburg by 29 October 2022.[3] On 7 November 2022 OFAC designated another four members of an ISIS cell operating in South Africa with a further eight business entities linked to the members who were stated to have played 'pivotal roles in enabling terrorism and other criminal activities in the region'.[4] These events provide reminders of the perceived presence of terrorism activity in South Africa and the Southern African region.

What links are there between these events and persons present in the territory of South Africa and other terrorism activity in the region and, more specifically, with the ongoing insurgency in Northern Mozambique? This chapter will illustrate how the conflict in the northern parts of Mozambique and the growing terrorist presence in the Southern African region has become a concern to Pretoria and explore South Africa's domestic response to terrorism in light thereof. The existence of activities related to Ansar al-Sunna will also be explored considering the prosecution of the Thulsie twins in South Africa. Growing evidence points towards a proliferation of funding emanating from Southern Africa being channelled to Ansar al-Sunna, but this may be eclipsed by Islamic State (IS) cells that are already present in the region.[5]

The subject of this chapter stretches wider than the pages devoted to it, and some thoughts had to be abandoned due to space constraints, while others were abandoned due to necessity. In the latter category, it is pointed out that this chapter was drafted without prejudice to the possible classification of the conflict in Mozambique as a non-international armed conflict or the status and designation of the fighters that are engaging in violent acts in Northern Mozambique and beyond. Also, the detail relating to the legislation, international agreements and various

DOI: 10.4324/9781003317647-4

mandates and authorisations applicable to forces operating in the area was not included in the present discussion.

Notwithstanding such omissions, it is hoped that the present chapter will provide a useful view of South Africa's security concerns in Mozambique and the growing threat of domestic terrorism in the region. The chapter will proceed to highlight South African concerns around the growing terrorist presence in Southern Africa in Section 3.2 and then discuss South Africa's domestic response to terrorism and the emerging links between Ansar al-Sunna and South Africa in Section 3.3. Section 3.4 deals with the consequences of the growing threat of terrorism in South Africa for regional stability and for the situation in Mozambique, before concluding.

3.2 South African concerns around the growing terrorist presence in Southern Africa

Before terrorism became a point of focus in Mozambique, maritime security linked to piracy off the east coast of Africa served as a focus point in Mozambique–South Africa defence relations. This was evidenced by the March 2000 defence cooperation agreement that envisaged military cooperation, the promotion of training, the exchange of military intelligence and border liaison.[6] That agreement was followed by a memorandum of understanding that included Tanzania on the conduct of combined maritime patrols within Mozambican territory in June 2011.[7] Mozambique, South Africa and Tanzania further strengthened the maritime security arrangements between them in December 2011 by signing another memorandum of understanding on maritime security cooperation.[8] All three international agreements mentioned remain in force.[9] These agreements served as the basis for the South African National Defence Force (SANDF) engagement in an SADC-linked counter-piracy effort in the Mozambican channel. The area covered by Operation Copper stretches up to the coast of Tanzania, includes the combating of crime at sea, and commenced in 2011.[10] It has a limited footprint on land that supports maritime and air operations being executed with South African platforms accompanied by Mozambican personnel, and it has been operating in the maritime area adjacent to the areas of Mozambique affected by terrorism for several years. Links between Somali pirates and terrorist groups were suspected, and some evidence of local cooperation or toleration emerged, although the threat of such cooperation appeared to have loomed larger than the actual impact, but the transnational nature and potential adverse impact of such cooperation on neighbouring states did not go unnoticed.[11]

Countries in the Southern African region were aware of growing discontent in Mozambique before terrorist links surfaced. Five years after the commencement of Operation Copper, by 2016, reports of clashes between the FRELIMO-run government and the RENAMO opposition pointed to government debt, corruption, unemployment, climate change pressures, and a lack of improvement of the conditions of ordinary citizens notwithstanding booming energy projects as underlying sources of the tension and discontent.[12] Messages began to spread that economic woes in the area were to blame on the Islamic Council of Mozambique that was accused of looting the wealth of Mozambique with FRELIMO. Shari'a law was championed as the solution to a more equitable distribution of riches.[13] This may have contributed to 'watering' the present conflict, if it could not be viewed as contributing to the 'seeding' thereof in an area – starting with the Cabo Delgado and Nampula provinces in Mozambique and extending far north up the East African coast – where people of a predominantly Muslim religion have lived for centuries.[14]

It did not take long for the IS to claim credit for successes in Mozambique after the October 2017 attacks in Mocímboa da Praia, and from time to time the black IS flag was flown in Mozambique.[15] With these developments, the conflict was sure to attract the attention of all the global powers that treated IS as a major threat.[16] The South African Minister of International Relations and Cooperation indicated that Mozambique and South Africa were talking about the security situation in Cabo Delgado in 2020, but public details were scarce.[17] The dramatic assault on Palma in March 2021 brought the conflict into sharper international focus, supported by an international media that would report on international interests being prejudiced amongst the grave consequences for the local population and Mozambique.

In relative terms, South Africa is a strong power in the Southern African region, but conflict and civil unrest in any of its neighbouring countries risk the increase of the already-present inflow of migrants into South Africa and will require South African resources to support its neighbours.[18] While South Africa has freely assisted in the past, the internal political cost thereof has been increasing with a growing uneasiness surrounding the effect of the high numbers of foreign nationals in South Africa on employment, crime, the draining of social security resources, and stability. Some unrest in South Africa has been directly driven by a perceived threat posed by foreign nationals[19] and frustrations over the porous nature of South African land borders with Mozambique and Zimbabwe.[20] A porous border is something that enables terrorist activities, and, although of international concern, it is overshadowed by greater international and regional political factors. Eyes always turn to South Africa to see how and whether it will act. However, a unilateral act in Mozambique is not an option that fits well with South Africa's stated foreign policy approach that supports non-intervention and multilateralism. South Africa is sensitive towards being seen as dictating to its neighbours and treads carefully, sometimes punching way below its potential diplomatic weight on regional issues, to avoid exacerbating international criticism of its neighbours or being perceived as a Southern African 'Big Brother'. The risk of less than effective South African action unfortunately leaves the door open to powers from outside the region to fill a gap and entrench their interests in a region that could otherwise have been filled by South African and regional efforts. The presence of natural resources is a further risk for an economically strong (in relative regional terms) South Africa that may be accused by opportunists of positioning itself to acquire rights and interests in the minerals and energy exploration and exploitation in the north of Mozambique.[21] Risks of terror attacks in South Africa were also emerging if South Africa chose to become involved in Mozambican counter-terror efforts and included open threats.[22]

3.3 South Africa's domestic response to terrorism and the emerging links between Ansar al-Sunna and South Africa

The South African policy, legislative and executive architecture in relation to terrorism falls beyond the scope of this chapter. Nevertheless, it is useful to note that the South African counter-terror legislative framework is extensive, and even if there is room for improvement, counter-terror policies are in place. South Africa has signed and ratified or acceded to most regional and international instruments relevant to terrorism and maintains standing internal structures aimed at coordinating the government's counter-terror response.[23]

Unfortunately, terrorism is a laden term in South Africa, and this must be considered as part of the bigger picture of South African counter-terror responses. The South African ruling political party – the African National Congress (ANC) – were once called 'terrorists' during their struggle against apartheid in the same manner that freedom fighters in the various other liberation movements were labelled terrorists. Internationally, Palestinian freedom fighters have frequently been labelled terrorists in the same manner, and the ANC cherishes its solidarity with the people of Palestine who continue to struggle against Israel. Naturally, the shared struggle between South African liberation movements and Palestinian liberation movements results in a deep political affinity in the ANC towards Palestinian freedom fighters and a concomitant resentment of their being labelled terrorists.[24] This dynamic produces a nuanced approach by South Africa that results in a more measured response where others may automatically react to the word 'terrorist'. It remains a politically sensitive term that must be used with caution in South African political and social conversation as the hero, and 'freedom fighter' of one person used to be labelled a criminal and 'terrorist' by another.

International sentiment and UN rhetoric supporting freedom fighters in the struggle against apartheid did a lot to change perceptions. However, when the Protocol Additional to the Geneva Conventions (GCs) of 12 August 1949 and Relating to the Protection of Victims of International Armed Conflicts of 8 June 1977[25] (API) elevated armed conflicts in which peoples are fighting against colonial domination and alien occupation and against racist regimes in the exercise of their right of self-determination to an international armed conflict as contemplated in article 2 to the Geneva Conventions of 12 August 1949,[26] international law stepped into the fray. Notwithstanding the customary international law status thereof, API conferred international legitimacy to South African freedom fighters and transformed a freedom fighter into a combatant.

This simplification of a rather complex situation is a possible explanation for the hesitancy of the South African government to enthusiastically join all international efforts against 'terrorism' since the late 1990s, particularly in instances where the target of such efforts could be perceived to include persons fighting for Palestinian freedom or other politically allied fighters.[27] In the mid-1990s it may also have created a false sense of security in that it was not expected that international terror would ever be directed against South Africa. That false sense of security was steadily challenged by increasing reports of links between international terror networks and South Africa. In 1998 it was reported that militant organisations such as the Algerian Islamic Salvation Front, Al-Qaeda, Hezbollah, Islamic Jihad and the Taliban attended conferences near Pretoria and that foreign militants considered South Africa a base for various activities.[28] In 2004 two South African nationals were arrested in Pakistan in the presence of a suspect in the US embassy bombings in East Africa in 1998, and disconcerting unconfirmed reports surfaced that they might have been planning to attack targets in South Africa.[29] Allegations against the South African Docrat brothers of links with terrorist organisations in 2007 further fuelled the spectre of terrorist cells existing in South Africa.[30]

By 2008 the South African Defence Minister expressed concern that Al-Qaeda may establish networks in South Africa.[31] The possibility of a terrorist attack being launched against a visiting foreign warship calling in a South African port is a dreaded spectre, and the October 2000 Al-Qaeda attack on the USS Cole in Aden, Yemen lent credibility to such a possibility. The expected number of international visitors when South Africa was preparing to host the 2010 FIFA World Cup soccer tournament meant that the likelihood of a terrorist attack had to be considered.[32] A former head of the Criminal Investigation Unit of the South African Police Service (SAPS) is reported to have stated that South Africa 'is a perfect place for terrorist networks to cool off, regroup, and plan finances and operations'.[33]

However, going somewhat further back in time, South Africa has had to deal with terrorist-related matters unrelated to Mozambique since the very birth of the democratic era in 1994 and before the first reports of terrorist camps in Mozambique surfaced around 2003.[34] One could start with the establishment of the People Against Gangsterism and Drugs (PAGAD) in 1995, noting that PAGAD was designated as a foreign terrorist organisation by the US State Department in 2001 after several bombings and killings.[35] In 1996 Israel lodged a formal complaint with South Africa regarding the existence of five Hezbollah training camps in South Africa.[36] Terrorists involved in the attacks on the US embassies in East Africa were arrested in Cape Town in 1999.[37] In 2002 the South African National Intelligence Agency warned that South Africa was being used to raise funds and serve as a safe haven for international terrorists, while 2004 saw the Minister of Home Affairs confirming that Al-Qaeda members are known to have used South African passports and that the suspected leader of Al-Qaeda in South Africa was reported to have evaded capture in the same year.[38] Twenty further significant events and incidents pointing to internationally linked terrorist activities in South Africa were recorded until 2010 when reports surfaced of militants being infiltrated from camps in Northern Mozambique into South Africa.[39]

Suspicions of strong links between IS and the insurgency in Mozambique have subsided since 2021, and while a link between specific local incidents and events in Mozambique may not always be forthcoming, answers to the more general question of links between terrorist activity in Mozambique and events in South Africa have become progressively clearer since 2010.[40] Terror financing links with South Africa of wider import were shown around the time of the January 2019 DusitD2 attacks in Kenya. Some of the suspects in the attack used funds transferred from Cape Town to Kenya to pay for weapons, vehicles, accommodation, bribes and surveillance.[41]

In a case that attracted much attention over the years, SAPS issued a public statement on 8 February 2022 informing South Africa that Brandon-Lee Thulsie and his brother, Tony-Lee Thulsie, following a guilty plea, were sentenced to 8 and 11 years of imprisonment, respectively, for terrorism-related crimes.[42] They were alleged to have been planning attacks on the US embassy, among other places, conspiring to commit terrorist acts elsewhere in South Africa, and were accused of attempting to leave South Africa to join the Islamic State in Iraq and the Levant (ISIL).[43] It was also reported that Renaldo Smith, a person associated with the Thulsie twins' residence, was reported as leaving for Mozambique with 15 others in 2018, and he was photographed when responsibility for an attack was claimed by IS in Mozambique.[44]

On 1 March 2022 the US Department of the Treasury's OFAC designated four 'ISIS and ISIS-M' financial facilitators based in South Africa as targets of the US domestic counter-terror sanctions regime.[45] The statements by the US at the time of the designation indicated strengthened suspicion of links between IS in South Africa and Mozambique with several South African IS sympathisers who were believed to have joined ISIS-M as combatants, taking into account that the US designation of ISIS-M is their synonym for Ansar al-Sunna in Mozambique.[46]

The South African National Terrorism Financing Risk Assessment of 31 March 2022 provides a rare insight into the South African government's own thinking of links between South Africa and terrorism in the region:

> On the African continent, terrorist groups continue to spread and influence terrorist activities across borders, entrenching themselves into existing conflicts, exploiting security vulnerabilities and enabling factors, and then causing cross-border spill overs. In Southern Africa, the attacks carried out by Al Sunnah Wa Jama'ah (ASWJ) in northern Mozambique, many of which having been claimed by the Islamic State Central Africa Province (ISCAP), is of growing security concern. ASWJ, through its links to regional terrorist groups, such as ISCAP, serves as an attractive option for FTFs to conduct 'violent' jihad when seeking to demonstrate their support of the ideology. South African authorities are increasingly concerned about the impact that this is having on Mozambique's neighbouring countries, as supporters may consider the conflict zone a viable operational theatre or safe haven from where to direct operations in the region. The possibility of retaliatory attacks in response to military deployment by SADC countries [*sic*] to assist in the stabilisation in northern Mozambique remains a concern. In July 2020, IS warned that it would retaliate with attacks if South Africa became involved in the conflict in Mozambique.[47]

The group attacking Palma on 24 March 2021 called itself Ansar al-Sunna, and it was reported to have included South African terrorist fighters.[48] The immediate local response to oppose the attacks included the actions of a South African private military and security company, Dyck Advisory Group.[49] South Africans working in Palma were also caught up in the violence and South African lives were lost during the attack with 43 requiring emergency evacuation and medical care.[50] Direct links to Ansar al-Sunna cannot be surprising following many years of warnings and reports.[51] Publicly disclosed links between terrorists and South Africa means increasing scrutiny and increasing pressure on government institutions that suffer from corruption, understaffing and other challenges. The South African Minister in the Presidency responsible for state security responded to the 2022 US designation of IS members operating in South Africa by stating that South Africa is 'resolved to combat terrorism and illicit financing activities' and that South Africa will 'not allow our territory to be used to fund terrorism in other countries', thereby indicating South Africa's intentions.[52]

This notwithstanding, South Africa's Financial Action Task Force (FATF)[53] Review of 2023 led to a 'grey-listing' for South Africa on 24 February 2023, thereby classifying South Africa as a jurisdiction under increased monitoring.[54] Eight areas of strategic deficiencies led to the grey-listing and two of the eight areas include explicit references to terrorism-related matters.[55]

3.4 Consequences of the growing threat of terrorism within South Africa for regional stability and for the situation in Mozambique

The August 1998 bombing of the US embassies in Kenya and Tanzania – the latter a SADC member state – and reports that one of the Tanzanian perpetrators, Khalfan Khamis Mohammed, had crossed into Mozambique shortly after the bombings and thereafter into South Africa before being arrested in 1999, should have caused concern in Pretoria, and calls rose for SADC to formulate its own regional counter-terror strategy by 2005.[56] Following the escalation of the insurgency in 2021, Mozambique – also an SADC member state – accepted assistance from international actors as far as the European Union (EU) to counter the threat.[57] The EU approved support in June 2021 and established a training mission in Mozambique aimed at providing 'training and support to the Mozambican armed forces to protect the civilian population and restore security in the Cabo Delgado province'.[58] After a request from Mozambique in May 2020, SADC deployed its SADC Mission in Mozambique (SAMIM) on 15 July 2021 'as a regional response to support the Republic of Mozambique to combat terrorism and acts of violent extremism'.[59] Troop-contributing countries include Angola, Botswana, the Democratic Republic of the Congo (DRC), Lesotho, Malawi, South Africa, Tanzania and Zambia and the EU provides support.[60]

Rwanda announced its deployment, at the request of Mozambique.[61] Troops arrived in August 2021, and their impact was generally assessed as positive,[62] but what does it mean when a SADC member state turns to powers from outside the SADC region to assist it in regaining control of the insurgency? What message does it send to SADC or to South Africa, if any, and what are the implications for relations between South Africa and Mozambique, particularly considering a strained relationship between South Africa and Rwanda in recent years?[63] On the one hand, the Mozambican decisions could be viewed as accepting any help that it can get in a desperate situation, where SADC or Mozambique's immediate neighbours did not act as quickly as desired, but it could also signal a lack of trust in SADC or South Africa to make any effective contribution that would be meaningful for Mozambique and its people. The message notwithstanding, a SADC technical mission made preliminary findings indicating that Ansar al-Sunna receives funding from sympathetic individuals and private organisations that include mobile platforms such as M-Pesa from South Africa[64] and South Africans continued to join the insurgents.[65]

By April 2021 widespread violence, insecurity and the deaths of more than 2 400 people, the displacement of over 500 000 civilians and the disruption of economic activities, especially farming, have been reported.[66] SADC member states 'noted' the insurgency 'with concern' in 2020.[67] A 'reasonable basis to suggest that' the insurgency 'may spill into neighbouring SADC countries if not addressed, especially those countries contiguous to Mozambique, namely Zimbabwe, Tanzania, South Africa, Eswatini, Zambia and Malawi' was found and South Africa expressed concerns that the situation may 'destabilise the region, reverse regional peace gains and dividends, increase the inflow of IDPs into South Africa and neighbouring countries, and disrupt possibilities of South Africa importing natural gas from Mozambique'.[68]

The July 2020 IS newsletter threatening the possible opening of a fighting front inside South Africa if the South African government becomes involved in Mozambique[69] is indicative of terror risks similar to those faced by Kenya for its involvement in Somalia.[70] Being a target and being used as a base of operations or a conduit for the channelling of funds that finance terrorist activities are factors that any responsible government must factor into its thinking and planning.

Terrorism transcends religion, culture and political affiliation. It constantly evolves in its targets, motivations, allegiances, enemies, means, methods and facilitators and does not respect previous political alliances. Terrorist cells have proven to be much more nimble and agile than any one country's security apparatus. Cooperation, information sharing, trust, sacrifice for the benefit of the safety of all people and a genuine concern and care for the people under the control of any government in the region are the only means of defeating terrorism. Governments themselves too often provide the motivation for terrorists to recruit followers through corruption, tribalism, factionalism and greed, and the solution to countering the actions that underlie these potentially is a discussion that is larger than countering terrorism.

South Africa pointed out that there are a range of implications flowing from the insurgency, including the fact that internally displaced persons might end up seeking refuge in South Africa and that South Africa's possible importation of natural gas from Mozambique may be affected.[71] All the national security agencies need to enhance their capabilities and skills, and combined with efficient communication and the timely sharing of intelligence, a regional effort is unavoidable as the same concerns are valid for all countries in the region. A supra-regional effort that includes organisations and states outside the region is possibly essential.[72]

The decades of relative calm and development in Southern Africa following the end of civil wars after independence and the wars of independence before that brought hard-won gains to the people of the region. All too often the images of the results of terrorism reflect a devastated landscape with the total ruin of infrastructure and the social fibre of the places ravaged by terrorism and the responses needed to eradicate it if left unchecked for too long.[73] Terrorism spreads more easily in poor communities left unsupported by poor governance. Governance that is more effective, responsive and free of corruption must be elevated among the priorities, and the 'business of good governance' should take up more space on agendas. This is especially sensitive in a region that is resource rich and where such riches must be alluring targets for terrorists looking for means to fund their activities. Such resources have the potential to draw in major powers and other smaller players that are not above using instability to reap economic rewards.

Governments becoming involved in operations against Ansar al-Sunnah in Mozambique would do well to learn from countries such as Cameroon that joined the fight against Boko Haram and suffered the consequences of attacks on home soil and Kenya. It must be assumed that IS sleeper cells in Eswatini, Lesotho, South Africa, Botswana and elsewhere may include hardened and experienced fighters with links to Ansar al-Sunnah in Mozambique considering the links that have already been established.[74] Involvement in Mozambique makes heightened vigilance at home imperative, and the point of non-involvement to avoid injury has already been passed.[75]

The South African Financial Intelligence Centre recently noted that terrorism financing in South Africa poses a 'direct threat to South Africa's national security as well as the integrity and reputation of its financial system'.[76] It expressed South Africa's increasing concern about the impact of regional links and violence on Mozambique's neighbours as any of these may be considered a haven from the conflict in Mozambique, while participation in operations in Mozambique may make the participating neighbours targets.[77] A closer scrutiny of cash transactions, border safeguards, charities and non-profit organisations, virtual currencies and organised crime is required, which was confirmed by South Africa's FATF grey-listing.[78]

The implications for a grey-listed country include reputational damage as its effectiveness in combating terror financing is placed in doubt; cross-border transactions become more difficult; and costs of transactions may be negatively affected.[79] For a country and a region that is desperate to see economic growth, further barriers to trade are not at all welcome although the South African government has indicated that it expects a limited impact.[80] The government can simply not afford that much-needed economic development and social upliftment that is still so urgently needed in the region, which are in any manner compromised by terrorism in the region.

3.5 Conclusion

The political, social, economic and human cost is too much to contemplate, and SADC already listed factors weakening counter-terrorism measures as 'inadequate legislation, weak institutions responsible for addressing terrorism, perceptions of social exclusion and corruption, a lack of information-sharing, inadequate cooperation between civil society and government, porous borders, rampant illegal migration, use of the region for training and mobilising terrorist groups, and a failure to harmonise legislation'.[81] Of course, the 'trick' for governments is not to list the factors but to do something about it.

If terrorism poses a significant threat to Southern Africa and its people based on publicly available information, one shudders to think what is available to intelligence services and governments. South Africa's concerns should not be those of her alone but should be the concern of every country in the Southern African region. South Africa's stability affects the region inordinately more considering the regional reliance on South African ports, industry and strength. If that is affected, the whole region will be affected.

It should also be clear that no state can address the terrorist threat in Southern Africa alone. Out-of-region assistance should be viewed as opportunities rather than threats, and continental and international cooperation must be leveraged with necessary caution to strengthen the local and regional responses. Ansar al-Sunna is linked internationally in any event; if anything, it is bound to become more integrated into the international terrorist network rather than less.

States may have to develop an appetite and plan for the realisation of risks associated with fighting terrorists. This will likely, if not immediately, include terror attacks locally and should not catch governments by surprise, having been duly warned and being aware of precedents for this in the past in other regions.

Notes

1 U.S. Department of the Treasury, 'Treasury Sanctions South Africa-based ISIS Organisers and Financial Facilitators' (1 March 2022) <https://home.treasury.gov/news/press-releases/jy0616>.

2 Pretoria, in the City of Tshwane Metropolitan Municipality, Gauteng, is the administrative and 'ultimate' capital of South Africa; see <www.gov.za/about-sa/south-africas-provinces>.

3 U.S. Embassy and Consulates in South Africa, 'Security Alert: US. Embassy Possible Attack' (26 October 2022).

4 Peter Fabricius, 'Are Red Flags About Islamic State in South Africa Alarmist?' *Institute for Security Studies* (11 November 2022); see also U.S. Department of the Treasury, 'Treasury Designates Members of ISIS Cell in South Africa' (7 November 2022).

5 UN Doc. S/2022/63 (28 January 2022) para 16, as quoted by Anneli Botha, 'Trans-Regionalisation of Terrorism in Eastern and Southern Africa' *EAPCCO CTCoE Issue Paper 5/2022* (16 April 2010) para 1.2.

6 Cooperation Agreement in the Field of Defence Between the Government of the Republic of South Africa and the Government of the Republic of Mozambique (16 March 2000).

7 Memorandum of Understanding Between the Government of the Republic of Mozambique and the Government of the Republic of South Africa on the Conduct of Combined Maritime Patrols within the Territory of the Republic of Mozambique (1 June 2011).

8 Memorandum of Understanding Between the Government of the Republic of Mozambique and the Government of the Republic of South Africa and the Government of the United Republic of Tanzania on Maritime Security Cooperation (13 December 2011).

9 See the South African Treaty Register <https://treaties.dirco.gov.za/dbtw-wpd/textbase/treatywebsearch.htm>.

10 Department of Defence, 'Annual Report 2011/12'8' (2012) 151 <www.gov.za/sites/default/files/gcis_document/201409/defence-annualreport1112a.pdf>; Reporting by Second Line of Defence (6 July 2013) <https://sldinfo.com/2013/06/south-africa-and-anti-piracy-operations/>.

11 World Bank, 'The Pirates of Somalia: Ending the Threat, Rebuilding a Nation' World Bank Vice-Presidency for Africa (11 April 2013); Robyn Kriel and Briana Duggan, 'Somali Pirate Kings Are Under Investigation for Helping ISIS and al-Shabaab' *CNN World* (10 July 2017); Jonathan Saul and Camila Reed, 'Shabaab-Somali Pirate Links Growing: UN Adviser' *Reuters* (20 October 2011); Samantha Farqhuhar, 'When Overfishing Leads to Terrorism' (2017) 21 (2) *World Affairs: The Journal of International Issues* 68.

12 Gustavo de Carvalho, Jonathan Rozen and Lisa Reppel, 'The Perfect Storm: Mozambique's Compounding Crises' *ISS Today* (22 July 2016); Tom van Rentergem, 'Al-Shabaab in Mozambique: Taking Stock of an Insurgency Under Cover' *Egmont Policy Brief 281* (June 2022); Enio Chingotuane and others, 'Strategic Options for Managing Violent Extremism in Southern Africa: The Case of Mozambique' *Friedrich Ebert Stiftung Situation Report* (October 2021).

13 Joseph Hanlon, 'Ignoring the Roots of Mozambique's War in a Push for Military Victory' *ACCORD Conflict and Resilience Monitor* 2021/2 (21 August 2021).

14 Ibid.

15 'Stemming the Insurrection in Mozambique's Cabo Delgado' *Crisis Group* (2021); 'Dozens Killed in Mozambique for Refusing to Join Terrorists' *Deutsche Welle* (22 April 2020); Jason Burke, 'Isis Claims Sub-Saharan Attacks in a Sign of African Ambitions' *The Guardian* (6 June 2019).

16 Hanlon (n 13).

17 'SANDF Stays Mum on Possible Assistance to Mozambique AFP' *SABC Africa Channel* (4 June 2020).

18 'South Africa Is Ready to Help Mozambique with Its Insurgency' *DefenceWeb* (3 September 2020); Chingotuane and others (n 12).

19 'South Africa "on the Precipice of Explosive Xenophobic Violence", UN Experts Warn' *UN News* (15 July 2022); Themba Hadebe, 'South Africa Events of 2020' *Human Rights Watch* (2020); Mamokhosi Choane, Lukong Stella Shulika and Mandla Mthombeni, 'An Analysis of the Causes, Effects and Ramifications of Xenophobia in South Africa' (2011) 3 (2) *Insight on Africa* (African Studies Association of India); Khadija Patel, 'What Caused the Xenophobic Attacks in South Africa?' *Al Jazeera* (6 April 2016).

20 Ralph Mathekga, 'Terrorism Left Unchecked in Southern Africa' *GIS Reports Online* (19 October 2020).

21 Ibid.

22 Aymenn Jawad Al-Tamimi, 'Islamic State Editorial on Mozambique' *Aymenn Jawad Al-Tamimi's Blog* (3 July 2020) <www.aymennjawad.org/2020/07/islamic-state-editorial-on-mozambique>.

23 The country report that South Africa submitted to the 11th UN Congress on Crime Prevention and Criminal Justice is most instructive and can be accessed at <www.saps.gov.za/resource_centre/publications/country_report/part_three.pdf>.

24 Mathekga (n 20).

25 Protocol Additional to the Geneva Conventions of 12 August 1949, and Relating to the Protection of Victims of International Armed Conflicts (Protocol I) (adopted 8 June 1977, entered into force 7 December 1978) 1125 UNTS 3.

26 Geneva Convention (I) for the Amelioration of the Condition of the Wounded and Sick in Armed Forces in the Field (adopted 12 August 1949, entered into force 21 October 1950) 75 UNTS 31; Geneva Convention (II) for the Amelioration of the Condition of Wounded, Sick and Shipwrecked Members of Armed Forces at Sea (adopted 12 August

1949, entered into force 21 October 1950) 75 UNTS 85; Geneva Convention (III) Relative to the Treatment of Prisoners of War (adopted 12 August 1949, entered into force 21 October 1950) 75 UNTS 135; and Geneva Convention (IV) Relative to the Protection of Civilian Persons in Time of War (adopted 12 August 1949, entered into force 21 October 1950) 75 UNTS 287.

27 Hussein Solomon, 'Playing Ostrich: Lessons Learned from South Africa's Response to Terrorism' *Africa Centre for Strategic Studies Africa Security Brief No 9* (31 January 2011); Brenda Githing'u, 'The Counterterrorism Conundrum: Exploring the Evolution of South Africa's Extremist Networks' *Hudson Institute* (23 October 2021).

28 Githing'u (n 27).

29 Staff Reporters, 'SA Men "Received Al-Qaeda Training"' *Mail & Guardian* (23 August 2004).

30 Michael Georgy, 'S Africa al Qaeda Suspect "Quiet, Religious" Dentist' *Reuters* (22 January 2007).

31 Githing'u (n 27).

32 Anneli Botha, 'Preparations for the 2010 FIFA World Cup: Vulnerability and Threat of Terrorism' *Real Instituto Elcano Working Paper 14/2010* (16 April 2010).

33 Solomon (n 27).

34 Ibid.

35 Ibid.

36 Ibid.

37 Ibid.

38 Ibid.

39 Ibid.

40 Austin Doctor, 'After Palma: Assessing the Islamic State's Position in Northern Mozambique' *George Washington University Program on Extremism Nexus Report* (August 2022).

41 Botha (n 5).

42 South African Police Service, 'Media Statement: Directorate for Priority Crimes Investigation (HAWKS)' (27 October 2022) <www.saps.gov.za/newsroom/msspeechdetail.php?nid=37994>.

43 Ibid.

44 Botha (n 5); 'Trans-Regionalisation of Terrorism in Eastern and Southern Africa' (2022) *Counter-Terrorism Centre of Excellence*, Issue Paper 5/2022 <https://eapcco-ctcoe.org/ct-issue-papers/17>.

45 U.S. Department of the Treasury, 'Treasury Sanctions South African-Based ISIS Organisers and Financial Facilitators' (1 March 2022) <https://home.treasury.gov/news/press-releases/jy0616>.

46 Peter Fabricius, 'US Sanctions Four Alleged ISIS Ringleaders in South Africa' *Institute for Security Studies* (4 March 2022); Doctor (n 40).

47 Financial Intelligence Centre, 'South African National Terrorism Financing Risk Assessment' <www.fic.gov.za/Documents/TF%20NRA%2031%20March%202022.pdf>.

48 Fernando Cardoso, 'Cabo Delgado: Insurgents, Jihadists or Terrorists?' *Instituto Marquês de Valle Flôr* (20 May 2021).

49 Ibid; David McKenzie and Ghazi Balkiz, 'ISIS-Linked Militants Are Threatening Huge Natural Gas Reserves the World Needs Badly Right Now' *CNN World* (28 October 2022); Doctor (n 40).

50 Christina Goldbaum, Eric Schmidt and Declan Walsh, 'As Militants Seize Mozambique Gas Hub, a Dash for Safety Turns Deadly' *New York Times* (28 March 2021); Githing'u (n 27).

51 Hussein Solomon, 'South Africa Provides Fertile Ground for Funders of Terrorism – Here's Why' *The Conversation* (10 November 2022).

52 'SA "Resolved" to Fight Terrorism – Gungubele' *DefenceWeb* (10 November 2022).

53 Financial Action Task Force, 'What We Do' <www.fatf-gafi.org/about/>.

54 See 'Jurisdictions under Increased Monitoring' *FATF* (24 February 2023) <www.fatf-gafi.org/en/publications/High-risk-and-other-monitored-jurisdictions/Increased-monitoring-february-2023.html>.
55 Media Statement by National Treasury, 'Listing of South Africa by the Financial Action Task Force as a "Jurisdiction under Increased Monitoring"' (24 February 2023) <www.treasury.gov.za/comm_media/press/2023/2023022401%20Media%20statement%20-%20Response%20to%20FATF.pdf>.
56 Michael Rifer, 'SADC and Terrorism' (2005) 14 (1) *African Security Review* 107.
57 EU, 'EUTM Mozambique' <www.eeas.europa.eu/eutm-mozambique_en?s=4411>; EU, 'European Union Training Mission in Mozambique (EUTM MOZ)' (15 October 2021) <https://emad.defensa.gob.es/en/Galerias/operaciones/46-UE-EUTM-Mozambique/files/trainingmozambique_15oct_0.pd.pdf>.
58 Ibid.
59 SADC, 'SADC Mission in Mozambique (SAMIM) in Brief' (10 November 2021) <www.sadc.int/latest-news/sadc-mission-mozambique-samim-brief>.
60 James Tasamba, 'EU Provides Additional Support to African Military Mission in Mozambique' *AA* (8 September 2022) <www.aa.com.tr/en/africa/eu-provides-additional-support-to-african-military-mission-in-mozambique/2680395>.
61 'Rwanda Deploys Joint Force to Mozambique' *Ministry of Defence of Rwanda* (10 July 2021) <www.mod.gov.rw/news-detail/rwanda-deploys-joint-force-to-mozambique-1>.
62 LUSA, 'Mozambique: Arrival of Rwandan Forces Was Very Positive' *Club of Mozambique* (21 February 2022); 'Rwandan Forces Display Confidence Amid Precarious Security Situation in Mozambique' *Africanews* (10 November 2022).
63 Liesl Louw-Vaudran, 'Coordination: Key to the Success of African Solutions for Mozambique' *Institute for Security Studies* (11 April 2022).
64 Githing'u (n 27).
65 Cardoso (n 48).
66 Clayton Hazvinei Vhumbunu, 'Insurgency in Mozambique: The Role of the Southern African Development Community' *ACCORD* (21 April 2021) <www.accord.org.za/conflict-trends/insurgency-in-mozambique-the-role-of-the-southern-african-development-community/>.
67 Ibid.
68 DefenceWeb (n 18).
69 Qaanitah Hunter, '"We Are Taking It Very, Very Seriously": Dlodlo on ISIS Threat' *News24* (19 July 2020); Al-Tamimi (n 22); also see 'Mozambique: Islamic State Threatens South Africa – AIM Report' *Club of Mozambique* (7 July 2020).
70 International Crisis Group, 'Al-Shabaab Five Years After Westgate: Still a Menace in East Africa' *ICG Africa Report No 265* (21 September 2018).
71 DefenceWeb (n 18); Hisham Aidi, 'Mozambique: A New Civil War?' *Policy Center for the New South PB 39/22* (27 May 2022); Amal El Ouassif and Seleman Yusuph Kitenge, 'Terorist Insurgency in Northern Mozambique: Context, Analysis, and Spillover Effects on Tanzania' *Policy Center for the New South* (1 December 2021).
72 DefenceWeb (n 18); Aidi (n 71); El Ouassif and Kitenge (n 71).
73 Mathekga (n 20).
74 Peter Fabricius, 'How Serious Is the Islamic State Threat to Attack South Africa?' *Institute for Security Studies* (23 July 2020).
75 Fabricius (n 46).
76 Financial Intelligence Centre, 'South African National Terrorism Financing Risk Assessment' (31 March 2022) <www.fic.gov.za/Documents/TF%20NRA%2031%20March%202022.pdf>.
77 Ibid, 4.
78 Fabricius (n 4).
79 See National Treasury Fact Sheet, 'What Does FATF Greylisting Mean for a Country?' <www.treasury.gov.za/comm_media/press/2023/2023022501%20FATF%20Grey%20Listing%20Fact%20Sheet.pdf>.

80 Tassilo Hummel, Bhargav Acharya and Alexander Winning, 'Financial Crime Watchdog Adds South Africa to "Grey List"' *Reuters* (24 February 2023).
81 Chingotuane and others (n 12).

Bibliography

Amal El Ouassif and Seleman Yusuph Kitenge, 'Terrorist Insurgency in Northern Mozambique: Context, Analysis, and Spillover Effects on Tanzania' *Policy Center for the New South* (1 December 2021).

Anneli Botha, 'Preparations for the 2010 FIFA World Cup: Vulnerability and Threat of Terrorism' *Real Instituto Elcano Working Paper 14/2010* (16 April 2010).

Anneli Botha, 'Trans-Regionalisation of Terrorism in Eastern and Southern Africa' *EAPCCO CTCoE Issue Paper 5/2022* (16 April 2010).

Austin Doctor, 'After Palma: Assessing the Islamic State's Position in Northern Mozambique' *George Washington University Program on Extremism Nexus Report* (August 2022).

Aymenn Jawad Al-Tamimi, 'Islamic State Editorial on Mozambique' *Aymenn Jawad Al-Tamimi's Blog* (3 July 2020) <www.aymennjawad.org/2020/07/islamic-state-editorial-on-mozambique>.

Brenda Githing'u, 'The Counterterrorism Conundrum: Exploring the Evolution of South Africa's Extremist Networks' *Hudson Institute* (23 October 2021).

Christina Goldbaum, Eric Schmidt and Declan Walsh, 'As Militants Seize Mozambique Gas Hub, a Dash for Safety Turns Deadly' *New York Times* (28 March 2021).

Clayton Hazvinei Vhumbunu, 'Insurgency in Mozambique: The Role of the Southern African Development Community' *ACCORD* (21 April 2021) <www.accord.org.za/conflict-trends/insurgency-in-mozambique-the-role-of-the-southern-african-development-community/>.

'Cooperation Agreement in the Field of Defence Between the Government of the Republic of South Africa and the Government of the Republic of Mozambique' (16 March 2000) <https://treaties.dirco.gov.za/dbtw-wpd/images/20000306MozambiqueCooperationDefence.pdf>.

Counter-Terrorism Centre of Excellence, *Issue Paper 5/2022* <https://eapcco-ctcoe.org/ct-issue-papers/>.

David McKenzie and Ghazi Balkiz, 'ISIS-Linked Militants are Threatening Huge Natural Gas Reserves the World Needs Badly Right Now' *CNN World* (28 October 2022).

Department of Defence Annual Report 2011/12 151 <www.gov.za/sites/default/files/gcis_document/201409/defence-annualreport1112a.pdf>.

'Dozens Killed in Mozambique for Refusing to Join Terrorists' *Deutsche Welle* (22 April 2020).

Enio Chingotuane and others, 'Strategic Options for Managing Violent Extremism in Southern Africa: The Case of Mozambique' *Friedrich Ebert Stiftung Situation Report* (October 2021).

EU, 'EUTM Mozambique' <www.eeas.europa.eu/eutm-mozambique_en?s=4411>; EU, 'European Union Training Mission in Mozambique (EUTM MOZ)' (15 October 2021) <https://emad.defensa.gob.es/en/Galerias/operaciones/46-UE-EUTM-Mozambique/files/trainingmozambique_15oct_0.pd.pdf>.

Fernando Cardoso, 'Cabo Delgado: Insurgents, Jihadists or Terrorists?' *Instituto Marquês de Valle Flôr* (20 May 2021).

Financial Action Task Force, 'What We Do' <www.fatf-gafi.org/about/>.

Financial Intelligence Centre, 'South African National Terrorism Financing Risk Assessment' (31 March 2022) <www.fic.gov.za/Documents/TF%20NRA%2031%20March%202022.pdf>.

Geneva Convention (I) for the Amelioration of the Condition of the Wounded and Sick in Armed Forces in the Field (1949) <https://treaties.un.org/Pages/showDetails.aspx?objid=080000028015847c&clang=_en>.

Geneva Convention (II) for the Amelioration of the Condition of Wounded, Sick and Shipwrecked Members of Armed Forces at Sea (1949) <https://treaties.un.org/Pages/showDetails.aspx?objid=08000002801591b0&clang=_en>.
Geneva Convention (III) Relative to the Treatment of Prisoners of War (1949) https://treaties.un.org/Pages/showDetails.aspx?objid=0800000280159839&clang=_en.
Geneva Convention (IV) Relative to the Protection of Civilian Persons in Time of War (1949) https://treaties.un.org/Pages/showDetails.aspx?objid=080000028015 8b1a&clang=_en.
Gustavo de Carvalho, Jonathan Rozen and Lisa Reppel, 'The Perfect Storm: Mozambique's Compounding Crises' *Institute for Security Studies* (22 July 2016).
Hisham Aidi, 'Mozambique: A new Civil War?' *Policy Center for the New South PB 39/22* (27 May 2022).
Hussein Solomon, 'Playing Ostrich: Lessons Learned from South Africa's Response to Terrorism' *Africa Centre for Strategic Studies Africa Security Brief No 9* (31 January 2011).
Hussein Solomon, 'South Africa Provides Fertile Ground for Funders of Terrorism – Here's Why' *The Conversation* (10 November 2022).
International Crisis Group, 'Al-Shabaab Five Years After Westgate: Still a Menace in East Africa' *ICG Africa Report No 265* (21 September 2018).
James Tasamba, 'EU Provides Additional Support to African Military Mission in Mozambique' *AA* (8 September 2022) <www.aa.com.tr/en/africa/eu-provides-additional-support-to-african-military-mission-in-mozambique/2680395>.
Jason Burke, 'Isis Claims Sub-Saharan Attacks in a Sign of African Ambitions' *The Guardian* (6 June 2019).
Jonathan Saul and Camila Reed, 'Shabaab-Somali Pirate Links Growing: UN Adviser' *Reuters* (20 October 2011).
Joseph Hanlon, 'Ignoring the Roots of Mozambique's War in a Push for Military Victory' *ACCORD Conflict and Resilience Monitor* 2021/2 (21 August 2021).
'Jurisdictions under Increased Monitoring' *FATF* (24 February 2023) <www.fatf-gafi.org/en/publications/High-risk-and-other-monitored-jurisdictions/Increased-monitoring-february-2023.html>.
Khadija Patel, 'What Caused the Xenophobic Attacks in South Africa?' *Al Jazeera* (6 April 2016).
Liesl Louw-Vaudran, 'Coordination: Key to the Success of African Solutions for Mozambique' *Institute for Security Studies* (11 April 2022).
LUSA, 'Mozambique: Arrival of Rwandan Forces Was Very Positive' *Club of Mozambique* (21 February 2022).
Mamokhosi Choane, Lukong Stella Shulika and Mandla Mthombeni, 'An Analysis of the Causes, Effects and Ramifications of Xenophobia in South Africa' (2011) 3 (2) *Insight on Africa* (African Studies Association of India).
Media Statement by National Treasury, 'Listing of South Africa by the Financial Action Task Force as a "Jurisdiction under Increased Monitoring"' (24 February 2023) <www.treasury.gov.za/comm_media/press/2023/2023022401%20Media%20statement%20-%20Response%20to%20FATF.pdf>.
'Memorandum of Understanding between the Government of the Republic of Mozambique and the Government of the Republic of South Africa and the Government of the United Republic of Tanzania on Maritime Security Cooperation' (13 December 2011) <https://treaties.dirco.gov.za/dbtw-wpd/images/20111213MultilateralMaritimeSecurity.pdf>.
'Memorandum of Understanding Between the Government of the Republic of Mozambique and the Government of the Republic of South Africa on the Conduct of Combined Maritime Patrols within the Territory of the Republic of Mozambique' (1 June 2011) <https://treaties.dirco.gov.za/dbtw-wpd/images/20110601MozambiqueMaritimePatrols.pdf>.
Michael Georgy, 'S Africa al Qaeda Suspect "Quiet, Religious" Dentist' *Reuters* (22 January 2007).

Michael Rifer, 'SADC and Terrorism' (2005) 14 (1) *African Security Review*.
'Mozambique: Islamic State Threatens South Africa – AIM Report' *Club of Mozambique* (7 July 2020).
National Treasury Fact Sheet, 'What Does FATF Greylisting Mean for a Country?' <www.treasury.gov.za/comm_media/press/2023/2023022501%20FATF%20Grey%20Listing%20Fact%20Sheet.pdf>.
Peter Fabricius, 'Are Red Flags About Islamic State in South Africa Alarmist?' *Institute for Security Studies* (11 November 2022).
Peter Fabricius, 'How Serious Is the Islamic State Threat to Attack South Africa?' *Institute for Security Studies* (23 July 2020).
Peter Fabricius, 'US Sanctions Four Alleged ISIS Ringleaders in South Africa' *Institute for Security Studies* (4 March 2022).
Protocol Additional to the Geneva Conventions of 12 August 1949, and Relating to the Protection of Victims of International Armed Conflicts (Protocol I) (1977) <https://treaties.un.org/Pages/showDetails.aspx?objid=08000002800f3586&clang=_en>.
Qaanitah Hunter, '"We Are Taking It Very, Very Seriously": Dlodlo on ISIS Threat' *News24* (19 July 2020).
Ralph Mathekga, 'Terrorism Left Unchecked in Southern Africa' *GIS Reports Online* (19 October 2020).
'Reporting by Second Line of Defence' (6 July 2013) <https://sldinfo.com/2013/06/south-africa-and-anti-piracy-operations/>.
Robyn Kriel and Briana Duggan, 'Somali Pirate Kings Are Under Investigation for Helping ISIS and al-Shabaab' *CNN World* (10 July 2017).
'Rwanda Deploys Joint Force to Mozambique' *Ministry of Defence of Rwanda* (10 July 2021) <www.mod.gov.rw/news-detail/rwanda-deploys-joint-force-to-mozambique-1>.
'Rwandan Forces Display Confidence Amid Precarious Security Situation in Mozambique' *Africanews* (10 November 2022).
SADC, 'SADC Mission in Mozambique (SAMIM) in Brief' (10 November 2021) <www.sadc.int/latest-news/sadc-mission-mozambique-samim-brief>.
Samantha Farqhuhar, 'When Overfishing Leads to Terrorism' (2017) 21 (2) *World Affairs: The Journal of International Issues*.
'SA Men "Received Al-Qaeda Training"' *Mail & Guardian* (23 August 2004).
'SANDF Stays Mum on Possible Assistance to Mozambique AFP' *SABC Africa Channel* (4 June 2020).
'SA "Resolved" to Fight Terrorism – Gungubele' *DefenceWeb* (10 November 2022).
'South Africa Is Ready to Help Mozambique with Its Insurgency' *DefenceWeb* (3 September 2020).
South African Police Service, 'Media Statement: Directorate for Priority Crimes Investigation (HAWKS)' (27 October 2022) <www.saps.gov.za/newsroom/msspeechdetail.php?nid=37994>.
South African Treaty Register <https://treaties.dirco.gov.za/dbtw-wpd/textbase/treatywebsearch.htm>.
'Stemming the Insurrection in Mozambique's Cabo Delgado' *Crisis Group* (2021).
Tassilo Hummel, Bhargav Acharya and Alexander Winning, 'Financial Crime Watchdog Adds South Africa to "Grey List"' *Reuters* (24 February 2023).
Themba Hadebe, 'South Africa Events of 2020' *Human Rights Watch* (2020).
Tom van Rentergem, 'Al-Shabaab in Mozambique: Taking Stock of an Insurgency Under Cover' *Egmont Policy Brief 281* (June 2022).
UN Doc. S/2022/63 (28 January 2022).
UN News, 'South Africa "on the Precipice of Explosive Xenophobic Violence", UN Experts Warn' (15 July 2022) <https://news.un.org/en/story/2022/07/1122612>.
U.S. Department of the Treasury, 'Treasury Designates Members of ISIS Cell in South Africa' (7 November 2022) <https://home.treasury.gov/news/press-releases/jy1084>.

U.S. Department of the Treasury, 'Treasury Sanctions South Africa-based ISIS Organisers and Financial Facilitators' (1 March 2022) <https://home.treasury.gov/news/press-releases/jy0616>.

U.S. Embassy and Consulates in South Africa, 'Security Alert: US. Embassy Possible Attack' (26 October 2022) <https://za.usembassy.gov/security-alert-u-s-embassy-possible-attack/>.

World Bank, 'The Pirates of Somalia: Ending the Threat, Rebuilding a Nation' *World Bank Vice-Presidency for Africa* (11 April 2013).

4 Armed conflict, climate change and the preparedness of international law through the lens of Mozambique

Jessie Phyffer

4.1 Introduction

Mozambique has since 2017 been in the throes of a non-international armed conflict (NIAC) in its northern province of Cabo Delgado.[1] Conflicts lead to deaths, damage to infrastructure and the environment, weakened state institutions and displacement, and the situation in Mozambique is no different.[2] As of writing, there have been thousands of deaths, almost one million internally displaced persons,[3] and damage to residential buildings, businesses, hospitals and schools in Mozambique.[4] These consequences, coupled with the fact that the region is no stranger to cyclones, leave the people and institutions of Mozambique especially vulnerable.[5] In 2019 Mozambique was hit by two devastating cyclones within six weeks of each other – 'Idai' made landfall in the Sofala province and 'Kenneth' in Cabo Delgado.[6] The storms led to death, displacement, the destruction of large swathes of crops and a cholera outbreak.[7] While not a new victim of tropical storms, climate change is likely to increase the frequency and severity of these events.[8] The people of Mozambique thus find themselves at the intersection of a horrific reality – armed conflict and climate change.

This chapter explores this intersection. The United Nations defines climate change as the human-induced 'long-term shifts in temperature and weather patterns'.[9] Much of the literature on armed conflict and climate change focuses on whether climate change will lead to an increase in the frequency and number of armed conflicts.[10] This is not the focus of this chapter. Rather, the chapter focuses on how the consequences of an armed conflict can be exacerbated by climatic events and whether international law is prepared to address this. In Section 4.2, the chapter looks at common consequences of both armed conflict and climate change and how these consequences are compounded when a climatic event occurs in a state where an armed conflict is already taking place. In light of these exacerbated consequences, Section 4.3 explores whether international humanitarian law (IHL), the Paris Agreement and international human rights law (IHRL), as the most relevant branches of international law, are prepared to deal with general compounded consequences. Section 4.4 focuses on the international law of displacement as it pertains to conflict and climate change. This specific

DOI: 10.4324/9781003317647-5

consequence of both events receives greater focus not only because it is uniquely miserable but also because the law on it is more extensive. Section 4.5 concludes the chapter.

4.2 The compounded consequences of armed conflict and climate change

The independent consequences of climate change and armed conflict can be devastating, but, when compounded, affected persons and states can find themselves in truly desperate circumstances.[11] This part focuses on the common consequences of an armed conflict and climate shocks. It explains the consequences of each event independently and how, when felt together, they are more severe using Mozambique as a case study.

4.2.1 Common consequences of armed conflict and climate shocks

The consequences of armed conflict are vast and wide-ranging. These include food and water insecurity, a disrupted energy supply, disrupted or non-existent education and health services, the outbreak of diseases, displacement and, of course, general safety concerns.[12] Armed conflicts force governments to reassess their national priorities, with national security, economic stability and critical infrastructure repair taking centre stage.[13] Governments are left weakened and overwhelmed by the reality of having to fight an armed conflict while still ensuring the delivery of basic services to affected and non-affected populations. Armed conflicts can, therefore, lead to paralysed governments and the collapse of state institutions.[14]

A weakened or paralysed government that does not have the capacity to respond and adapt to the consequences of an armed conflict will also likely not have the capacity to plan for and respond and adapt to the impacts of climate change. Tropical storms made more intense by climate change can lead to food and water insecurity, damage to infrastructure and, as a consequence, displacement and disruption to health, education and electricity services.[15] Where climatic events occur in states already embroiled in armed conflict, the effects of both disasters converge and have the potential to worsen the situation.[16] With state institutions already weakened by a conflict, it becomes difficult for a state to respond adequately to or address the impacts of climate change.[17]

Climate mitigation[18] and adaptation[19] plans can be relegated to the bottom of the priority list as a state struggles to keep control of its territory and ensure the safety of its population.[20] The Paris Agreement, to which Mozambique is a party,[21] calls on all state parties to pursue mitigation and adaptation measures in their approaches to addressing climate change.[22] Parties are to communicate these measures through their nationally determined contributions (NDCs).[23] While not bound by the plans they set out in their NDCs, states must strive to achieve the mitigation and adaptation goals they set themselves.[24] Climate mitigation and adaptation can be an enormous challenge even at the best of times, but where an armed conflict has already stretched a state to its limits, its ability to abide by its NDCs is severely limited.[25]

In addition to mitigation and adaptation, the Paris Agreement has a third goal – free-flowing exchange of finances to ensure climate-resilient development.[26] The issue of financing climate mitigation and adaptation techniques and technologies in developing countries specifically is a salient feature of the Paris Agreement.[27] These funds can help states meet the goals they set for themselves in their NDCs, but states embroiled in conflicts are less likely to receive climate-related financing.[28] Financing climate-related projects in conflict zones places security risks on staff, local communities and others that are involved in the project.[29] Poorly managed climate funding can also exacerbate conflicts in certain regions and result in funds being misappropriated.[30] All of this can deter future climate investment.[31] In a developing country such as Mozambique, which contributes very little to climate change but is very vulnerable to its impacts, the consequences of this can be dire.

The consequences of the conflict in Mozambique have been compounded by the COVID-19 pandemic and climate shocks.[32] The conflict in Cabo Delgado has severely damaged infrastructure, which has disrupted health services and water and electricity supply.[33] Mozambique's health sector is also suffering from a shortage of key staff, the closure of several health centres across Cabo Delgado due to safety concerns, and a total or partial destruction of electricity systems.[34] The education, housing and market-related sectors have also not escaped unscathed with several schools being partially or completely destroyed and damage to residential dwellings and market-related buildings across Cabo Delgado.[35] Conflict-related damage has caused food insecurity and malnutrition and worsened an already-precarious water and sanitation situation.[36] This is mostly driven by displacement[37] but is also a result of damage to economic hubs and infrastructure.[38]

The already dire situation was aggravated by tropical cyclones Idai and Kenneth, both of which made landfall in 2019.[39] The storms destroyed thousands of hectares of crops, exacerbating food insecurity.[40] They also caused significant damage to infrastructure including residential dwellings and educational facilities, water facilities and infrastructure and critical health facilities, resulting in a cholera outbreak.[41] Additionally, several thousands of people were displaced – some for the second time, having already been displaced by conflict.[42] Mozambique is particularly vulnerable to climate change and related shocks because of its geographic location.[43] It is prone to droughts, flooding and tropical storms,[44] and the cyclones, specifically Kenneth that made landfall in Cabo Delgado, have exacerbated an already-precarious situation.

4.2.2 Internal displacement

Displacement is a guaranteed consequence of armed conflict.[45] In addition to facing violence at the hands of armed groups, people are forced to flee their homes and lose their livelihoods as vital infrastructure is destroyed.[46] State institutions weakened by armed conflicts are not able to provide necessary care and support for those both temporarily and permanently displaced,[47] which, in turn, impacts food and water security of displaced persons, their access to health and education and their ability to gain autonomy over their livelihoods.[48] Displaced persons are also vulnerable to sexual violence in camps,[49] and children face the risk of being abducted or recruited into armed groups.[50] States also suffer the effects of displacement. The cost of maintaining displacement camps can stretch an already-overstretched budget of a state embroiled in war.[51]

Climatic events can also lead to displacement.[52] The consequences of this type of displacement are much the same as those faced when displacement is caused by conflict. There can be damage to critical health infrastructure and the subsequent spread of diseases, food and water insecurity and permanent loss of homes and livelihoods.[53] In a state that is geographically vulnerable to climatic events and is already in the middle of an armed conflict, people can find themselves displaced by, first, an armed conflict and then by a climatic event.[54] Persons displaced by conflict are vulnerable, and they are likely to feel the impacts of climate change more intensely.[55]

The conflict in Mozambique has led to hundreds of thousands of people being internally displaced.[56] Many of these people have been displaced multiple times due to 'consecutive climate shocks'.[57] Kenneth affected 170 000 people who, in one way or another, had already had their safety and security eroded by the conflict.[58] The cyclones damaged critical health and water infrastructure, leading to a cholera outbreak and disrupted access to medication.[59] Mozambique's geography makes it particularly vulnerable to consecutive climatic events, meaning that several thousands of people can experience displacement multiple times in their lifetimes.[60]

4.2.3 Sectional conclusion

The consequences of an armed conflict are always dire, and the situation in Mozambique is no exception. Affected people face violence, food and water insecurity, the collapse of state institutions, health risks and displacement. Institutions that are already weakened by a protracted armed conflict will be expected to also deal with the severe consequences of more frequent and severe climate shocks. Where a climatic event occurs during an armed conflict, the consequences of each are likely to be compounded, as is the case in Mozambique.

4.3 International law at the intersection of armed conflict and climate change

This part of the chapter looks to international law to assess whether, if at all, it is prepared for the compounded consequences of armed conflict and climate change. For the sake of brevity, this part will only look at the preparedness of the most relevant international law, namely, IHL, the Paris Agreement and AU texts and IHRL.

4.3.1 International humanitarian law

Where an armed conflict exists, IHL applies as the *lex specialis*. It must, therefore, be the starting point for the search for any rules that may address climate change or the consequences thereof in a state where an armed conflict is ongoing. The search is rather short. IHL does not address climate change mitigation nor adaptation in any way, but, in limited circumstances, it can be interpreted to protect the environment. The protection of the environment during an armed conflict can be an incidental mitigation measure because an intact environment is better at capturing carbon emissions than a destroyed one. The environment is directly protected where there is an international armed conflict.[61] However, no such protection exists where there is an NIAC, such as in Mozambique. In those types of armed conflicts, protection of the environment has to be read in to existing principles and provisions.

The core customary principles of IHL – the principle of distinction, proportionality and military necessity – can offer some environmental protection.[62] The principle of distinction requires parties to a conflict to distinguish between military and civilian objects at all times and prohibits the targeting of civilian objects.[63] By default, the environment is civilian in nature and, therefore, cannot be targeted unless it becomes a military object, and even then it cannot be indiscriminately attacked.[64] The principle of proportionality requires that the military objective of an attack must be proportional to the damage likely to occur.[65] Accordingly, this principle prohibits attacks that cause unnecessary damage to the environment.[66] Finally, the principle of military necessity requires that all acts on the battlefield must seek to achieve a military objective.[67] Any acts that recklessly damage the environment are prohibited under this principle,[68] as are any means and methods of warfare that are likely to cause widespread and long-term damage to the environment.[69]

Treaty law is also able to incidentally protect the environment during an NIAC. Such protection is primarily aimed at civilians, which means that any environmental protection is purely incidental. This incidental protection is found in Common Article 3 to the Geneva Conventions,[70] and articles 4(2)(g), 13, 14, 15, 16 and 17 of Additional Protocol II.[71] Common Article 3 protects civilians from a range of offences, including torture, cruel and degrading treatment and outrages upon personal dignity, and where damaging the environment will constitute the commission of any of these offences, Common Article 3 incidentally protects the environment.[72] Article 4(2)(g) of Additional Protocol II protects civilians from pillage, and this can, in a very limited way, protect civilian-owned pieces of the environment.[73]

Articles 13 and 14 of Additional Protocol II concern the protection of civilians and indispensable civilian objects and offer the same type of environmental protection offered by the principle of distinction.[74] Articles 14 and 15 provide very narrow protection to certain parts of the environment where they are used for specific civilian purposes: article 14 prevents the use of starvation as a war tactic, thus protecting agricultural land from attack; and article 15 protects dams and dykes from attack, thus protecting select parts of the aquatic environment. These, in a way, align with Rule 45 of the ICRC's customary study, which prohibits parties from destroying the environment as a means of warfare.[75] Article 16 protects places of cultural and religious importance, which provides narrow and incidental protection to religiously and culturally significant parts of the environment. Finally, article 17 protects civilians from forced migration. Not only does this protect the environment from degradation caused by mass migration,[76] but it also prevents armed groups from intentionally destroying the environment to such an extent that it forces civilians to migrate.[77]

The foregoing shows that IHL's protection of the environment is incidental, narrow and incomplete.

4.3.2 The Paris Agreement and African Union instruments

The Paris Agreement, the premier international law instrument on climate change, requires state parties to draw up NDCs that represent their most ambitious plans to mitigate climate change and set out their national adaptation plans.[78] Where a state finds itself embroiled in an armed conflict, it can be difficult, if not impossible, for it to meet its mitigation targets or implement its adaptation plans. The Paris Agreement provides no guidance on how a state is to mitigate or adapt to climate change when it is in the middle of an armed conflict, but it does allow states to set their own mitigation and adaptation targets, as Mozambique has done.[79] In this way, it arguably allows states facing armed conflict some grace when addressing climate change. Displacement can also arguably be considered a form of forced adaptation – people move because they have to.[80] Nevertheless, the Paris Agreement itself does not provide any guidance on how a state should cope with the consequences of armed conflict.[81] Additionally, any guidance offered by the Paris Agreement applies to states only and not to non-state armed groups in a conflict, meaning that such groups have no mitigation or adaptation obligations. The Paris Agreement, therefore, is not particularly helpful to states facing both conflict and climate change.

The AU is acutely aware of the potential of climate change to be a threat multiplier. Though not binding, the AU's Climate Change and Resilient Development Strategy for the period 2022–2023 provides guidance on how African states can ensure that the impacts of climate change do not lead to more conflict.[82] This strategy, however, does not provide guidance on how states are to cope with the compounded consequences of conflict and climate change. Preventing climate-induced conflict is a good adaptation technique,[83] but there is a need for guidance on how to deal with situations where conflict and climate change have already met. The overall silence of the climate change regime is a further indictment of international law's lack of preparedness for the convergence of conflict and climate change.

4.3.3 International human rights law

IHRL is always applicable and, as such, it is important to consider what rules, if any, it has to address the consequences of conflict and climate change.[84] The Paris Agreement barely acknowledges human rights in the context of climate change,[85] but this does not change the reality that climate change is likely to impact most human rights, including the right to life; the right to food; the right to water; the right to housing; the right to health; and the right to education.[86] Although IHRL always applies, during an armed conflict where IHL is the *lex specialis*, the latter's more specific protection also applies.[87] As such, where the consequences of an armed conflict are multiplied by the consequences of a climatic event, affected populations will receive the minimum protections offered by IHRL and IHL.

While IHL obligations rest on both state and non-state armed groups, IHRL obligations are only state obligations.[88] Whether these obligations extend to non-state parties in an armed conflict is less clear.[89] This raises an issue where a non-state armed group exercises territorial control. Ronen argues that where a non-state armed group exercises territorial or governmental control in the same way a state usually does, it should be conferred with international human rights obligations.[90] Similarly, Constantinides's study of Security Council Resolutions in this respect shows that the Security Council considers that the *de facto* authorities with territorial control in the Democratic Republic of the Congo, Georgia and Afghanistan had and have IHRL obligations.[91] Sassòli, however, considers that these are minority views and that the issue is not settled.[92]

The applicability of IHRL at all times, even during an armed conflict, may be an indication that international law is at least somewhat prepared to deal with the compounded consequences of armed conflict and climate change. However, it is only states that bear these human rights obligations. According to Sassòli, where a climatic event occurs in territory held by non-state armed groups, IHRL might not apply at all. This potentially leaves large swathes of people with no human rights protection beyond the little that is offered by IHL. These glaring gaps in protection are an indication of the insufficiency of IHRL when addressing the compounded consequences of conflict and climate change.

4.3.4 Sectional conclusion

International law is not prepared to address the compounded consequences of armed conflict and climate change. IHL provides superficial and insufficient guidance on how to approach climate change during an armed conflict. If the Paris Agreement provides any guidance on how to manage climate change during an armed conflict, it is incidental at best and barely sufficient to be considered helpful. IHRL is perhaps the most helpful body of law because it finds continued application and sets minimum standards for treatment, but it does not bind non-state armed groups, rendering it incapable of meaningfully addressing the compounded consequences felt by victims of conflict and climate change. International law is, therefore, underprepared, if prepared at all, for the realities of the impacts of climate change in areas plagued by armed conflict.

4.4 Internally displaced persons at the intersection of IHL and IHRL

Displacement, as a uniquely miserable consequence of armed conflict and climate shocks, makes it deserving of more, albeit brief, attention. The continuous applicability of IHRL means that whether people are displaced by conflict or by a climatic event, they have rights guaranteed to them under the International Covenant on Economic, Social and Cultural Rights;[93] the Convention on the Elimination of All

Forms of Discrimination against Women;[94] and the Convention on the Rights of the Child,[95] to name but a few. Be that as it may, displacement as a result of either conflict or climatic events risks, *inter alia*, the rights to health, education, food, water and housing.[96]

Where a person has been displaced within the context of an armed conflict, IHL provides civilian protections to those not taking part in hostilities.[97] In a NIAC, Common Article 3 applies to displaced and non-displaced persons as do articles 4 and 5 of Additional Protocol II, which protect civilians against inhuman treatment and sexual violence.[98] Additional Protocol II also ensures that medical personnel are not prohibited from servicing displaced persons[99] and that children are not to be recruited as child soldiers.[100] During situations of an armed conflict and, specifically NIACs, IHL applies to the entire geographic area of the state.[101] As such, persons who are displaced in a state where an armed conflict is taking place, even if not displaced by that armed conflict, will be protected by both IHRL and IHL. However, where displaced persons are living in occupied territory, they will be protected only by IHL. People in Cabo Delgado displaced by the conflict and once again by Kenneth are, therefore, covered by IHL wherever they are, but not by IHRL in occupied territory.

This protection is reaffirmed in the AU Convention for the Protection and Assistance of Internally Displaced Persons in Africa (Kampala Convention),[102] to which Mozambique is a party.[103] This convention focuses on displaced persons in Africa and covers persons who have been displaced by conflict as well as by 'natural or human-made disasters'.[104] The Convention calls for displaced persons to have their basic needs met,[105] for states to protect the dignity and uphold the human rights of displaced persons[106] and to ensure that displaced persons receive the protections guaranteed to them under IHL.[107] The Convention, however, applies only to states, meaning that displaced persons in territory controlled by armed non-state actors or armed groups are not similarly protected.

Accordingly, any displaced persons in state-controlled territory will be protected by IHL and IHRL. Additionally, the Kampala Convention ensures that displaced persons in Africa receive these protections from their states when the need arises. As such, internally displaced people in state-controlled Mozambique are protected, to a very large extent, by international law. On the other hand, displaced persons in occupied territory receive only IHL and not IHRL protection. Ultimately, while international law seems somewhat prepared to deal with displaced persons under state control, this cannot make up for the general lack of preparedness of international law in addressing the compounded consequences of climate change and conflict, especially for displaced persons in occupied territory.

4.5 Conclusion

At the time of writing, Mozambique's six-year-long conflict has resulted in several thousands of deaths and displacements. In the midst of this, Mozambique has been hit by a number of tropical storms and cyclones that have led to more deaths and displacements, and due to its geographic location, the state is likely to experience more severe storms in the coming years. International law is not prepared for this reality. IHL, the Paris Agreement and, to a lesser extent, IHRL are not prepared for this reality. Displaced persons seem to be quite well covered in Africa, but displacement is but one consequence of conflict and climate change, and extensive protection extends only to those in state-controlled territory. Beyond displacement, international law has not planned for this future and its silence, though already not unnoticed by the people of Mozambique, will be deafening to future generations.

Notes

1 Internal Displacement Monitoring Centre, 'Global Report on Internal Displacement (GRID) 2021: Internal Displacement in a Changing Climate' (2021) 31 <www.internal-displacement.org/sites/default/files/publications/documents/grid2021_idmc.pdf>. See Chapter 6 of this edited volume for an in-depth assessment of the NIAC in Mozambique.
2 ICRC, 'When Rain Turns to Dust: Understanding and Responding to the Combined Impact of Armed Conflicts and the Climate and Environment Crisis on People's Lives' (2020) 8.
3 International Crisis Group, 'Winning Peace in Mozambique's Embattled North' (10 February 2022).
4 UNDP, 'Infrastructure Damage Assessment Cabo Delgado – Mozambique' (August 2022) <www.undp.org/sites/g/files/zskgke326/files/2022-09/UNDP_220906_ENG-IDA%20Report_0.pdf> (IDA).
5 Ibid, 3.
6 IFRC, 'Displacement in a Changing Climate: Localised Humanitarian Action at the Forefront of the Climate Crisis' 27 <www.ifrc.org/sites/default/files/2021-11/2021-Climate-Displacement-Report-Final.pdf>.
7 Ibid.
8 GRID (n 1) 96.
9 UN, 'What Is Climate Change?' <www.un.org/en/climatechange/what-is-climate-change>.
10 See, for example, Halvard Buhaug, Nils Petter Gleditsch and Ole Magnus Theisen, 'Implications of Climate Change for Armed Conflict' in Robin Mearns and Andrew Norton (eds), *Social Dimensions of Climate Change: Equity and Vulnerability in a Warming World* (World Bank Publications 2010) 75–101; Clionadh Raleigh and Henrik Urdal, 'Climate Change, Environmental Degradation and Armed Conflict' (2007) 26 (6) *Political Geography* 674; Betsy Hartmann, 'Rethinking Climate Refugees and Climate Conflict: Rhetoric, Reality and the Politics of Policy Discourse' (2010) 22 *Journal of International Development* 234–239.
11 ICRC (n 2) 8.
12 Ibid, 12; GRID (n 1) 2.
13 ICRC (n 2) 18.
14 UN Doc. A/50/60 (25 January 1995) para 13.
15 ICRC (n 2) 8; GRID (n 1) 88; IFRC (n 6) 13–15.
16 ICRC (n 2) 8, 18.
17 Ibid, 18.
18 Mitigation means '[a]n anthropogenic intervention to reduce the anthropogenic forcing of the climate system'. See Martin Parry and others, 'Climate Change 2007: Impacts, Adaptation, and Vulnerability' (Contribution of Working Group II to the Fourth Assessment Report of the Intergovernmental Panel on Climate Change, CUP 2007) 878.
19 Adaptation means '[a]djustment in natural or human systems in response to actual or expected climatic stimuli or their effects', Ibid, 869.

20 ICRC (n 2) 18.
21 UNTC, 'Paris Agreement' (United Nations Treaty Collection, 9 February 2023).
22 Paris Agreement to the United Nations Framework Convention on Climate Change (adopted 12 December 2015, entered into force 4 November 2016) 3156 UNTS 79, articles 4 and 6 for mitigation and article 7 for adaptation (Paris Agreement).
23 Ibid, article 4(2).
24 Ibid; see also Mark Roelfsema and others, 'Taking Stock of National Climate Policies to Evaluate Implementation of the Paris Agreement' (2020) 11 *Nature Communications* 1, 2.
25 ICRC (n 2) 8.
26 Article 2(1)(c) of the Paris Agreement (n 22).
27 See, for example, articles 2(2), 6(8), (9) and (10).
28 UNDP, 'Climate Finance for Sustaining Peace: Making Climate Finance Work for Conflict-Afflicted and Fragile Contexts' (UNDP 2021) 30.
29 Ibid, 31.
30 Ibid.
31 Ibid.
32 Republic of Mozambique Ministry of Land and Environment, 'Update of the First Nationally Determined Contribution to the United Nations Framework Convention on Climate Change Period 2020–2025' (1 November 2021) 13 <https://unfccc.int/sites/default/files/NDC/2022-06/NDC_EN_Final.pdf> (Mozambique Updated NDC); IFRC (n 6) 28.
33 GRID (n 1) 31; IFRC (n 6) 28; OCHA, 'Humanitarian Response Plan: Mozambique' (June 2022) 7, 8.
34 IDA (n 4) 22; OCHA (n 33) 7, 8.
35 IDA (n 4) 9, 12, 18; OCHA (n 33) 7.
36 IDA (n 4) 28; OCHA (n 33) 7; GRID (n 1) 31.
37 OCHA (n 33) 7.
38 IDA (n 4) 12; GRID (n 1) 31.
39 GRID (n 1) 31; IFRC (n 6) 27.
40 IFRC (n 6) 27.
41 IFRC (n 6) 27, 28; Mozambique Updated NDC (n 32) 29.
42 IFRC (n 6) 27, 28.
43 Ibid, 27.
44 GRID (n 1) 31; Mozambique Updated NDC (n32) 28, 29.
45 Marguerite Contat Hickel, 'Protection of Internally Displaced Persons Affected by Armed Conflict: Concept and Challenges' (2001) 83 *International Review of the Red Cross* 699, 700.
46 ICRC, 'Internally Displaced Persons and International Humanitarian Law' (ICRC 6 April 2022) 2.
47 ICRC (n 2) 8, 18; OCHA (n 33) 7.
48 ICRC (n 2) 16.
49 Ibid, 27; OCHA (n 33) 53; Global Protection Cluster, 'Cabo Delgado Province Protection Analysis Update' 2 (2022) (Protection Analysis Update).
50 OCHA (n 33) 53, ICRC (n 46) 6; Protection Analysis Update (n 49) 2.
51 GRID (n 1) 17; ICRC (n 2) 16.
52 GRID (n 1) 2.
53 Ibid, 21; IFRC (n 6) 13, 27.
54 GRID (n 1) 2.
55 Rajendra K Pachauri and others, 'Climate Change 2014: Synthesis Report' (Contribution of Working Groups I, II and III to the Fifth Assessment Report of the Intergovernmental Panel on Climate Change, IPCC 2014) 54 <www.ipcc.ch/site/assets/uploads/2018/05/SYR_AR5_FINAL_full_wcover.pdf>.
56 OCHA (n 33) 7.

57 Ibid, 5.
58 IFRC (n 6) 13.
59 Ibid, 27, 28.
60 OCHA (n 33) 5, 6. This happened when 500 people displaced by Idai were once again displaced by storm Chalane: see IFRC (n 6) 27.
61 Articles 35(3) and 55(1) Protocol Additional to the Geneva Conventions of 12 August 1949, and Relating to the Protection of Victims of International Armed Conflicts (Protocol I) (adopted 8 June 1977, entered into force 7 December 1978) 1125 UNTS 3 (Additional Protocol I) protect the environment from widespread, long-term and severe damage. It is also a rule of customary international law for international armed conflicts, see ICRC, *Guidelines on the Protection of the Natural Environment in Armed Conflict* (ICRC 2020) para 47.
62 ICRC, 'Rule 43: Application of General Principles on the Conduct of Hostilities to the Natural Environment' <https://ihl-databases.icrc.org/en/customary-ihl/v1/rule43> reinforces that these core principles apply to the protection of the natural environment.
63 ICRC (n 61) paras 18, 99.
64 Ibid.
65 Ibid, para 115.
66 Ibid.
67 Ibid, paras 101–103.
68 ICRC, 'Rule 44: Due Regard for the Natural Environment in Military Operations' <https://ihl-databases.icrc.org/en/customary-ihl/v1/rule44> also reads, in part, 'in the conduct of military operations, all feasible precautions must be taken to avoid, and in any event to minimize, incidental damage to the environment'.
69 ICRC, 'Rule 45: Causing Serious Damage to the Natural Environment' <https://ihl-databases.icrc.org/en/customary-ihl/v1/rule45>.
70 The 1949 Geneva Convention I for the Amelioration of the Condition of the Wounded and Sick in Armed Forces in the Field (adopted 12 August 1949, entered into force 21 October 1950) 75 UNTS 31; the 1949 Geneva Convention II for the Amelioration of the Condition of Wounded, Sick and Shipwrecked Members of Armed Forces at Sea (adopted 12 August 1949, entered into force 21 October 1950) 75 UNTS 85; the 1949 Geneva Convention III Relative to the Treatment of Prisoners of War (adopted 12 August 1949, entered into force 21 October 1950) 75 UNTS 135; and the 1949 Geneva Convention IV Relative to the Protection of Civilian Persons in Time of War (adopted 12 August 1949, entered into force 21 October 1950) 75 UNTS 287.
71 Protocol Additional to the Geneva Conventions of 12 August 1949, and Relating to the Protection of Victims of Non-International Armed Conflicts (Protocol II) (adopted 8 June 1977, entered into force 7 December 1978) 1125 UNTS 609 (Additional Protocol II).
72 Jeanique Pretorius, 'Enhancing Environmental Protection in Non-International Armed Conflict: The Way Forward' (2018) 78 *Zeitschrift für ausländisches öffentliches Recht und Völkerrecht* 903, 905–906.
73 Ibid, 907–908.
74 Ibid, 908–913.
75 ICRC (n 69).
76 Sumudu Anopama Atapattu, 'A New Category of Refugee: 'Climate Refugees' and a Gaping Hole in International Law' in Simon Behrman and Avidan Kent (eds), *Climate Refugees: Beyond the Legal Impasse?* (Routledge 2018) 34, 38.
77 Pretorius (n 72) 914–915.
78 Articles 4(2) and 7 of the Paris Agreement (n 22).
79 Mozambique Updated NDC (n 32).
80 UNHCR, 'Climate Change, Displacement and Human Rights' 1 (UNCHR March 2022) <www.unhcr.org/6242ea7c4.pdf>; Atapattu (n 76) 35; GRID (n 1) 56.
81 It should be noted that neither the United Nations Framework Convention on Climate Change (adopted 9 May 1992, entered into force 21 March 1994) 1771 UNTS 107 nor

the Kyoto Protocol to the United Nations Framework Convention on Climate Change (adopted 11 December 1997, entered into force 16 February 2005) 2303 UNTS 162 contains any guidance on armed conflict and climate change.

82 AU, 'African Union Climate Change and Resilient Development Strategy and Action Plan (2022–2032)' VII (2022), 36–37.

83 Ibid, 36.

84 Erik V Koppe, 'Climate Change and Human Security During Armed Conflict' (2014) 68 *Human Rights and International Legal Discourse* 68, 76.

85 The Preamble to the Paris Agreement (n 22) states that when taking action on climate change, parties should consider their human rights obligations; see also Alan Boyle, 'Climate Change, the Paris Agreement and Human Rights' (2018) 67 *International and Comparative Law* 759, 769–773 for a discussion on the shortcomings of the Paris Agreement concerning its lack of inclusion of human rights.

86 OHCHR, 'Understanding Human Rights and Climate Change' 13, 16–19 (submission of the Office of the High Commissioner for Human Rights to the 21st Conference of the Parties to the United Nations Framework Convention on Climate Change 2015, OHCHR 2015).

87 Koppe (n 84) 76, 79.

88 Yael Ronen, 'Human Rights Obligations of Territorial Non-State Actors' (2013) 46 (1) *Cornell International Law Journal* 21, 25.

89 Marco Sassòli, *International Humanitarian Law: Rules, Controversies, and Solutions to Problems Arising in Warfare* (Edward Elgar Publishing 2019) para 9.23.

90 Ronen (n 88) 26, 27.

91 Aristotle Constantinides, 'Human Rights Obligations and Accountability of Armed Opposition Groups: The Practice of the UN Security Council' (2010) 4 *Human Rights & International Legal Discourse* 89, 101.

92 Sassòli (n 89) paras 9.23, 9.24.

93 International Covenant on Economic, Social and Cultural Rights (adopted 16 December 1966, entered into force 3 January 1976), 993 UNTS 3. It should be noted that Mozambique has not taken any action in respect of this treaty; see OHCHR, 'Treaties: Status of Ratification' (2014) <https://indicators.ohchr.org/>. However, at least one author is of the view that the Convention is customary international law; see Eleanor D Kinney, 'The International Human Right to Health: What Does this Mean for Our Nation and World' (2001) 34 (4) *Indiana Law Review* 1457, 1464.

94 Convention on the Elimination of All Forms of Discrimination against Women (adopted 18 December 1979, entered into force 3 September 1981) 1249 UNTS 1. Mozambique has ratified this Convention; see OHCHR (n 93).

95 Convention on the Rights of the Child (adopted 20 November 1989, entered into force 2 September 1990) 1577 UNTS 3. Mozambique has ratified this Convention; see OHCHR (n 93).

96 Atapattu (n 76) 36; UNCHR (n 80) 16–19.

97 Hickel (n 45) 701.

98 ICRC (n 46) 4.

99 Additional Protocol II (n 71) articles 9, 10, 11.

100 Ibid, article 4(3).

101 ICRC, 'Updated Commentary on the Geneva Conventions of August 12 1949' paras 456–459 (ICRC 2016) <https://ihl-databases.icrc.org/en/ihl-treaties/gci-1949/article-3/commentary/2016?activeTab=undefined>; see also Sassòli (n 89) para 6.47.

102 African Union Convention for the Protection and Assistance of Internally Displaced Persons in Africa (Kampala Convention) (adopted 23 October 2009, entered into force 6 December 2012) 3014 UNTS 3.

103 African Union, 'List of Countries Which Have Signed, Ratified/Acceded to the African Union Convention for the Protection and Assistance of Internally Displaced Persons in Africa (Kampala Convention)' (AU, 27 April 2022).

104 Kampala Convention (n 103) article I(j).
105 Ibid, article III(1)(j).
106 Ibid, articles III(1)(c), (d).
107 Ibid, article III(1)(e).

Bibliography

Alan Boyle, 'Climate Change, the Paris Agreement and Human Rights' (2018) 67 *International and Comparative Law*.

Aristotle Constantinides, 'Human Rights Obligations and Accountability of Armed Opposition Groups: The Practice of the UN Security Council' (2010) 4 *Human Rights & International Legal Discourse*.

AU, 'African Union Climate Change and Resilient Development Strategy and Action Plan (2022–2032)' VII (2022) <https://au.int/sites/default/files/documents/42276-doc-CC_Strategy_and_Action_Plan_2022-2032_23_06_22_ENGLISH-compressed.pdf>.

African Union Convention for the Protection and Assistance of Internally Displaced Persons in Africa (2009) <https://au.int/en/treaties/african-union-convention-protection-and-assistance-internally-displaced-persons-africa>.

AU, 'List of Countries Which Have Signed, Ratified/Acceded to the African Union Convention for the Protection and Assistance of Internally Displaced Persons in Africa (Kampala Convention)' (AU, 27 April 2022) <https://au.int/sites/default/files/treaties/36846-sl-AFRICAN_UNION_CONVENTION_FOR_THE_PROTECTION_AND_ASSISTANCE_OF_INTERNALLY_DISPLACED_PERSONS_IN_AFRICA_KAMPALA_CONVENTION_1.pdf>.

Betsy Hartmann, 'Rethinking Climate Refugees and Climate Conflict: Rhetoric, Reality and the Politics of Policy Discourse' (2010) 22 *Journal of International Development*.

Clionadh Raleigh and Henrik Urdal, 'Climate Change, Environmental Degradation and Armed Conflict' (2007) 26 (6) *Political Geography*.

Convention on the Elimination of All Forms of Discrimination against Women (1979) <https://treaties.un.org/Pages/showDetails.aspx?objid=080000028000309d&clang=_en>.

Convention on the Rights of the Child (1989) <https://treaties.un.org/Pages/showDetails.aspx?objid=08000002800007fe&clang=_en>.

Crisis Group Africa Briefing, 'Winning Peace in Mozambique's Embattled North' Crisis Group (10 February 2022) <www.crisisgroup.org/africa/southern-africa/mozambique/winning-peace-mozambiques-embattled-north>.

Eleanor D Kinney, 'The International Human Right to Health: What Does This Mean for Our Nation and World' (2001) 34 (4) *Indiana Law Review*.

Erik V Koppe, 'Climate Change and Human Security During Armed Conflict' (2014) 68 *Human Rights and International Legal Discourse*.

Geneva Convention (I) for the Amelioration of the Condition of the Wounded and Sick in Armed Forces in the Field (1949) <https://treaties.un.org/Pages/showDetails.aspx?objid=080000028015847c&clang=_en>.

Geneva Convention (II) for the Amelioration of the Condition of Wounded, Sick and Shipwrecked Members of Armed Forces at Sea (1949) <https://treaties.un.org/Pages/showDetails.aspx?objid=08000002801591b0&clang=_en>.

Geneva Convention (III) Relative to the Treatment of Prisoners of War (1949) <https://treaties.un.org/Pages/showDetails.aspx?objid=0800000280159839&clang=_en>.

Geneva Convention (IV) Relative to the Protection of Civilian Persons in Time of War (1949) <https://treaties.un.org/Pages/showDetails.aspx?objid=080000028015 8b1a&clang=_en>.

Global Protection Cluster, 'Cabo Delgado Province Protection Analysis Update' 2 (Global Protection Cluster 2022) <www.globalprotectioncluster.org/sites/default/files/2022-11/20221114_pc_prot_analysis_cd_final_cleared_gpc_1.pdf>.

Halvard Buhaug, Nils Petter Gleditsch and Ole Magnus Theisen, 'Implications of Climate Change for Armed Conflict' in Robin Mearns and Andrew Norton (eds), *Social Dimensions of Climate Change: Equity and Vulnerability in a Warming World* (World Bank Publications 2010).

ICRC, 'Guidelines on the Protection of the Natural Environment in Armed Conflict' (ICRC 2020) <www.icrc.org/en/document/guidelines-protection-natural-environment-armed-conflict-rules-and-recommendations-relating>.

ICRC, 'Internally Displaced Persons and International Humanitarian Law' (6 April 2022) <www.icrc.org/en/document/internally-displaced-persons-and-international-humanitarian-law-factsheet>.

ICRC, 'International Humanitarian Law and International Human Rights Law: Similarities and Differences' (ICRC 2003) <www.icrc.org/en/doc/assets/files/other/ihl_and_ihrl.pdf>.

ICRC, 'Rule 43: Application of General Principles on the Conduct of Hostilities to the Natural Environment' <https://ihl-databases.icrc.org/en/customary-ihl/v1/rule43>.

ICRC, 'Rule 44: Due Regard for the Natural Environment in Military Operations' <https://ihl-databases.icrc.org/en/customary-ihl/v1/rule44>.

ICRC, 'Rule 45: Causing Serious Damage to the Natural Environment' <https://ihl-databases.icrc.org/en/customary-ihl/v1/rule45>.

ICRC, 'Updated Commentary on the Geneva Conventions of August 12 1949' <https://ihl-databases.icrc.org/en/ihl-treaties/gci-1949/article-3/commentary/2016?activeTab=undefined>.

ICRC, 'When Rain Turns to Dust: Understanding and Responding to the Combined Impact of Armed Conflicts and the Climate and Environment Crisis on People's Lives' (ICRC 2020) 8 <www.icrc.org/sites/default/files/topic/file_plus_list/rain_turns_to_dust_climate_change_conflict.pdf>.

IFRC, 'Displacement in a Changing Climate: Localised Humanitarian Action at the Forefront of the Climate Crisis' (IFRC 2021) 27 <www.ifrc.org/sites/default/files/2021-11/2021-Climate-Displacement-Report-Final.pdf>.

Internal Displacement Monitoring Centre, 'Global Report on Internal Displacement (GRID) 2021: Internal Displacement in a Changing Climate' (2021) 31 <www.internal-displacement.org/sites/default/files/publications/documents/grid2021_idmc.pdf>.

International Covenant on Economic, Social and Cultural Rights (1966) <https://treaties.un.org/Pages/showDetails.aspx?objid=080000028002b6ed&clang=_en>.

Jeanique Pretorius, 'Enhancing Environmental Protection in Non-International Armed Conflict: The Way Forward' (2018) 78 *ZaöRV*.

Kyoto Protocol to the United Nations Framework Convention on Climate Change (1997) <https://treaties.un.org/Pages/showDetails.aspx?objid=0800000280021a16&clang=_en>.

Marco Sassòli, *International Humanitarian Law: Rules, Controversies, and Solutions to Problems Arising in Warfare* (Edward Elgar Publishing 2019).

Marguerite Contat Hickel, 'Protection of Internally Displaced Persons Affected by Armed Conflict: Concept and Challenges' (2001) 83 *International Review of the Red Cross*.

Mark Roelfsema and others, 'Taking Stock of National Climate Policies to Evaluate Implementation of the Paris Agreement' (2020) 11 *Nature Communications*.

Martin Parry and others, 'Climate Change 2007: Impacts, Adaptation, and Vulnerability' (Contribution of Working Group II to the Fourth Assessment Report of the Intergovernmental Panel on Climate Change, CUP 2007) <www.ipcc.ch/site/assets/uploads/2018/03/ar4_wg2_full_report.pdf>.

OCHA, 'Humanitarian Response Plan: Mozambique' (June 2022) <www.humanitarianresponse.info/sites/www.humanitarianresponse.info/files/documents/files/mozambique_humanitarian_response_plan_2022.pdf>.

OHCHR, 'Treaties: Status of Ratification' *OHCHR* (2014) <https://indicators.ohchr.org/>.

OHCHR, 'Understanding Human Rights and Climate Change' (submission of the Office of the High Commissioner for Human Rights to the 21st Conference of the Parties to the

United Nations Framework Convention on Climate Change 2015) <www.ohchr.org/sites/default/files/Documents/Issues/ClimateChange/COP21.pdf>.

Paris Agreement to the United Nations Framework Convention on Climate Change (2015) <https://treaties.un.org/Pages/showDetails.aspx?objid=0800000280458f37&clang=_en>.

Protocol Additional to the Geneva Conventions of 12 August 1949, and Relating to the Protection of Victims of International Armed Conflicts (1977) <https://treaties.un.org/Pages/showDetails.aspx?objid=08000002800f3586&clang=_en>.

Protocol Additional to the Geneva Conventions of 12 August 1949, and Relating to the Protection of Victims of Non-International Armed Conflicts (1977) <https://treaties.un.org/Pages/showDetails.aspx?objid=08000002800f3cb8&clang=_en>.

Rajendra K Pachauri and others, 'Climate Change 2014: Synthesis Report' (Contribution of Working Groups I, II and III to the Fifth Assessment Report of the Intergovernmental Panel on Climate Change, IPCC 2014) <www.ipcc.ch/site/assets/uploads/2018/05/SYR_AR5_FINAL_full_wcover.pdf>.

Republic of Mozambique Ministry of Land and Environment, 'Update of the First Nationally Determined Contribution to the United Nations Framework Convention on Climate Change Period 2020–2025' (1 November 2021) <https://unfccc.int/sites/default/files/NDC/2022-06/NDC_EN_Final.pdf>.

Sumudu Anopama Atapattu, 'A New Category of Refugee: "Climate refugees" and a Gaping Hole in International Law' in Simon Behrman and Avidan Kent (eds), *Climate Refugees: Beyond the Legal Impasse?* (Routledge 2018).

UN Doc. A/50/60 (25 January 1995).

UN, 'What Is Climate Change?' (United Nations) <www.un.org/en/climatechange/what-is-climate-change>.

UNDP, 'Climate Finance for Sustaining Peace: Making Climate Finance Work for Conflict-Afflicted and Fragile Contexts' (2021) <www.undp.org/publications/climate-finance-sustaining-peace-making-climate-finance-work-conflict-affected-and-fragile-contexts>.

UNDP, 'Infrastructure Damage Assessment Cabo Delgado – Mozambique' (August 2022) <www.undp.org/sites/g/files/zskgke326/files/2022-09/UNDP_220906_ENG-IDA%20Report_0.pdf>.

UNHCR, 'Climate Change, Displacement and Human Rights' (March 2022) <www.unhcr.org/6242ea7c4.pdf>.

United Nations Framework Convention on Climate Change (1992) <https://treaties.un.org/Pages/showDetails.aspx?objid=080000028004 31ce&clang=_en>.

Yael Ronen, 'Human Rights Obligations of Territorial Non-State Actors' (2013) 46 (1) *Cornell International Law Journal*.

5 The relationship between Ansar al-Sunna and the Islamic State

A transactional alliance?

Aniel de Beer

5.1 Introduction

Terrorism tends to flourish in states with social inequality and ineffective governments.[1] This has also been the case in Mozambique.[2] Rich offshore gas reserves estimated to be worth more than $60 million were discovered in 2010 in Cabo Delgado, Northern Mozambique, one of Mozambique's poorest provinces.[3] The hopes of the local inhabitants that the discovery would lead to economic benefits and improved living conditions were quickly dashed amid allegations of corruption and the monopoly of resources by a small fraction of the governing elite.[4] An early overestimation of the financial benefits expected from the natural gas discovery also led to poor economic decision making by public officials, including risky borrowing, and resulted in Mozambique economically underperforming.[5] Instead of improvements, various provinces in Mozambique saw poverty rates rise in the aftermath of the natural gas find.[6]

Cabo Delgado, in particular, has been described as both Mozambique's richest and its poorest province.[7] Despite housing one of the largest offshore gas fields in Africa worth billions of dollars and a wealth of rubies and graphite, the province has the highest rates of inequality, illiteracy and child malnutrition in Mozambique.[8] The combination of the natural gas find in Cabo Delgado, a further deterioration in already poor living conditions and perceptions of government corruption provided for an explosive mix.[9] These factors fuelled the perception of the state's failure to deliver in the province as well as a deep feeling of social injustice – fertile ground for an insurgency.[10]

Against this background, Ansar al-Sunna emerged in 2007 as an Islamist sect that initially isolated itself from surrounding society.[11] In late 2015 it started to build its own mosques and religious schools, engaging in proselytising activities and offering education to the local population, including women. Although the group was popular among unemployed and marginalised young people, some of its traditions put it into conflict with local Muslim communities opposed to the perceived interference with the area's Islamic traditions.[12] In October 2017 the conflict escalated when community leaders in Mocímboa da Praia issued a complaint to the local authorities in the district and 30 members of Ansar al-Sunna were arrested.[13] A few days later, the remainder of the group attacked police commands and stations

DOI: 10.4324/9781003317647-6

in a pre-dawn raid in Mocímboa da Praia, killing two officers.[14] The fighters occupied the town for nearly two days.[15] This was the beginning of an armed insurgency against the state of Mozambique.[16] The state responded with mass arrests, leading to further radicalisation among the area's youth.[17]

The insurgency has since increasingly relied on violence. What started as the targeting of police stations and administrative buildings morphed into brutal guerrilla attacks against civilians in smaller and isolated villages, as well as violent raids on cities and strategic gas installations in Cabo Delgado's coastal towns of Macomia, Mocímboa da Praia and Palma.[18]

In March 2021 Ansar al-Sunna launched a bloody, multi-day assault on Palma killing dozens of people, including foreign workers.[19] This attack garnered considerable press coverage for the insurgency both regionally and within the global jihadist enterprise of IS, the latter quickly claiming credit for the assault.[20] In the same month, the United States (US) termed the insurgency 'ISIS-Mozambique' and designated Ansar al-Sunna as a foreign terrorist organisation.[21]

However, numerous questions remain regarding the nature and intensity of the connection between the Islamic State (IS) and Ansar al-Sunna. This chapter explores this connection.

5.2 Ansar al-Sunna: acts of terrorism and the spread of a local insurgency

Terrorism has become a recurring feature of local conflicts and civil wars in Africa.[22] The violence between the armed forces of the state of Mozambique and Ansar al-Sunna has been described as a non-international armed conflict.[23] Whether during international or non-international armed conflicts, the intentional use of terror as a means of warfare is prohibited.[24] The Geneva Conventions and their Additional Protocols specifically prohibit and criminalise terrorism and acts of terror against civilians committed during armed conflict.[25]

Article 3 is common to all four Geneva Conventions (Common Article 3), and Additional Protocol II applies to non-international armed conflicts,[26] such as the conflict in Mozambique. Common Article 3 prohibits, inter alia, violence to life and person, murder, mutilation, torture, cruel treatment and the taking of hostages.[27] Article 4(1) read with article 4(2)(d) of Additional Protocol II prohibits acts of terrorism against 'all persons who do not take a direct part or who have ceased to take part in hostilities'. Article 13(2) of Additional Protocol II states that '[t]he civilian population as such, as well as individual civilians, shall not be the object of attack. Acts or threats of violence the primary purpose of which is to spread terror among the civilian population are prohibited.'[28] Although different legal regimes may apply, acts of terrorism, whether committed during armed conflict or in peacetime, share a common characteristic: violence intended to provoke terror among civilians.[29]

There can be little doubt that the excessively gruesome and shocking nature of the violence committed by Ansar al-Sunna is aimed at provoking fear and terror among civilians and that the violent acts, which include mass killings and beheadings,[30] are prohibited under international humanitarian law (IHL). Furthermore, while the acts of Ansar al-Sunna might have initially been limited to domestic terrorism where the group had no ties outside Mozambique and victims were local inhabitants, the insurgency later launched attacks against foreign targets within Mozambique.[31] This included attacks against foreign corporations and firms involved in a natural gas project in Cabo Delgado, such as the US Anadarko Petroleum Corporation, as well as an attack on a construction vehicle belonging to a firm subcontracted by Total South Africa.[32]

If the acts of Ansar al-Sunna meet the requirements for acts of terrorism that are prohibited under IHL, why is it important whether the insurgency is also an affiliate of IS? An alleged link with IS tends to invite international scrutiny and attention beyond that afforded to 'ordinary' civil wars, even where these civil wars include acts of immense brutality. Links with IS also invoke the fear of the spread of the operations of an insurgency such as Ansar al-Sunna beyond the borders of Mozambique.[33] IS seeks to create a caliphate, as its previous successes in Syria and Iraq have shown. This, in addition to attacks against foreign interests in Mozambique, has focused international attention on the conflict in Cabo Delgado.

However, the exact nature of the connection between Ansar al-Sunna and IS remains unclear. The next part will examine the nature of this link.

5.3 The relationship between Ansar al-Sunna and the Islamic State

5.3.1 Origins

Indications of a connection between Ansar al-Sunna and IS started in May 2018, when a photo of six Ansar al-Sunna group members allegedly pledging allegiance to IS in front of an IS flag was shared on social media and internet platforms. The photo was accompanied by a message from the insurgency, stating that a pledge of allegiance to IS caliph Abu Bakr al-Baghdadi would soon follow.[34] However, no official communication or pledge by Ansar al-Sunna leadership on an affiliation with IS has ever been publicly circulated.[35]

On 18 April 2019 IS claimed its first official attack in the Democratic Republic of the Congo (DRC) and introduced its new Central African Province (ISCAP).[36] Less than two months later, it claimed responsibility for an attack in Mozambique and stated that Mozambique was part of the Central African Province of IS.[37] An official IS video, published on 24 July 2019, showed a group including fighters in Mozambique pledging allegiance to IS.[38] Between June 2019 and November 2021, the media department of IS claimed 53 attacks in Mozambique, including the particularly bloody attack on Palma in March 2021, and published photos of war spoils.[39] In 2021 the US State Department designated Ansar al-Sunna (which it named 'ISIS-Mozambique') as a foreign terrorist organisation.[40] The following year, IS described Ansar al-Sunna as 'Wilayat Mozambique' – a province of IS in Africa.[41] IS also extolled the virtues of 'the soldiers of the Caliphate in Mozambique'.[42]

Notwithstanding the atmosphere created by these statements and evidence suggesting some level of association and communication between Ansar al-Sunna and

IS, the nature, extent and degree of the connection remains open to debate.[43] This is partly due to a paucity of information on the insurgency's leaders and the secrecy of its communications.[44]

In considering the nature of the relationship between the two groups, this part will consider whether the two groups have a shared ideology and target(s). It will then discuss the organisational structure of the insurgency and debate whether IS has command and control over Ansar al-Sunna. Lastly, it will examine whether there is evidence of any provision of resources and/or support by IS to the insurgency.

5.3.2 Is Ansar al-Sunna an IS affiliate?

5.3.2.1 Ideology, goals and targets

In a study analysing various hypotheses as to why terrorist groups form alliances, Asal and others found that groups that form alliances tend to, among other things, have a common ideology and motivation.[45] In terms of ideology and targets, the primary target of IS has been 'apostate' regimes in the Arab world, such as the Assad regime in Syria and the Abadi regime in Iraq.[46] IS aims to purify the Islamic community by attacking Shi'a and other religious minorities as well as rival jihadist groups.[47] Its goal is to conquer and control territory – establishing and expanding a caliphate where Muslims can live under its version of Islamic law.[48] In territory it controls, it then uses mass executions, public beheadings, rape, and symbolic crucifixion to terrorise the population into submission. At the same time, it provides basic services; a confusing but effective mix that garners them some support or acquiescence, though driven by fear, from the population.[49]

At its height, the actions of IS were more akin to a revolutionary war, as it used artillery, forces and tanks to conquer new areas, undermining morale in the army and police and forcing a sectarian backlash.[50] IS had thousands of foreign fighters under its banner[51] and also managed to inspire 'lone wolves' that had little or no contact with IS, but found its ideology and methods appealing and acted on their own.[52] However, IS's position has greatly deteriorated since the loss of territory in Iraq and Syria and the killing of its operatives and senior leaders in counterterrorism operations.[53] This has forced the group to go underground to launch kidnappings, assassinations and suicide bombings in Iraq and Syria.[54] Claiming attacks wherever territory is captured is thus important to IS to show of strength and garner international media attention.[55]

There is little evidence that Ansar al-Sunna has any concern for the global nature and objectives of IS. Shared support for Islam and a radical jihadist ideology cannot by itself provide evidence of a firm link between Ansar al-Sunna and IS.[56] However the powerful influence of a global terrorist organisation such as IS may be, the origin and lifespan of terrorist groups such as Ansar al-Sunna are in the first place determined by local factors, namely, socio-political conflicts inherent in particular societies.[57] Like many radical Islamist groups in Africa, Ansar al-Sunna first and foremost is a local insurgent group.[58] Its core propellants are local inequalities associated with the exploitation of resource wealth in the region and governmental abuse.[59] The insurgency also argues for a puritanical Islamic government as a cure for decades of political exclusion, unemployment and poverty.[60]

Furthermore, the insurgency does not seem to share a strong common ideology with IS when it comes to capturing and ruling territory as a *de facto* state.[61] Since it lost Mocímboa da Praia in August 2021, there have been no clear attempts by Ansar al-Sunna to capture and hold territory.[62] The focus since has been on brutal, isolated attacks in urban areas.[63] Operationally, Ansar al-Sunna has decentralised its operations by regrouping its fighters into smaller, more autonomous, and geographically dispersed units, and has focused on inland attacks in 2022.[64]

Arguably, terrorism in Mozambique therefore is less shaped by a common ideology with IS than by the desire to assert power locally and to obtain material benefits.[65]

5.3.2.2 Organisation and command

Some scholars contend that 'a terrorist affiliate is a terrorist organisation that accepts the leadership of another terrorist organisation but remains organisationally distinct'.[66] Affiliates are expected to align with the overall goal of the central organisation but at the same time enjoy a large degree of autonomy.[67] Unlike Al-Qaeda, IS lacks stringent criteria for affiliates.[68] However, it has emphasised three general elements when deciding on whether to accept a pledge of allegiance: unity in jihad and a designated leadership; territorial consolidation;[69] and direct communication with IS.[70] As far as communication is concerned, Somalia heads the ISCAP office and acts as the intermediary between IS's leadership and Ansar al-Sunna.[71] However, while Ansar al-Sunna does communicate with IS, the majority of its engagement with the IS transnational network in fact is through other affiliates across the African continent.[72]

Although Ansar al-Sunna itself seems to have a designated leadership, there seems to be a lack of command and control by IS over Ansar al-Sunna. There is little to no evidence that IS plays a substantive role in designing, organising or overseeing Ansar al Sunna's military activities.[73] This includes the attack on Palma in 2021.[74] While affiliates may have a high degree of autonomy, arguably the combination of the absence of firm evidence of a common ideology with IS discussed earlier as well as the lack of command and control by the latter over the actions of the insurgency suggests something less than a firm alliance. Ansar al-Sunna acts more like a 'sovereign affiliate' and has been described as 'a local insurgency with a regional character'.[75] Most of the group's members are made up of Mozambicans, including poor fishermen, frustrated petty traders, former farmers, and unemployed youths.[76]

The composition of the group's leadership also suggests that local leaders have command and control and value local operational experience when recruiting members.[77] The majority of Ansar al-Sunna's leaders are from Northern Mozambique or the surrounding regions, although there is some uncertainty regarding its official leadership.[78] Abu Yasir Hassan, also known as Yaseer

Hassan or Abu Qasim, has been identified as heading the group.[79] Abu Yasir is from Tanzania, but migrated to Mozambique, providing support for the regional character of the insurgency.[80] Another key leader of the group is Bonomade Machude Omar, who head the Military and External Affairs department and who was born in Cabo Delgado.[81] Ansar al-Sunna's recruitment pools are also local and regional: Many fighters from Tanzania[82] are among the militants' leaders, and its leaders have ties with Somalia, Kenya, Uganda, the DRC, Tanzania, Sudan and Saudi Arabia.[83]

The local and regional influence when it comes to both its members and leaders mitigates against IS exercising overall command and control of Ansar al-Sunna or directing its operations. The next part considers the extent of support provided by IS to Ansar al-Sunna.

5.3.2.3 Resources and support

It has been suggested that there are various possible affiliations between terrorist organisations.[84] An affiliation may be based on a sharing of resources, where the parties become dependent on one another with no end date for the partnership being foreseen (a 'pooled' alliance).[85] However, it is also possible that only one party is dependent on the other for resources, in which case it constitutes a subordinate affiliation.[86] Where the sharing arrangement and termination date are less defined, it constitutes an 'integrated' partnership.[87] Finally, there are instances of temporal and transactional partnerships where both parties maintain their own resources and authority, and only come together for a short period to realise a common objective (a 'reciprocal' alliance).[88]

As to the provision of resources by IS to Ansar al-Sunna, some scholars argue that there is evidence of direct material support from IS's leadership and network to Ansar al-Sunna.[89] They point to Ansar al-Sunna's improvement in strength, weaponry, tactics, violence and propaganda since 2017, when it was using small arms such as machetes to launch attacks. By 2021, the insurgency was executing complex operations with coordination across maritime and land-based forces,[90] and by 2022 it was allegedly using 'drone squads' to surveil potential targets and counterinsurgent forces.[91] As far as funding is concerned, the US also contends that IS members and associates in South Africa are involved in facilitating the transfer of funds from the top of the IS hierarchy to branches across Africa.[92] However, counter-insurgence measures and the disparate distribution of its fighting units may complicate the insurgency putting funds and resources into the hands of its fighters, creating incentives for its units to use looting, extortion and kidnapping for ransom to sustain itself.[93] The insurgency further tends to rely on regional militant networks in Central and Southern Africa, including other alleged IS affiliates, to provide funding, sustainability and growth.[94]

Accordingly, although there has been an improvement in weaponry and tactics since Ansar al-Sunna pledged allegiance to IS, there is little evidence of ongoing weapons and funding being provided by IS to the insurgency on an ongoing basis, and there does not seem to be a subordinate affiliate relationship where

Ansar al-Sunna is dependent on IS for resources.[95] The connection between Ansar al-Sunna and IS, therefore, appears to be a temporal and transactional partnership where both parties, for the most part, maintain their own resources and authority and come together only for a short period to realise a common objective.[96]

In addition to this, there are motivations for IS, Ansar al-Sunna and other stakeholders to support a connection between the two groups, which will be explored in the next part.

5.4 Motivations for an exaggerated link

Supporting a connection between the two groups is a strategic arrangement of mutual benefit to both the IS central leadership and Ansar al-Sunna, and both groups have exploited the connection for reputational and propaganda value.[97] IS has suffered significant losses in recent years,[98] where it could previously rely on attacks where territory was captured to garner attention and show strength.[99] Scholars have argued that IS often exaggerates its own prowess and role in global attacks to the point of absurdity.[100] By claiming responsibility for the deadly attack in Palma, for example, IS leveraged loose ties with Ansar al-Sunna to create the impression of a global struggle.[101]

Supporting a connection with IS is also in Ansar al-Sunna's interest. It has been said that terrorism does not work if no one is watching.[102] Ansar al-Sunna primarily benefits from its affiliation with IS, not through the provision of direct resources, militants or funding, but through branding, and its relationship with IS is strongest in the informational space.[103]

There are also other role players benefiting from exaggerating a link between the insurgency and IS. First, due to the discovery and exploitation of the gas fields in Palma by foreign actors, global interests are at stake. A link with IS may legitimise and galvanise international military action, which will be complex if it were only a local insurgency.[104] Other stakeholders benefiting from a link between IS and Ansar al-Sunna are private security companies attempting to obtain lucrative contracts to suppress the insurgency.[105] Therefore, the reliance on a relationship between IS and Ansar al-Sunna often is opportunistic.

5.5 Conclusion

Important questions remain concerning the precise nature of IS's relationship with Ansar al-Sunna.[106] The IS media department's publication of videos, photos and accounts of attacks in Mozambique indicate some level of organisational interaction.[107] However, it appears that the affiliation is in the nature of a transactional agreement, with each party exploiting the connection when it suits them. There is no firm evidence that Ansar al-Sunna is aligned with the ideology of IS.

The connection seems fluid, at times more intense, depending on the propaganda value of an attack for both groups and at times more distant. Ansar al-Sunna mostly relies on a link with IS for publicity value as opposed to any reliance on IS for resources or direction concerning strategy or the appointment of leaders.

Ansar al-Sunna remains a local insurgency with regional connections and relies on these regional connections for much of its support. Similarly, IS also claims attacks opportunistically, especially where territory is captured. Thus, the nature of the affiliation between IS and Ansar al-Sunna arguably, at least at the time of writing this chapter, remains a transactional arrangement, with most of the atmosphere around a firm alliance being created by the groups themselves or by other stakeholders with interests in tying the conflict in Mozambique to IS.

That said, the goals of IS may evolve. IS has had to adapt since its loss of territory. In future, holding territory and the establishment of another caliphate may start to fade as a core goal, as it was the establishment of territorial control that resulted in the formation of the international coalition to defeat IS.[108] IS may then start to rely increasingly on its regional connections and their acts of terror as evidence of the strength of IS globally, to bolster the group in the eyes of its supporters and to attract more members – irrespective of whether territory is captured or held by regional affiliates. The prospect of growing support for IS and its strategies based on terrorising civilian populations may be the most disturbing consequence of the transactional alliance between IS and Ansar al-Sunna in Mozambique.

Notes

1 Olaniyi Evans and Ikechukwu Kelikume, 'The Impact of Poverty, Unemployment, Inequality, Corruption and Poor Governance on Niger Delta Militancy, Boko Haram Terrorism and Fulani Herdsmen Attacks in Nigeria' (2006) 8 (2) *International Journal of Management, Economics and Social Sciences* 68, where the authors note that 'inequality and unemployment are positively related to terrorism, meaning the higher the levels of inequality and unemployment in the country, the higher the level of terrorism'; see further Tim Krieger and Daniel Meierrieks, 'Does Income Inequality Lead to Terrorism?' *Centre for Economic Studies and Information Working Paper No 5821* (2016) 7, 22.

2 Austin Doctor, 'After Palma: Assessing the Islamic State's Position in Northern Mozambique' *Programme on Extremism at the George Washington University* (The George Washington University 2022) 14.

3 Felix Makonye, 'The Cabo Delgado Insurgency in Mozambique: Origin, Ideology, Recruitment Strategies and Social, Political and Economic Implications for Natural Gas and Oil Exploration' (2020) 1 (3) *African Journal of Terrorism and Insurgency Research* 65, 68.

4 Makonye (n 3) 65, 68; Amal El Ouassif and Seleman Yusuph Kitenge, 'Terrorist Insurgency in Northern Mozambique: Context, Analysis, and Spillover Effects on Tanzania' *Policy Centre for the New South* (November 2021) 9.

5 David Mihalyi and Thomas Scurfield, 'How Africa's Prospective Petroleum Producers Fell Victim to the Resource Curse' (2021) 8 *The Extractive Industries and Society* 225.

6 Vijay Prashad, 'Why the Discovery of Natural Gas in Mozambique Has Produced Tragedy' *Mail and Guardian* (3 September 2021).

7 Joseph Hanlon, 'Mozambique' in Albert Awedoba and others (eds), *Africa Yearbook: Politics, Economy and Society South of the Sahara in 2019* (Brill 2020) 497.

8 Ibid.

9 Amanda M Makosso and Auréole Collinet, 'Islamic State Central Africa Province (ISCAP): A Threat to Regional Stability and Security' (2021) 4 (1) *Journal of Intelligence, Conflict, and Warfare* 107–108.

10 Ouassif and Kitenge (n 4) 8–10; Makonye (n 3) 64'.
11 Tore Refslund Hamming, 'The Islamic State in Mozambique' *Lawfare* (24 January 2021). The author clarifies that while Ansar al-Sunna is referred to as Al-Shabaab by the locals, Ansar Al-Sunna bears no relation to the Somalia-based Al-Qaeda affiliate. Accordingly, this chapter uses the name 'Ansar-Al Sunnah' to refer to the insurgency in Northern Mozambique.
12 Ibid. These traditions included opposing formal educational institutions, praying in the mosque wearing shoes and praying only three times per day.
13 Ibid.
14 Clayton Hazvinei Vhumbunu, 'Insurgency in Mozambique: The Role of the Southern African Development Community' *ACCORD* (21 April 2021); Adrian Frey 'Armed Men Attack Police Stations in Mocímboa da Praia – AIM Report' *Club of Mozambique* (5 October 2017).
15 Hamming (n 11); Doctor (n 2) 5.
16 Hamming (n 11).
17 Ibid.
18 Ouassif and Kitenge (n 4) 9–10. In August and September 2020, Ansar al-Sunna launched brutal attacks on two barracks in Mocimboa de Praia, killing 50 people. Fighters also beheaded as many as 50 people at the local soccer field in the village of Muatide in early November 2020.
19 Hanlon (n 7); Christina Goldbaum, 'ISIS Claims Responsibility for Mozambique Attack' *New York Times* (30 March 2021).
20 Doctor (n 2) 6, 18.
21 Office of the Spokesperson, 'State Department Terrorist Designations of ISIS Affiliates and Leaders in the Democratic Republic of the Congo and Mozambique' (10 March 2021) (U.S. Department of State).
22 Jakkie Cilliers, 'Terrorism and Africa' (2010) (12) 4 *African Security Studies* 102; Anneli Botha, 'Background: Terrorism in Africa' 9 Paper Presented at the Institute for Security Studies Terrorism Seminar, 18–19 September 2003, Colosseum Hotel, Pretoria, South Africa 5–6.
23 See Chapter 6 of this book.
24 See International Committee of the Red Cross, 'Challenges for IHL – Terrorism: Overview' (29 October 2010) <www.icrc.org/en/document/challenges-ihl-terrorism>.
25 Ibid.
26 See the Protocol Additional to the Geneva Conventions of 12 August 1949, and Relating to the Protection of Victims of Non-International Armed Conflicts (Protocol II) (adopted 8 June 1977, entered into force 7 December 1978) 1125 UNTS 609, Common Article 3 to the Geneva Conventions of 12 August 1949.
27 See Common Article 3, ibid.
28 Article 51(2) of Protocol I to the Geneva Conventions, which applies to international armed conflicts, contains the same wording as article 13(2) of Additional Protocol II. Protocol II elaborates on protections for victims caught up in internal conflicts such as civil wars. It does not apply to internal disturbances such as riots, demonstrations and isolated acts of violence. For more on the classification of armed conflicts, see Chapter 6 in this book. See also Protocol Additional to the Geneva Conventions of 12 August 1949, and Relating to the Protection of Victims of International Armed Conflicts (Protocol I) (adopted 8 June 1977, entered into force 7 December 1978) 1125 UNTS 3.
29 Although the conflict in Mozambique is governed by IHL, it is interesting to note that numerous UN resolutions, the Draft Comprehensive Convention on International Terrorism, 2006, sectoral treaties prohibiting terrorism, national legislation and domestic and international jurisprudence also consistently reflect intentional violence with the purpose of spreading fear among civilians as an element of terrorism. For a

comprehensive analysis in this regard, see Aniel de Beer, 'Peremptory Norms of General International Law (*Jus Cogens*) and the Prohibition of Terrorism' (Brill Nijhoff 2019) 17–60.

30 See Luís Nhachote, 'Humanising Security in Cabo Delgado: A CSO Report on the Drivers of Conflict and Its Impact on Civilians' *The Investigative Journalism Centre, Mozambique* (August 2021) <africaportal.org>, 11. Makonye (n 3) 67 also notes the viciousness of attacks against defenceless civilians in remote villages, where the insurgents hack people to death using knives and machetes, behead victims, burn homes and set vehicles ablaze.

31 Domestic terrorism becomes transnational terrorism where the terrorists, victims or targets represent different states and nationalities. Seung-Whan Choi, *New Explorations into International Relations: Democracy, Foreign Investment, Terrorism and Conflict* (University of GA Press 2016) 220; David Pilling, 'Anadarko Petroleum Attacked Mozambique' *Financial Times* (22 February 2020).

32 Makosso and Collinet (n 9).

33 Makosso and Collinet (n 9) 101–102, 107–108. See further UN Doc. S/2021/682 (27 July 2021) para 6; Kenneth Kunaka, 'An Analysis of the Transnational Diffusion of Terrorism in Africa: The Case of Ansar Al-Sunna Armed Group in Northern Mozambique' (2021) 11 (2) *African Journal on Terrorism* 5.

34 Brenda Mugeci Githing'u and Tore Refslund Hamming, 'The Arc of Jihad': The Ecosystem of Militancy in East, Central and Southern Africa' 44 *International Centre for the Study of Radicalisation* (2021).

35 Tom van Rentergem, 'Al-Shabaab in Mozambique: Taking Stock of an Insurgency Under Cover' *Egmont Policy Brief* (June 2022); Githing'u and Hamming (n 34) 45–46.

36 Githing'u and Hamming (n 34) 21.

37 Ibid.

38 Ibid, 44.

39 Ibid; Doctor (n 2) 5.

40 Doctor (n 2) 6; Goldbaum (n 19); Office of the Spokesperson (n 21).

41 Tara Candland and others, 'The Rising Threat to Central Africa: The 2021 Transformation of the Islamic State's Congolese Branch' (2022) 15 (6) *Combating Terrorism Centre Sentinel* 1–16.

42 Doctor (n 2) 16.

43 James Barnett, 'The "Central African" Jihad: Islamism and Nation-Building in Mozambique and Uganda' (2020) *Current Trends in Islamist Ideology*; Jason Warner and Charlotte Hulme, 'The Islamic State in Africa: Estimating Fighter Numbers in Cells Across the Continent' (2018) 7 (11) *CTC Sentinel* 21–22.

44 Githing'u and Hamming (n 34) 45; Eric Morier-Genoud, 'Tracing the History of Mozambique's Mysterious and Deadly Insurgency' *The Conversation* (18 February 2019). However, see Office of the Spokesperson (n 21): The U.S. State Department is of the view that the entire insurgency pledged allegiance to IS.

45 Victor H Asal and others, 'With Friends Like These: Why Terrorist Organisations Ally' (2016) 19 (1) *International Public Management Journal* 1.

46 Ibid.

47 Ibid.

48 Ibid. Daniel Byman, 'Buddies or Burdens? Understanding the Al-Qaeda Relationship with Its Affiliate Organisations' (2014) 23 (3) *Security Studies* 8.

49 Ibid.

50 Byman (n 48) 6.

51 Doctor (n 2) 12. See CENTCOM, 'Fight Against ISIS in 2022' (12 January 2023), noting that in 2014 IS swept through Iraq and Syria, 'carved out a third of each country, and created the Islamic State'.'

52 Byman (n 48) 7.

53 Eric Schmitt and Helene Cooper, 'Senior ISIS Leader in Somalia Killed in US Special Operations Raid' *New York Times* (26 January 2023); CENTCOM (n 51).
54 See CENTCOM (n 51).
55 Richard English, *Does Terrorism Work? A History* (OUP 2016) 228; de Beer (n 29) 51–52.
56 For more on religiously-motivated terrorism, see generally David C Rapoport, 'The Four Waves of Modern Terrorism' in AK Cronin and JM Ludes (eds), *Attacking Terrorism: Elements of a Grand Strategy* (Georgetown University Press 2004)25, 47. Rapoport argues that terrorism occurs in cycles, driven by certain events and objectives. He contends that the fourth wave of terrorism is driven by religious objectives and explores, inter alia, the role of Islam.
57 See Michael Aondona Chiangi, 'Critically Examining David Rapoport's Four Waves Theory of Modern Terrorism in the Light of Factual Historical Events' (2021) 11 (2) *African Journal on Terrorism* 24.
58 Hilary Matfess, 'In Africa, All Jihad Is Local' *Foreign Policy* (16 May 2019); Doctor (n 2) 13.
59 See Hamming (n 11).
60 Makonye (n 3) 65.
61 Asal and others (n 45).
62 Doctor (n 2) 12.
63 Ibid. Emily Estelle, 'The Islamic State Resurges in Mozambique' *Foreign Policy* (16 June 2021).
64 Doctor (n 2) 10.
65 Ouassif and Kitenge (n 4) 13; International Crisis Group 'Stemming the Insurrection in Mozambique's Cabo Delgado' (11 June 2021).
66 Byman (n 48); Mahmut Cengiz and Kutluer Karademir, 'Why Salafi-Jihadist Terrorist Groups Pledge Allegiance to Al Qaeda or ISIS' (2020) 7 (2) *International Journal on Criminology* 10.
67 Doctor (n 2) 17; Warner and Hume (n 43) 21–28.
68 See Githing'u and Hamming (n 34) 8.
69 Jacob Zenn, 'The Islamic State's Provinces on the Peripheries: Juxtaposing the Pledges from Boko Haram in Nigeria and Abu Sayyaf and Maute Group in the Philippines' (2019) 13 (1) *Perspectives on Terrorism* 87; Githing'u and Hamming (n 34) 23.
70 Daniel Milton and Muhammad al'Ubaydi, 'Pledging Bay'a: A Benefit or Burden to the Islamic State?' (2015) 8 (3) *CTC Sentinel* 1; Githing'u and Hamming (n 34) 8.
71 UN Doc. S/2021/68 (3 February 2021); UN Doc. S/2021/486 (1 June 2021).
72 Doctor (n 2) 4.
73 Ibid, 17.
74 See ACLED, 'Cabo Delgado Monthly March 2021' (15 April 2021) <www.caboligado.com/monthly-reports/cabo-ligado-monthly-march-2021>, stating that '[t]here is no evidence from the Palma attack that IS controls the strategic direction of the insurgency'.
75 Jason Warner, *The Islamic State in Africa: The Emergence, Evolution, and Future of the Next Jihadist Battlefront* (OUP 2022); Doctor (n 2) 14.
76 International Crisis Group (n 65) 1.
77 Doctor (n 2) 13; Office of the Spokesperson (n 21).
78 Githing'u and Hamming (n 34) 45–46; João Feijó, 'From the "Faceless Enemy" to the Hypothesis of Dialogue: Identities, Pretensions and Channels of Communication with the Machababs, Destaque Rural' (2021) 130 *Observatorio do Meio Rural* <https://omrmz.org/omrweb/wpcontent/uploads/DR-130-Cabo-Delgado-Pt-e-Eng.pdf>.
79 U.S. Department of State, 'Designations of ISIS-Mozambique, JNIM, and Al-Shabaab Leaders' <www.state.gov/designations-of-isis-mozambique-jnim-and-al-shabaab-leaders> (6 August 2021); Centro de Jornalismo Investigativo, 'Bonomado Machude Omar ou Ibn Omar: The Mozambican face of terrorism in Cabo Delgado' (22 September 2020) <https://cjimoz.org/news/en/bonomado-machude-omar-ou-ibnomar-the-mozambican-face-of-terrorism-in-cabo-delgado/>; Nhachote (n 30).
80 Hamming (n 11) 46.

81 U.S. Department of State (n 79); Centro de Jornalismo Investigativo (n 79); Nhachote (n 30).
82 International Crisis Group (n 65).
83 Doctor (n 2) 14; Makonye (n 3) 65.
84 See Tricia Bacon, 'Strange Bedfellows or Brothers in Arms: Why Terrorist Groups Ally' (PhD thesis, Georgetown University, 2013) 753.
85 Ibid, 754.
86 Ibid.
87 Ibid.
88 Ibid, 755.
89 Doctor (n 2) 17.
90 Doctor (n 2) 5; International Crisis Group (n 65); Tyler Lycan, Christopher Faulkner and Austin C Doctor, 'Making Waves: Militant Maritime Operations Along Africa's Eastern Coast' *War on the Rocks* (4 November 2022).
91 See 'Mozambique Army Intercepts ISIS Drones Using Israeli MCTECH Systems – Israel Defence Report' *Club of Mozambique* (7 March 2022).
92 Ned Price, 'Designation of ISIS Organisers and Financial Facilitators Based in South Africa – United States Department of State' (1 March 2022).
93 Doctor (n 2) 12.
94 Ibid, 14. The IS affiliate in the DRC has allegedly helped fund Ansar Al-Sunna.
95 See Bacon (n 84) 754 for more on subordinate affiliate relationships.
96 Ibid.
97 Doctor (n 2) 15, Barnett (n 43).
98 Githing'u and Hamming (n 34).
99 English (n 55) 11; De Beer (n 29) 612.
100 Byman (n 48) 5.
101 Goldbaum (n 19).
102 Byman (n 48) 4.
103 Warner and Hume (n 43); Doctor (n 2).
104 Ouassif and Kitenge (n 4) 7; 'Mozambique Palma Attack: Why IS Involvement Is Exaggerated' *BBC News* (17 April 2021).
105 Borges Nhamirre, 'Resort to Private Military Companies to Fight the Insurgency in Cabo Delgado: Without Transparency and with Disastrous Results' *Centro de Integridade Pública* (2020) <https://cipmoz.org/wp-content/uploads/2020/12/insurgency-in-Cabo-Delgado.pdf>; Daniel Sixto, 'Russian Mercenaries: A String of Failures in Africa' *Foreign Policy Research Institute* (2020).
106 Doctor (n 2) 6.
107 Githing'u and Hamming (n 34) 23.
108 At its height, the Islamic State held about a third of Syria and 40 per cent of Iraq. By December 2017 it had lost 95 per cent of its territory, including its two biggest properties, Mosul, Iraq's second-largest city, and the Northern Syrian city of Raqqa, its nominal capital. Wilson Centre, 'Timeline: The Rise, Spread and Fall of the Islamic State' (28 October 2019).

Bibliography

ACLED, 'Cabo Delgado Monthly March 2021' (15 April 2021) <www.caboligado.com/monthly-reports/cabo-ligado-monthly-march-2021>.

Adrian Frey, 'Armed Men Attack Police Stations in Mocímboa da Praia – AIM Report' *Club of Mozambique* (5 October 2017).

'Advisory Opinion on the Legal Consequences of the Construction of a Wall in the Occupied Palestinian Territory' *ICJ Reports* (2004) 136.

Amal El Ouassif and Seleman Yusuph Kitenge, 'Terrorist Insurgency in Northern Mozambique: Context, Analysis, and Spillover Effects on Tanzania' *Policy Centre for the New South* (November 2021).

Amanda M Makosso and Auréole Collinet, 'Islamic State Central Africa Province (ISCAP): A Threat to Regional Stability and Security' (2021) 4 (1) *Journal of Intelligence, Conflict, and Warfare*.

Aniel de Beer, *Peremptory Norms of General International Law (Jus Cogens) and the Prohibition of Terrorism* (Brill Nijhoff 2019).

Anneli Botha, 'Background: Terrorism in Africa' Paper Presented at the Institute for Security Studies Terrorism Seminar, 18–19 September 2003, Colosseum Hotel, Pretoria, South Africa 5–6 <www.africaportal.org>.

Austin Doctor, 'After Palma: Assessing the Islamic State's Position in Northern Mozambique' *Programme on Extremism at the George Washington University* (The George Washington University 2022).

Borges Nhamirre, 'Resort to Private Military Companies to Fight the Insurgency in Cabo Delgado: Without Transparency and with Disastrous Results' *Centro de Integridade Pública* (2020) <https://cipmoz.org/wp-content/uploads/2020/12/insurgency-in-Cabo-Delgado.pdf>.

Brenda Mugeci Githing'u and Tore Refslund Hamming, 'The Arc of Jihad': The Ecosystem of Militancy in East, Central and Southern Africa' 44 *International Centre for the Study of Radicalisation* (2021) <https://icsr.info/wp-content/uploads/2021/11/ICSR-Report-The-Arc-of-Jihad-The-Ecosystem-of-Militancy-in-East-Centraland-Southern-Africa.pdf>.

CENTCOM, 'Fight Against ISIS in 2022' (12 January 2023) <www.wilsoncenter.org/article/centcom-fight-against-isis-2022>.

Centro de Jornalismo Investigativo, Bonomado Machude Omar ou Ibn Omar: The Mozambican face of terrorism in Cabo Delgado' (22 September 2020) <https://cjimoz.org/news/en/bonomado-machude-omar-ou-ibnomar-the-mozambican-face-of-terrorism-in-cabo-delgado/>.

Christina Goldbaum, 'ISIS Claims Responsibility for Mozambique Attack' *New York Times* (30 March 2021).

Clayton Hazvinei Vhumbunu, 'Insurgency in Mozambique: The Role of the Southern African Development Community' (21 April 2021) <www/accord.org.za/conflict-trends/insurgency-in-mozambique-the-role-of-the-southern-african-development-community>.

Daniel Byman, 'Buddies or Burdens? Understanding the Al-Qaeda Relationship with Its Affiliate Organisations' (2014) 23 (3) *Security Studies*.

Daniel Milton and Muhammad al'Ubaydi, 'Pledging Bay'a: A Benefit or Burden to the Islamic State?' (2015) 8 (3) *CTC Sentinel* 1 <www.ctc.usma.edu/pledging-baya-a-benefit-or-burden-to-theislamic-state>.

Daniel Sixto, 'Russian Mercenaries: A String of Failures in Africa' *Foreign Policy Research Institute* (2020) <www.fpri.org/article/2023/01/wagner-group-redefined-threats-and-responses>.

David C Rapoport, 'The Four Waves of Modern Terrorism' in AK Cronin and JM Ludes (eds), *Attacking Terrorism: Elements of a Grand Strategy* (Georgetown University Press 2004).

David Mihalyi and Thomas Scurfield, 'How Africa's Prospective Petroleum Producers Fell Victim to the Resource Curse' (2021) 8 *The Extractive Industries and Society*.

David Pilling, 'Anadarko Petroleum Attacked Mozambique' *Financial Times* (22 February 2020).

Emily Estelle, 'The Islamic State Resurges in Mozambique' *Foreign Policy* (16 June 2021) <https://foreignpolicy.com/2021/06/16/mozambique-islamic-state-terrorism-france-total/>.

Eric Morier-Genoud, 'Tracing the History of Mozambique's Mysterious and Deadly Insurgency' *The Conversation* (18 February 2019).

Eric Schmitt and Helene Cooper, 'Senior ISIS Leader in Somalia Killed in US Special Operations Raid' *New York Times* (26 January 2023).

Felix Makonye, 'The Cabo Delgado Insurgency in Mozambique: Origin, Ideology, Recruitment Strategies and Social, Political and Economic Implications for Natural Gas and Oil Exploration' (2020) 1 (3) *African Journal of Terrorism and Insurgency Research*.

Hilary Matfess, 'In Africa, All Jihad Is Local' *Foreign Policy* (16 May 2019).
ICRC, 'Challenges for IHL – Terrorism: Overview' (29 October 2010) <www.icrc.org/en/document/challenges-ihl-terrorism>.
International Crisis Group, 'Stemming the Insurrection in Mozambique's Cabo Delgado' (11 June 2021) <www.crisisgroup.org/africa/southern-africa/mozambique/303-stemming-insurrection-mozambiques-cabo-delgado>.
Jacob Zenn, 'The Islamic State's Provinces on the Peripheries: Juxtaposing the Pledges from Boko Haram in Nigeria and Abu Sayyaf and Maute Group in the Philippines' (2019) 13 (1) *Perspectives on Terrorism*.
Jakkie Cilliers, 'Terrorism and Africa' (2010) 12 (4) *African Security Studies*.
James Barnett, 'The "Central African" Jihad: Islamism and Nation-Building in Mozambique and Uganda' *Currents Trends in Islamist Ideology* (29 October 2020) Hudson Institute <https://www.hudson.org/node/43467>.
Jason Warner, *The Islamic State in Africa: The Emergence, Evolution, and Future of the Next Jihadist Battlefront* (OUP 2022).
Jason Warner and Charlotte Hulme, 'The Islamic State in Africa: Estimating Fighter Numbers in Cells Across the Continent' (2018) 7(11) *CTC Sentinel*.
João Feijó, 'From the "Faceless Enemy" to the Hypothesis of Dialogue: Identities, Pretensions and Channels of Communication with the Machababs, Destaque Rural' (2021) *Observatorio do Meio Rural* <https://omrmz.org/omrweb/wpcontent/uploads/DR-130-Cabo-Delgado-Pt-e-Eng.pdf>.
Joseph Hanlon, 'Mozambique' in Albert Awedoba and others (eds), *Africa Yearbook: Politics, Economy and Society South of the Sahara in 2019* (Brill 2020).
Kenneth Kunaka, 'An Analysis of the Transnational Diffusion of Terrorism in Africa: The Case of Ansar Al-Sunna Armed Group in Northern Mozambique' (2021) 11 (2) *African Journal on Terrorism*.
Luís Nhachote, 'Humanising Security in Cabo Delgado: A CSO Report on the Drivers of Conflict and Its Impact on Civilians' *The Investigative Journalism Centre, Mozambique* (August 2021) <africaportal.org>.
Mahmut Cengiz and Kutluer Karademir, 'Why Salafi-Jihadist Terrorist Groups Pledge Allegiance to Al Qaeda or ISIS' (2020) 7 (2) *International Journal on Criminology*.
Marnie Sayles, 'Relative Deprivation and Collective Protest: An Impoverished Theory?' (1984) 54 (4) *Sociological Inquiry*.
Michael Aondona Chiangi, 'Critically Examining David Rapoport's Four Waves Theory of Modern Terrorism in the Light of Factual Historical Events' (2021) 11 (2) *African Journal on Terrorism*.
'Mozambique Army Intercepts ISIS Drones Using Israeli MCTECH Systems – Israel Defence Report' *Club of Mozambique* (7 March 2022).
'Mozambique Palma Attack: Why IS Involvement is Exaggerated' *BBC News* (17 April 2021).
Ned Price, 'Designation of ISIS Organisers and Financial Facilitators Based in South Africa – United States Department of State' (1 March 2022) <www.state.gov/designation-of-isisorganizers-and-financial-facilitators-based-in-south-africa>.
New Zealand, 'New Zealand Terrorism Suppression Act' (2002) <https://www.legislation.govt.nz/act/public/2002/0034/latest/DLM152702.html>.
Office of the Spokesperson, 'State Department Terrorist Designations of ISIS Affiliates and Leaders in the Democratic Republic of the Congo and Mozambique' (10 March 2021) <www.state.gov/state-department-terrorist-designations-of-isis-affiliates-and-leaders-in-thedemocratic-republic-of-the-congo-and-mozambique/>.
Olaniyi Evans and Ikechukwu Kelikume, 'The Impact of Poverty, Unemployment, Inequality, Corruption and Poor Governance on Niger Delta Militancy, Boko Haram Terrorism

and Fulani Herdsmen Attacks in Nigeria' (2006) 8(2) *International Journal of Management, Economics and Social Sciences*.

Protocol Additional to the Geneva Conventions of 12 August 1949, and Relating to the Protection of Victims of International Armed Conflicts (Protocol I) (1977) <https://treaties.un.org/Pages/showDetails.aspx?objid=08000002800f3586&clang=_en>

Protocol Additional to the Geneva Conventions of 12 August 1949, and Relating to the Protection of Victims of Non-International Armed Conflicts (Protocol II) (1977) <https://treaties.un.org/Pages/showDetails.aspx?objid=08000002800f3cb8&clang=_en>.

Richard English, *Does Terrorism Work? A History* (OUP 2016) 228.

Seung-Whan Choi, *New Explorations into International Relations: Democracy, Foreign Investment, Terrorism and Conflict* (University of GA Press 2016).

Tara Candland and others, 'The Rising Threat to Central Africa: The 2021 Transformation of the Islamic State's Congolese Branch' (2022) 15 (6) *Combating Terrorism Centre Sentinel*.

Tehmina S Khan and others, 'From Commodity Discovery to Production' *World Bank Policy Research Working Paper* 7823 (2016) <https://openknowledge.worldbank.org/handle/10986/25134>.

Thomas Hegghammer, 'The Ideological Hybridisation of Jihadi Groups' (2009) 18 *Current Trends in Islamist Ideology*.

Tim Krieger and Daniel Meierrieks, 'Does Income Inequality Lead to Terrorism?' *Centre for Economic Studies and Information Working Paper No 5821* (March 2016) <https://www.ifo.de/DocDL/cesifo1_wp5821.pdf>.

Tom van Rentergem, 'Al-Shabaab in Mozambique: Taking Stock of an Insurgency Under Cover' *Egmont Policy Brief* (June 2022) <www.egmontinstitute.be/app/uploads/2022/06/PB-281-Tom-VR_Al-Shabab-in-Mozambique.pdf?type=pdf>.

Tore Refslund Hamming, 'The Islamic State in Mozambique' *Lawfare* (24 January 2021).

Tricia Bacon, 'Strange Bedfellows or Brothers in Arms: Why Terrorist Groups Ally' (PhD thesis, Georgetown University, 2013).

Tyler Lycan, Christopher Faulkner and Austin C Doctor, 'Making Waves: Militant Maritime Operations Along Africa's Eastern Coast' *War on the Rocks* (4 November 2022).

UN Doc. S/2021/68 (3 February 2021).

UN Doc. S/2021/486 (1 June 2021).

'United Nations Thirteenth Report of the Secretary-General on the Threat Posed by ISIL (Da'esh) to International Peace and Security and the Range of United Nations Efforts in Support of Member States in Countering the Threat' (27 July 2021) S/2021/682.

U.S. Department of State, 'Designation of Abu Yasir Hassan as a Specially Designated Global Terrorist' (11 March 2021) <www.federalregister.gov/documents/2021/03/11/2021-04907/designation-of-abu-yasirhassan-as-a-specially-designated-global-terrorist>.

U.S. Department of State, 'Designations of ISIS-Mozambique, JNIM, and Al-Shabaab Leaders' (6 August 2021) <www.state.gov/designations-of-isis-mozambique-jnim-and-al-shabaab-leaders>.

Victor H Asal and others, 'With Friends Like These: Why Terrorist Organisations Ally' (2016) 19 (1) *International Public Management Journal*.

Vijay Prashad, 'Why the Discovery of Natural Gas in Mozambique Has Produced Tragedy' *Mail and Guardian* (3 September 2021).

Wilson Centre, 'Timeline: The Rise, Spread and Fall of the Islamic State' (28 October 2019) <www.wilsoncenter.org/article/timeline-the-rise-spread-and-fall-the-islamic-state>.

Part II

International humanitarian law perspectives

6 The law of armed conflict and the classification of the situation in Cabo Delgado as a non-international armed conflict

Najimdeen Bakare and Ayodele Ojedokun

6.1 Introduction

A conflict can be an international armed conflict (IAC) or a non-international armed conflict (NIAC) based on the actors and whether it displays different levels of low or high-intensity violence.[1] There is consensus with regard to the set of rules applicable to international and non-international armed conflicts. These variations in definition and regulation are embodied in the Geneva Conventions and subsequent Additional Protocols I–III (AP I–III). According to the ICRC, 'the entirety of the four Geneva Conventions, as well as the rules of Additional Protocol I apply to international armed conflicts, while Article 3 Common to the four Geneva Conventions and Additional Protocol II (APII) apply to non-international armed conflicts'.[2] Thus, this chapter addresses conflict classification through the lens of Common Article 3 (CA3)[3] and APII[4] under the law of non-international armed conflict (NIAC). As a case study, the chapter classifies the situation in Cabo Delgado, Northern Mozambique as a NIAC within the epistemic and legal prism of international humanitarian law (IHL). It examines the minimum threshold that qualifies the conflict as a NIAC and analyses the impact of an intervention by foreign troops on the classification.

The socio-political and economic causes of the conflict do not fallen into the scope of the chapter; the focus is on locating the conflict in the domain of IHL. The chapter is structured in five parts. The first part is this introduction. The second part contextualises and classifies the conflict situation in Cabo Delgado, Mozambique, and explains the applicability of the minimum threshold of CA3. The third part addresses the applicability of APII to the conflict. The fourth part examines the intervention of foreign state armed forces in the conflict and explores the consequences of their involvement in conflict classification. The fifth part then draws some conclusions.

6.2 The threshold level of a Common Article 3 conflict and the situation in Mozambique

CA3 to the four Geneva Conventions provides a minimum set of humanitarian principles applicable to 'armed conflict not of an international character'.[5] There is no clarification of the meaning of this term in treaty law.[6] However, the Appeals Chamber of the International Criminal Tribunal for the former Yugoslavia (ICTY)

DOI: 10.4324/9781003317647-8

in *Tadić* clarified that an armed conflict not of an international character exists when there is 'protracted armed violence between governmental authorities and organised armed groups or between such groups within a state'.[7] This clarification remains the authoritative definition of an armed conflict not of an international character and is grounded in its acceptance by states in their practice and *opinio juris*, conferring on the definition of the status of international custom.[8]

The Trial Chamber of the ICTY in *Tadić* explained that the approach of the Appeals Chamber notes that situations that amount to a CA3 armed conflict are determined as a result of the 'intensity of the conflict and organisation of the parties to the conflict'.[9] It should be noted that these elements pre-date their reformulation by the Trial Chamber in *Tadić*.[10] The dual elements separate an armed conflict from events or situations below the threshold of an armed conflict.[11] A determination of the existence of a NIAC in terms of the elements described, with the aid of indicators, is mapped out in the jurisprudence of tribunals.[12] The application of these indicators is flexible and depends on the circumstances being assessed.[13] The jurisprudence of the tribunals affirmed that none of the indicators is determinative but merely indicative in the assessment of a NIAC.[14] It has been argued that the tribunals' 'findings seem to contradict' their assertion of the indicative role of some indicators.[15] Scholars have argued for adopting a minimum threshold approach and for advancing some indicators as determinative rather than indicative.[16] These elements of armed conflict and the indicators will be discussed below in relation to the situation in Cabo Delgado.

An assessment of the organisational capacity applies only to an armed group of a non-state party;[17] the armed forces of the state are presumed to be organised.[18] It is necessary to highlight the degree of organisation that qualifies an armed group as a party to a conflict. The Trial Chamber II of ICTY in *Boskoski* noted that the degree of organisation that qualifies a non-state group as a party to a CA3 conflict 'has not been specifically defined in legal text or in jurisprudence'.[19] Nevertheless, an armed group qualifies as a party to a CA3 conflict if it is 'sufficiently organised',[20] however, at a minimal level.[21] The extent of an armed group's organisational nature requires an objective analysis and is identified through one or more of the following indicators.[22]

The first indicator is the presence of a command structure in a group.[23] This indicator is believed by Kleffner and Bradley to play a determinative role in the identification of an organised armed group.[24] The authors of this chapter agree with this position. Logically, what distinguishes a group that is organised from that which is disorganised is the presence of an identifiable authority which coordinates the activities of the group. It is important to note that the indicator does not require the same level of structure as that of a state armed force.[25] The discussion now turns to an analysis of the command structure of the Ansar al-Sunna group.

The facts relating to the leadership structure of Ansar al-Sunna are unclear.[26] Most armed groups operate in secrecy, and this is true particularly of Islamist groups.[27] Attacks on media personnel in Cabo Delgado contribute to the non-availability of detailed facts regarding the conflict.[28] The following person is named to be a member of the leadership of the insurgent group, namely, Bonomade Machude

Omar. He is believed to have led various attacks in Cabo Delgado, in particular, the first attack in 2017 and the Palma attack in 2021.[29] He is a senior military official within the ranks of the group and directs communications of the group.[30] Other notable leaders include Abu Yasir Hassan and Abu Dardai Jongo.[31] The minimal facts available suggest that the group has a form of structure; although it is not sophisticated, it can be likened to a 'leadership and lower-level fighters' structure.[32] Nevertheless, it is evident that a form of control is exerted over members and this undoubtedly has aided the strength of the insurgent group to carry out military attacks.

The ability of a group to carry out operations in an organised manner, such as by displaying a unified military strategy, indicates a well-organised group.[33] For instance, Ansar al-Sunnah carried out coordinated attacks simultaneously in various geographical locations in Cabo Delgado.[34] The level of logistics it displays indicates an armed group that is well organised.[35] In this regard, Ansar al-Sunna possesses the ability to train and recruit new members. Most of its members are recruited from neighbouring Tanzania,[36] it is of the utmost importance to note that the nationality of a member of an armed group does not have a consequential effect on the classification of an armed group as a party to a conflict. Furthermore, some of its members are recruited locally through the abduction of civilians during raids.[37] The total membership of the group is estimated to range from 1 500 to 4 000 members.[38] These members receive military training locally in Cabo Delgado and, in 2019, it was reported that they received training support from an armed group based in the Democratic Republic of the Congo (DRC) and in Uganda.[39] The method of gaining access to weapons and military equipment is by raiding military bases in Cabo Delgado[40] and outside the borders of Mozambique.[41] It was reported that over 300 members of the insurgent group had attacked a military base located in Kitaya village in Tanzania and escaped with weapons and ammunition.[42] The weapons and ammunition in possession of the insurgent group include sophisticated equipment such as 82-millimetre mortars, rocket-propelled grenades (RPGs), machine guns and grenade launchers.[43]

The ability of a group to discipline its members and assert the implementation of the basic principles of CA3 indicates a sufficiently organised armed group.[44] Ansar al-Sunna, as in the case of other jihadist groups, in their practice does not conform to IHL principles as enshrined in the provisions of CA3. The reason for non-conformity to the principles of IHL by Ansar al-Sunna is not entirely clear. It could be because of an absence of an internal disciplinary mechanism to assert compliance by its members with the rules and instructions of the group leadership or it may be a deliberate act of non-conformity. The authors argue that Islamist armed groups conform to Shari'a law or to the principles of jihad rather than to humanitarian laws.[45] However, non-conformity to humanitarian principles does not denote a lack of organisation as explained by the Trial Chamber in *Boskoski*.[46] The authors argue that Ansar al-Sunna, by reason of their organisational structure, possesses the capacity to implement CA3.

The element of 'protracted armed violence' connotes the intensity and not the duration of the conflict.[47] Thus, a conflict, though of short duration but of severe intensity, amounts to a NIAC,[48] and a conflict where the fighting is less severe but is protracted in nature also is a NIAC. The criteria highlighted by Trial Chamber I in the *Haradinaj* case must be present in both instances. The indicators are as follows:

> The number, duration and intensity of individual confrontations; the type of weapons and other military equipment used; the number and calibre of munitions fired; the number of persons and type of forces partaking in the fight; the number of causalities; the extent of material destruction; and the number of civilians fleeing combat zones. The involvement of the UN Security Council may also be a reflection of the intensity of a conflict.[49]

As a matter of law, there is no agreed period that determines a shift from an internal disturbance to a NIAC. Nevertheless, objective criteria determine if a NIAC exists.[50] It is difficult to ascertain precisely when the violence in Cabo Delgado became a NIAC. However, it is recorded that the hostilities between the Mozambique Defence Armed Forces (FADM) and Ansar al-Sunna commenced sometime in 2017 and continue. Thus, the duration indicator of a NIAC is present.[51]

The armed confrontation between the parties to the conflict has caused severe material destruction in the Cabo Delgado province.[52] The use of sophisticated weapons, such as assault rifles, RPGs, anti-aircraft guns, improvised bombs with explosives and armoured carriers in numerous armed confrontations with the FADM and other parties to the conflict further confirms the intensity of the conflict.[53] More than 1 513 attacks have been recorded against civilian targets as well as against the military.[54] For instance, the attack on Palma commenced on 24 March 2021 and lasted for ten days,[55] causing many deaths and the displacement of over 38 000 people, with the damage caused estimated at US$113 million.[56]

The protracted nature of the conflict has caused it to spread to other provinces in Mozambique. It is reported that Ansar al-Sunna extended its military operation in the Niassa province in November 2022.[57] Many districts in Cabo Delgado province, namely, Ibo, Macomia, Meluco, Mocímboa da Praia and Mueda, have been affected by the intensity of the conflict.[58] These deadly confrontations and attacks by Ansar al-Sunna on civilians have resulted in the deaths of over 4 000 people.[59] The UN refugee agency estimates that nearly a million people have been displaced in fleeing from the combat zone.[60] At its summit in 2020 the African Union noted the violence against civilians as a result of the severity of the conflict.[61]

The foregoing assessment of the indicators in relation to the impact Ansar al-Sunna's military operations in the Cabo Delgado area of Mozambique has had confirms that the group is sufficiently organised in the context of a CA3-type conflict and that an argument that establishes that the confrontation between the FADM and Ansar al-Sunna meets the minimum threshold of protracted armed violence applicable to a CA3-type conflict is sound. The authors argue that an armed conflict not of an international character exists in Cabo Delgado and that the hostilities between the parties are regulated by CA3 of the Geneva Conventions.

6.3 The threshold of Additional Protocol II conflict and application to the situation in Cabo Delgado

APII is the most comprehensive treaty regulating non-international armed conflict. After the adoption of CA3, it became evident that the laws regulating NIACs were insufficiently developed.[62] The explicit delineation of the material field of application and the comprehensive nature of the Protocol elevate its scope of application beyond the threshold of a CA3-type conflict.[63]

It is crucial, first, to identify whether Mozambique is a state party to APII and whether hostilities between the armed forces of Mozambique and an organised armed group exist on the territory of Mozambique. Ancillary issues to the classification of the conflict in Mozambique as an APII-type conflict are whether Ansar al-Sunna has a responsible command and whether the group controls territory within Mozambique so as to enable it to carry out a sustained and concerted military operation and can implement the Protocol.[64]

First, a responsible command signifies a level of organisation of an armed group; the notion of 'responsible command' is 'inherent in the idea of organisation'.[65] This level of organisation must be structured but does not necessarily have to match a 'rigid military hierarchy'.[66] APII fails to give an exact description of what the notion of 'responsible command' entails.[67] Hence, for the purpose of classifying an APII-type conflict, the International Committee of the Red Cross (ICRC) Commentary clarifies that 'responsible command' means 'an organisation capable, on the one hand, of planning and carrying out sustained and concerted military operations and, on the other, of imposing discipline in the name of a *de facto* authority'.[68] Clearly, an armed group with a one-man leadership and without a structure of ranks cannot be described as having a responsible command. It would be impossible for the group to have the capacity to achieve the detailed obligations imposed by the Protocol on parties to a conflict.

Second, the control of territory by an armed group performs a dual function based on a literal interpretation of the provisions as illustrated in the phrase '*as to enable* them to carry out sustained and concerted military operations and to implement this protocol'.[69] The role of the territory controlled is to be regarded as a 'functional'[70] or 'enabling element',[71] as 'there is no requirement of territorial control in and of itself'.[72] The requisite size of the territory under control is such that permits the fulfilment of the dual obligations. The extent of the territory under control, however, is inconsequential, provided the control is 'sufficient' and 'stable' to carry out military operations and to implement the Protocol.[73] The nature of control over territory does not entail an administrative or governmental form of control.[74]

Third, the 'sustained' and 'concerted' nature of an APII-type conflict denotes a 'continuous and planned military operation'.[75] Perhaps, it can be described as a more ferocious version of protracted armed violence. Bradley is of the opinion that the difference between 'protracted armed violence' and a 'sustained military operation' is based not on the intensity of the conflict but on its duration.[76] In her explanation of the intensity of an APII-type conflict, Bradley argues that the nature of the conflict is such that it represents a conflict 'prolonged in time'.[77] Thus, duration is of the essence in an APII-type conflict. The realisation of this factor of a conflict is dependent on a higher threshold of organisation[78] and intensity.[79] However, in considering the continuous nature of military operations, the calculation can incorporate intervals in the exercise of hostilities.[80]

Lastly, the requirement of a capacity for 'implementation of the Protocol' is problematic. It is uncertain whether the actual implementation of the Protocol is required or if the ability to implement the Protocol will suffice.[81] A majority of judicial opinion and scholarship holds the view that an ability to implement the Protocol is sufficient to meet the material condition of application.[82] In practice, there is a danger that the actual implementation of the Protocol raises too high a threshold and that an organised armed group that violates the Protocol might be deemed insufficiently organised, undermining the essence of the Protocol.

According to the ICRC database on state parties to APII, Mozambique became a state party to the Protocol on 12 November 2002.[83] The classification of hostilities in Cabo Delgado as a CA3-type conflict confirms that there exists in Mozambique a conflict between the armed forces of a member state to the Protocol – the FADM and an organised armed group (Ansar al-Sunna). Furthermore, the group qualifies to be recognised as an organised armed group exhibiting a level of organisation of a party to an APII-type conflict. The authors note that there is uncertainty regarding the exact command structure of Ansar al-Sunna.[84] Nevertheless, the ability of the group to implement a sustained and well-coordinated military operation in Cabo Delgado confirms the presence of an organised group with an organised internal structure.[85] Furthermore, the capacity of the group to evolve technically in its operations confirms the level of development of its organisation. Recently, the group introduced the use of an improvised explosive device, a technological development that demonstrates the presence of an advanced group led by a well-organised command.[86]

The group's ability to control territory in Cabo Delgado demonstrates its organisational capacity to rise above the threshold of the CA3 to the Geneva Conventions.[87] The control of territory strongly indicates the existence of a sustained military operation:[88] Control of Nangade district, Palma and Meluco district by Ansar al-Sunna demonstrates a high level of organisation and reflects the intensity of the conflict.[89] Most of the territory formerly under the control of the insurgents now is controlled by government forces. It is reported that three major bases of the insurgency were destroyed by the forces of the Southern African Development Community Mission in Mozambique (SAMIM) in November 2021;[90] the Nangade base was reclaimed in March 2022.[91] The restoration of governmental control over territory as a result of military operations points to the fact that previously Ansar al-Sunna controlled those territories. The sustained nature of the conflict, in general, confirms the stability of the group's control that enabled it to carry out a sustained and concerted military operation.

The violation of the provisions of APII by Ansar al-Sunna may raise doubt about the group's organisational capacity. There have been numerous and deliberate attacks on civilians in Cabo Delgado, actions that amount to acts of terrorism and are a violation of APII.[92] It is settled jurisprudence that a consistent violation of humanitarian law does not denote the absence of organisation.[93]

There is substantial evidence that confirms the existence of sustained and well-planned hostilities in Cabo Delgado by Ansar al-Sunna, for instance, the planning and tactical execution of military operations in the following areas: Nangade;[94] Palma (displacing about 38 000 civilians);[95] and Ancuabe (displacing about 20 000 civilians).[96] Additionally, the group's tactical coordination of military operations is demonstrated by the attacks that took place simultaneously in the southern and northern districts of Cabo Delgado sometime in June 2022. ACLED noted that these events demonstrate the 'degree of strategic coordination among insurgents'.[97] The sustained nature of the conflict has necessitated the incorporation of local militias into the structures of the FADM.[98] Recently, there has been a decrease in the violence but hostilities have not ended.[99]

The authors conclude that, based on the facts, the conflict in Cabo Delgado confirms the existence of an APII-type conflict and that the material scope of application that will trigger APII is applicable.

6.4 The intervention of foreign state military in Cabo Delgado and, consequently, the effect on the classification

The concept of an 'internationalised' armed conflict is without a legal basis in treaty law. At best, it refers to a term in IHL practice that is used to describe the transformation of an existing non-international armed conflict into an international armed conflict.[100] In some instances this process creates a proxy war or a mixed conflict.[101] In this part, the authors consider a dynamic that may affect the classification of the existing NIAC in Cabo Delgado as a result of the involvement of foreign states in the conflict.

The concept of an 'internationalisation' of a NIAC hinges on intervention by the military force of a foreign state in an existing conflict.[102] It is important to note that economic and political support by a third state of any party to the conflict does not identify the foreign state as being a party to an existing conflict.[103] Whether an existing conflict becomes internationalised or remains a NIAC predominantly is determined by a military role in the conduct of the intervening state and the group against which they exercise military operations.[104] The intervention by a foreign state can be at the invitation or with the consent of the territorial state. In some instances, intervention is without the consent of the territorial state.[105]

In an existing conflict there are two likely scenarios that occur: the intervention of a foreign state acting on the invitation and directly in support of the territorial state or the foreign state acting in support of an armed group against the territorial state. The former reflects the current situation in Cabo Delgado and is the focus of this discussion. These scenarios are distinct and require the application of separate legal regimes.[106] Where a foreign state intervenes at the invitation and in support of the territorial state against an organised armed group, the implication is that it fights the non-state group, and the conflict remains a non-international armed conflict.[107] This conclusion corresponds to Sassòli's view that 'the actors involved is what differentiate NIACs from IACs'.[108]

The conflict in Cabo Delgado has been joined by Rwanda, deploying 1 000 personnel from the Rwandan defence force and Rwanda national police,[109] with a mandate of 'conducting combat and security operations' in support of the FADM against Ansar al-Sunna. The SADC regional mission, comprising the national forces from Angola, Botswana, the DRC, Lesotho, Malawi, South Africa, Tanzania and Zimbabwe, was deployed on 15 July 2021 and mandated to support Mozambique to combat terrorism and acts of violent extremism. The mandates of the foreign states that are involved in the conflict are evidence that they are engaged in military operations against Ansar al-Sunna. By virtue of their mandates and their actions, the conflict in the Cabo Delgado province remains a non-international armed conflict.

The provisions of CA3, which regulates all NIACs,[110] are applicable to the conflict between Ansar al-Sunna and the foreign military forces involved in the conflict in Cabo Delgado.

6.5 Conclusion

This chapter analysed the conflict in Cabo Delgado between the Mozambican defence force and Ansar al-Sunna as well as the intervention by foreign states. The nature of the parties involved in the conflict confirms that a non-international armed conflict is ongoing in Cabo Delgado. This conclusion is supported by the evidence that the state of armed violence that exists between the state of Mozambique and a sufficiently organised non-state armed group, Ansar al-Sunna, is of a protracted nature. On an estimation of the trajectory, complexion and nature of the hostilities and their duration, it is concluded the conflict meets the threshold of a CA3-type conflict and APII-type conflict. Finally, it is submitted that the intervention in the conflict by external parties does not have a consequential influence on the prior classification of the hostilities as a non-international armed conflict. However, a reassessment may be required if in the future an external state were to act in support of the non-state armed force.

Notes

1 Elizabeth Wilmshurst, *International Law and the Classification of Conflicts* (OUP 2012).
2 ICRC, 'Classification of Conflict' *ICRC Casebook* <https://casebook.icrc.org/glossary/classification-conflict>.
3 Geneva Convention I for the Amelioration of the Condition of the Wounded and Sick in Armed Forces in the Field (adopted 12 August 1949, entered into force 21 October 1950) 75 UNTS 31 (Geneva Convention I).
4 Protocol Additional to the Geneva Conventions of 12 August 1949 and Relating to the Protection of Victims of Non-International Armed Conflicts (Protocol II) (adopted 8 June 1977, entered into force 7 December 1978) 1125 UNTS 609.
5 Geneva Convention I (n 3).
6 The lack of definition was deliberate during the diplomatic conference. See Sandesh Sivakumaran, *The Law of Non-International Armed Conflict* (OUP 2012) 161.
7 *Prosecutor v Dusko Tadic a/k/a 'Dule'* (Decision on the Defence Motion for Interlocutory Appeal on Jurisdiction) (2 October 1995) para 70.
8 See for the definition of international custom article 38(b) Statute of the International Court of Justice (adopted 26 June 1945) XV UNCIO 355; Sivakumaran (n 6) 166.

9 *Prosecutor v Dusko Tadic a/k/a 'Dule'* IT-94-I-T (7 May 1997) para 562.
10 The ICRC Commentary confirmed that these elements form part of the indicators mapped by Pictet. See Convention (1) for the amelioration of the condition of the wounded and sick in armed forces in the field, Geneva, 12 August 1949, Commentary of 01.01.2016, article 3 not of an international character, para 424.
11 These situations, according to the Trial Chamber, include banditry, unorganised and short-lived insurrections, or terrorist activities that are not subject to international humanitarian law. See *Tadic* (Opinion and Judgment) (n 9) para 562.
12 *Prosecutor v Ljube Boskoski, Johan Tarculovski* (Judgment) IT-04–82-T (10 July 2008); *Prosecutor v Ramush Haradinaj, Idriz Balaj, Lahi Brahimaj* (Judgment) IT-04–84-T (3 April 2008).
13 *Boskoski* (n 12) para 198.
14 Ibid.
15 Jann Kleffner, 'The Legal Fog of an Illusion: Three Reflections on "Organisation" and "Intensity" as Criteria for the Temporal Scope of the Law of Non-International Armed Conflict' (2019) 95 *International Law Studies* 161, 168.
16 For examples, see Kleffner (n 15)168–170; Martha M Bradley, 'Revisiting the Notion of "Organised Armed Group" in Accordance with Common Article 3: Exploring the Inherent Minimum Threshold Requirement' (2018) *African Yearbook on International Humanitarian Law* 50, 75–77.
17 For a distinction between a party to the conflict and an armed group of a non-state party to the conflict, see Kleffner (n 15) 170–172.
18 Kleffner (n 15) 170.
19 *Boskoski* (n 12) para 194. For scholarly arguments on the degree of organisation, see Bradley (n 16) 66–77.
20 *Boskoski* (n 12) 198.
21 Ibid, para 197.
22 Dapo Akande, 'Classification of Conflict' in Ben Saul and Dapo Akande (eds), *The Oxford Guide to International Humanitarian Law* (OUP 2020) 41.
23 *Boskoski* (n 12) para 199.
24 Kleffner (n 15)169; Bradley (n 16) 77.
25 ICRC Commentary 2016 (n 10) para 429; *Boskoski* (n 12) para 197.
26 Tomas Queface, 'Research on the Insurgency in Mozambique' *Cabo Ligado* <www.caboligado.com/monthly-reports/cabo-ligado-monthly-august-2022>.
27 A consideration of the *modus operandi* of other similar groups operating on the African continent confirms this fact, for instance, Boko Haram in Northern Nigeria.
28 ACLED, 'Organised Political Violence and Reported Fatalities in Cabo Delgado (1 January 2020–31 March 2022)' <www.caboligado.com/monthly-reports/cabo-ligado-monthly-march-2022>.
29 Ibid; U.S. Department of State, 'Designations of ISIS – Mozambique, JNIM, and al-Shabaab Leaders' (6 August 2021) <www.state.gov/designations-of-isis-mozambique-jnim-and-al-shabaab-leaders/>.
30 Ibid.
31 Ibid; ACLED (n 28).
32 RULAC, 'Non-international Armed Conflicts in Mozambique' *RULAC* (18 May 2023) <www.rulac.org/browse/conflicts/non-international-armed-conflicts-in-mozambique#collapse2accord>.
33 *Boskoski* (n 12) para 200.
34 For instance, the statement issued by the Ministry of Defence confirms that the attack on Palma some time in 2021 came from three different directions, namely, Manguna crossroads, Nhica do Rovuma road and the airfield. See International Crisis Group, 'Stemming the Insurrection in Mozambique's Cabo Delgado' (11 June 2021) 18 <www.crisisgroup.org/africa/southern-africa/mozambique/303-stemming-insurrection-mozambiques-cabo-delgado>.

35 *Boskoski* (n 12) para 201.
36 Daveed Gartenstein-Ross, Emelie Chace-Donahue and Colin P Clarke, 'The Evolution and Escalation of the Islamic State Threat to Mozambique' *Foreign Policy Research Institute* (13 April 2021) <www.fpri.org/article/2021/04/the-evolution-and-escalation-of-the-islamic-state-threat-to-mozambique/>.
37 RULAC (n 32).
38 Ibid; International Crisis Group (n 34) 17–18.
39 Gartenstein-Ross and others (n 36).
40 International Crisis Group African Report (n 34) 11.
41 George Obulutsa, 'Militant from Mozambique Staged Deadly Attack in Tanzania, Police Says' *Reuters* (23 October 2020).
42 Ibid.
43 International Crisis Group (n 34) 15.
44 *Boskoski* (n 12) para 202.
45 Alix Culbertson, 'Mozambique Conflict: Why Will One Million People Have Been Forced to Flee Their Homes?' *Sky News* (29 March 2021); see also Amnesty International, 'Mozambique: "What I Saw Is Death": War Crimes in Mozambique's Forgotten Cape' (2 March, 2021) 9.
46 Boskoski (n 12) para 204–205; Yoram Dinstein, *Non-International Armed Conflicts in International Law* (OUP 2021) 65.
47 Sivakumaran (n 6)168; *Haradinaj* (n 12) para 49.
48 The Inter-American Commission in the *La-Tablada* case focused on the nature of the hostilities rather than on the duration of the conflict, which lasted only 30 hours. See *Juan Carlos Abella v Argentina*, Case 11. 137, 18 November 1997, OEA/Se.L/V/II.98, Doc.38 rev, 1997 para 155 <https://casebook.icrc.org/case-study/inter-american-commission-human-rights-tablada>.
49 *Haradinaj* (n 12) para 49.
50 Akande (n 22) 41.
51 RULAC (n 32).
52 See the detailed analysis of the destruction in Sections 6.3 and 6.4.
53 ACLED Report (n 28) <www.caboligado.com/reports/cabo-ligado-weekly-10-16-october-2022>.
54 Ibid <www.caboligado.com/reports/cabo-ligado-weekly-14-20-november-2022>.
55 See BBC News, 'Mozambique Town Palma "Retaken" from Militants Islamists' *BBC News* (5 April 2021)
56 ACLED (n 28) <www.caboligado.com/monthly-reports/cabo-ligado-monthly-march-2021>.
57 Ibid <www.caboligado.com/monthly-reports/cabo-ligado-monthly-feb-2022>.
58 Ibid.
59 'Mozambique Insurgency: Why 24 Countries Have Sent Troops' *BBC News* (23 May 2022).
60 UNHCR, 'Nearly 1 Million People Have Fled Five Years of Northern Mozambique Violence' (4 October 2022).
61 Peter Fabricius, 'AU Finally Takes Official Note of Northern Mozambique Jihadist Insurgency' *Daily Maverick News* (11 February 2020).
62 Noam Zamir, *Classification of Conflicts in International Humanitarian Law: The Legal Impact of Foreign Intervention in Civil Wars* (Edward Elgar 2017) 69.
63 Sylvain Vité, 'Typology of Armed Conflict in International Humanitarian Law: Legal Concepts and Actual Situations' (2009) 91 *International Review of the Red Cross* 69, 79.
64 APII (n 4) article 1(1).
65 Tilman Rodenhauser, *Organising Rebellion: Non-state Armed Groups Under International Humanitarian Law, Human Rights Law, and International Criminal Law* (OUP 2018) 85.

66 Sylvie Junod, 'Additional Protocol II: History and Scope (1983) 33 *American University Law Review* 29, 37.
67 For a comprehensive scholarly discussion on the exact content of a responsible command, see Martha M Bradley, 'Revisiting the Scope of Application of Additional Protocol II: Exploring the Inherent Minimum Threshold Requirements' (2019) *African Yearbook on International Humanitarian Law* 81, 92–102.
68 ICRC, 'Protocol Additional to the Geneva Conventions of 12 August 1949, and Relating to the Protection of Victims of Non-International Armed Conflicts (Protocol II), 8 June 1977, Commentary of 01.01.1987, Article 1 – Material Field of Application' para 4463 <https://ihl-databases.icrc.org/en/ihl-treaties/apii-1977/article-1/commentary/1987?activeTab=undefined>.
69 Article 1(1) Protocol II (n4)
70 Marco Sassòli, *International Humanitarian Law: Rules, Controversies, and Solutions to Problems Arising in Warfare* (Edward Edgar Publishing 2019) 184.
71 Sivakumaran (n 6) 186.
72 Ibid, 185.
73 APII ICRC Commentary (n 68) para 4466.
74 Yoram Dinstein, 'Concluding Remarks on Non-International Armed Conflicts' in Kenneth Watkin and Andrew J Norris (eds), 'Non-International Armed Conflict in the Twenty-First Century' (2012) 88 *International Law Study* 399, 404.
75 APII ICRC Commentary (n 68) para 4469.
76 Martha M Bradley, 'Additional Protocol II: Elevating the Minimum Threshold of Intensity?' (2020) *International Review of the Red Cross* 1125, 1146.
77 For a scholarly view of the intensity threshold in APII-type conflict, see Bradley (n 76) 1144.
78 *Boskoski* (n 12) para 197.
79 Anthony Cullen, *The Concept of Non-International Armed Conflict in International Humanitarian Law* (CUP 2010) 104. The higher threshold of intensity of APII-type conflicts prevents the immediate application of the Protocol in the early stages of most NIACs, hence the application of CA3 pending the fulfilment of the continuous and planned material requirements in the Protocol. See also APII ICRC Commentary (n 68) para 4469.
80 See Dinstein (n 46) 64 citing Limaj para 168.
81 Sivakumaran (n 6) 189.
82 For a scholarly analysis of judicial decisions, see Bradley Protocol II (n 67) 111–118; see also Sivakumaran (n 6) 189.
83 ICRC, 'International Humanitarian Law Databases' <https://ihl-databases.icrc.org/en/ihl-treaties/treaties-and-states-parties?title=&topic=&state=MZ&from=&to=&sort=state&order=ASC>.
84 For more discussion on this, see Section 6.2 of this chapter on the command structure of Ansar al-Sunnah.
85 See the discussion on the command structure of Ansar al-Sunnah under Section 6.2.
86 ACLED (n 28).
87 Territorial control is not an element of consideration in assessing a CA3-type conflict; this condition is necessary only in the determination of an APII-type conflict. See Dinstein (n 46) 55.
88 The ICRC Commentary noted: 'sustained and concerted military operation which effectively determine the control of a territory'; see APII ICRC Commentary (n 68) para 4468.
89 ACLED (n 28). ACLED reported, 'The expansion into Meluco is an opportunity for insurgents to gather more supplies and force pro-government forces to spread themselves thinner, but it also increases the group's capacity to threaten the N380 and, by extension, Macomia town itself' <www.caboligado.com/monthly-reports/cabo-ligado-monthly-jan-2022>.

90 Ibid <www.caboligado.com/monthly-reports/cabo-ligado-monthly-nov-2021>.
91 Ibid <www.caboligado.com/monthly-reports/cabo-ligado-monthly-march-2022>.
92 See analysis under Section 6.2 of this chapter.
93 See the authors' argument on this discussion in Section 6.2.
94 The Ansar al-Sunnah on 8 December 2020 launched three simultaneous military operations in Nangade district <www.polgeonow.com/2021/04/cabo-delgado-conflict-map-2021.html>.
95 ACLED (n 28).
96 Ibid <www.caboligado.com/monthly-reports/cabo-ligado-monthly-june-2022>.
97 In June 2022 Ansar al-Sunna launched coordinated attacks in the southern district of Ancuabe, also attacking the northern regions of Macomia, Nangade, Palma, Mocímboa da Praia, and Muidumbe. For greater detail, see <www.caboligado.com/monthly-reports/cabo-ligado-monthly-june-2022>.
98 ACLED (n 28).
99 Ibid.
100 Kubo Mačák, *Internationalized Armed Conflicts in International Law* (OUP 2018) 32.
101 For a definition of a mixed conflict, see Akande (n 22) 48–49.
102 Sivakumaran (n 6) 222. The term 'internationalisation' clearly does not create a distinct type of conflict; literally it describes the transformation of an existing NIAC into an IAC.
103 Mačák (n 100) 32.
104 Sivakumaran (n 6) 222.
105 Scholarly discussion regarding the role of consent of an intervening state in an existing conflict is polarised. The authors will not explore the implication of a lack of consent by a territorial state to the intervention of a foreign state in an existing conflict. For scholarly discussion of this issue, see Akande (n 22) 52–56; see also Mačák (n 100) 32–37.
106 When a foreign state acts in support of an armed group against a territorial state it is important to determine the relationship between the foreign state and the armed group. Two tests are suggested for determining the relationship between a third state and a non-state group, namely, the 'effective control test' by the ICJ and an 'overall control test' by the ICTY. The choice among scholars and tribunals is for the 'overall control test'. For scholarly discussion, see Mačák (n 100) 37–47; Akande (n 22) 44–47; Sivakumaran (n 6) 225–228.
107 Emily Crawford and Alison Pert, *International Humanitarian Law* (2nd edn, OUP 2020) 79.
108 Sassòli (n 70) para 6.31 at 180.
109 'Rwanda Deploys 1 000 Soldiers to Mozambique's Cabo Delgado' *Aljazeera News* (10 July 2021).
110 Crawford and Pert (n 107) 66; Dinstein (n 46) 23.

Bibliography

ACLED, 'Organised Political Violence and Reported Fatalities in Cabo Delgado (1 January 2020–31 March 2022)' <www.caboligado.com/monthly-reports/cabo-ligado-monthly-march-2022>.

ACLED Report <www.caboligado.com/monthly-reports/cabo-ligado-monthly-nov-2021>.

ACLED Report <www.caboligado.com/monthly-reports/cabo-ligado-monthly-jan-2022>.

ACLED Report <www.caboligado.com/monthly-reports/cabo-ligado-monthly-march-2022>.

ACLED Report <www.caboligado.com/monthly-reports/cabo-ligado-monthly-june-2022>.

ACLED Report <www.caboligado.com/reports/cabo-ligado-weekly-14-20-november-2022>.

Alix Culbertson, 'Mozambique Conflict: Why Will One Million People Have Been Forced to Flee Their Homes?' *Sky News* (29 March 2021).

Amnesty International, 'Mozambique: "What I Saw Is Death": War Crimes in Mozambique's Forgotten Cape' *Amnesty International* (2 March 2021) <www.amnesty.org/en/documents/afr41/3545/2021/en/>.

Anthony Cullen, *The Concept of Non-International Armed Conflict in International Humanitarian Law* (CUP 2010).
Dapo Akande, 'Classification of Conflict' in Ben Saul and Dapo Akande (eds), *The Oxford Guide to International Humanitarian Law* (OUP 2020).
Daveed Gartenstein-Ross, Emelie Chace-Donahue and Colin P Clarke, 'The Evolution and Escalation of the Islamic State Threat to Mozambique' *Foreign Policy Research Institute* (13 April 2021) <www.fpri.org/article/2021/04/the-evolution-and-escalation-of-the-islamic-state-threat-to-mozambique/>.
Eliseeva Anastasya, 'African Values in War: A Tool on Traditional Customs and IHL' (ICRC 2021) <www.icrc.org/en/document/african-customs-tool-traditional-customs-and-ihl>.
Elizabeth Wilmshurst, *International Law and the Classification of Conflicts* (OUP 2012).
Emily Crawford and Alison Pert, *International Humanitarian Law* (2nd edn, CUP 2020).
Geneva Convention (I) for the Amelioration of the Condition of the Wounded and Sick in Armed Forces in the Field (1949) <https://treaties.un.org/Pages/showDetails.aspx?objid=080000028015847c&clang=_en>.
George Obulutsa, 'Militant From Mozambique Staged Deadly Attack in Tanzania, Police Says' *Reuters* (23 October 2020).
Hans Speier, 'The Social Types of War' (1941) 46 *American Journal of Sociology* 445–454 <www.jstor.org/stable/2769917>.
ICRC, 'Classification of Conflict' *ICRC Casebook* <https://casebook.icrc.org/glossary/classification-conflict>.
ICRC, 'IHL and Non-State Armed Groups' (International Humanitarian Law and the Challenges of Contemporary Armed Conflicts Recommitting to Protection in Armed Conflict on the 70th Anniversary of the Geneva Conventions, Report, 2019).
ICRC, 'International Humanitarian Law: A Branch of International Law Governing the Conduct of States and Individuals: Situations of Application' *ICRC Casebook* <https://casebook.icrc.org/law/fundamentals-ihl#b_iii_1>.
ICRC, 'Protocol Additional to the Geneva Conventions of 12 August 1949, and Relating to the Protection of Victims of Non-International Armed Conflicts (Protocol II), 8 June 1977, Commentary of 01.01.1987, Article 1 – Material Field of Application' para 4463 <https://ihl-databases.icrc.org/en/ihl-treaties/apii-1977/article-1/commentary/1987?activeTab=undefined>.
ICRC, 'Convention (1) for the amelioration of the condition of the wounded and sick in armed forces in the field, Geneva, 12 August 1949, Commentary of 01.01.2016, article 3 – Conflicts not of an international character' <https://ihl-databases.icrc.org/en/ihl-treaties/gci-1949/article-3/commentary/2016>.
ICRC, 'Urbanisation of Armed Conflicts' (International Humanitarian Law and the Challenges of Contemporary Armed Conflicts Recommitting to Protection in Armed Conflict on the 70th Anniversary of the Geneva Conventions, Report, 2019).
ICRC, International Committee of the Red Cross, 'International Humanitarian Law Databases' <https://ihl-databases.icrc.org/en/ihl-treaties/treaties-and-states-parties?title=&topic=&state=MZ&from=&to=&sort=state&order=ASC>.
International Crisis Group, 'Making the Most of the EU's Integrated Approach to Mozambique' (31 January 2023) <www.crisisgroup.org/africa/east-and-southern-africa/mozambique/making-most-eus-integrated-approach-mozambique>.
International Crisis Group, 'Stemming the Insurrection in Mozambique's Cabo Delgado' (11 June 2021) <www.crisisgroup.org/africa/southern-africa/mozambique/303-stemming-insurrection-mozambiques-cabo-delgado>.
Jann Kleffner, 'The Legal Fog of an Illusion: Three Reflections on "Organisation" and "Intensity" as Criteria for the Temporal Scope of the Law of Non-International Armed Conflict' (2019) 95 *International Law Studies*.
John A Vasquez, 'Capability, Types of War, Peace' (1986) 39 *The Western Political Quarterly*.
John A Vasquez and Brandon Valeriano, 'Classification of Interstate Wars' (2010) 72 *The Journal of Politics*.

Juan Carlos Abella v Argentina Case 11. 137, 18 November 1997, OEA/Se.L/V/II.98, Doc.38 rev, 1997 <https://casebook.icrc.org/case-study/inter-american-commission-human-rights-tablada>.

Kubo Maćák, *Internationalized Armed Conflicts in International Law* (OUP 2018).

Marco Sassòli, *International Humanitarian Law: Rules, Controversies, and Solutions to Problems Arising in Warfare* (Edward Edgar 2019).

Martha M. Bradley, 'Additional Protocol II: Elevating the Minimum Threshold of Intensity?' (2020) 102(915) *International Review of the Red Cross*.

Martha M. Bradley, 'Revisiting the Notion of "Organised Armed Group" in Accordance with Common Article 3: Exploring the Inherent Minimum Threshold Requirement' (2018) 1 *African Yearbook on International Humanitarian Law*.

Martha M. Bradley, 'Revisiting the Scope of Application of Additional Protocol II: Exploring the Inherent Minimum Threshold Requirements' (2019) 1 *African Yearbook on International Humanitarian Law*.

Michael Schmitt, 'Classification of Cyber Conflict' (2012) 17 *Journal of Conflict and Security Law*.

'Mozambique Insurgency: Why 24 Countries Have Sent Troops' *BBC News* (23 May 2022).

'Mozambique Town Palma "Retaken" from Militants Islamists' *BBC News* (5 April 2021).

'Mozambique: State Confirms Attack on Palma, Near Total's Cabo Delgado LNG Project' *Club of Mozambique* (25 March 2021).

MS Mate, 'Dhammaghoṣa and Bherighoṣa of Aśoka' (1991) 51/52 *Bulletin of the Deccan College Research Institute*.

Muhammed Munir, *The Law of War and Peace in Islam: Causes and Conduct of Jihad and Non-State Islamic Actors Under Islamic Law* (Edwin Mellen Press 2019).

Noam Zamir, *Classification of Conflicts in International Humanitarian Law: The Legal Impact of Foreign Intervention in Civil Wars* (Edward Elgar 2017).

OCHA, 'Mozambique Annual Country Report 2022 – Country Strategic Plan 2017–2022' (3 April 2023) <https://reliefweb.int/report/mozambique/mozambique-annual-country-report-2022-country-strategic-plan-2017-2022?gclid=Cj0KCQjwmZejBhC_ARIsAGhCqnfcJnKoeSkBPhjOoWF5LTP5WhDevBzOzB_bxoyKpbvrAei3Ud9yMa8aApUGEALw_wcB>.

OCHA, 'UNICEF Mozambique Humanitarian Situation Report No 1 January 2023' (24 February 2023) <https://reliefweb.int/report/mozambique/unicef-mozambique-humanitarian-situation-report-no-1-january-2023?gclid=Cj0KCQjwmZejBhC_ARIsAGhCqncPg-eCL9xe2RpMEm_hxDJfq207V6W1KlomhQDAnbwOSxHndk88MmwaAjAjEALw_wcB>.

Oona A Hathaway and others, 'Consent Is Not Enough: Why States Must Respect the Intensity Threshold in Transnational Conflict' (2016) 165 *University of Pennsylvania Law Review*.

Peter Fabricius, 'AU Finally Takes Official Note of Northern Mozambique Jihadist Insurgency' *Daily Maverick* (11 February 2020).

Prosecutor v Dusko Tadic a/k/a 'Dule' (Decision on the Defence Motion for Interlocutory Appeal on Jurisdiction) (2 October 1995).

Prosecutor v Dusko Tadic a/k/a 'Dule' IT-94-I-T (7 May 1997).

Prosecutor v Enver Hardzihasanovic, Mehmed Alagic and Amir Kubura (Decision on Interlocutory Appeal Challenging Jurisdiction in Relation to Command Responsibility) IT-01–47-AR72 (16 July 2003).

Prosecutor v Ljube Boskoski, Johan Tarculovski (Judgment) IT-04–82-T (10 July 2008).

Prosecutor v Ramush Haradinaj, Idriz Balaj, Lahi Brahimaj (Judgment) IT-04–84-T (3 April 2008).

Protocol Additional to the Geneva Conventions of 12 August 1949 and Relating to the Protection of Victims of Non-International Armed Conflicts (Protocol II) (1977) <https://treaties.un.org/Pages/showDetails.aspx?objid=08000002800f3cb8&clang=_en>.

Rogier Bartels, 'The Classification of Armed Conflicts by International Criminal Courts and Tribunals' (2020) 20 *International Criminal Law Review*.

RULAC, 'Non-international Armed Conflicts in Mozambique' *RULAC* (18 May 2023) <www.rulac.org/browse/conflicts/non-international-armed-conflicts-in-mozambique#collapse2accord>.

'Rwanda Deploys 1000 Soldiers to Mozambique's Cabo Delgado' *Aljazeera News* (10 July 2021).

'SADC Mission in Mozambique (SAMIM) in Brief' *SADC* (10 November 2021) <www.sadc.int/latest-news/sadc-mission-mozambique-samim-brief>.

Sandesh Sivakumaran, *The Law of Non-International Armed Conflict* (OUP 2012).

Statute of the International Court of Justice (1946) <https://treaties.un.org/Pages/showDetails.aspx?objid=080000028004ca91&clang=_en>.

Stephen C Neff, 'The Law of Armed Conflict from Part IV – Grotius as a Legal Scholar' in Randall Lesaffer and Janne E Nijman (eds), *The Cambridge Companion to Hugo Grotius* (CUP 2021).

Sylvain Vité, 'Typology of Armed Conflict in International Humanitarian Law: Legal Concepts and Actual Situations' (2009) 91 *International Review of the Red Cross.*

Sylvie Junod, 'Additional Protocol II: History and Scope' (1983) 33 *American University Law Review.*

Theodor Meron, 'Classification of Armed Conflict in the Former Yugoslavia: Nicaragua's Fallout' (1998) 92 *American Journal of International Law.*

Tilman Rodenhauser, *Organising Rebellion: Non-state Armed Groups Under International Humanitarian Law, Human Rights Law, and International Criminal Law* (OUP 2018).

Tomas Queface, 'Research on the Insurgency in Mozambique' *Cabo Ligado* <www.caboligado.com/monthly-reports/cabo-ligado-monthly-august-2022>.

UNHCR, 'Gender-Based Violence Response Delgado Cabo Delgado, Northern Mozambique, Cabo Delgado GBV Factsheet – October 2022' (14 November 2022) <https://reliefweb.int/report/mozambique/unhcr-mozambique-cabo-delgado-gbv-factsheet-october-2022>.

UNHCR, 'Mozambique | Gender-Based Violence Incidents Report – Gender-Based Violence (GBV) Incidents Trends Analysis Cabo Delgado | July – December 2021' (6 June 2022) <https://reliefweb.int/report/mozambique/mozambique-gender-based-violence-gbv-incidents-trends-analysis-cabo-delgado-july-december-2021>.

UNHCR, 'Nearly 1 Million People Have Fled Five Years of Northern Mozambique Violence' (4 October 2022) <www.unhcr.org/news/briefing/2022/10/633be4474/nearly-1-million-people-fled-five-years-northern-mozambique-violence.html>.

U.S. Department of State, 'Designations of ISIS – Mozambique, JNIM, and Al-Shabaab Leaders' (6 August 2021) <www.state.gov/designations-of-isis-mozambique-jnim-and-al-shabaab-leaders/>.

Vienna Convention on the Law of Treaties (1969) <https://treaties.un.org/Pages/showDetails.aspx?objid=080000028003902f&clang=_en>.

Yolande Diallo, 'African Traditions and Humanitarian Law' (1976) 16 (185) *International Review of the Red Cross.*

Yoram Dinstein, 'Concluding Remarks on Non-International Armed Conflicts' in Kenneth Watkin and Andrew J Norris (eds), 'Non-International Armed Conflict in the Twenty-First Century' (2012) 88 *International Law Study.*

Yoram Dinstein, *Non-International Armed Conflicts in International Law* (CUP 2021).

7 Ansar al-Sunna (IS-affiliates) engaging in a mosaic of violence in Mozambique

Terrorists, rebels or both – legal implications and challenges

Gus Waschefort, Jessie Phyffer and Martha M. Bradley

7.1 Introduction

The 2019 International Committee of the Red Cross (ICRC) Contemporary Report flags the applicability of international humanitarian law (IHL) to states fighting organised armed groups designated as terrorists.[1] Three specific challenges are highlighted. First, states often deny the existence of non-international armed conflict (NIAC) on their territory and label organised armed groups exclusively as terrorists.[2] Second, there is a tendency to consider conflict-related violence as acts of terrorism only.[3] Lastly, in their view, some states regard organised armed groups they designate as terrorists as creating a counter-terrorism response that is not constrained by IHL.[4] The consequence of the misapplication of a 'label' is that it may be enlisted in an effort to limit the application of IHL, which is the primary legal framework for the conduct of hostilities in a situation of NIAC. The authors are mindful that labelling an organised armed group as a terrorist organisation is not inherently wrong but rather caution that the 'terrorist' designation can be used as a smokescreen behind which IHL and international human rights law (IHRL) responses are diluted. This chapter responds to the situation in Cabo Delgado where the Mozambican government[5] and other states[6] purport Ansar al-Sunna,[7] an Islamic State (IS) affiliate group, to be a terrorist organisation.

Cabo Delgado in Northern Mozambique has, since 2017, experienced ongoing violence.[8] The violence between the state armed forces of Mozambique and Ansar al-Sunna has escalated to being designated a NIAC.[9] IS has long been considered a terrorist group that makes use of terror tactics, and the IS endorsement of Ansar al-Sunna in Mozambique has led to the view that Ansar al-Sunna is a terrorist organisation, not an organised armed group.[10] This label affects the tools available to combat the activities of Ansar al-Sunna. Terrorists committing acts of terror are regulated by national law and several regimes of international law – IHRL in peace time, whereas during an armed conflict, if the terrorist group qualifies as an organised armed group, it is regulated by IHL (as the *lex specialis*), IHRL and the applicable international law on counter-terrorism.[11] In a situation such as that in Mozambique the question is whether traditionally conceived terrorist groups such

DOI: 10.4324/9781003317647-9

as Ansar al-Sunna that legally qualify as an organised armed group in an armed conflict must be brought within the ambit of IHL.

The differentiation between terrorist activities and those of organised armed groups in a NIAC in terms of the applicable legal framework is summarised by the International Criminal Tribunal for the former Yugoslavia (ICTY) in *Tadić*.[12] In this case, the Trial Chamber considered the nature of the violence between an organised armed group and its adversary to be regarded as meeting the minimum threshold of protracted armed conflict to be 'used solely for the purpose, as a minimum of distinguishing an armed conflict from banditry, unorganised and short-lived insurrections, or terrorist activities which are not subject to international humanitarian law'.[13]

This chapter is set out as follows: the following part explores the activities of Ansar al-Sunna in Mozambique. Next, terrorism within international law and IHL is explored. The chapter then explores the regulation of the insurgency in Mozambique. Lastly, the conclusion makes clear that applying IHL as the primary regime of international law to the situation in Cabo Delgado increases the number of legal tools available to the government of Mozambique in combating Ansar al-Sunna.

7.2 Ansar al-Sunna in Mozambique

Initially, Ansar al-Sunna was an isolated Islamic sect focused on building communities that practised Shari'a law.[14] Before the current outbreak of violence, their activities, though not directed against the state of Mozambique, led to clashes with less fundamentalist local Muslim communities.[15] The catalysing event of the current violence against the state of Mozambique took place in Mocímboa da Praia on 5 October 2017 when Ansar al-Sunna launched a coordinated retaliatory attack against a prison and three police stations in an attempt to rescue members of the group who were being detained.[16] The attacks were committed by local people and, at this point, were purposively aimed only at the police.[17] The larger purpose was to demonstrate the rejection of the secular state and the institution of Shari'a law.[18]

Since the attack in October 2017, the violence perpetrated by Ansar al-Sunna has escalated from guerrilla attacks on small, isolated villages to full-blown violence across a number of regions in Cabo Delgado.[19] The group exercises a 'high level of brutality'[20] with actions that range from highly targeted individual attacks[21] to indiscriminate violence against civilians, civilian homes,[22] and state and military installations and personnel.[23] Beheadings, abductions, extrajudicial killings, sexual violence, arson and the recruitment of child soldiers are commonplace.[24] Machetes, automatic weapons and homemade explosives are employed.[25] A particularly brutal instance of machete-related violence is the beheading of 50 people in a football stadium in Muidumbe.[26] The group has also launched coordinated military attacks, the most notable example of which is the March 2021 attack on the town of Palma, which was besieged by about 200 Ansar al-Sunna fighters for four days during which the fighters killed several local and foreign civilians, destroyed much of the town's infrastructure and displaced almost 40 000 people.[27] The attack is considered to have been well-coordinated: The fighters had three main targets – the airfield, the army barracks and the city's banks and a food storage warehouse.[28] Survivors of the attack report that people were beheaded and their bodies left in the streets.[29] Although the Ansar al-Sunna fighters do not wear uniforms, they are easily recognisable to local people who describe them as having long beards, carrying machetes and wearing black headdresses with the IS emblem.[30]

It has proved difficult to determine the structure of the group.[31] The situation is complex both religiously and politically, and the leaders of the group are not known.[32] In addition, the nature of the relationship between the group and IS is unclear.[33] The insurgency is considered 'inherently local' and 'uses jihadist ideology as an organising tool' but shows little regard to wider jihadist goals.[34] Nevertheless, Ansar al-Sunna has been linked to and pledged allegiance to IS, and IS confirms that 'a contingent of the mujahideen' in Mozambique joined their wider terror network.[35] The suggestion is that the insurgency in Mozambique, much like insurgencies elsewhere, is fragmented.[36] The local population maintain that there is only one group perpetrating the violence but the group has a 'smaller unit active in different areas'.[37]

The link with IS resulted in the United States designating Ansar al-Sunna a foreign terrorist organisation and placing it on the sanctions list.[38] Mozambique's position is less resolved. Initially, fearing international attention, the Mozambican government made little information about the group public.[39] In lieu of labelling it a terrorist organisation or an organised armed group Mozambique at first dismissed Ansar al-Sunna as 'criminals', 'thugs' and 'common bandits',[40] but the continuing use of terror tactics and the intensity of Mozambique's military response forced Mozambique to classify Ansar al-Sunna as terrorists.[41] Other entities classify Ansar al-Sunna as an organised armed group that is party to a NIAC in Mozambique.[42] The classification of the conflict is addressed more systemically in Chapter 6 of this volume but to better contextualise the content in the rest of this chapter, the classification is briefly discussed here.

A survey of reports indicates that the requirements that trigger Additional Protocol II (APII) as codified in article 1(1) of the treaty are met.[43] Ansar al-Sunna has exercised continuous control over villages in Cabo Delgado.[44] At various stages during the conflict, control over these villages may have exchanged hands between Ansar al-Sunna and the actors supporting the Mozambican government but, as of at least 2021, Ansar al-Sunna has exercised effective control over some parts of Mozambican territory.[45] In the *Akayesu* case, Trial Chamber I of the International Criminal Tribunal for Rwanda (ICTR) declared that the spatial dimension of territory was not instructive; rather, what is important is what control of territory enables the organised armed group to do.[46] This factor is a functional test that the organised armed group is able to maintain sustained and concerted military operations and has the ability to apply APII.[47] The *Sesay* case, adjudicated by the Special Court for Sierra Leone, stresses that APII continues to apply to a situation regardless of whether the geographic area under control by the organised armed group has shrunk.[48]

Reports further reveal that, at stages, the Palma district changed hands between Ansar al-Sunna and the government.[49] At the time of writing the government had not retaken control over Namacunde.[50] Sufficient territory is controlled by Ansar al-Sunna as of February 2023 to enable it to continue to launch sustained and concerted military operations. In 2022, 16 out of 17 districts in Cabo Delgado were attacked by Ansar al-Sunna.[51] These attacks continued at the beginning of 2023.[52] Thus, APII continues to apply. The question of which branch of international law – the law on terrorism or IHL – should apply to this situation is the focus of this chapter and will be answered in the next parts.

7.3 Terrorism in international law

This part explores how international law regulates terrorism. The purpose is to illustrate that IHL, as the *lex specialis* during a NIAC, will apply where a group, ordinarily conceived of as a terrorist group that uses terror tactics, is considered an organised armed group if it meets the necessary threshold.

7.3.1 Terrorism in international law

To comprehend how terrorism impacts (or does not impact) the application of IHL, it is important to set out international law's current approach to terrorism. Rosalyn Higgins commented in 1997 that 'terrorism is not a discrete topic of international law with its own substantive legal norms'.[53] The events of 11 September 2001 in the United States and the rise of terrorism as the persistent global threat in a post-Cold War world has resulted in a dramatic increase in terrorism-related treaties, institutions, state practice, United Nations (UN) resolutions (Security Council and General Assembly) and domestic legal developments. Several commentators have weighed in on the issue, suggesting that these developments give rise to a discrete topic of international law on terrorism. Others argue that the lack of an agreed definition of 'terrorism' in peace time hampers the emergence of a terrorism regime in international law.

Since the 1930s there have been several attempts to define terrorism in international law.[54] The first international legal text to offer a definition of terrorism was the League of Nations' 1937 Convention for the Prevention and Punishment of Terrorism. Article 1(2) defines acts of terrorism, for the purposes of that convention, as 'criminal acts directed against a state and intended or calculated to create a state of terror in the minds of particular persons, or a group of persons or the general public'.[55] This Convention never entered into force, but its definition of terrorism has served as an inspiration for several texts that have been drawn up as part of the UN's attempt to develop a legal framework for the crime of international terrorism.[56]

In the 1970s several Western states brought the issue of terrorism to the attention of the UN and its member states[57] in response to the actions of the Palestinian Liberation Organisation (PLO) at the 1972 Munich Olympics.[58] In these new rounds of discussion, it became clear that a universal definition of terrorism would remain elusive, primarily, as a result of a theoretical debate on the differences between acts of terrorism and attempts by national liberation movements to exercise the right to self-determination.[59] In addition to this hurdle, there is a debate around whether a state can be a perpetrator of terrorism and, as such, whether in peace time a universal definition includes only acts committed against a state and not by a state.[60] These theoretical issues, to a lesser extent the state terrorism debate, have caused an impasse in adopting a universal definition for terrorism.[61]

Nevertheless, the sense of the importance of addressing terrorism on an international plane remains. In 1994 the General Assembly adopted the Declaration on Measures to Eliminate International Terrorism that sought to address the rise in international terrorism in one comprehensive international document.[62] This Declaration does not define terrorism; instead it describes the term using wording similar to that in the 1937 Convention on the Prevention and Punishment of Terrorism and states that terrorist acts are '[c]riminal acts intended or calculated to provoke a state of terror in the general public, a group of persons or particular persons for political purposes'.[63] Although this is similar to the wording of the 1937 Convention, this description, and not definition, differs by recognising that terrorism is not limited to acts directed against a state.

The elusive nature of a universal definition of terrorism led the UN to adopt a sectoral approach to the issue with crime-specific conventions that cover acts that are typically associated with terrorism.[64] None of the Conventions attempts to define terrorism; instead they clarify that certain criminal acts are deemed terrorist in nature.[65] The International Convention for the Suppression of Terrorist Bombings (Terrorist Bombing Convention) criminalises placing and discharging lethal devices in certain circumstances;[66] the International Convention for the Suppression of the Financing of Terrorism, 1999 (Terrorism Financing Convention) makes it an offence to provide or collect funds that are channelled towards the commission of certain offences;[67] and the International Convention for the Suppression of Acts of Nuclear Terrorism, 2005 (Nuclear Terrorism Convention) criminalises nuclear terrorism.[68] The Conventions call on state parties to adopt domestic legislation that criminalises the acts set out in them, especially where those acts are intended to provoke a state of fear among the general public.[69] Although a universal definition of terrorism cannot, and indeed should not, be distilled from the sectoral conventions, the Conventions and the texts that precede them offer an element that differentiates terrorism from other acts of violence, that the primary purpose of an act of terrorism is to spread fear in a civilian population.[70]

In addition, and importantly for this chapter, of the three Conventions, the application of two is generally excluded from acts *in bello*. Article 19 of the Terrorist Bombing Convention and article 4 of the Nuclear Terrorism Convention state that they do not apply to actions taken by armed forces during an armed conflict as these terms are understood under IHL.[71] The Terrorism Financing Convention is less clear as to its application during armed conflict, but it uses the language of IHL to distinguish between civilians and combatants in stating that acts funded for the purposes of targeting persons not taking an active part in hostilities are deemed an offence under the Convention.[72] A nugatory reading of this wording suggests that financing activities that target combatants is not an offence; it means that the Convention does not apply during a NIAC which, essentially, is the same position as in the other conventions. In this circumstance the international law on terrorism makes it clear that IHL applies as the *lex specialis* where there is an armed conflict.[73] This approach has been adopted by the Ad Hoc Committee on Measures to Eliminate Terrorism in its most ambitious project yet.

7.3.2 Terrorism and international humanitarian law

The Ad Hoc Committee has worked on a further text for almost two decades – the Draft Comprehensive Convention on International Terrorism (Draft Convention).[74] The Draft Convention is intended to comprehensively fill the gaps left by the sectoral conventions and, more importantly, to provide a universal definition of terrorism that is acceptable to all states.[75] Part of this work addresses the relationship between terrorism and IHL.

Article 3 (previously 18) of the 2013 Report of the Ad Hoc Committee attempts to address the difficulty caused by a potential overlap between IHL and the international law on terrorism. Paragraph 2 of the proposed article reads: 'The activities of armed forces during an armed conflict, as those terms are understood under international humanitarian law, which are governed by that law, are not governed by the present Convention'. Paragraph 5 of the same article reads: 'The present Convention is without prejudice to the rules of international law applicable in armed conflict, in particular those rules applicable to acts lawful under international humanitarian law'.

According to Perera, read together with article 3, these two paragraphs explicitly state that acts that are committed by both state and non-state armed forces in times of armed conflict will not be governed by the Draft Convention and instead will be governed by IHL as the *lex specialis*.[76] This position essentially is the same as that taken in the Terrorism Bombing Convention and the Nuclear Terrorism Convention.[77] An 'armed force' as defined under IHL includes organised armed groups.[78] Thus, acts ordinarily seen as terrorism under the UN framework on terrorism are considered acts of terrorism if committed by an armed force during an armed conflict, even where their primary purpose is to spread fear.

Accordingly, the proposed article 3 of the Draft Convention places IHL in the forefront. This position is a step forward for the law on terrorism and for IHL, but no significant progress has been made on the Draft Convention.[79] The guidance provided by the Draft Convention is *lex ferenda* rather than *lex lata*, but this position is *lex ferenda* in the Terrorism Bombing Convention, which Mozambique has ratified,[80] and in the Nuclear Terrorism Convention, which Mozambique has only signed.[81]

7.3.3 Acts of terror committed during non-international armed conflicts

Following the logic that identifies IHL as the *lex specialis* during times of conflict, the question arises as to how IHL addresses acts of terrorism committed during a NIAC. Because this edited volume is concerned with Mozambique, this section answers the question by examining the actions of Ansar al-Sunna in Mozambique.

Article 4 of APII codifies fundamental guarantees to those it protects by strictly prohibiting certain acts. Acts (and threats) of terrorism are strictly prohibited by article 4(2)(d). Article 31 of the Vienna Convention on the Law of Treaties is employed to determine the meaning of the phrase 'acts of terrorism'.[82] Terrorism is defined as 'the systematic use of terror especially as a means of coercion'.[83] The 1987 ICRC Commentaries to article 4(2)(d) define acts of terrorism as acts directed against not only people (civilians) but also civilian installations.[84] Bellal and Maslen explain that such acts of terror include the deliberate destruction of medical facilities, schools and homes, as well as the torture or murder of civilians or those *hors de combat* where the intent is to terrorise the civilian population.[85]

Ansar al-Sunna frequently attacks civilians.[86] Their acts include kidnappings and beheadings.[87] Houses often are burned down when civilian villages are the object of attack.[88] Frequently, attacks against civilians include the destruction of an entire village.[89] For example, on 23 June 2018, Ansar al-Sunna attacked a village in Maganja de Costa, Cabo Delgado and destroyed 120 houses.[90] Violence against civilians has been committed since 30 November 2017 with an increasing frequency during military engagements between Ansar al-Sunna and the Mozambican government forces.[91] At the time of writing, in the most recent act of terror, Ansar al-Sunna attacked the Ntamba village in the district of Mueda, Cabo Delgado on 24 January 2023.[92] The casualties suffered during this event are unknown.[93]

Article 13(2) of APII prohibits an attack in the conduct of hostilities where its primary purpose is to spread terror among the civilian population. Here the term 'primary' is instructive. Article 13(2) prohibits those attacks against civilians which, predominantly or fundamentally, are aimed at terrorising the civilian population.[94] The 1987 Commentaries to this article explain that such attacks are frequent and inflict particularly cruel suffering on the civilian population.[95] The Commentaries take cognisance that any attack is likely to intimidate the civilian population, but they clearly state that article 13(2) outlaws attacks that have the 'primary' purpose of spreading terror.[96] Attacks that primarily target military objectives then are not considered acts of terrorism in terms of this article. In *Prosecutor v Galić* the ICTY defined 'terror' as 'extreme fear'.[97] Owing to the limited engagement with Ansar al-Sunna, apart from IS endorsing its attacks, the purpose of an attack against the civilian population is not expressly stated by the perpetrators. The frequency and brutality of attacks aimed at civilian villages, which regularly include beheadings and mass destruction of civilian huts,[98] does seem to meet the threshold of 'particularly reprehensible' acts, and it may be concluded that these attacks are prohibited by article 13(2) of APII.

An analysis of the nature of the attacks, the context in which they occur (APII-type NIAC) and the reality that Ansar al-Sunna, an organised armed group that is party to the conflict, is the perpetrator of these attacks shows that even though Ansar al-Sunna is designated a terrorist group, IHL applies. Thus, Mozambique cannot escape accepting the reality that IHL applies by classifying (however unwillingly) Ansar al-Sunna as a terrorist organisation. As *Prosecutor v Galić* clarifies, 'the moniker applied by a state in its public pronouncements does not affect the applicable law or the applicable rules, which are rooted in the prevailing circumstances of each case'.[99]

This discussion turns to the regulation of the insurgency in Cabo Delgado, specifically in terms of regional legal frameworks.

7.4 The regulation of the insurgency in Cabo Delgado

Though the violence between Mozambique and Ansar al-Sunna amounts to an APII-type NIAC, the nature and characteristics of Ansar al-Sunna as a group and the tactics that they employ, as well as their affiliations are such that it is not improper for states to designate the group as a terror group as well. What is important is that the implications of a group, as both a party to a NIAC and a terror group, be properly understood so as to avoid any limitation on the protective reach of international law or of purposive excess on the part of states.[100] Several states have domestic counter-terror frameworks in terms of which they formally designate foreign groups as terror groups, as the United States has done in relation to Ansar al-Sunna.[101] However, the present discussion focuses on the response by Mozambique, and designation is used in a broader sense to incorporate political rhetoric. Feasibly, the designation of Ansar al-Sunna as a terror group may have an impact on two aspects regarding the state's response as it relates to the state's international law obligations: (i) the treatment of members of the group, including lethal targeting and detention, and (ii) the accountability measures that may be used in respect of the group.

7.4.1 The military response to Ansar al-Sunna

The primary regimes of international law for the protection of the liberty and physical integrity of individuals are IHRL and IHL. In the context of Mozambique, the state's obligations in terms of IHRL are augmented by its obligations in terms of the regional African human rights system. These regimes co-apply during an armed conflict, and IHRL always applies. In contrast, the body of rules and principles aimed at regulating terrorism, whether conceived of as an independent regime of international law or as a patchwork of enactments, is aimed at suppressing and combating terrorism and, appropriately, is silent on the treatment of individual members of such groups and the tactics that may be used in the suppression of terrorism through military or police action. In its General Comment on the Right to Life, the African Commission on Human and Peoples' Rights (African Commission) confirms:

> Organised crime and terrorism can pose significant threats to the enjoyment of the right to life and require a robust state response, but one that at all times takes into account the requirements of international human rights law. . . . Derogation from the right to life is not permissible in a time of emergency, including a situation of armed conflict, or in response to threats such as terrorism.[102]

Beyond doubt, no enhanced powers afforded to the state allow for a differential treatment of individuals or groups designated as terrorist that departs from or relaxes the application of IHRL and/or IHL. As a matter of international law, a rhetoric of terrorism or even a formal designation of groups or individuals as 'terrorists' does not dilute the protective norms of IHRL or IHL. Police or military action against an individual or group, terrorist or otherwise, and whether it is aimed at using force or taking detainees, has to comply with IHRL when conducted outside of situations of armed conflict and both IHL and IHRL when conducted within the context of armed conflict. Outside of lawful derogation from certain derogable rights there are no exceptions.[103]

The catalogue of IHL violations for which terror groups, in general, and Ansar al-Sunna, in particular, are responsible is extensive. For present purposes the emphasis is placed on those violations that most directly relate to the characterisation as a 'terror group'. Notwithstanding a lack of agreement on a definition of terrorism, there is substantial, if not universal, agreement that terrorism involves acts intentionally directed at civilian populations and intended to create fear among members of the civilian population.[104] This viewpoint is articulated in the second rule in the ICRC Customary IHL study: 'Acts or threats of violence the primary purpose of which is to spread terror among the civilian population are prohibited'.[105]

The rule directly reflects the fact that acts or threats of terror are proscribed in identical terms in both Additional Protocols: 'The civilian population as such, as well as individual civilians, shall not be the object of attack. Acts or threats of violence the primary purpose of which is to spread terror among the civilian population are prohibited'.[106] This proscription is significant, as generally APII is characterised as providing a lower threshold of protection compared to the equivalent provisions in API.[107] Moreover, when acts of violence are intentionally directed at members of the civilian population during a NIAC or are indiscriminate, the circumstance amounts to a violation of the principles of distinction and/or proportionality.[108] Acts of terror, thus, are conceptually inconsistent with lawful warfare in terms of IHL. The effect is that such acts amount to violations of IHL when committed during an armed conflict and not that they fall outside of the applicability of IHL.

The IHL formulation of 'violence the primary purpose of which is to spread terror among the civilian population' brings us no closer to an agreed definition of 'terror' or 'terrorism', yet quintessential and high-threshold acts of terror often are easy to identify. Much of the conduct of Ansar al-Sunna leaves no doubt that it meets the threshold of violence that spreads terror among the civilian population or fulfils any other definition of terrorism. This level of violence is exemplified by the November 2020 beheading of more than 50 civilians mentioned earlier and the attack on the town of Palma in March 2021 which lasted for four days in which civilians were also targeted and beheaded. Having established that state responses to acts of terror and the groups responsible for such acts must be IHRL and IHL compliant, the question arises as to the most appropriate international mechanisms through which Mozambique can respond to the violence instigated by Ansar al-Sunna.

7.4.2 Accountability measures in respect of Ansar al-Sunna

A unique feature of IHL is that it creates obligations for non-state actors on the international plane. By acting in a manner inconsistent with its obligations under IHL, Ansar al-Sunna as a group and its individual members are guilty of violations of international law. However, IHL does not have robust enforcement or accountability mechanisms of its own. Consequently, international criminal law (ICL) and its better-developed accountability mechanisms, particularly the International Criminal Court (ICC), together with domestic prosecutions, offer better avenues for accountability. Unfortunately, although an early signatory to the Rome Statute, Mozambique has not ratified the statute.[109] The implications of a failure to ratify are considered after a discussion of the applicable substantive offences.

The Rome Statute does not proscribe an offence of terrorism. The Netherlands introduced a resolution in the lead-up to the 2011 Kampala Review Conference of the Rome Statute which aimed at the introduction of such an offence.[110] This move, however, was not favoured by participating states, primarily because (i) there is no agreed definition of terrorism; (ii) such an offence may politicise the ICC; and (iii) acts of terror are already encapsulated in the crimes against humanity and war crimes, which fall within the Court's jurisdiction.[111] Accordingly, violations committed by Ansar al-Sunna that may be characterised as acts of terror and which ostensibly violate the IHL prohibition on acts or threats of terror-related violence may be prosecuted either as crimes against humanity or as war crimes (should the Court have jurisdiction).

These crimes are differentiated primarily by their respective underlying contextual elements. Using Ansar al-Sunna's campaigns of civilian beheadings as an illustrative example, it is instructive to have regard to the Rome Statute's elements of crimes. This conduct may amount to the crime against humanity of murder, the elements of which are:

1 The perpetrator killed one or more persons.
2 The conduct was committed as part of a widespread or systematic attack directed against a civilian population.
3 The perpetrator knew that the conduct was part of or intended the conduct to be part of a widespread or systematic attack against a civilian population.[112]

The conduct also may amount to the war crime of 'violence to life and person, in particular murder':

1 The perpetrator killed one or more persons.
2 Such person or persons were either *hors de combat*, or were civilians, medical personnel, or religious personnel taking no active part in the hostilities.
3 The perpetrator was aware of the factual circumstances that established this status.
4 The conduct took place in the context of and was associated with an armed conflict not of an international character.
5 The perpetrator was aware of factual circumstances that established the existence of an armed conflict.[113]

The contextual elements of the crime against humanity are reflected in the requirement that the conduct be committed as part of a widespread or systematic attack directed against a civilian population and that the perpetrator acted knowing that their conduct formed part of this attack. 'Widespread' or 'systematic' are alternative and not cumulative criteria, nor are they synonymous terms. 'Widespread' speaks to the scale of the attack and the number of targeted victims,[114] whereas 'systematic' speaks to the level of organisation and planning of an attack.[115] In contrast, the contextual element of the applicable war crime is reflected in the need for the conduct to take place in the context of a NIAC with a nexus to the conflict and that the perpetrators acted with an awareness of the factual circumstances that established the existence of the armed conflict.

As previously mentioned, the existence of an armed conflict is a question of fact and there is little doubt that the Cabo Delgado insurgency meets the threshold of an APII-type NIAC. Thus, the evidentiary threshold of establishing the contextual elements for a war crimes prosecution is not complicated. On the other hand, the contextual elements of crimes against humanity impose a comparatively high evidentiary threshold that cannot be established *a fortiori* based on the existence of an armed conflict.

It is suggested that a central feature of an ongoing 'populist' onslaught against human rights is a representation that states are required extensively to protect the rights of perpetrators but are not afforded the necessary tools to combat organised crime or terrorism.[116] In fact, the tools exist, but states fail to subscribe to them or fail to use them, for example, the failure of Mozambique to ratify the Rome Statute. Even immediate ratification of the Rome Statute by Mozambique will not allow the ICC to exercise jurisdiction over the situation in Cabo Delgado as the Rome Statute enters into force between two and three months after ratification[117] and applies only prospectively.[118] However, the Rome Statute provides a mechanism by which a state that is not a party can activate the jurisdiction of the ICC on an *ad hoc* basis and in a manner not limited to prospective temporal jurisdiction.[119] A referral is to be made by lodging a declaration by the state with the registrar of the Court.[120] From a state's perspective, an *ad hoc* referral should be an attractive option as, unlike the jurisdiction of the Court in respect of state parties or premised on a Security Council referral, the state maintains significant control over the temporal, personal and territorial scope of the ICC's *ad hoc* jurisdiction.[121] The state shares with the Court jurisdiction that it enjoys by virtue of its sovereignty, and, thus, it decides how much of its jurisdiction it wishes to share.[122] Côte d'Ivoire was the first state to afford the Court *ad hoc* jurisdiction in 2005.[123] The confidence the experience inspired led Côte d'Ivoire to ratify the Rome Statute in 2013.

7.5 Conclusion

There is nothing inherently problematic in designating Ansar al-Sunna as a terror organisation or to suppress, in part, their activities through counter-terror treaties and to respond to their violence through a domestic counter-terror framework. Indeed, the designation may be of material use to the state in its response to the group by, for example, facilitating the implementation of sanctions, disrupting the financial position of the group, facilitating inter-state intelligence sharing and so forth. However, the designation, formal or informal, cannot be used to usurp the protection offered through IHRL and IHL, in the event that the latter has objectively been triggered. The protective reach IHRL and IHL provide often falls victim to a political rhetoric on terrorism. A domestic counter-terror framework, which falls outside the scope of this contribution, must comply with the state's IHL and IHRL obligations.

The authors of this contribution agree with the conclusion in the ICRC 2019 Challenges Report that, when engaging non-state armed groups designated as terrorists in a counter-terrorism operation, a state should assess the situation, objectively and exclusively, on the basis of the facts and in accordance with the recognised criteria for conflict classification under IHL.[124] The application of IHL appropriately enhances the scope of the actions that the state lawfully can utilise to combat Ansar al-Sunna. The Rome Statute offers a viable path for asserting accountability by members of Ansar al-Sunna and provides Mozambique with a mechanism by which to activate the jurisdiction of the ICC on an *ad hoc* basis. Lastly, we conclude by citing the ICRC 2019 Contemporary Challenges Report: 'IHL does not hinder states from fighting terrorism effectively, while setting out a baseline of humanity that all states have agreed to respect, even in the most exceptional situations'.[125]

Notes

1 ICRC, *International Humanitarian Law and the Challenges of Contemporary Armed Conflicts* (2019) 58 (Contemporary Challenges Report).
2 Ibid, 68.
3 Ibid.
4 Ibid.
5 Tom van Rentergem, 'Al-Shabaab in Mozambique: Taking Stock of an Insurgency Under Cover' *Egmont Policy Brief* 281 (June 2022) 3.
6 See the Global Coalition to Defeat ISIS, 'Joint Communiqué by Ministers of the Global Coalition to Defeat ISIS' (11 May 2022).
7 Ansar al-Sunna is known locally as Al-Shabaab but is not linked to Al-Shabaab Somalia. See Amnesty International, 'Mozambique: "What I Saw Is Death": War Crimes in Mozambique's Forgotten Cape' (2021) 9.
8 International Crisis Group, 'Mozambique'.
9 See Chapter 6 of this book.
10 Counter Terrorism Guide, 'Islamic State of Iraq and Ash-Sham (ISIS)' *Counter Terrorism Guide* (September 2022) <www.dni.gov/nctc/ftos/isis_fto.html>; U.S. Department of State, 'Country Reports on Terrorism 2021: Mozambique' <https://www.state.gov/reports/country-reports-on-terrorism-2021/>; Liesl Louw-Vaudran, 'The Many Roots of Mozambique's Deadly Insurgency' *Institute for Security Studies* (8 September 2022); UNODC, 'UNODC Supports Mozambican Authorities to Tackle Terrorism and Its Financing in the Country' (18 August 2022) <https://www.unodc.org/rosaf/stories/2022/August/unodc-supports-mozambican-authorities-to-tackle-terrorism-and-its-financing-in-the-country.html>.
11 ICRC, Contemporary Challenges Report (n 1) 59.
12 *Prosecutor v Dusko Tadic a/k/a 'Dule'* (Opinion and Judgment) IT-94–1-T (7 May 1997) para 561.

13 Ibid.
14 Eric Morier-Genoud, 'The Jihadi Insurgency in Mozambique: Origins, Nature and Beginning' (2020) 14 (3) *Journal of East African Studies* 396, 397–400; see also Tore Refslund Hamming, 'The Islamic State in Mozambique' *Lawfare Blog* (24 January 2021).
15 Hamming (n 14).
16 Ibid; Amnesty International (n 7) 9.
17 Morier-Genoud (n 14) 397, 398.
18 Ibid, 398.
19 Hamming (n 14).
20 Dorina A Bekoe, Stephanie M Burchard and Sarah A Daly, 'Extremism in Mozambique: Interpreting Group Tactics and the Role of the Government's Response in the Crisis in Cabo Delgado' *Institute for Defense Analyses* (March 2020) 12.
21 Ibid, 10.
22 Ibid, 8 and 9; Global Centre for the Responsibility to Protect, 'Mozambique' *Global Centre for the Responsibility to Protect* (31 May 2023) <www.globalr2p.org/countries/mozambique/>; Human Rights Watch, 'Mozambique: Events of 2022' <www.hrw.org/world-report/2023/country-chapters/mozambique>; Amnesty International (n 7) 12.
23 Bekoe and others (n 20) 9.
24 Ibid, 8 and 9; Global Centre for the Responsibility to Protect (n 22); Human Rights Watch (n 22).
25 Bekoe and others (n 20) 12; Amnesty International (n 7) 10.
26 Amnesty International (n 7) 12.
27 Tim Lister, 'The March 2021 Palma Attack and the Evolving Terror Threat to Mozambique' *Combating Terrorism Centre at West Point* (April/May 2021); '40 000 Displaced in North Mozambique After Assault in Palma' *Africanews* (20 April 2021).
28 Lister (n 27).
29 Ibid.
30 Amnesty International (n 7) 10.
31 Bekoe and others (n 20) 12.
32 Ibid, 8 and 12; Opperman opines that at the start of the crisis there was 'no overarching leader or structure'; see Jasmine Opperman, 'Is Northern Mozambique Faced with an Emerging Extremist Threat?' *Daily Maverick* (31 May 2018).
33 Hamming (n 14); see also Chapter 5 of this book.
34 Hamming (n 14); Amnesty International (n 7) 9.
35 Amnesty International (n 7) 9; Bekoe and others, (n 20) 12; Hamming (n 14).
36 Hamming (n 14).
37 Bekoe and others (n 20) 12.
38 U.S. Department of State, 'State Department Terrorist Designations of ISIS Affiliates and Leaders in the Democratic Republic of the Congo and Mozambique' (10 March 2021); 'Sanctions List Search' *Office of Foreign Assets* <https://sanctionssearch.ofac.treas.gov/Details.aspx?id=31372>.
39 Bekoe and others (n 20) 12; Rentergem (n 5) 3.
40 Bekoe and others (n 20) 12; Peter Fabricus, 'Is another Boko Haram or Al-Shabaab Erupting in Mozambique?' *Institute for Security Studies* (14 June 2018).
41 Makaita Noel Mutasa and Cyprian Muchemwa, 'Ansar Al-Sunna Mozambique: Is It the Boko Karam of Southern Africa' (2022) 17 (3) *Journal of Applied Security Research* 332, 341; Rentergem (n 5) 3; Bekoe and others (n 20) 21, 23; Audu Bulama Bukarti and Sandun Munasinghe, 'The Mozambique Conflict and Deteriorating Security Situation' *Tony Blair Institute for Global Change* (19 June 2020).
42 See Chapter 6 of this book for an in-depth assessment. See also Amnesty International (n 7) 8; RULAC, 'Non-International Armed Conflicts in Mozambique' (18 May 2023) <www.rulac.org/browse/conflicts/non-international-aarmed-conflicts-in-mozambique#collapse2accord>.

43 U.S. Department of State (n 10); UN News, 'Five Years of Violence in Northern Mozambique Has Forced Nearly a Million to Flee' (4 October 2022) <https://news.un.org/en/story/2022/10/1129217>; 'Mozambique: Is Cabo Delgado the Last Islamic State Outpost?' *BBC News* (5 May 2020); Djordje Djukic and Evan Centanni, 'Mozambique Insurgency: Close-up Map of Control in April 2021' *Political Geography Now* (22 April 2021) <www.polgeonow.com/2021/04/cabo-delgado-conflict-map-2021.html>.
44 U.S. Department of State (n 10); *UN News* (n 43); *BBC News* (n 43); Djukic and Centanni (n 43).
45 International Crisis Group, 'Making the Most of the EU's Integrated Approach to Mozambique' (31 January 2023).
46 *Prosecutor v Akayesu* (Judgment) ICTR-96–4-T (2 September 1998) para 626.
47 Ibid; *Prosecutor v Sesay, Kallon and Gbao (RUF accused)* (Trial Judgment) SCSL-04–15-T (2 March 2009) para 966 supports this functional approach. For a comprehensive discussion of territorial control under article 1(1) of Additional Protocol II, see Martha M Bradley, 'Classifying Non-International Armed Conflicts: The "Territorial Control" Requirement Under Additional Protocol II in an Era of Complex Conflicts' (2020) *Journal of International Humanitarian Legal Studies* 349, 384.
48 *Sesay* (n 47) paras 947 and 948; see also Bradley (n 47) 379–381.
49 International Crisis Group, 'Stemming the Insurrection in Mozambique's Cabo Delgado' (11 June 2021).
50 Ibid.
51 Ibid.
52 ACLED, 'Organised Political Violence in Mozambique (1 January 1997–3 February 2023)' <https://acleddata.com/cabo-ligado-mozambique-conflict-observatory/>.
53 Rosalyn Higgins, 'The General International Law of Terrorism' in Rosalyn Higgins and Maurice Flory (eds), *Terrorism and International Law* (Routledge 1997) 13–14.
54 Amrith Rohan Perera, 'The Draft United Nations Comprehensive Convention on International Terrorism' in Ben Saul (ed), *Research Handbook in International Law and Terrorism* (2nd edn, Edward Elgar 2020) 120.
55 Convention for the Prevention and Punishment of Terrorism (1937).
56 Perera (n 54) 121.
57 Ibid.
58 In an attempt to get Israel to release 236 prisoners, eight armed men of the Palestine Liberation Organisation (PLO) held members of the Israeli Olympic team hostage; 17 people died, 11 members of the Israeli team, five members of the PLO and one West German policeman. See James Doubek, '50 Years Ago, the Munich Olympics Massacre Changed How We Think About Terrorism' *NPR* (4 September 2022) <www.npr.org/2022/09/04/1116641214/munich-olympics-massacre-hostage-terrorism-israel-germany>.
59 Perera (n 54) 122.
60 Ibid, 125.
61 Ibid, 124–125.
62 UNGA, 'Declaration on Measures to Eliminate International Terrorism', *UN Doc. A/Res/49/60* (17 February 1995); Rohan Perera, 'Declaration on Measures to Eliminate International Terrorism, 1994 and the 1996 Supplementary Declaration Thereto' *UN Audio Visual Library of International Law* <https://legal.un.org/avl/pdf/ha/dot/dot_e.pdf>.
63 Sec I(3) of the Declaration on Measures to Eliminate International Terrorism (n 62).
64 Perera (n 54) 122.
65 Samuel Witten, 'The International Convention for the Suppression of Terrorist Bombings' in Ben Saul (ed), *Research Handbook in International Law and Terrorism* (2nd edn, Edward Elgar 2020) 109, 111.
66 Article 2 of the International Convention for the Suppression of Terrorist Bombings (adopted 15 December 1997, entered into force 23 May 2001) 2149 UNTS 256 (Terrorist Bombing Convention).

67 Article 2 of the International Convention for the Suppression of the Financing of Terrorism (adopted 9 December 1999, entered into force 10 April 2002) 2178 UNTS 197 (Terrorism Financing Convention).
68 Article 2 of the International Convention for the Suppression of Acts of Nuclear Terrorism (adopted 13 April 2005, entered into force 7 July 2007) 2445 UNTS 89 (Nuclear Terrorism Convention).
69 Article 5 of the Terrorist Bombings Convention (n 66); article 6 of the Nuclear Terrorism Convention (n 68); article 2(1)(b) of the Terrorism Financing Convention (n 67).
70 Waschefort argues that the *mens rea* element of terrorism is to spread fear; see Gus Waschefort, 'Drawing the Boundaries Between Terrorism and Crimes Against Humanity' (2007) 22 (2) *SA Public Law* 457, 469.
71 Article 19 of the Terrorist Bombing Convention (n 66); article 4 of the Nuclear Terrorism Convention (n 68).
72 Article 2(1)(b) of the Terrorism Financing Convention (n 67).
73 It should be noted that the International Convention Against the Taking of Hostages (adopted 17 December 1979, entered into force 3 June 1983) 1316 UNTS 205 does not cover hostage taking that occurs during an armed conflict. Article 12 reads in part that '[t]he present Convention shall not apply to an act of hostage taking committed in the course of armed conflicts as defined in the Geneva Conventions'. This treaty was drawn up before the advent of the Ad Hoc Committee and does not use the word 'terrorism' or 'terrorist' but, nevertheless, it is considered a terrorism-related text; see Robert Rosenstock, 'International Convention Against the Taking of Hostages: Another International Community Step Against Terrorism' (1980) 9 (2) *Denver Journal of International Law and Policy* 169.
74 UN Doc. A/57/37; UNGA Res. 3034 (XXVII).
75 Perera (n 54) 124–125.
76 Ibid, 127. It should be noted that Perera refers to the 2002 Report of the Ad Hoc Committee, but the relevant text, that is, article 3 (previously 18) of the 2002 and 2013 reports, is the same.
77 Article 19 of the Terrorist Bombing Convention (n 66); article 4 of the Nuclear Terrorism Convention (n 68).
78 ICRC, 'Rule 4: Definition of Armed Forces' <https://ihl-databases.icrc.org/en/customary-ihl/v1/rule4>. Rule 4 reads: 'The armed forces of a party to the conflict consist of all organised armed forces, groups and units which are under a command responsible to that party for the conduct of its subordinates'. Mozambique has ratified this Convention.
79 In 2021 and 2022, the General Assembly adopted a resolution in which it recommended that the Sixth Committee convene a working group aimed at finalising the Draft Convention; see UNGA, '2021 Political Declaration on the Implementation of the United Nations Global Plan of Action to Combat Trafficking in Persons' (10 November 2021) UN Doc. A/C.6/76/L.11, para 25; and UNGA, 'Measures to Eliminate International Terrorism' (20 December 2022) UN Doc. A/RES/77/113 para 25.
80 UNTS, 'International Convention for the Suppression of Terrorist Bombings'.
81 UNTS, 'International Convention for the Suppression of Acts of Nuclear Terrorism'.
82 Article 31(1) of the Vienna Convention on the Law of Treaties (adopted 22 May 1969, entered into force 27 January 1980) 1155 UNTS 331 (VCLT).
83 *Merriam-Webster's Dictionary and Thesaurus* (Merriam-Webster 2020) 840.
84 ICRC, 'Protocol Additional to the Geneva Conventions of 12 August 1949, and Relating to the Protection of Victims of Non-International Armed Conflicts (Protocol II), 8 June 1977, Commentary of 01.01.1987; article 13 – Protection of the civilian population' para 4538 <https://ihl-databases.icrc.org/en/ihl-treaties/apii-1977/article-13/commentary/1987?activeTab=undefined> (ICRC Commentaries); see also Annyssa Bellal and Stuart Maslen, *The Additional Protocols to the Geneva Conventions in Context* (OUP 2022) 210 para 13.8.

85 Bellal and Maslen (n 84) 210 para 13.8.
86 ACLED, 'Organised Political Violence in Mozambique (1 January 1997–3 February 2023)' <https://acleddata.com/cabo-ligado-mozambique-conflict-observatory/>.
87 Ibid.
88 Ibid.
89 Ibid.
90 Ibid.
91 Ibid.
92 Ibid.
93 Ibid.
94 Article 13(2) reads: 'The civilian population as such, as well as individual civilians, shall not be the object of attack. Acts or threats of violence the primary purpose of which is to spread terror among the civilian population are prohibited'. See Protocol Additional to the Geneva Conventions of 12 August 1949; and Relating to the Protection of Victims of Non-International Armed Conflicts (Protocol II) (adopted 8 June 1977, entered into force 7 December 1978) 1125 UNTS 609 (Additional Protocol II).
95 ICRC Commentaries (n 84) para 4785.
96 Ibid, para 4786.
97 *Prosecutor v Galić* (Judgment and Opinion) IT-98–29F (5 December 2003) para 135. For an overview of acts of violence intended to terrorise the civilian population, see Bellal and Maslen (n 84) 211 paras 3.12–3.16.
98 ACLED (n 86).
99 Bellal and Maslen (n 84) 208.
100 This is exemplified by the US position (although it has evolved over time) regarding the applicability of IHL and IHRL to the 'war on terror'. Borelli comments: 'With regard to the US, it seems clear that the choice of detaining individuals abroad as part of the 'war on terror' is based, at least in part, on the assumption that by keeping them outside national territory, the military or the other agencies will not be restricted by standards of national (and international) legal protection in the same way as if they were held on national territory'. See Silvia Borelli, 'Casting Light on the Legal Black Hole: International Law and Detentions Abroad in the "War on Terror"' (2005) 87 (857) *International Review of The Red Cross* 39, 44.
101 The US refers to the group as 'Islamic State of Iraq and Syria – Mozambique (ISIS-Mozambique)'; see U.S. Department of State (n 38).
102 African Commission on Human and Peoples' Rights, 'General Comment No 3 on the African Charter on Human and Peoples' Rights: The Right to Life (Article 4)' (PULP 2015) paras 2 and 7.
103 For example, article 4(1) of the International Covenant on Civil and Political Rights (adopted 16 December 1966, entered into force 23 March 1976) 999 UNTS 171, which Mozambique ratified during 1993, provides that '[i]n time of public emergency which threatens the life of the nation and the existence of which is officially proclaimed, the States Parties to the present Covenant may take measures derogating from their obligations under the present Covenant to the extent strictly required by the exigencies of the situation, provided that such measures are not inconsistent with their other obligations under international law and do not involve discrimination solely on the ground of race, colour, sex, language, religion or social origin'. While the right to life and prohibition against torture are non-derogable, the right to liberty and security of person is derogable'.
104 Waschefort (n 70) 469.
105 ICRC, 'Rule 2: Violence Aimed at Spreading Terror among the Civilian Population'.
106 Articles 13(2) and 51(2) of Additional Protocol II (n 94).
107 There are exceptions to the general rule; for example, Additional Protocol I provides a lower threshold of protection to children against use for participation in hostilities and

recruitment. Compare article 4(3)(c) of Additional Protocol II (n 94) with article 77(2) of Protocol Additional to the Geneva Conventions of 12 August 1949, and Relating to the Protection of Victims of International Armed Conflicts (Protocol I) (adopted 8 June 1977, entered into force 7 December 1978)1125 UNTS 3 (Additional Protocol I).

108 See Rules 1, 7, 11 and 12 of the ICRC Customary IHL Study, which apply to both NIAC and IAC (ICRC, 'Rule 1: The Principle of Distinction between Civilians and Combatants) <https://ihl-databases.icrc.org/en/customary-ihl/v1/rule1>; ICRC, 'Rule 7: The Principle of Distinction between Civilian Objects and Military Objectives' <https://ihl-databases.icrc.org/en/customary-ihl/v1/rule7>; ICRC, 'Rule 11: Indiscriminate Attacks' <https://ihl-databases.icrc.org/en/customary-ihl/v1/rule11>; ICRC, 'Rule 12: Definition of Indiscriminate Attacks' <https://ihl-databases.icrc.org/en/customary-ihl/v1/rule12>.

109 ICC, 'The States Parties to the Rome Statute' ICC Doc. ICC-ASP/8/20 <https://asp.icc-cpi.int/states-parties>.

110 See paras 40 and 51 of ICC, 'Eight Session of the Assembly of the Parties' (18–26 November 2009) <https://asp.icc-cpi.int/sites/asp/files/asp_docs/ASP8/OR/or-asp8-vol.i-eng.annexes.pdf>.

111 Ibid, paras 50–51.

112 Article 7(1)(a) in ICC, 'Elements of Crimes' (2013) <www.icc-cpi.int/sites/default/files/Publications/Elements-of-Crimes.pdf>.

113 Ibid, article 8(2)(c)(i).

114 See, for example, *Prosecutor v Jean-Pierre Bemba Gombo* (Judgment pursuant to article 74 of the Statute) ICC-01/05–01/08 (21 March 2016) para 163; *Prosecutor v Germain Katanga* (Judgment pursuant to article 74 of the Statute) ICC-01/04–01/07 (7 March 2014) para 1123; *Prosecutor v Laurent Gbagbo* (Decision on Confirmation of Charges against Laurent Gbago) ICC-02/11–01/11 (12 June 2014) para 222.

115 *Katanga* (n 114) para 1123; *Prosecutor v Blaśkič* (Trial Judgment) IT-95–14-T (3 March 2000) para 658; *Prosecutor v Brdanin* (Judgment) IT-99–36-T (1 September 2004) para 135; *Prosecutor v Dragoljub Kunarac, Radomir Kovac and Zoran Vukovic* (Trial Judgment) IT-96–23-T & IT-96–23/1-T (22 February 2001) para 429.

116 See, for example, Joan Fitzpatrick, 'Speaking Law to Power: The War Against Terrorism and Human Rights' (2003) 14 (2) *European Journal of Human Rights* 241, 242 where she comments: 'For many years sceptical, stand-offish, and self-righteous, the United States now exercises its hegemony more corrosively than ever on the international human rights regime, with the increasingly bold campaign against the International Criminal Court (ICC) serving as the most vivid example of American exceptionalism'.

117 Article 126 of the Rome Statute of the International Criminal Court (adopted 17 July 1998, entered into force 1 July 2002) 2187 UNTS 3.

118 Ibid, article 11(2).

119 Ibid, articles 12(2)–(3), read with article 11(2).

120 Ibid, article 12(3).

121 Carsten Stahn, Mohamed M El Zeidy and Héctor Olásolo, 'The International Criminal Court's Ad Hoc Jurisdiction Revisited' (2005) 99 (2) *American Journal of International Law* 421, 423.

122 Ibid.

123 ICC, 'Registrar Confirms That the Republic of Côte d'Ivoire Has Accepted the Jurisdiction of the Court' (15 February 2005) <www.icc-cpi.int/news/icc-registrar-confirms-republic-cote-divoire-has-accepted-jurisdiction-court>.

124 Contemporary Challenges Report (n 1) 59.

125 Ibid.

Bibliography

'40 000 Displaced in North Mozambique After Assault in Palma' *Africanews* (20 April 2021).

ACLED, 'Organised Political Violence in Mozambique (1 January 1997–3 February 2023)' <https://acleddata.com/cabo-ligado-mozambique-conflict-observatory/>.

African Commission on Human and Peoples' Rights, 'General Comment No 3 on the African Charter on Human and Peoples' Rights: The Right to Life (Article 4)' (PULP 2015).

Amnesty International, 'Mozambique: "What I Saw Is Death": War Crimes in Mozambique's Forgotten Cape' (2 March 2021).

Amrith Rohan Perera, 'The Draft United Nations Comprehensive Convention on International Terrorism' in Ben Saul (ed), *Research Handbook in International Law and Terrorism* (2nd edn, Edward Elgar 2020).

Annyssa Bellal and Stuart Maslen, *The Additional Protocols to the Geneva Conventions in Context* (OUP 2022).

Audu Bulama Bukarti and Sandun Munasinghe, 'The Mozambique Conflict and Deteriorating Security Situation' *Tony Blair Institute for Global Change* (19 June 2020) <www.institute.global/insights/geopolitics-and-security/mozambique-conflict-and-deteriorating-security-situation>.

Carsten Stahn, Mohamed M El Zeidy and Héctor Olásolo, 'The International Criminal Court's Ad Hoc Jurisdiction Revisited' (2005) 99 (2) *American Journal of International Law*.

Convention for the Prevention and Punishment of Terrorism (1937) <https://www.loc.gov/item/2021667893/>.

Djordje Djukic and Evan Centanni, 'Mozambique Insurgency: Close-up Map of Control in April 2021' *Political Geography Now* (22 April 2021) <www.polgeonow.com/2021/04/cabo-delgado-conflict-map-2021.html>.

Dorina A Bekoe, Stephanie M Burchard and Sarah A Daly, 'Extremism in Mozambique: Interpreting Group Tactics and the Role of the Government's Response in the Crisis in Cabo Delgado' *Institute for Defense Analyses* (March 2020).

Eric Morier-Genoud, 'The Jihadi Insurgency in Mozambique: Origins, Nature and Beginning' (2020) 14 (3) *Journal of East African Studies*.

Global Centre for the Responsibility to Protect, 'Mozambique' (31 May 2023) <www.globalr2p.org/countries/mozambique/>.

Global Coalition to Defeat ISIS, 'Joint Communiqué by Ministers of the Global Coalition to Defeat ISIS' (11 May 2022) <https://theglobalcoalition.org/en/communique-global-coalition-morocco/>.

Gus Waschefort, 'Drawing the Boundaries Between Terrorism and Crimes Against Humanity' (2007) 22 (2) *SA Public Law*.

Human Rights Watch, 'Mozambique: Events of 2022' <www.hrw.org/world-report/2023/country-chapters/mozambique>.

ICC, 'Eight Session of the Assembly of the Parties' (18–26 November 2009) <https://asp.icc-cpi.int/sites/asp/files/asp_docs/ASP8/OR/or-asp8-vol.i-eng.annexes.pdf>.

ICC, 'Elements of Crimes' (2013) <www.icc-cpi.int/sites/default/files/Publications/Elements-of-Crimes.pdf>.

ICC, 'Registrar Confirms that the Republic of Côte d'Ivoire Has Accepted the Jurisdiction of the Court' *International Criminal Court* (15 February 2005) <www.icc-cpi.int/news/icc-registrar-confirms-republic-cote-divoire-has-accepted-jurisdiction-court>.

ICC, 'The States Parties to the Rome Statute' ICC Doc ICC-ASP/8/20 <https://asp.icc-cpi.int/states-parties>.

ICRC, 'International Humanitarian Law and the Challenges of Contemporary Armed Conflicts' (2019).

ICRC, 'Protocol Additional to the Geneva Conventions of 12 August 1949, and Relating to the Protection of Victims of Non-International Armed Conflicts (Protocol II), 8 June 1977, Commentary of 01.01.1987; art 13 – Protection of the civilian population' <https://ihl-databases.icrc.org/en/ihl-treaties/apii-1977/article-13/commentary/1987?activeTab=u ndefined>.

ICRC, 'Rule 1: The Principle of Distinction between Civilians and Combatants <https://ihl-databases.icrc.org/en/customary-ihl/v1/rule1>.

ICRC, 'Rule 2: Violence Aimed at Spreading Terror Among the Civilian Population' <https://ihl-databases.icrc.org/en/customary-ihl/v1/rule2>.

ICRC, 'Rule 4: Definition of Armed Forces' <https://ihl-databases.icrc.org/en/customary-ihl/v1/rule4>.

ICRC, 'Rule 7: The Principle of Distinction between Civilian Objects and Military Objectives' <https://ihl-databases.icrc.org/en/customary-ihl/v1/rule7>.

ICRC, 'Rule 11: Indiscriminate Attacks' <https://ihl-databases.icrc.org/en/customary-ihl/v1/rule11>.

ICRC, 'Rule 12: Definition of Indiscriminate Attacks' <https://ihl-databases.icrc.org/en/customary-ihl/v1/rule12>.

International Convention Against the Taking of Hostages (1979) <https://treaties.un.org/Pages/showDetails.aspx?objid=0800000280056c38&clang=_en>.

International Convention for the Suppression of Acts of Nuclear Terrorism (2005) <https://treaties.un.org/Pages/showDetails.aspx?objid=0800000280057ab0&clang=_en>.

International Convention for the Suppression of the Financing of Terrorism (1999) <https://treaties.un.org/Pages/showDetails.aspx?objid=080000028004f335&clang=_en>.

International Convention for the Suppression of Terrorist Bombings (1997) <https://treaties.un.org/Pages/showDetails.aspx?objid=0800000280048c82&clang=_en>.

International Covenant on Civil and Political Rights (1966) <https://treaties.un.org/Pages/showDetails.aspx?objid=0800000280004bf5&clang=_en>.

International Crisis Group, 'Making the Most of the EU's Integrated Approach to Mozambique' (31 January 2023) <www.crisisgroup.org/africa/east-and-southern-africa/mozambique/making-most-eus-integrated-approach-mozambique>.

International Crisis Group, 'Mozambique' *Crisis Group* <www.crisisgroup.org/africa/east-and-southern-africa/mozambique>.

International Crisis Group, 'Stemming the Insurrection in Mozambique's Cabo Delgado' *International Crisis Group* (11 June 2021) <www.crisisgroup.org/africa/southern-africa/mozambique/303-stemming-insurrection-mozambiques-cabo-delgado>.

'Islamic State of Iraq and Ash-Sham (ISIS)' *Counter Terrorism Guide* (September 2022) <www.dni.gov/nctc/ftos/isis_fto.html>.

James Doubek, '50 Years Ago, the Munich Olympics Massacre Changed How We Think About Terrorism' *NPR* (4 September 2022) <www.npr.org/2022/09/04/1116641214/munich-olympics-massacre-hostage-terrorism-israel-germany>.

Jasmine Opperman, 'Is Northern Mozambique Faced with an Emerging Extremist Threat?' *Daily Maverick* (31 May 2018).

Joan Fitzpatrick, 'Speaking Law to Power: The War Against Terrorism and Human Rights' (2003) 14 (2) *European Journal of Human Rights*.

Liesl Louw-Vaudran, 'The Many Roots of Mozambique's Deadly Insurgency' *Institute for Security Studies* (8 September 2022).

Makaita Noel Mutasa and Cyprian Muchemwa, 'Ansar Al-Sunna Mozambique: Is It the Boko Haram of Southern Africa' (2022) 17 (3) *Journal of Applied Security Research*.

Martha M. Bradley, 'Classifying Non-International Armed Conflicts: The "Territorial Control" Requirement Under Additional Protocol II in an Era of Complex Conflicts' (2020) 11(2) *Journal of International Humanitarian Legal Studies*.

Merriam-Webster's Dictionary and Thesaurus (Merriam-Webster 2020).

'Mozambique: Is Cabo Delgado the Last Islamic State Outpost?' *BBC News* (5 May 2020).

Peter Fabricus, 'Is Another Boko Haram or Al-Shabaab Erupting in Mozambique?' *Institute for Security Studies* (14 June 2018).

Prosecutor v Ahmad Muhammad Harun ('Ahmad Harun') and Ali Muhammad Ali Abd-Al-Rahman ('Ali Kushayb') (Decision on the Prosecution Application under Article 58(7) of the Statute) ICC-02/05–01/07 (27 April 2007).

Prosecutor v Akayesu (Judgment) ICTR-96–4-T (2 September 1998).

Prosecutor v Blaśkič (Trial Judgment) IT-95–14-T (3 March 2000).

Prosecutor v Brdanin (Judgment) IT-99–36-T (1 September 2004).

Prosecutor v Dragoljub Kunarac, Radomir Kovac and Zoran Vukovic (Trial Judgment) IT-96–23-T & IT-96–23/1-T (22 February 2001).

Prosecutor v Dusko Tadic a/k/a 'Dule' (Opinion and Judgment) IT-94–1-T (7 May 1997).
Prosecutor v Galić (Judgment and Opinion) IT-98–29F (5 December 2003).
Prosecutor v Germain Katanga (Judgment pursuant to Article 74 of the Statute) ICC-01/04–01/07 (7 March 2014).
Prosecutor v Jean-Pierre Bemba Gombo (Judgment pursuant to Article 74 of the Statute) ICC-01/05–01/08 (21 March 2016).
Prosecutor v Laurent Gbagbo (Decision on Confirmation of Charges against Laurent Gbago) ICC-02/11–01/11 (12 June 2014).
Prosecutor v Sesay, Kallon and Gbao (RUF accused) (Trial Judgment) SCSL-04–15-T (2 March 2009).
Protocol Additional to the Geneva Conventions of 12 August 1949, and Relating to the Protection of Victims of International Armed Conflicts (Protocol I) (1977) <https://treaties.un.org/Pages/showDetails.aspx?objid=08000002800f3586&clang=_en>.
Protocol Additional to the Geneva Conventions of 12 August 1949; and Relating to the Protection of Victims of Non-International Armed Conflicts (Protocol II) (1977) <https://treaties.un.org/Pages/showDetails.aspx?objid=08000002800f3cb8&clang=_en>.
Robert Rosenstock, 'International Convention Against the Taking of Hostages: Another International Community Step Against Terrorism' (1980) 9 (2) *Denver Journal of International Law and Policy*.
Rohan Perera, 'Declaration on Measures to Eliminate International Terrorism, 1994 and the 1996 Supplementary Declaration Thereto' *Audio Visual Library of International Law* <https://legal.un.org/avl/pdf/ha/dot/dot_e.pdf>.
Rome Statute of the International Criminal Court (1998) <https://treaties.un.org/Pages/showDetails.aspx?objid=0800000280025774&clang=_en>.
Rosalyn Higgins, 'The General International Law of Terrorism' in Rosalyn Higgins and Maurice Flory (eds), *Terrorism and International Law* (Routledge 1997).
RULAC, 'Non-International Armed Conflicts in Mozambique' (18 May 2023) <www.rulac.org/browse/conflicts/non-international-aarmed-conflicts-in-mozambique#collapse2accord>.
Samuel Witten, 'The International Convention for the Suppression of Terrorist Bombings' in Ben Saul (ed), *Research Handbook in International Law and Terrorism* (2nd edn, Edward Elgar 2020).
'Sanctions List Search' *Office of Foreign Assets* <https://sanctionssearch.ofac.treas.gov/Details.aspx?id=31372>.
Silvia Borelli, 'Casting Light on the Legal Black Hole: International Law and Detentions Abroad in the "War on Terror"' (2005) 87 (857) *International Review of the Red Cross*.
Tim Lister, 'The March 2021 Palma Attack and the Evolving Terror Threat to Mozambique' *Combating Terrorism Center at West Point* (April/May 2021) <https://ctc.westpoint.edu/the-march-2021-palma-attack-and-the-evolving-jihadi-terror-threat-to-mozambique/>.
Tom van Rentergem, 'Al-Shabaab in Mozambique: Taking Stock of an Insurgency Under Cover' *Egmont Policy Brief 281* (June 2022) <www.egmontinstitute.be/app/uploads/2022/06/PB-281-Tom-VR_Al-Shabab-in-Mozambique.pdf?type=pdf>.
Tore Refslund Hamming, 'The Islamic State in Mozambique' *Lawfare Blog* (24 January 2021).
UN Doc. A/57/37.
UN Doc. A/C.6/76/L.11 (10 November 2021).
UNGA Res. A/RES/49/60 (17 February 1995).
UNGA Res. A/RES/77/113 (20 December 2022).
UNGA Res. A/RES/3034 (18 December 1972).
UN News, 'Five Years of Violence in Northern Mozambique Has Forced Nearly a Million to Flee' (4 October 2022) <https://news.un.org/en/story/2022/10/1129217>.
UNODC, 'UNODC Supports Mozambican Authorities to Tackle Terrorism and Its Financing in the Country' <www.unodc.org/southernafrica/en/aml/terrorism.html>.
UNTC, 'International Convention for the Suppression of Acts of Nuclear Terrorism' <https://treaties.un.org/pages/ViewDetailsIII.aspx?src=TREATY&mtdsg_no=XVIII-15&chapter=18&Temp=mtdsg3&clang=_en>.

U.S. Department of State, 'State Department Terrorist Designations of ISIS Affiliates and Leaders in the Democratic Republic of the Congo and Mozambique' (10 March 2021) <www.state.gov/state-department-terrorist-designations-of-isis-affiliates-and-leaders-in-the-democratic-republic-of-the-congo-and-mozambique/>.

U.S. Department of State, Bureau of Counterterrorism, 'Country Reports on Terrorism 2021: Mozambique' <www.state.gov/reports/country-reports-on-terrorism-2021/mozambique/>.

Vienna Convention on the Law of Treaties (1969) <https://treaties.un.org/Pages/showDetails.aspx?objid=080000028003902f&clang=_en>.

8 Sexual and gender-based violence in Cabo Delgado

Implications for international humanitarian law and international criminal law

Emma Charlene Lubaale and Brenda Akia

8.1 Introduction

Cabo Delgado, a northern province of Mozambique, has been recently prominent for a conflict dating back to 2017 but, also, for acts of violence against women. Various rights groups, including Human Rights Watch, Amnesty International, the United Nations Children's Fund (UNICEF) and the United Nations High Commissioner for Refugees, report that the position of women in this conflict is at the extreme on a vulnerability continuum.[1] There is evidence of women being raped, forced marriage and human trafficking during this conflict.[2] The reports also reveal that sexual slavery, forced labour and physical and economic violence are pervasive.[3] There is evidence that Islamist armed groups use hundreds of kidnapped women as sex slaves and force them into marriages.[4] A recent report indicates that between 2018 and 2021 these Islamist armed groups kidnapped and enslaved over 600 women during the attacks in Cabo Delgado.[5] These armed groups have targeted and forced women to marry members of the groups. Many of the kidnapped and abducted women have been sexually abused and enslaved, and some have been sold to foreign fighters at prices ranging from US$600 to US$1 800.[6] In an interview, a 34-year-old male former abductee declared that the leaders of the Islamist armed group forced him to identify and abduct young and good-looking women from the region of Cabo Delgado.[7] These women were abducted to provide sexual services and to perform chores for Islamist armed group members returning from military operations.[8] Reports reveal that women who fail to cooperate are punished through being flogged, deprived of food, detained, tortured and, in some instances, killed.[9]

Acts committed against women in Cabo Delgado constitute rape, forced marriage, sexual slavery, human trafficking and forced labour. Until now there has been no analysis on the implications of these occurrences for international humanitarian law (IHL). This neglect leaves unresolved, the issue whether IHL prohibits the various forms of Sexual and Gender-based Violence (SGBV) in Cabo Delgado. Moreover, although the atrocities are largely committed by organised armed groups, there hasn't been an analysis of the prospects of holding the perpetrators criminally responsible in terms of international criminal law (ICL), individually or in the form of command responsibility.

DOI: 10.4324/9781003317647-10

The Rome Statute of the International Criminal Court (ICC Statute) provides an enforcement platform for the prosecution of crimes of sexual violence that amount to violations of international humanitarian law in article 8. Mozambique has signed but not ratified the ICC Statute,[10] thus, posing challenges in prosecuting perpetrators for the crimes committed in Cabo Delgado. In light of these unresolved issues, the primary aim in this chapter is to assess whether the sexual and gender-based atrocities in Cabo Delgado are prohibited under Common Article 3 of the Geneva Conventions and Additional Protocol II.[11] If the foregoing are positively resolved, a secondary aim is to determine whether the perpetrators can be held criminally responsible in terms of ICL.

8.2 Acts of sexual and gender-based violence in Cabo Delgado and international humanitarian law

During a non-international armed conflict (NIAC) each party to the conflict is bound to adhere to various humanitarian provisions, at a minimum. These provisions are entrenched in Article 3 common to all the Four Geneva Conventions: 'As soon as Common Article 3 applies, the obligation to respect its provisions is automatic and absolute for State and non-State Parties to the conflict alike'.[12] Common Article 3 has been developed and supplemented by Additional Protocol II of 1977 and together they constitute the yardstick by which parties to a NIAC are to measure their engagement during wartime. In this section, Article 3 Common to the Four Geneva Conventions and Additional Protocol II are analysed to assess whether, explicitly or by interpretation, they prohibit the various SGBV acts committed during the conflict in Cabo Delgado.

8.2.1 Common Article 3(1)(a): torture and SGBV in Cabo Delgado

In terms of Article 3(1)(a) Common to all Geneva Conventions torture is a prohibited act.[13] Torture along with other listed acts 'are and shall remain prohibited',[14] which means that the 'prohibitions are absolute and admit no exception'.[15] The provision does not provide meaning in the use of the term 'torture'. In terms of the ICRC Commentary, 'torture' in comparison to 'cruel treatment' entails a higher threshold of pain or suffering which is severe and which results from a specific purpose or motivation.[16] For the purposes of IHL the International Criminal Tribunal for the former Yugoslavia (ICTY) defines torture as the

> intentional infliction, by act or omission, of severe pain or suffering, whether physical or mental, for such purposes as to obtain information or a confession, to punish, intimidate or coerce the victim or a third person, or to discriminate, on any ground, against the victim or a third person.[17]

In addition, a good faith interpretation envisaged by article 31(1) of the Vienna Convention of the Law of Treaties (VCLT) provides a basis for giving meaningful content to the term.[18] Article 31(1) of the VCLT envisages recourse to the ordinary meaning of words to give content to provisions and the wording of treaties. In its ordinary sense 'torture' means 'the action or practice of inflicting severe pain or suffering on someone as a punishment or in order to force them to do or say something'.[19] Taking this ordinary meaning into account, it is plausible to conclude that the acts of SGBV in Cabo Delgado are prohibited by article 3(1)(a); notably, rape, trafficking for sexual exploitation, forced marriage and sexual slavery. In the forthcoming paragraphs, the following acts of SGBV will be considered to determine whether these acts constitute torture for purposes of Common Article 3(1)(a). Rape has been defined as follows:

1 The perpetrator invaded the body of a person by conduct resulting in penetration, however slight, of any part of the body of the victim or of the perpetrator with a sexual organ, or of the anal or genital opening of the victim with any object or any other part of the body.
2 The invasion was committed by force, or by threat of force or coercion, such as that caused by fear of violence, duress, detention, psychological oppression or abuse of power, against such person or another person, or by taking advantage of a coercive environment, or the invasion was committed against a person incapable of giving genuine consent.[20]

The act of penetrating the body of a person, in and of itself, amounts to torture provided it meets the severity threshold of torture, which is severe pain or suffering. The same is to be said of other SGBV acts, such as trafficking for sexual exploitation. As noted in the introduction, some of the abducted women have been sold to foreign fighters for a price ranging from US$600 to US$1 800, which is tantamount to trafficking for sexual exploitation. Trafficking of this nature for sexual exploitation amounts to torture if it meets the threshold of severe pain and suffering.

Reports are abound of the deplorable circumstances and conditions under which trafficked women live. They are tortured, raped, subjected to forced labour, starved and enslaved.[21] The pain inflicted on them, psychological or physical, often is intended to force them to engage in sexual conduct, labour, prostitution and all forms of conduct against their will. These conditions fit squarely within the definition of torture – 'the action or practice of inflicting severe pain or suffering on someone as a punishment or in order to force them to do or say something'.

It has been reported that forced marriage is rampant during the conflict in Cabo Delgado. Islamist armed groups are identified as the primary culprits. Forced marriage refers to a situation where an individual is forced to marry another person through threat, the use of physical violence or mental abuse.[22] In the Cabo Delgado conflict forced wives, categorised according to age and beauty, reportedly are distributed among fighters based on merit and rank;[23] higher-ranking fighters enjoy the privilege of choosing their wives, while lower-ranking officers are merely assigned.[24] Once the women are forcibly married, the acts of sexual violence, including rape, reportedly continue, resulting in forced pregnancies, forced childbearing and forced parenthood.[25] In *The Prosecutor v Dominic Ongwen* case (*Ongwen*) Trial Chamber of the International Tribunal for Rwanda described the atrocity of forced marriage as follows:

'The harm suffered from forced marriage can consist of being ostracised from the community, mental trauma, the serious attack on the victim's dignity, and the deprivation of the victim's fundamental rights to choose his other spouse'.[26] The Chamber added: 'Beyond its illegality, [forced marriage also has] social, ethical and even religious effects which have a serious impact on the victim's physical and psychological well-being'.[27] The prosecution in the *Ongwen* case alludes to this heinous act in the statement that to the armed group's women are

> spoils of war, awarded as prizes without any more say in the matter than if they had been animals or inanimate objects . . . [They were] regarded . . . as . . . possessions: sometimes valued, but ultimately disposable and replaceable.[28]

From these descriptions of forced marriage, it is evident, in accordance with the definition of torture, that severe pain and suffering are integral to the act of forced marriage and are intended to keep women in forced marriages.

Sexual slavery is another atrocity that women experience during the Cabo Delgado conflict. It is described as follows:

1 The perpetrator exercised any or all of the powers attaching to the right of ownership over one or more persons, such as by purchasing, selling, lending or bartering such a person or persons or by imposing on them a similar deprivation of liberty.
2 The perpetrator caused such person or persons to engage in one or more acts of a sexual nature.[29]

Members of the armed groups exercise ownership over women, who are forced into marriage.[30] The women are deprived of their liberty and, as noted, some are sold to foreign fighters at a price. These activities involve engagement in acts of a sexual nature. Reports revealed that women who resist forceful entry into marriage, engaging in conduct of a sexual nature or being sold to foreign fighters, are subjected to severe flogging, detention, rape and murder.[31] Effectively, these women are exploited in forced marriages and forced labour; they have been trafficked and subjected to forms of sexual exploitation resulting in severe pain and suffering.

On the above analysis, the forms of SGBV in Cabo Delgado fall within the ambit of torture. This view is supported in the decisions of various international criminal tribunals, some of which establish a nexus between acts of gender-based violence and torture. In *Prosecutor v Delalić and Others* the Trial Chamber of the ICTY noted:

> Rape causes severe pain and suffering both physical and psychological . . . it is difficult to envisage circumstances where in which rape by, or at the instigation of a public official . . . could be considered as occurring for a purpose that does not, in some way, involve punishment, coercion, discrimination or intimidation.[32]

The Chamber concluded: 'Whenever rape and other forms of sexual violence meet the aforementioned criteria, then they shall constitute torture, in the same manner as any other acts that meet these criteria'.[33] Similarly, in the *Brđanin* Trial Judgment, the ICTY concluded:

> Some acts, like rape, appear by definition to meet the severity threshold. Like torture, rape is a violation of personal dignity and is used for such purposes as intimidation, degradation, humiliation and discrimination, punishment, control or destruction of a person. Severe pain or suffering, as required by the definition of the crime of torture, can be said to be established once rape has been proved, since the act of rape necessarily implies such pain or suffering.[34]

On these grounds it is concluded that the various acts of SGBV in Cabo Delgado constitute torture and, accordingly, that Common Article 3(1)(a) covers SGBV.

8.2.2 Common Article 3(1)(a): cruel treatment and SGBV in Cabo Delgado

Common Article 3 also prohibits cruel treatment. None of the four Geneva Conventions and the Additional Protocols has defined 'cruel treatment'. However, as previously noted, article 31 of the VCLT recognises the ordinary meaning accorded words as giving meaningful content to treaty provisions. 'Cruel treatment' refers to 'the intentional infliction of severe physical or mental pain or suffering upon a person'.[35] In line with the ordinary meaning of 'cruel treatment', the ICTY Trial Chamber in *The Prosecutor v Delalić and others*[36] defined it as 'treatment which causes serious mental or physical suffering or constitutes a serious attack upon human dignity, which is equivalent to the offence of inhuman treatment in the framework of the grave breaches provisions of the Geneva Conventions'.

Based on the above definition, an act constitutes cruel treatment if it causes mental or physical pain or suffering. Unlike in the definition of torture where pain and suffering are for purposes of forcing an individual to do or say something, this is not a requirement to establish cruel treatment, suggesting the threshold for proving cruel treatment is somewhat lower than for torture.[37] Nevertheless, Common Article 3 prohibits cruel treatment in absolute terms. Moreover, from the definition of cruel treatment in the *Delalić* case above, 'cruel treatment' and 'inhuman treatment' are used synonymously. A similar approach is evident in the Elements of Crime for the ICC. Notably, in defining 'inhuman treatment', the definition is identical to that for 'cruel treatment': 'The perpetrator inflicted severe physical or mental pain or suffering upon one or more persons'.[38]

The detailed unpacking of various categories of SGBV in Cabo Delgado in the preceding part on torture leads to the conclusion the acts of SGBV during the Cabo Delgado conflict constitute cruel treatment in accordance with Common Article 3(1)(a). Notably, abducting women, enslaving them, exercising ownership over them, selling them to foreign fighters as forced wives, beating and flogging them for failing to meet the sexual demands of fighters or performing forced labour are acts that cause physical and mental pain. They are an attack on the dignity of women. If the acts of forced marriage, the trafficking of women, sexual slavery, rape and forced labour are measured against the definition of cruel treatment, the logical conclusion is that they constitute cruel treatment. Although Common Article 3 does not explicitly mention any of the foregoing acts committed against women in Cabo Delgado, a good faith interpretation of the provision justifies the conclusion that they fall within the definition of cruel treatment.

8.2.3 Article 4(2)(e) of Additional Protocol II and SGBV in Cabo Delgado

Both Common Article 3(1)(c) and article 4(2)(e) of Additional Protocol II prohibit 'outrages upon personal dignity, in particular humiliating and degrading treatment'. However, the provision in Additional Protocol II is more elaborate in that it provides a broader catalogue of acts constituting outrage upon personal dignity. Thus, for this purpose, the provision in Additional Protocol II will be discussed since it supplements and develops the provision in Common Article 3. Additional Protocol II applies to NIACs 'which take place in the territory of a High Contracting Party between its armed forces and dissident armed forces or other organised armed groups which, under responsible command, exercise such control over a part of its territory as to enable them to carry out sustained and concerted military operations and to implement this Protocol'.[39] As has been shown by Bakare and Ojedokun in Chapter 6, the conflict in Cabo Delgado, arguably, is classified as a NIAC, thus meeting the foregoing threshold. In terms of article 4(2)(e) of Additional Protocol II, the following acts are prohibited during NIACs: 'outrages upon personal dignity, in particular humiliating and degrading treatment, rape, enforced prostitution and any form of indecent assault'.[40]

As noted, various acts, including rape, enforced prostitution and indecent assault, are pervasive during the Cabo Delgado conflict. These acts are explicitly prohibited in article 4(2)(e) of Additional Protocol II and, thus, it may be concluded that they are prohibited under IHL. However, there are acts that constitute SGBV that are not mentioned explicitly, such as forced marriage, human trafficking and forced pregnancy. Does an interpretation of article 4(2)(e), the phrase 'humiliating and degrading treatment', especially, adequately cover these unmentioned acts? The starting point to answer this question is to unpack the meaning of the notion of 'humiliating and degrading treatment'.

Additional Protocol II does not provide a definition of the term. Again, in accordance with article 31 of the VCLT, which makes provision for giving the ordinary meaning to words used in treaties, the ordinary meaning is invoked to give meaningful content. To degrade people is to cause them 'to feel that they have no value'.[41] The acts of trafficking, causing them to marry against their will and so forth, certainly amount to treating women and girls as though they have no value. To humiliate people is to make them 'feel ashamed or stupid'.[42] The act of using force, fraud or coercion to get women and girls to engage in activities such as labour, commercial sex or sexual slavery, undoubtedly creates feelings of shame and stupidity. The same can be said of forced marriage: To enter into a marriage that is not an expression of full and free consent creates feelings of shame and stupidity as though they have no mind of their own in their decisions. On this interpretation it can be concluded that the acts committed in Cabo Delgado, such as forced marriage and human trafficking, not mentioned explicitly under article 4(2)(e), fall within the ambit of 'humiliating and degrading treatment' and, therefore, are prohibited under IHL.

8.2.4 Article 4(2)(f) of Additional Protocol II and SGBV in Cabo Delgado

Article 4(2)(f) of Additional Protocol II prohibits 'slavery and the slave trade in all their forms'. Slavery constitutes 'the activity of legally owning other people who are forced to work for or obey you'.[43] Ownership of a person is at the heart of this definition and a lack of freedom/liberty of the person owned. Acts including forced marriage, human trafficking and kidnapping may not constitute ownership in the strict sense of the word. The Islamist armed groups in Cabo Delgado have dealt with abducted women as though they own them, even offering them for sale to foreign fighters. The ICC Elements of Crime codify that the act of selling a person is a factor that determines if a perpetrator exercises ownership of a person.[44] If selling a person is considered a factor proving ownership, it may be concluded that by offering women for sale they are subjected to slavery.

Regarding forced marriage, especially, the perpetrators exercise a form of control over forced wives akin to ownership. Moreover, the act of depriving a person of liberty has been interpreted to constitute one way by which a perpetrator exercises ownership of a person.[45] Forced wives have no freedom and an attempt to exercise freedom, for example through attempted escape, incurs penalties, including beating, flogging, torture or even death. Suffice it to note that acts constituting human trafficking and forced marriage are much broader than slavery, though aspects of slavery are subsumed under these acts. The ICRC has addressed 'slavery and the slave trade in all their forms' and in doing so identifies 'the purchase of wives' as a form of slavery.[46]

To conclude, IHL treaties are often criticised for failing to deal strongly with SGBV.[47] These treaties do not mention several acts of SGBV pervasive in conflict situations, including those reported in Cabo Delgado. Because of this silence it may be argued that under IHL SGBV in Cabo Delgado is not prohibited. Although the criticism levelled against these treaties holds weight and cannot easily be dismissed, the analysis in this part indicates that the criticism is overstated. Notably, SGBV that takes the form of rape, enforced prostitution and indecent assault is explicitly prohibited. The catalogue of acts that constitute SGBV could and should be more broadly defined, but an interpretation in good faith of the prohibitions that are explicitly mentioned, such as torture, cruel treatment and slavery, creates an entry point by which acts of SGBV not mentioned can be prohibited. The downside to consideration based on interpretation arises from discretion being exercised in interpreting provisions of IHL treaties where interpretation may not always cover all acts of SGBV perpetrated during conflict. Moreover, a convergence of IHL and ICL in the context of criminal accountability results in a further constraint on interpretation because the principle of legality, strongly entrenched in ICL, not only requires crimes to be interpreted strictly but also prohibits the extension of crimes (prohibited acts) by analogy.[48]

8.3 Sexual violence crimes committed in Cabo Delgado: the nexus between IHL and ICL for purposes of criminal accountability

The earlier parts have found that rape, enforced prostitution and other forms of sexual violence committed against civilians in Cabo Delgado by armed groups are prohibited under IHL. This finding has three major implications. First, perpetrators of crimes of sexual violence committed against civilians can be prosecuted for serious violations of IHL. The second implication is that all persons, including heads of state and persons acting in an official capacity, who participate in the planning, preparation or execution of the crimes as serious violations of IHL can be held individually criminally responsible in their individual capacity or through command responsibility. Third, there is reinforcement of responsible command embodied in IHL,[49] which includes the legal duty of a military commander and civilian superior to comply with the laws of war, including preventing, punishing or reporting crimes committed in armed conflict and to effectively supervise their subordinates' compliance.[50]

These three implications manifest an interplay between ICL and IHL regarding crimes of sexual violence committed during armed conflict. The criminalisation of sexual violence crimes as war crimes in the statutes of the ICTY, ICTR and ICC provides a legal basis for the prosecution of sexual violence crimes as war crimes. For example, article 5(g) of the ICTY Statute lists rape as a crime against humanity and gives the ICTY Tribunal the legal basis to prosecute crimes amounting to grave breaches of the Geneva Conventions of 12 August 1949 and a violation of the laws or customs of war pursuant to articles 2 and 3 of the ICTY Statute.[51] These provisions are based on IHL instruments, namely, the four Geneva Conventions of 1949[52] and the two Additional Protocols.[53] According to ICTY jurisprudence, what ultimately distinguishes a war crime from a purely domestic offence is the fact that a war crime is shaped by or dependent upon the environment – the armed conflict – in which it is committed.[54] The sexual violence crimes need not have been planned or supported by some form of policy and the armed conflict need not have been causal to the commission of the crime.[55] However, the existence of an armed conflict must, at a minimum, have played a substantial part in the perpetrator's ability to commit a crime, his decision to commit it, the manner in which it was committed or the purpose for which it was committed.[56] The determination of what constitutes a war crime, therefore, is dependent on the laws and customs of war at the time when an act charged in an indictment was committed.[57]

To prosecute and secure a conviction for sexual violence crimes as war crimes, the prosecution has to show that the sexual violence crimes meet the common elements of war crimes recognised under the ICTY Statute, that is, the sexual violence crimes (i) were closely linked to the armed conflict; (ii) were directed against any civilian population; and (iii) that the accused commander knew or had reason to know of the commission of the sexual violence crime.[58]

Once the common elements of war crimes are met, article 7 of the ICTY Statute, which provides for individual criminal responsibility, including commission, command responsibility, planning, instigation, ordering, committing or otherwise aiding and abetting, is applied to hold an accused criminally responsible. In the *Čelebići camp* case, the prosecutor charged Zdravko Mucic, the camp commander, Zejnil Delalić, later a commander in the Bosnian army, and Hazim Delić, a deputy commander[59] under command responsibility pursuant to article 7(3) for crimes of sexual violence, such as rape committed by the guards at Čelebići prison camp.[60]

To determine criminal liability for sexual violence crimes pursuant to article 7(3), the ICTY prosecution had to prove the legal elements of command responsibility to establish a link between those in command and the sexual violence crimes committed by subordinates. That is, a superior–subordinate relationship had to be established as a legal element of command responsibility, proving that (i) the accused commander was senior to the perpetrators in a formal or informal hierarchy (*de jure* or *de facto* superior) and that the accused commander had effective control (the material ability to prevent or punish the commission of crimes) over his or her subordinates;[61] (ii) the commander (a) knew or (b) had reason to know that his or her subordinate was committing a crime or had done so;[62] and (iii) the commander failed to take the necessary and reasonable measures to (a) prevent the acts or (b) punish the perpetrators thereof.[63] Based on an evaluation of the legal elements, only Mucic was found criminally responsible for rape based on his role as a *de facto* commander for failing to prevent, stop or punish his subordinates for committing sex crimes in the Čelebići prison camp.[64] If a decision is made to prosecute the sexual violence crimes committed in Cabo Delgado, the Čelebići prison camp case and other ICTY jurisprudence on sexual violence crimes offer precedence on the legal principles surrounding their prosecution to ensure that victims get justice.

The ICTR Statute in article 4 expressly lists rape, enforced prostitution and any form of indecent assault as war crimes amounting to violations of Article 3 Common to the Geneva Conventions and of Additional Protocol II. Based on the examination of the ICTR jurisprudence, for an accused to be prosecuted and held criminally responsible for sexual violence crimes the prosecution has to show that the sexual violence crimes meet the common elements of war crimes recognised under the ICTR Statute, that is, that the sexual violence crimes (i) were closely linked to the armed conflict; (ii) were directed against any civilian population; and (iii) that the accused commander knew or had reason to know of the commission of the crime.[65] To hold an accused criminally responsible for sexual violence crimes, the judges relied on either article 6(1) or (3) of the ICTR Statute that provides for individual criminal responsibility, including command responsibility, planning, instigation, ordering, committing or otherwise aiding and abetting and enabled them to prosecute and adjudicate sexual violence crimes as grave breaches and serious violations of IHL and convict accused persons for sexual violence crimes as war crimes.

A significant case in the prosecution of sexual violence crimes at the ICTR that provides precedence for the prosecution of sexual violence crimes committed in Cabo Delgado is that of *Prosecutor v Jean Paul Akayesu*. Jean Paul Akayesu was *bourgmestre* of Taba commune from April 1993 until June 1994. He was charged with sexual violence crimes as crimes against humanity, genocide and violations of Article 3 Common to the Geneva Conventions and of article 4(2)(e) of Additional Protocol II (outrage upon personal dignity, in particular rape, degrading and humiliating treatment and indecent assault).[66] *Akayesu* is the first case under international criminal law to find that sexual violence crimes such as rape can amount to crimes against humanity, genocide, torture and causing serious bodily and mental harm, as well as a violation of personal dignity.[67] The *Akayesu* case also is the first to define rape under international criminal law.[68] Although there is no commonly accepted definition of rape, variations in the form of rape may include acts that involve the insertion of objects and/or the use of bodily orifices not considered to be intrinsically sexual.[69] In the view of the Tribunal, thrusting a piece of wood into the sexual organs of a woman as she lay dying constituted an act of rape.[70] Consequently, sexual violence crimes committed in Cabo Delgado may be found to amount to acts of torture, causing serious bodily and mental harm and a violation of personal dignity.

In respect of prosecution under the ICC, it presents a challenge because Mozambique has signed but not ratified the ICC Statute.[71] This means that, should the avenue of prosecution be taken into consideration, the solution available is to either equip the domestic courts in Mozambique to prosecute sexual violence crimes that amount to crimes under international humanitarian law, establish an international criminal tribunal or hybrid tribunal to exclusively prosecute the sexual violence crimes committed in Cabo Delgado or for the government of Mozambique to ratify the ICC Statute to give the ICC jurisdiction to prosecute the sexual violence crimes committed in Cabo Delgado.

If the sexual violence crimes committed in Cabo Delgado are prosecuted by domestic courts or an established international tribunal, the ICC Statute and the ICC jurisprudence on sexual violence crimes provide significant guidance and precedence relating to the legal principles and modes of criminal responsibility of prosecuting sexual violence crimes to the courts that prosecute the sexual violence crimes committed in Cabo Delgado. ICC jurisprudence and Statute that reinforce a link between IHL and ICL which creates the ICC as an enforcement platform for the ICC to adjudicate grave breaches and serious violations of international humanitarian law, including sexual violence crimes,[72] has established clear precedence on the prosecution of sexual violence crimes under ICL. For example, under article 8 of the ICC Statute, war crimes that constitute grave breaches of the Geneva Convention of 12 August 1949, including forced pregnancy, rape, sexual slavery, enforced prostitution, enforced sterilisation or any other form of sexual violence also constituting a grave breach of the Geneva Conventions committed against persons protected under the Geneva Convention are criminalised. Additionally, articles 25 and 28 of the ICC Statute provide for individual criminal responsibility, including commission, ordering, soliciting, inducing and commanding responsibility that provide avenues through which individuals shall be held individually criminally responsible for sexual violence crimes such as war crimes.

These ICC provisions on sexual violence crimes as war crimes led to the ICC's first and second convictions on sexual violence crimes in the cases of Bosco Ntaganda in

July 2019[73] and Dominic Ongwen,[74] for sexual violence crimes as war crimes under ICL. In *Prosecutor v Bosco Ntaganda*, Ntaganda was charged with sexual violence crimes, such as rape and sexual slavery.[75] To hold Ntaganda criminally responsible for sexual violence crimes as war crimes, the ICC found that the rape and sexual slavery of the victims were associated with a non-international armed conflict and, therefore, fulfilled the requisite requirement of a nexus.[76] The Court added that provided there is a nexus in relation to the armed conflict, then rape and sexual slavery against any person is prohibited and, therefore, that members of the same armed force are not *per se* excluded as potential victims of the war crimes of rape and sexual slavery under article 8(2)(e)(vi).[77] The ICC found Bosco Ntaganda criminally liable for war crimes of rape and sexual slavery committed in Ituri province in Eastern Congo between 2002 and 2003.[78] In *Prosecutor v Dominic Ongwen*, Ongwen was charged with 70 counts of crimes against humanity and war crimes, including sexual violence crimes of rape, forced marriage, torture, sexual slavery, forced pregnancy and outrages upon personal dignity, committed against civilians and children under 15 years of age in Northern Uganda between 1 July 2002 and 31 December 2005.[79] The Trial Chamber found Ongwen individually criminally responsible for sexual violence crimes as war crimes pursuant to article 8(2) of the ICC Statute.[80] Dominic Ongwen appealed his conviction and the judgement will be delivered in due course.

Perpetrators of sexual violence crimes in Cabo Delgado can be prosecuted pursuant to command responsibility for the sexual violence crimes committed by their subordinates. The recognition of command responsibility in article 28 of the ICC Statute demonstrates an interplay between ICL and IHL regarding holding military commanders or civilian superiors criminally responsible for sexual violence crimes as war crimes pursuant to command responsibility.[81] Command responsibility places legal obligations on commanders to take reasonable and necessary steps to prevent and suppress the commission of crimes by persons under their command or to report to competent authorities if the crimes are committed.[82] Command responsibility is a well-established norm of customary and conventional international law.[83] This means that it can be applied to impute criminal responsibility to the military commanders or civilian superiors in the armed conflict in Cabo Delgado for sexual violence crimes committed by their subordinates.

As an IHL construct, command responsibility provides for responsible command and the responsibility of commanders by virtue of the powers of control they exercise over their subordinates.[84] The law of war imposes, on a military officer in a position of command, an affirmative duty to take such steps as are within his power and appropriate to the circumstances to control those under his command for the prevention of acts that are violations of the law of war.[85] This means that IHL presupposes that violations of the law of war are to be avoided through the control of the operations of war by commanders who to some extent are responsible for the acts of their subordinates.[86] Therefore, if a commander fails in his duty recognised under IHL to prevent, repress and punish subordinates for the commission of sexual violence crimes, the failure translates into a prosecutorial strategy for holding military commanders or civilian superiors criminally responsible under ICL.[87] At the ICC the definition of command responsibility comprising the legal elements that must be proved to hold a military commander or civilian superior criminally responsible are (i) the existence of a superior–subordinate relationship (the hierarchical relationship, whether military or civilian); (ii) effective command and control and effective authority and control; (iii) the superior's violations of the duty to act, which includes (a) the failure to exercise control properly over the subordinates and (b) the failure to adopt reasonable and necessary measures to prevent, repress or to submit the crimes to the competent authorities; (iv) the causal nexus between the superior's omission and the crime committed by the subordinate; and, in relation to knowledge, (v) that the military commander or civilian superior had knowledge of the crimes; (vi) that the military commander should have known of the crimes; and (vii) that the civilian superior consciously disregarded information that clearly indicated the perpetration of crimes.[88]

8.4 Conclusion

This chapter set out to determine whether under IHL the sexual violence crimes committed in Cabo Delgado are prohibited and, second, if ICL ensures accountability for these crimes. The analysis establishes that IHL prohibits these crimes, either explicitly or by interpretation. Also, a nexus is established between IHL and ICL. Based on this finding, it may be argued that under ICL regulations relating to command responsibility and modes of individual criminal responsibility, such as ordering, commission, instigation, aiding and abetting, soliciting, inducing and assisting, there are options for prosecuting the mass criminality of the sexual violence crimes and giving victims justice for crimes committed in Cabo Delgado. These modes of liability are critical because, otherwise, it will be impossible to prosecute all the perpetrators of sexual violence crimes committed in Cabo Delgado. Moreover, the jurisprudence of international criminal courts and tribunals, such as the ICTY, ICTR and the ICC, that reinforce the link between ICL and IHL offers examples of precedence to prosecutors and judges on how effectively to prosecute the sexual violence crimes committed in Cabo Delgado.

Mozambique has signed but has not ratified the ICC Statute. This situation poses a challenge for the prosecution by the ICC of the sexual violence crimes committed in Cabo Delgado. Therefore, there is a recommendation that to ensure accountability for the sexual violence crimes in Cabo Delgado, the government of Mozambique should ratify the ICC Statute giving the ICC jurisdiction to investigate and prosecute the sexual violence crimes. A further recommendation is that the government of Mozambique prosecute the perpetrators of the sexual violence crimes committed in Cabo Delgado in its domestic courts since it bears the primary responsibility to ensure that there is accountability for international crimes.[89]

Notes

1 Amnesty International, 'Mozambique 2021' <www.amnesty.org/en/location/africa/southern-africa/mozambique/report-mozambique/>; Amnesty International, 'Mozambique: Cabo Delgado Conflict Country's "Most Critical" Human Rights Situation' (29 March 2022); Human Rights Watch, 'Mozambique Events of 2021'; UNICEF, 'UNICEF

Statement on Abduction of Minors in Cabo Delgado' (5 October 2022); UNICEF, 'Mozambique Humanitarian Situation Report No 3' (31 March 2022) 1–10; UNHCR, 'Gender-Based Violence Response Cabo Delgado, Northern Mozambique' (April 2022); Human Rights Watch, 'Cabo Delgado: 600 Women, Girls Kidnapped Since 2018, Some Sold to Foreign Fighters' *Club of Mozambique* (8 December 2021); Human Rights Watch, 'Mozambique: Hundreds of Women, Girls Abducted' (7 December 2021).

2 UNHCR, 'Gender-Based Violence Response Cabo Delgado, Northern Mozambique' (April 2022).

3 Ibid.

4 Human Rights Watch, 'Mozambique Events of 2021'.

5 Human Rights Watch, 'Cabo Delgado' (n 1).

6 Ibid.

7 Human Rights Watch, 'Mozambique: Hundreds of Women, Girls Abducted' (7 December 2021).

8 Ibid.

9 Ibid.

10 About the ICC: State parties to the ICC <www.aba-icc.org/about-the-icc/states-parties-to-the-icc/>. Mozambique signed the ICC Statute on 20 December 2000 but has not ratified it.

11 Protocol Additional to the Geneva Conventions of 12 August 1949, and Relating to the Protection of Victims of Non-International Armed Conflicts (Protocol II) (adopted 8 June 1977, entered into force 7 December 1978) 1125 UNTS 609 (Additional Protocol II).

12 International Committee of the Red Cross, 'Commentary of 2020 Article 3: Conflicts Not of An International Character', para 538 (ICRC 2020 Commentary).

13 See article 3 of all four Geneva Conventions: Geneva Convention (I) for the Amelioration of the Condition of the Wounded and Sick in Armed Forces in the Field (adopted 12 August 1949, entered into force 21 October 1950) 75 UNTS 31; Geneva Convention (II) for the Amelioration of the Condition of Wounded, Sick and Shipwrecked Members of Armed Forces at Sea (adopted 12 August 1949, entered into force 21 October 1950) 75 UNTS 85; Geneva Convention (III) relative to the Treatment of Prisoners of War (adopted 12 August 1949, entered into force 21 October 1950) 75 UNTS 135; Geneva Convention (IV) relative to the Protection of Civilian Persons in Time of War (adopted 12 August 1949, entered into force 21 October 1950) 75 UNTS 287.

14 Common Article 3 (n 13).

15 ICRC 2020 Commentary (n 12) para 618.

16 ICRC 2020 Commentary para 664.

17 ICTY, *Prosecutor v Dragoljub Kunarac and Others*, Case No IT-96–23&23/1 (Appeals Chamber), 12 June 2002, para 497.

18 Article 31(1), Vienna Convention on the Law of Treaties (adopted 23 May 1969, entered into force 27 January 1980) 1155 UNTS 331 (VCLT).

19 Definitions from *Oxford Languages*, 'Torture' <https://languages.oup.com/google-dictionary-en/>.

20 Article 7(1)(g)-1 and article 8(2)(b)(xxii)-1, ICC Elements of Crime.

21 United Nations Women, 'Trafficked: Three Survivors of Human Trafficking Share Their Stories' (29 July 2019).

22 ICC, *The Prosecutor v Dominic Ongwen*, Trial Chamber IX, Case No ICC-02/04–01/15, 4 February 2021 (*Ongwen* case) para 2748.

23 Human Rights Watch, 'Mozambique: Hundreds of Women, Girls Abducted' (7 December 2021); Human Rights Watch, 'Cabo Delgado' (n 1).

24 Ibid.

25 Ibid.

26 *Ongwen* case (n 22) para 2749.

27 *Ongwen* case (n 22) para 2748.

28 *Ongwen* case (n 22) Prosecution's Pre-Trial Brief, paras 500–501.
29 Article 8(2)(b)(xxii)-2 ICC Elements of Crime. See also *Prosecutor v Kunarac, Kovac and Vukovic*, Trial Chamber, Judgment, Case No IT96–23-T and 23/1, especially para 542. It was noted that 'indications of enslavement include . . . control and ownership; the restriction or control of an individual's autonomy . . . freedom of movement . . . the accruing of some gain to the perpetrator. The consent . . . is often rendered impossible by . . . the threat or use of force or other forms of coercion; the fear of violence, deception or false promises . . . captivity, psychological oppression'.
30 UNICEF, 'Mozambique Humanitarian Situation Report No 3' (31 March 2022); UNHCR, 'Gender-Based Violence Response Cabo Delgado, Northern Mozambique' (April 2022).
31 Human Rights Watch, 'Mozambique: Hundreds of Women, Girls Abducted' (7 December 2021).
32 *Prosecutor v Delalić & Others* Judgment of 16 November 1998, Case IT-96–21 (*Celebici* case) para 495.
33 Ibid, para 496.
34 *Brđanin* Trial Judgment, ICTY (2004) para 485.
35 Vocabularly.com, 'Inhuman Treatment' <www.vocabulary.com/dictionary/inhuman%20 treatment>.
36 ICTY, *Delalić* Trial Judgment, 1998 para 551. See also *Naletilić and Martinović* Trial Judgment, 2003, para 246; *Kordić and Čerkez* Trial Judgment, 2001 para 256; *Blaškić* Trial Judgment, 2000 paras 154–155; *Limaj* Trial Judgment, 2005 para 231; *Orić* Trial Judgment, 2006 para 351; *Haradinaj* Trial Judgment, 2008 para 126; *Mrkšić* Trial Judgment, 2007 para 514; *Lukić and Lukić* Trial Judgment, 2009 para 957; and *Tolimir* Trial Judgment, 2012 para 853.
37 ICRC 2020 Commentary, paras 651 and 665. See also ICTY *Delalić* Trial Judgment, 1998 para 551, where cruel treatment was defined as 'treatment which causes serious mental or physical suffering or constitutes a serious attack upon human dignity, which is equivalent to the offence of inhuman treatment in the framework of the grave breaches provisions of the Geneva Conventions'.
38 Articles 8(2)(a)(ii)-2, War crime of inhuman treatment, ICC Elements of Crimes.
39 Additional Protocol II (n 10).
40 Ibid, article 4(2)(e).
41 *Cambridge Online Dictionary*, 'degrade' <https://dictionary.cambridge.org/dictionary/english/degrading>.
42 *Oxford Learner's Dictionary*, 'humiliate' <www.oxfordlearnersdictionaries.com/definition/american_english/humiliate>.
43 *Cambridge Dictionary* 'slavery' <https://dictionary.cambridge.org/dictionary/english/slavery>.
44 Article 8(2)(b)(xxii)-2, War crime of sexual slavery, ICC Elements of Crime.
45 Ibid.
46 ICRC, 'Protocol Additional to the Geneva Conventions of 12 August 1949, and Relating to the Protection of Victims of Non-International Armed Conflicts (Protocol II), 8 June 1977, Commentary of 01.01.1987, Article 4(2)(f) – Slavery and the Slave Trade, para 4541.
47 See, for example, Judith Gardam, 'Women, Human Rights and International Humanitarian Law' (1998) 324 *International Review of the Red Cross* 421–432; Judith Gardam and Michelle Jarvis, *Women, Armed Conflict and International Law* (Kluwer Law International 2001); Helen Durham, 'Women, Armed Conflict and International Law' (2002) 84 *International Review of the Red Cross* 655–659.
48 Article 22, *nullum crimen sine lege*, Rome Statute of the International Criminal Court (adopted 17 July 1998, entered into force 1 July 2002) 2187 UNTS 3 (Rome Statute).
49 ICRC, 'The Tokyo War Crimes Trial Responsibility for War Crimes Against Prisoners' <https://casebook.icrc.org/case-study/tokyo-war-crimes-trial>.
50 The *Hirota* case, Three Judgments of the International Military Tribunal for the Far East 1 (1948); 20 Record of Proceedings of the International Military Tribunal for the Far

East (1946–1949) (Lib of Cong microfilm, reel 37 of 37) 49, 791, and 816, reprinted in John R Pritchard and others (eds), *The Tokyo War Crimes Trial* (1981).
51 *Prosecutor v Dragoljub Kunarac, Radomir Kova and Zoran Vukovic,* Case No IT-96–23/-23/1-A (Judgment of 12 June 2002) para 58.
52 Geneva Conventions (n 27).
53 The Geneva Convention of 12 August 1949, article 27; article 75(2)(b); Protocol Additional I to the Geneva Conventions of 12 August 1949, and Relating to the Protection of Victims of International Armed Conflicts (adopted 8 June 1977, entered into force 7 December 1978) 1125 UNTS 3 (Additional Protocol I); article 76(1) Additional Protocol II (n 11).
54 *Kunarac, Kova and Vukovic* (n 51) para 58.
55 Ibid.
56 Ibid.
57 Ibid, paras 67 and 195.
58 Ibid, para 55.
59 *Delalić* (n 36) para 4.
60 Andrew D Mitchell, 'The Failure to Halt, Prevent or Punish: The Doctrine of Command Responsibility for War Crimes' (2000) 22 *Sydney Law Review* 381, 401. Also see *Delalić* (n 36) para 4.
61 Barbara Goy, Michelle Jarvis and Giulia Pinzauti, 'Linking Sexual Violence to Senior Officials' in Michelle Jarvis and Serge Brammertz (eds), *Prosecuting Conflict-Related Sexual Violence at the ICTY* (OUP 2016) 243. Also see *Kunarac, Kovac and Vukovic* (n 51) para 396; a superior-subordinate relationship must exist for the recognition of command responsibility.
62 *Prosecutor v Nasser Orić* Case No IT-03–68-A, (Judgment of 3 July 2008) para 18.
63 ICTY Statute, article 7(3).
64 *Delalić* (n 36) para 775. Also see Olivia Swaak-Goldman, '*Prosecutor v Delalić,* No IT-96–21-T' (1999) 93 *American Journal of International Law* 514, 517.
65 ICTR Statute, article 4.
66 *Prosecutor v Akayesu* Case No ICTR-96–4-A (Judgment of 1 June 2001) para 7.
67 Ibid, paras 687, 731, 734.
68 *Prosecutor v Akayesu*, Case No ICTR-96–4-T (Judgment of 2 September 1998) para 688; a physical invasion of a sexual nature committed on a person under circumstances that are coercive.
69 *Akayesu* (n 68) para 686.
70 Ibid.
71 ICC, About the ICC: State parties to the ICC <www.aba-icc.org/about-the-icc/states-parties-to-the-icc/>. Mozambique signed the ICC Statute on 20 December 2000 but has not ratified it.
72 Article 8, ICC Statute.
73 *Prosecutor v Bosco Ntaganda*, ICC-01/04–02/06, with public Annexes A, B, and C, (Judgement of 8 July 2019) 536–537. The ICC found Bosco Ntaganda criminally liable for war crimes and crimes against humanity, including sexual violence, crimes committed in Ituri province in Eastern Congo between 2002 and 2003.
74 *Ongwen* (n 22) 216. The 2016 conviction of Jean-Pierre Bemba for rape as crimes against humanity and war crimes was overturned by the Appeals Chamber in 2018.
75 *Ntaganda* (n 73) paras 965 and 1196.
76 Ibid, para 986.
77 Ibid, para 965.
78 Ibid, paras 974–975, 1188 and 1199.
79 *Ongwen* (n 22) paras 32, 35–36.
80 Ibid, paras 3047, 3049, 3062, 3074, 3080, 3083–3084, 3100 and 3116.
81 Article 28, ICC Statute.

82 Additional Protocol I (n 53) article 87(1).
83 *Prosecutor v Zejnil Delalić, Zdravko Mucic, Hazim Delic and Esad Landzo* Case No IT-96–21-T (Judgment of 16 November 1998) para 333 (*Delalić and others*).
84 *Prosecutor v Jean Pierre Bemba Gombo*, "Judgment pursuant to Article 74 of the Statute," ICC-01/05–01/08–3343, (Judgment of 21 March 2016), para 172.
85 United Nations War Crimes Commission, Law Reports of Trials of War Criminals: Trial of General Tomoyuki Yamashita, United States Military Commission, Manila; Case No 21 (8 October-7 December 1945) The Supreme Court of the United States (4 February 1946) 93 <www.loc.gov/rr/frd/Military_Law/pdf/Law-Reports_Vol-4.pdf>.
86 Ibid, 43.
87 Ibid. According to the Court, the purpose of the law of war is to protect the civilian population and prisoners of war from brutality.
88 See Article 28, ICC Statute, on the definition of command responsibility.
89 Article 1, ICC Statute.

Bibliography

Additional Protocol to the Geneva Convention of 12 August 1949 and Relating to the Protection of Victims of Non-International Armed Conflict (Protocol II) (1977) <https://treaties.un.org/Pages/showDetails.aspx?objid=08000002800f3cb8&clang=_en>.

Amnesty International, 'Mozambique 2021' <www.amnesty.org/en/location/africa/southern-africa/mozambique/report-mozambique/>.

Amnesty International, 'Mozambique: Cabo Delgado Conflict Country's "Most Critical" Human Rights Situation' (29 March 2022).

Andrew D Mitchell, 'The Failure to Halt, Prevent or Punish: The Doctrine of Command Responsibility for War Crimes' (2000) 22 *Sydney Law Review*.

Arthur T O'Reilly, 'Command Responsibility: A Call to Realign Doctrine with Principles' (2004) 20 *American University International Law Review*.

Barbara Goy, Michelle Jarvis and Giulia Pinzauti, 'Linking Sexual Violence to Senior Officials' in Michelle Jarvis and Serge Brammertz (eds), *Prosecuting Conflict-Related Sexual Violence at the ICTY* (OUP 2016).

Blaškić, Trial Judgment (2000).

Brđanin, Trial Judgment, ICTY (2004).

Charter of the International Military Tribunal for the Far East, 19 January 1946 <www.un.org/en/genocideprevention/documents/atrocity-crimes/Doc.3_1946%20Tokyo%20Charter.pdf>.

Christin B Coan, 'Rethinking the Spoils of War: Prosecuting Rape as a War Crime in the International Criminal Tribunal for the Former Yugoslavia' (2001) 26 *North Carolina Journal of International Law and Commercial Regulation*.

'Degrade' *Cambridge Online Dictionary* <https://dictionary.cambridge.org/dictionary/english/degrading>.

Delalić, Trial Judgment (1998).

Eunice Jethá and others, 'Domestic Violence in Mozambique: From Policy to Practice' (2021) *BMC Public Health*.

Geneva Convention (I) for the Amelioration of the Condition of the Wounded and Sick in Armed Forces in the Field (1949) https://treaties.un.org/Pages/showDetails.aspx?objid=080000028015847c&clang=_en.

Geneva Convention (II) for the Amelioration of the Condition of Wounded, Sick and Shipwrecked Members of Armed Forces at Sea (1949) <https://treaties.un.org/Pages/showDetails.aspx?objid=08000002801591b0&clang=_en>.

Geneva Convention (III) Relative to the Treatment of Prisoners of War (1949) <https://treaties.un.org/Pages/showDetails.aspx?objid=0800000280159839&clang=_en>.

Geneva Convention (IV) Relative to the Protection of Civilian Persons in Time of War (1949) <https://treaties.un.org/Pages/showDetails.aspx?objid=080000028015 8b1a&clang=_en>.

Gerhard Werle, *Principles of International Criminal Law* (OUP 2009).

Haradinaj, Trial Judgment (2008).

Helen Durham, 'Women, Armed Conflict and International Law' (2002) 84 *International Review of the Red Cross*.

Hirota Case, 'Three Judgments of the International Military Tribunal for the Far East' 1 (1948) 20 *Record of Proceedings of the International Military Tribunal for the Far East* (1946–1949) (Lib of Cong microfilm, reel 37 of 37) 49, 791, and 816, reprinted in John R Pritchard and others (eds), *The Tokyo War Crimes Trial* (1981).

Human Rights Watch, 'Cabo Delgado: 600 Women, Girls Kidnapped Since 2018, Some Sold to Foreign Fighters' *Club of Mozambique* (8 December 2021).

Human Rights Watch, 'Mozambique Events of 2021' <www.hrw.org/world-report/2022/country-chapters/mozambique#>.

Human Rights Watch, 'Mozambique: Hundreds of Women, Girls Abducted' (7 December 2021) <www.hrw.org/news/2021/12/07/mozambique-hundreds-women-girls-abducted>.

'Humiliate' *Oxford Learner's Dictionary* <www.oxfordlearnersdictionaries.com/definition/american_english/humiliate>.

ICC, 'About the ICC: State Parties to the ICC' <www.aba-icc.org/about-the-icc/states-parties-to-the-icc/>.

ICRC, 'Commentary of 2020 Article 3: Conflicts Not of An International Character' (2020).

ICRC, 'The Tokyo War Crimes Trial Responsibility for War Crimes Against Prisoners' <https://casebook.icrc.org/case-study/tokyo-war-crimes-trial>.

ICRC, 'Protocol Additional to the Geneva Conventions of 12 August 1949, and Relating to the Protection of Victims of Non-International Armed Conflicts (Protocol II), 8 June 1977, Commentary of 01.01.1987, Article 4(2)(f) – Slavery and the Slave Trade.

ICTY, *Delalić*, Trial Judgment, 1998.

ICTY, *Prosecutor v Dragoljub Kunarac and Others*, Case No IT-96–23&23/1 (Appeals Chamber), 12 June 2002.

'Inhuman Treatment' *Vocabularly.com* <www.vocabulary.com/dictionary/inhuman%20treatment>.

International Military Tribunal for the Far East, judgment of 4 November 1948 <https://crimeofaggression.info/documents/6/1948_Tokyo_Judgment.pdf>.

International Military Tribunal for the Far East, judgment of 12 November 1948 <https://crimeofaggression.info/documents/6/1948_Tokyo_Judgment.pdf>.

John Pritchard and Sonia M Zaide (eds), *The Tokyo War Crimes Trial: The Complete Transcripts of the Proceedings of the International Military Tribunal for the Far East* (Garland 1981).

Judith Gardam, 'Women, Human Rights and International Humanitarian Law' (1998) 324 *International Review of the Red Cross*.

Judith Gardam and Michelle Jarvis, *Women, Armed Conflict and International Law* (Kluwer Law International 2001).

Kordić and Čerkez, Trial Judgment, 2001.

Limaj, Trial Judgment, 2005.

Lukić and Lukić, Trial Judgment, 2009.

Lynn Lawry, Kirsten Johnston and Jana Asher, 'Evidence-Based Documentation of Gender-Based Violence' in Anne-Marie de Brouwer and others (eds), *Sexual Violence as an International Crime: Interdisciplinary Approaches* (Intersentia 2013).

Mrkšić, Trial Judgment, 2007.

Naletilić and Martinović, Trial Judgment, 2003.

Olivia Swaak-Goldman, '*Prosecutor v Delalić*, No IT-96–21-T' (1999) 93 *American Journal of International Law*.

Orić, Trial Judgment, 2006.

Prosecutor v Akayesu, Case No ICTR-96–4-A (Judgment of 1 June 2001).

Prosecutor v Akayesu, Case No ICTR-96–4-T (Judgment of 2 September 1998).

Prosecutor v Bosco Ntaganda, ICC-01/04–02/06, with public Annexes A, B, and C, (Judgement of 8 July 2019).

Prosecutor v Delalić & Others, Judgment of 16 November 1998, Case IT-96–21 (*Celebici* case).

The Prosecutor v Dominic Ongwen, Trial Chamber IX, Case No ICC-02/04–01/15, 4 February 2021.

Prosecutor v Dragoljub Kunarac, Radomir Kova and Zoran Vukovic, Case No IT-96–23/-23/1-A (Judgment of 12 June 2002).

Prosecutor v Jean Pierre Bemba Gombo, "Judgment pursuant to Article 74 of the Statute," ICC-01/05–01/08–3343, (Judgment of 21 March 2016).

Prosecutor v Kunarac, Kovac and Vukovic, Trial Chamber, Judgment, Case No IT96–23-T and 23/1.

Prosecutor v Nasser Orić, Case No IT-03–68-A, (Judgment of 3 July 2008).

Prosecutor v Zejnil Delalić, Zdravko Mucic, Hazim Delic and Esad Landzo, Case No IT-96–21-T (Judgment of 16 November 1998).

Protocol Additional to the Geneva Conventions of 12 August 1949, and Relating to the Protection of Victims of International Armed Conflicts (Protocol I) (1977) <https://treaties.un.org/Pages/showDetails.aspx?objid=08000002800f3586&clang=_en>.

Protocol Additional to the Geneva Conventions of 12 August 1949, and Relating to the Protection of Victims of Non-International Armed Conflicts (Protocol II) (1977) <https://treaties.un.org/Pages/showDetails.aspx?objid=08000002800f3cb8&clang=_en>.

Rome Statute of the International Criminal Court (1998) <https://treaties.un.org/Pages/showDetails.aspx?objid=0800000280025774&clang=_en>.

'Slavery' *Cambridge Dictionary* <https://dictionary.cambridge.org/dictionary/english/slavery>.

Tolimir, Trial Judgment, 2012.

'Torture' *Oxford Languages* <https://languages.oup.com/google-dictionary-en/>.

UNHCR, 'Gender-Based Violence Response Cabo Delgado, Northern Mozambique' (April 2022) <https://reliefweb.int/report/mozambique/unhcr-mozambique-cabo-delgado-gender-based-violence-response-factsheet-april-2022>.

UNICEF, 'Mozambique Humanitarian Situation Report No 3' (31 March 2022) <www.unicef.org/>.

UNICEF, 'UNICEF Statement on Abduction of Minors in Cabo Delgado' (5 October 2022) <www.unicef.org/mozambique/en/press-releases/unicef-statement-abduction-minors-cabo-delgado>.

United Nations War Crimes Commission, 'Law Reports of Trials of War Criminals: Trial of General Tomoyuki Yamashita, United States Military Commission, Manila; Case No 21' (8 October–7 December 1945) The Supreme Court of the United States (4 February 1946) 93 <www.loc.gov/rr/frd/Military_Law/pdf/Law-Reports_Vol-4.pdf>.

United Nations Women, 'Trafficked: Three Survivors of Human Trafficking Share Their Stories' (29 July 2019) <www.unwomen.org/>.

Vienna Convention on the Law of Treaties (1969) <https://treaties.un.org/Pages/showDetails.aspx?objid=080000028003902f&clang=_en>.

9 Towards the protection of the environment in Cabo Delgado

Looking beyond the existing legal framework and engaging Ansar al-Sunna

Quillene M. Vertue

9.1 Introduction

Though humanity has always counted its war casualties in terms of dead and wounded soldiers and civilians, destroyed cities and livelihoods, the environment has often remained the unpublicised victim of war. Water wells have been polluted, crops torched, forests cut down, soils poisoned and animals killed to gain military advantage.[1]

For decades Mozambique has been ensnared in the web of armed conflict;[2] the northern province of Cabo Delgado, especially, consistently experiences cycles of violence.[3] Towards the end of 2017, Cabo Delgado again fell victim to violence when an Islamist insurgent group, Ansar al-Sunna, launched attacks on the Mozambican armed forces as well as on civilians.[4] As discussed in Chapter 6, the conflict in Cabo Delgado is classified as a non-international armed conflict (NIAC).[5] In 2022 the International Committee of the Red Cross (ICRC) assessed that globally around 524 armed groups were in a position to cause violence sufficient to be of humanitarian concern.[6] The level of violence carried out by Ansar al-Sunna (the insurgents) appeared to peak in 2022[7] but, at the time of writing, the conflict in Cabo Delgado was ongoing.[8]

Since the seventh or eighth century Islam has had a presence in Mozambique;[9] the highest proportion of the Muslim population is in Cabo Delgado.[10] In the late 1990s the tension escalated between diverse forms of practice in Islam and, on separating from the Islamic Council in the northern region,[11] a group of young men established an organisation they gave the name Ansar al-Sunna. According to reports, Islamic fundamentalism is a driver in Ansar al-Sunna's insurgency[12] and is reflected in the goal of implementing Shari'a law (an Islamic legal system)[13] which encompasses combating Western influence[14] and rejecting secular education.[15] It is noted that since 2019 the insurgents have claimed allegiance to the Islamic State (IS).[16]

As a result of poverty, decades of under-investment and neglect by the government, Cabo Delgado has become known as 'Mozambique's forgotten cape' and, now, as the face of a violent insurgency.[17] The tactics and strategies employed by Ansar al-Sunna have been labelled as 'unconventional'[18] and 'brutal'.[19] Research

DOI: 10.4324/9781003317647-11

indicates that a NIAC often is fought in a region that is a biodiversity hotspot,[20] regularly is linked to the presence of rich natural resources[21] and that non-state armed groups (NSAGs) add substantially to the damage caused to the environment during a NIAC.[22] Notably, the ICRC flags in its reports the destruction of the environment during armed conflict and non-state armed groups as contemporary challenges of armed conflict.[23] Though the environmental destruction caused by Ansar al-Sunna is not well documented, it has been reported that the insurgents burn, destroy and pillage[24] properties, villages, farms and public infrastructure.[25] In addition, due to the escalation of violence in this region, it is estimated that more than one million people have been internally displaced.[26] A cause for great concern and an amplification of the significance of this NIAC are that Cabo Delgado is recognised as a biodiversity hotspot[27] and is rich in natural resources such as gold, graphite, marble, timber and liquid natural gas,[28] giving it the label of 'a resource-rich war zone'.[29] Cabo Delgado is a region all the more vulnerable to environmental damage. A joint study prepared by the Institute for Security Studies and the Judicial Training Institute of Mozambique found that according to the people in Cabo Delgado, the main drivers in the armed conflict are natural resources and poor governance.[30]

An armed conflict has a serious effect on the environment.[31] Note that the consequence of environmental damage caused during an armed conflict continues for decades after the conflict has ended.[32] The protection of the environment is seldom regarded as a top priority, whether during international armed conflicts (IACs) or NIACs.[33] The dominant type of armed conflict is non-international in character,[34] but scholarly attention and suggestions for the solution, specifically regarding environmental protection, are scant.[35] The current situation in Mozambique demonstrates this paucity of attention and serves as a practical example of the two contemporary challenges flagged by the ICRC as mentioned earlier.

In addition, treaty law regulating the protection of the environment during NIACs is regarded as weak, leaving the environment susceptible to destruction and exploitation by non-state actors party to the armed conflict.[36] The ICRC and the International Law Commission (ILC) have endeavoured to address the lacuna found in the law regulating the protection of the environment during NIACs. First, in 2020 the ICRC released Updated Guidelines on the Protection of the Natural Environment in Armed Conflict (Updated Guidelines),[37] which aim to represent developments in treaty law and customary international humanitarian law (IHL).[38] The Updated Guidelines encompass a set of existing IHL rules and recommendations providing protection to the environment during armed conflict and seek to act as a reference for all parties to the armed conflict, including other actors able to influence the conduct of parties to an armed conflict.[39] Second, in 2022, the ILC adopted 27 Draft Principles with Commentaries, specifically dedicated to the Protection of the Environment in Relation to Armed Conflicts (PERAC).[40] The PERAC Principles are the product of 11 years of dedication by two Special Rapporteurs,[41] as well as members of the ILC, to this topic in response to a request made by the United Nations Environment Programme (UNEP) in 2009 to assess the legal framework regulating the protection of the environment during armed conflict and advise on its expansion, codification and clarification.[42] In line with the mandate of the ILC progressively to develop and codify the law,[43] the PERAC Principles are a combination of codification and progressive development,[44] with an ultimate aim of strengthening the legal framework regulating the protection of the environment during all cycles of armed conflict, thus, before, during and after an armed conflict.[45]

This chapter aims to contribute a better understanding of the current legal framework, providing protection for the environment during NIACs. Where the existing legal framework falls short of this ideal, the chapter seeks to offer recommendations that are a complement to the existing legal framework and provide a 'blueprint' or pathway for engaging with Ansar al-Sunna on this issue. This chapter is divided into four sections, including the introduction. Section 9.2 explores examples of environmental damage caused by Ansar al-Sunna and the threat posed to the environment in justification of underlining the practical need for engagement as reflected by the chapter title. Section 9.3 turns to the existing legal framework or lack thereof, which regulates the protection of the environment during NIACs. This section examines treaty law and PERAC Principles and provides the reader with brief recommendations as to the way forward and looks beyond the existing legal framework to alternative ways of engaging with Ansar al-Sunna. Lastly, a conclusion is drawn in the fourth section.

9.2 Ansar al-Sunna's insurgency: environmental damage and the threat posed to the 'forgotten cape'

The environment can be either directly targeted or endure incidental harm as a consequence of the means and methods used in warfare.[46] It has been observed that, generally, NIACs break out in a biodiversity hotspot.[47] Thus, the degradation of biodiversity becomes an irreparable consequence.[48] The purpose of this section to examine the threat Ansar al-Sunna poses to this specific biodiversity hotspot[49] by investigating the means and methods of warfare employed through the tactics used by Ansar al-Sunna and their impact on the environment.

A 2021 report of key biodiversity areas that contains a red list of ecosystems and species under threat in Mozambique lists four key biodiversity areas in Cabo Delgado.[50] This section will briefly look at two key biodiversity areas identified.[51] First, the Palma region contains an assortment of endemic (or close to endemic) and rare species belonging to a range of plant and animal groups, of which 17 species trigger the criteria for designating a key biodiversity area.[52] In 2021 the armed conflict between the insurgents and the national defence forces came to the Palma region.[53] It is reported that the insurgents burned down two-thirds of the buildings in Palma and pillaged the town throughout the night.[54] Second, Quiterajo, a coastal area in the Macomia district incorporates the Quirimbas National Park.[55] The Quirimbas Archipelago and the national park lie on the coastline of Cabo Delgado and are declared a United Nations Educational, Scientific and Cultural Organisation (UNESCO) Biosphere Reserve.[56] This region boasts various species of plants, birds, wild animals and reptiles.[57] Quiterajo, as claimed in research reports, is one of four regions marked for preserving coastal forests and related vegetation types.[58] In 2022 the insurgents launched an attack in the Quiterajo region, killing three members of the armed forces.[59] It is reported that the insurgents burned down a barrack.[60]

It is stated that the insurgency has 'secured more advanced materials, expertise, and other resources that it initially lacked'.[61] Examples are landmines and improvised explosive devices (IEDs).[62] Reports suggest that the insurgents looted a landmine from the Namoto border post armoury, which became the basis of an IED used in 2021 against the forces of the Southern African Development Community (SADC).[63] This allegation suggests that the insurgents are developing new tactics and also heralds a return by Mozambique to using landmines.[64] After the report of their first use in 2021, IEDs have been used increasingly and the development of this tactic indicates that the insurgency is receiving external assistance.[65] This assistance and a greater capability to use IEDs significantly intensify the conflict.[66] According to a retired general in the South African National Defence Force (SANDF): '[The use of land]mines and IEDs change[s] the whole ball game',[67] and is true also with regard to the effect on the environment.[68] Information with regard to the effect of explosive weapons on the environment is limited, but research suggests that the use of explosive devices such as landmines and IEDs has a devastating and lasting effect,[69] including the contamination of the soil and rivers, the destruction of ecosystems and the killing of animals, essentially, they 'tip the world out of balance'.[70]

A major tactic the insurgents employ is an incendiary attack.[71] Incendiary weapons include mines, bombs, rockets, grenades, shells, flamethrowers and other containers of incendiary substance.[72] These weapons rely for their effectiveness on a chemical reaction on impact causing heat or flames, which set fire to the surroundings and injure persons.[73] It has been reported the insurgents are armed with automatic weapons and rocket-propelled grenade launchers.[74] Homes and other property have been destroyed, and the insurgents have burned down a mosque[75] and a church.[76] The use of incendiary weapons impacts the environment in various ways.[77] For example, trees and plants are damaged, the protective layer of soil cover is destroyed making it vulnerable to erosion and the wildlife population is affected, all of which disrupts the ecology.[78]

Furthermore, as mentioned earlier, Cabo Delgado is a 'resource-rich war zone';[79] a driver of the armed conflict is the wealth of natural resources.[80] It is reported that the insurgency is funded by the extraction of gemstones and participation in the trade in illegal gemstones.[81] Cabo Delgado is known for the illegal trafficking of timber, but the involvement of the insurgents in logging has not been proven.[82] At the time of writing, there is insufficient evidence to establish whether the insurgents are involved in the exploitation of natural resources; any change in the situation offers a significant threat to the environment.

Lastly, human displacement has significant environmental implications.[83] In Cabo Delgado, displaced civilians, particularly children (at least 45 per cent of those displaced), women, girls, those with disabilities and the elderly, are exceptionally vulnerable to exploitation.[84] In addition, there are signs of systemic collapse as the internally displaced place a strain on their new locations causing rising tension between the residents and the refugees and aggravating a situation of already limited access to basic human needs such as healthcare, water and sanitation.[85] This process creates a legacy of a seriously damaging environmental footprint.[86]

The biodiversity found in Cabo Delgado makes it especially vulnerable to environmental damage and highlights the imminent threat the armed conflict and the brutality that the insurgency offer this region. It exemplifies this despairing judgement: 'Like climate change, conflicts are unfair. They increase the vulnerability of . . . [what is] . . . already vulnerable'.[87]

9.3 An overview of the legal framework protecting the environment during NIACs as it relates to NSAGs

This section explores the extent of the existing legal framework's ability to regulate the protection of the environment during NIACs and the fit of non-state armed groups in this framework. There are two main 'sources' of International Humanitarian Law (IHL):[88] first, treaty law, specifically the four Geneva Conventions[89] and the Additional Protocols;[90] second, customary international law,[91] which fills the gaps in treaty law,[92] like, for example, specific Rules in the Updated Guidelines of the ICRC.[93] Customary IHL is of significant value as some of its rules are binding on state and non-state parties to an armed conflict.[94] States implicitly confer an international legal personality on non-governmental forces party to the armed conflict, such as non-state armed groups, by which they possess rights and responsibilities under these rules.[95] Henckaerts and Wiesener note that increasingly it is accepted that treaty law and customary law bind non-state armed groups party to an armed conflict.[96] Certain PERAC Principles comprise elements of treaty law as well as of customary international law.[97] Accordingly, this is the sequence followed in this section: first, a brief examination of IHL treaty provisions regulating NIACs. and, second, it investigates certain PERAC Principles. In conclusion, some alternative avenues that could strengthen engagement with Ansar al-Sunna on this issue are provided. Section 9.2 illustrated environmental damage is a serious corollary to the violence generated by a NIAC; the discussion in Section 9.3 focuses on Ansar al-Sunna and in line with the tone set in Section 9.2 endeavours to establish a practical link between the insurgency and the PERAC Principles.

9.3.1 Treaty law regulating NIACs

Under treaty law, Common Article 3 (CA3) to the four Geneva Conventions[98] and Additional Protocol II (APII)[99] regulate NIACs.[100] Regrettably, CA3, which binds all parties to a NIAC,[101] and APII that is binding on non-state armed groups[102] do not directly provide protection to the environment.[103]

There is a scholarly argument in favour of the view that specific prohibitions under CA3 have an environmental dimension under the categories governing 'violence to life',[104] 'cruel treatment',[105] 'torture',[106] 'outrages on personal dignity'[107] and 'degrading treatment'.[108] However, with regard to the suggestion that CA3 indirectly prohibits environmental damage in a NIAC, Smith observes: 'Common Article 3 is neither the strongest nor the most convincing provision in this regard'.[109]

Meron maintains that if a broad interpretation of certain provisions of APII is adopted,[110] then indirect protection of the environment may be possible.[111] One of these provisions is the prohibition of pillage under article 4(2)(g) of APII,[112] which can be applicable to the exploitation of natural resources and is a possible instrument for holding non-state armed groups accountable.[113] Pretorius cautions against following a broad approach as it may cause parties to a NIAC to disregard their obligations should the precise responsibilities under APII be unclear.[114] In conclusion, clearly neither CA3 nor APII provides direct protection to the environment and to interpret them in terms of such protection is a doubtful project.[115]

9.3.2 Selected draft principles of the ILC on PERAC: addressing Ansar al-Sunna

This part explores the work of the ILC on PERAC to determine the extent to which non-state armed groups, such as Ansar al-Sunna, are addressed. Treaty law proved weak in regulating the protection of the environment during armed conflict.[116] The PERAC Principles seek specifically to develop the law progressively and to strengthen the protection of the environment during armed conflict.[117] During a 2019 United Nations General Assembly (UNGA) debate on the topic, member states raised a concern relating to the responsibilities and obligations of non-state armed groups in respect of their role in causing environmental damage and being held accountable under international law.[118] The concern raised is attended to in the final report of the ILC and is referenced in the Commentary on scope in Principle 1[119] reads: 'In addition to states, several draft principles are addressed to international organisations, or to parties to an armed conflict, including non-state armed groups, or to other relevant actors, such as civil society organisations'.[120]

Limitation on length means this section examines Principle 8 on human displacement and Principle 16 on the prohibition of pillage. These principles are selected for relevance to the insurgency in Cabo Delgado and for practical reasons.[121] Other principles, such as Principle 13 on the general protection of the environment during armed conflict[122] and Principle 18 on protected zones,[123] bearing in mind the United Nations Educational, Scientific and Cultural Organisation (UNESCO) Biosphere Reserve in Cabo Delgado,[124] also apply.

9.3.2.1 Principle 8 on human displacement

Internal displacement is a serious consequence of the armed conflict in Cabo Delgado.[125] As mentioned earlier, approximately 1 million people have been internally displaced.[126] Draft Principle 8 reads:

> States, international organisations and other relevant actors should take appropriate measures to prevent, mitigate and remediate harm to the environment in areas where persons displaced by armed conflict are located, or

through which they transit, while providing relief and assistance for such persons and local communities.[127]

The purpose of the Principle is the acknowledgement of an interrelationship between aiding those displaced by armed conflict and lessening the environmental consequences of the displacement.[128] Though Draft Principle 8 does not make specific reference to non-state armed groups, they are referred to in the Commentary, which states that non-state armed groups are included under 'other relevant actors'.[129] On behalf of Nordic countries, Sweden proposed that non-state armed groups are added to the non-exhaustive list in paragraph (7) of the Commentary to the Principle to indicate who are 'other relevant actors'.[130] The Special Rapporteur agreed.[131] This Principle is a burden-sharing mechanism, if only a recommendation by referencing the term 'should',[132] and implies that Ansar al-Sunna would need to take action to prevent and alleviate environmental degradation in regions hosting persons displaced by the armed conflict and provide relief aid to the displaced and local communities.[133]

9.3.2.2 Draft Principle 16 on the prohibition of pillage

Principle 16 prohibits the pillage of natural resources and reiterates the prohibition in general.[134] According to the Updated Guidelines of the ICRC, 'pillage', which is a violation of IHL, refers to the seizure of property, not necessarily by way of violence or force, but without the implied or direct consent of the property owner.[135] Draft Principle 16 is of specific importance for NIACs as the Commentary to this principle states that the exploitation of natural resources previously caused environmental stress in affected areas and mentions the illegal exploitation of natural resources as a driver of NIACs.[136] As mentioned in Section 9.2, natural resources and poor governance are driving forces behind the insurgency in Cabo Delgado[137] but, at the time of writing, there is insufficient proof to conclude that the insurgents have exploited natural resources though it may occur in the future. In paragraph (7) of the Commentary to Principle 16 the prohibition on illegal exploitation of natural resources covers the activities of non-state armed groups.[138] Further, under the Rome Statute, pillaging during IACs and NIACs can be prosecuted as a war crime.[139]

In light of a weak treaty regime regulating NIACs, this brief overview of the Draft Principles demonstrates that they make a critical contribution. The Draft Principles are not legally binding on non-state armed groups or states.[140] Principle 8 on human displacement, for example, employs 'should' and not the enforceable 'shall' and is not an explicit obligation placed on states and non-state actors.[141] Draft Principle 16 on the prohibition of pillage, on the other hand, has elements of customary and treaty law,[142] indicating an obligation on states as well as on non-state armed groups such as Ansar al-Sunna. Other Draft Principles that have not been discussed and perhaps do not have customary and treaty law elements, will need to attain customary law status to be legally binding; per article 38(1)(b) of the Statute of the International Court of Justice there should be evidence of general practice and such practice should be accepted as law.[143] Establishing whether a rule has attained customary international law status is a challenging, contentious and 'time-consuming' process.[144] In relation to customary international law and its binding nature, the PERAC Principles aim to strengthen the existing legal framework and progressively develop the law.[145]

Considering the immediate and alarming situation in Cabo Delgado, a logical course of action in the future is to explore alternative avenues that could strengthen engagement with Ansar al-Sunna. These avenues could include, for example, incorporating non-Western-based instruments such as Islamic law[146] in conjunction with soft law instruments and turning towards the significant role of key players such as the ICRC and Geneva Call[147] in engaging with these groups and disseminating the PERAC Principles and Updated Guidelines of the ICRC.[148] Finally, Islamic law can be the source of a code of conduct[149] for the actions of Ansar al-Sunna and enable the insurgents to take 'ownership of the law'[150] and be a guide to protect the environment.[151]

9.4 Conclusion

This chapter promotes a better understanding of the existing legal framework regulating the protection of the environment as it relates to non-state armed groups. It surveys the current position and indicates what can be done in the future. The aim is to identify gaps in the legal framework and provide possible avenues for filling them in the face of the dire situation in Cabo Delgado. The second part elaborates on the threat posed to a biodiversity hotspot by the tactics employed by Ansar al-Sunna. It reveals that Cabo Delgado is vulnerable to environmental damage. The third part discusses the existing legal framework regulating the protection of the environment as it relates to non-state armed groups. CA3 and APII are considered, but neither treaty provision offer direct protection to the environment during a NIAC. Second, attention is given to PERAC Principles. Principle 8 on human displacement and Principle 16 on the prohibition of pillage are of practical significance, but the principles are not necessarily legally binding. The debate rests on the interpretation of the wording in the principles and whether they present elements of treaty or customary law. The PERAC Principles are a critically important contribution. This chapter looks beyond the existing legal framework and proposes that humanitarian organisations such as the ICRC and Geneva Call focus on the value of Islamic law to the engagement with non-state armed groups, like Ansar al-Sunna which can inform a potential code of conduct. This chapter suggests drawing on Islamic law, the PERAC Principles and the Updated Guidelines of the ICRC in engaging with Ansar al-Sunna. The goal of looking beyond the existing legal framework is to further the project by which the environment no longer is the 'unpublicised victim of war'.

Notes

1 UN, 'International Day for Preventing the Exploitation of the Environment in War and Armed Conflict: 6 November' <www.un.org/en/observances/environment-in-war-protection-day#:~:text=Though%20humanity%20has%20always%20counted,the%20unpublicized%20victim%20of%20war.>.

2 See generally RULAC, 'Non-international Armed Conflicts in Mozambique' (18 May 2023).
3 Jokin Alberdi and others, 'Ayuda en Acción: War, Forced Displacement and Responses to the Crisis in Cabo Delgado: Mozambique' *Alliance 2015* (22 March 2023) 11–13.
4 RULAC (n 2).
5 Ibid.
6 ICRC, 'Why the ICRC Talks to Armed Groups' (1 March 2023).
7 Monique Bennett and Nnaemeka Ohamadike, 'How to Silence the Guns in Cabo Delgado' *Good Governance Africa* (12 April 2023) <https://gga.org/how-to-silence-the-guns-in-cabo-delgado/>.
8 Cabo Ligado, 'Mozambique Conflict Observatory' <www.caboligado.com/>, which is a website specifically dedicated to monitoring the insurgency in Cabo Delgado and providing the user with information and weekly updates concerning the conflict.
9 Dorina A Bekoe, Stephanie M Burchard and Sarah A Daly, 'Extremism in Mozambique: Interpreting Group Tactics and the Role of the Government's Response in the Crisis in Cabo Delgado' *Institute for Defense Analyses IDA* (March 2020) 3.
10 Emily Estelle and Jessica Trisko Darden, 'Combating the Islamic State's Spread in Africa: Assessment and Recommendations for Mozambique' *American Enterprise Institute* (February 2021) 5–6.
11 Bekoe and others (n 9) 4.
12 Clayton Hazvinei Vhumbunu, 'Insurgency in Mozambique: The Role of the Southern African Development Community' *ACCORD* (21 April 2021); Saide Habibe, Salvador Forquilha and João Pereira, 'Islamic Radicalisation in Northern Mozambique: The Case of Mocímboa da Praia' *IESE Scientific Council* (September 2019) 10 <www.iese.ac.mz/wp-content/uploads/2019/12/cadernos_17eng.pdf>.
13 'Islam' *History* (29 June 2023) <www.history.com/topics/religion/islam>.
14 Habibe and others (n 12) 10.
15 Bekoe and others (n 9) 4, 22.
16 Julia Stanyard and others, 'Insurgency, Illicit Markets and Corruption: The Cabo Delgado Conflict and Its Regional Implications' *Global Initiative Against Transnational Organised Crime* (February 2022) 9–15.
17 Amnesty International, 'Mozambique: "What I Saw Is Death": War Crimes in Mozambique's Forgotten Cape' (2021) 5.
18 Vhumbunu (n 12).
19 Bekoe and others (n 9) 1–19.
20 Thor Hanson and others, 'Warfare in Biodiversity Hotspots' (2009) 23 (3) *Conservation Biology*. See also Vanessa Murphy and Helen Obregón Gieseken, 'Fighting Without a Planet B: How IHL Protects the Natural Environment in Armed Conflict' *ICRC Humanitarian Law and Policy* (25 May 2021).
21 See UNEP, 'From Conflict to Peacebuilding: The Role of Natural Resources and the Environment' (UNEP 2009) 30.
22 Thibaud de la Bourdonnaye, 'Greener Insurgencies? Engaging Non-State Armed Groups for the Protection of the Natural Environment During Non-International Armed Conflicts' (2020) 102 (914) *International Review of the Red Cross* 579. For examples of armed groups causing damage to the environment during a NIAC, see in general 'Witnessing the Environmental Impacts of War: Environmental Case Studies From Conflict Zones Around the World' *Zoï Environment Network* (November 2020) <https://zoinet.org/wp-content/uploads/2018/01/Witnessing-the-environmental-impacts-of-war_EN.pdf>.
23 See ICRC, 'Twelve Issues for 2022: What States Can Do to Improve Respect for International Humanitarian Law' (21 March 2022); ICRC, 'ICRC Report on IHL and the Challenges of Contemporary Armed Conflicts: Recommitting to the Protection in Armed Conflict on the 70th Anniversary of the Geneva Conventions' (22 November 2019) 50–55, 66–68.

24 Sources refer to 'looting'. However, for the purposes of this chapter, the term 'pillage' will be employed. It is acknowledged that the terms 'pillage', 'plunder' and 'looting' have been utilised synonymously by international courts and tribunals and therefore share a common legal interpretation – all refer to the 'unlawful appropriation of public or private property in armed conflict'. See ILC, 'Report of the International Law Commission on the Work of Its Seventy-third Session (18 April–3 June and 4 July–5 August 2022) UN Doc. A/77/10, para (5) of the Commentary to Draft Principle 16 and footnote 697.

25 Vhumbunu (n 12). See also in general Bekoe and others (n 9) 13.

26 European Commission: European Civil Protection and Humanitarian Aid Operations, 'Mozambique: Factsheet' (7 March 2023) <https://civil-protection-humanitarian-aid.ec.europa.eu/where/africa/mozambique_en>.

27 WCS, Government of Mozambique and USAID, 'Key Biodiversity Areas (KBAs) Identified in Mozambique: Factsheets VOL. II: Red List of Threatened Species and Ecosystems, Identification and Mapping of Key Biodiversity Areas (KBAs) in Mozambique' Combo Program (2021) 8.

28 Nicolaas C Steenkamp, 'Cabo Delgado, the Dark Treasure Trove of Mozambique' *African Mining* (1 June 2022) <www.africanmining.co.za/2022/06/01/cabo-delgado-the-dark-treasure-trove-of-mozambique/>.

29 Ashoka Mukpo, 'Gas Fields and Jihad: Mozambique's Cabo Delgado Becomes a Resource-Rich War Zone' Mongabay: News and Inspiration from Nature's Frontline (26 April 2021) <https://news.mongabay.com/2021/04/gas-fields-and-jihad-mozambiques-cabo-delgado-becomes-a-resource-rich-war-zone/>.

30 Martin Ewi and others, 'Violent Extremism in Mozambique: Drivers and Links to Transnational Organised Crime' *Institute for Security Studies* (5 September 2022) 1, 19 (ISS Report).

31 ICRC, 'When Rain Turns to Dust: Understanding and Responding to the Combined Impact of Armed Conflicts and the Climate and Environment Crisis on People's Lives' (2020) 16–17.

32 ICRC, 'Guidelines on the Protection of the Natural Environment in Armed Conflict' (25 September 2020) 11.

33 Indrė Lechtimiakytė, 'Preservation of Environment in Times of Non-International Armed Conflict. Legal Framework, Its Sufficiency and Suggestion' (2013) 20 (2) *Jurisprudence* 569.

34 Annyssa Bellal, 'The War Report: Armed Conflicts in 2018' *Geneva Academy of International Humanitarian Law and Human Rights* (April 2019) 19; Jeanique Pretorius, 'Protecting the Environment in Non-International Armed Conflicts Means Looking Beyond International Humanitarian Law Alone' Conflict and Environment Observatory (15 March 2019) <https://ceobs.org/environmental-protection-in-non-international-armed-conflicts-finding-the-way-forward/>.

35 Lechtimiakytė (n 33) 569–570.

36 Jeanique A Pretorius, 'The Protection of the Natural Environment in Non-International Armed Conflict under International Treaty Law' (LLD thesis, University of Pretoria 2018) 86, 239.

37 The first version was released in 1994. See Updated Guidelines of the ICRC (n 32) 4–14.

38 Updated Guidelines of the ICRC (n 32) 13.

39 Ibid, 13–14.

40 UN Doc. A/77/10 (n 24) 96–187. See also UNGA Res. 77/104 (7 December 2022), 1–2.

41 For a record of the ILC's work on this topic, see ILC, 'Analytical Guide to the Work of the International Law Commission, Protection of the Environment in Relation to Armed Conflicts' (9 June 2023) <https://legal.un.org/ilc/guide/8_7.shtml>.

42 UNEP, 'Protecting the Environment During Armed Conflict: An Inventory and Analysis of International Law' (November 2009) 6.
43 The General Assembly created the ILC to undertake its mandate as stipulated in article 13(1)(a) of the Charter of the United Nations (adopted 26 June 1945, entered into force 24 October 1945) 1 UNTS XVI (UN Charter). Article 1 of the Statute of the ILC, adopted in UNGA Res. 174 (II) of 21 November 1947, as amended by Resolutions 485 (V) of 12 December 1950, 984 (X) of 3 December 1955, 985 (X) of 3 December 1955 and 36/39 of 18 November 1981.
44 Doug Weir and Stavros-Evdokimos Pantazopoulos, 'If Not Us, Who? How States – With the Help of Civil Society – Can Implement the Legal Framework Protecting the Environment from Armed Conflict' *ICRC Humanitarian Law and Policy* (10 June 2021).
45 UN Doc. A/77/10 (n 24), para (2) of the General Commentary and Principles 1 and 2; Doug Weir, 'The PERAC Legal Framework, Frequently Asked Questions' *CEOBS* (September 2022) <https://ceobs.org/perac-principles-frequently-asked-questions/#1663073164735-f59acb18-3a80>.
46 Updated Guidelines of the ICRC (n 32) 11.
47 Hanson and others (n 20); Murphy and Gieseken (n 20).
48 Updated Guidelines of the ICRC (n 32) 11.
49 Report on KBAs identified in Mozambique (n 27) 8–9.
50 Ibid.
51 Two other key biodiversity areas identified and not discussed in detail here are Vamizi and Taratibu. See Report on KBAs identified in Mozambique (n 27) 8–23.
52 Report on KBAs identified in Mozambique (n 27) 16–17.
53 Ibid, 16.
54 Mozambique Conflict Observatory (n 8) <www.caboligado.com/reports/cabo-ligado-weekly-22-28-march-2021#:~:text=26%20March%202021%3A%20Palma,trapped%20inside%20the%20Amarula%20hotel>.
55 Report on KBAs identified in Mozambique (n 27) 20.
56 Ibid; Mukpo (n 29); UNESCO, 'Quirimbas Biosphere Reserve, Mozambique' (April 2019).
57 Report on KBAs identified in Mozambique (n 27) 20.
58 Ibid, 21. See Jonathan Timberlake and others, 'Coastal Dry Forest in Northern Mozambique' (2011) 144 (2) *Plant Ecology and Evolution* 126, 135.
59 Report on KBAs identified in Mozambique (n 27) 20; Mozambique Conflict Observatory (n 8) <www.caboligado.com/reports/cabo-ligado-weekly-25-apri-8-may-2022>.
60 Ibid.
61 Bekoe and others (n 9) 13.
62 Ibid; Erika Gibson, 'SADC Forces Tread Dangerous Ground in Mozambique: Landmines and IEDs Are Now Being Used by Insurgents, "Changing the Course of the Conflict"' *Business Day* (19 September 2021).
63 Stanyard and others (n 16) 36.
64 Mozambique Conflict Observatory (n 8) <www.caboligado.com/reports/cabo-ligado-weekly-6-12-september-2021>.
65 Ibid.
66 Ibid.
67 As quoted by journalist Erika Gibson (n 62).
68 Updated Guidelines of the ICRC (n 32) 96–99.
69 Action on Armed Violence, 'The Broken Land: The Environmental Consequences of Explosive Weapon Use' (2020) 4 <https://aoav.org.uk/wp-content/uploads/2020/04/The-Broken-Land-v4.pdf>.
70 Ibid.
71 ISS Report (n 30) 11–12.

72 ICRC, 'How Does Law Protect War? Incendiary Weapons'.
73 Ibid.
74 Mozambique Conflict Observatory (n 8) <www.caboligado.com/reports/cabo-ligado-weekly-6-12-february-2023>; see also Amnesty International (n 17) 10.
75 Mozambique Conflict Observatory (n 8) <www.caboligado.com/reports/cabo-ligado-weekly-24-30-may-2021>.
76 Ibid <www.caboligado.com/reports/cabo-ligado-weekly-4-10-july-2022>; 'Insurgent Attacks Intensify in Ancuabe District of Cabo Delgado' *Zitmar News* (21 June 2022) <www.zitamar.com/insurgent-attacks-intensify-in-ancuabe-district-of-cabo-delgado/>.
77 Updated Guidelines of the ICRC (n 32) 94.
78 Ibid.
79 Mukpo (n 29).
80 ISS Report (n 30) 19.
81 Stanyard and others (n 16) 32–33.
82 Ibid, 31.
83 Doug Weir, 'How Does War Damage the Environment?' *CEOBS* (4 June 2020) <https://ceobs.org/how-does-war-damage-the-environment/>.
84 Vhumbunu (n 12).
85 Ibid; ICRC, 'Mozambique: How Does Armed Conflict in Cabo Delgado Affect Access to Basic Services Like Water, Sanitation and Health?' (9 March 2023).
86 Weir (n 83).
87 ICRC (n 31) 16.
88 ICRC, 'Sources of IHL: Treaties and Customary Law' <https://blogs.icrc.org/ir/en/international-humanitarian-law/sources-ihl-treaties-customary-law/>.
89 Geneva Convention (I) for the Amelioration of the Condition of the Wounded and Sick in Armed Forces in the Field (adopted 12 August 1949, entered into force 21 October 1950) 75 UNTS 31 (First Geneva Convention); Geneva Convention (II) for the Amelioration of the Condition of Wounded, Sick and Shipwrecked Members of Armed Forces at Sea (adopted 12 August 1949, entered into force 21 October 1950) 75 UNTS 85 (Second Geneva Convention); Geneva Convention (III) Relative to the Treatment of Prisoners of War (adopted 12 August 1949, entered into force 21 October 1950) 75 UNTS 135 (Third Geneva Convention); Geneva Convention (IV) Relative to the Protection of Civilian Persons in Time of War (adopted 12 August 1949, entered into force 21 October 1950) 75 UNTS 287 (Fourth Geneva Convention) (the Four Geneva Conventions).
90 Protocol Additional to the Geneva Conventions of 12 August 1949 and relating to the Protection of Victims of International Armed Conflicts (adopted 12 December 1977, entered into force 7 December 1979) 1125 UNTS 3 (AP I); Protocol Additional to the Geneva Conventions of 12 August 1949, and relating to the Protection of Victims of Non-International Armed Conflicts (adopted 12 December 1977, entered into force 7 December 1978) 1125 UNTS 609 (AP II).
91 ICRC (n 88); Jean-Marie Henckaerts and Louise Doswald-Beck (eds), *International Committee of the Red Cross, Customary International Humanitarian Law: Volume 1: Rules* (CUP 2005) read together with Jean-Marie Henckaerts and Louise Doswald-Beck (eds), *International Committee of the Red Cross: Customary International Humanitarian Law: Volume II: Practice: Part 1* (CUP 2005).
92 ICRC, 'Customary Law' (June 2023).
93 See, for example, Rules 14, 23.A and 29 of the Updated Guidelines of the ICRC (n 32) 74–75, 94–95 and 111–112 which are binding on Ansar al-Sunna due to its customary law status.
94 ICRC (n 92).
95 ICRC, 'Non-International Armed Conflict: VIII. Who Is Bound by the Law of Non-International Armed Conflicts?' <https://casebook.icrc.org/law/non-international-armed-conflict#chapter9>. See also Marco Sassóli, 'Taking Armed Groups Seriously: Ways

to Improve Their Compliance with International Humanitarian Law' (2010) 1 *International Humanitarian Legal Studies*.

96 Jean-Marie Henckaerts and Cornelius Wiesener, 'Human Rights Obligations of Non-State Armed Groups: An Assessment Based on Recent Practice' in Ezequiel Heffes, Marcos D Kotlik and Manuel J Ventura (eds), *International Humanitarian Law and Non-State Actors: Debates, Law and Practice* (TMC Asser Press 2020) ch 8, 199.

97 UN Doc. A/77/10 (n 24), para (3) of the General Commentary; Weir (n 45).

98 The Four Geneva Conventions (n 89).

99 AP II (n 90).

100 Marco Sassòli, *International Humanitarian Law: Rules, Controversies, and Solutions to Problems Arising in Warfare* (Edward Elgar 2019) 213–219.

101 Jelena Pejic, 'The Protective Scope of Common Article 3: More Than Meets the Eye' (2011) 93 *International Review of the Red Cross* 1, 9–10. In addition, the customary law status of CA3 has been confirmed by the International Court of Justice in *Case Concerning Military and Paramilitary Activities in and Against Nicaragua (Nicaragua v United States of America)* (Judgment) [1986] ICJ Rep 14, para 218.

102 Henckaerts and Wiesener (n 96), ch 8, 198. See AP II (n 90) article 1.

103 Jeanique Pretorius, 'Enhancing Environmental Protection in Non-International Armed Conflict: The Way Forward' (2018) 78 *Zeitschrift Für Ausländisches Öffentliches Recht Und Völkerrecht* 904, 906.

104 The four Geneva Conventions (n 89), article 3(1)(a).

105 Ibid.

106 Ibid.

107 Ibid, article 3(1)(c).

108 Ibid; Pretorius (n 103) 906; Tara Smith, 'The Protection of the Environment and Natural Resources in Armed Conflict' in Sergey Sayapin and others (eds), *International Conflict and Security Law: A Research Handbook* (TMC Asser Press 2022) ch 20, 432; Carl E Bruch, 'All's Not Fair in (Civil) War: Criminal Liability for Environmental Damage in Internal Armed Conflict' (2001) 25 (3) *Vermont Law Review* 695, 709–710.

109 Tara Smith, 'The Prohibition of Environmental Damage During the Conduct of Hostilities in Non-International Armed Conflict' (PhD thesis, National University of Ireland Galway, 2013) 54. This author agrees with Smith's observation.

110 For example, articles 14, 15 and 16 of AP II (n 90); Smith (n 108) 433; see also Pretorius (n 103) 906–913.

111 Theodor Meron, 'Chapter XX Comment: Protection of the Environment During Non-International Armed Conflicts' in Richard Grunawalt, John King and Ronald McClain (eds), *Protection of the Environment in Armed Conflict and Other Military Operations* (Naval War College International Law Studies 1996) 353; Smith (n 108) 432.

112 AP II (n 90); Smith (n 108) 432–433.

113 Smith (n 108) 433. See also Daniëla Dam, 'International Law and Resource Plunder: The Protection of Natural Resources During Armed Conflict' (2009) 19 (1) *Yearbook of International Environmental Law* 27, 53.

114 Pretorius (n 36) 62–63.

115 Pretorius (n 103) 931–932.

116 Pretorius (n 36) 86, 239.

117 Weir (n 45).

118 Stravos Pantazopoulos, 'Report: 2019's UN General Assembly Debate on the Protection of the Environment in Relation to Armed Conflicts' *CEOBS* (December 2019) <https://ceobs.org/report-2019s-un-general-assembly-debate-on-the-protection-of-the-environment-in-relation-to-armed-conflicts/>. See, for example, statements made by the Republic of Korea, Egypt, Cyprus, Colombia in UN Doc. A/C.6/74/SR.30. For statements made by the Islamic Republic of Iran and Portugal and Mexico, see UN Doc. A/C.6/74/SR.29.

119 UN Doc. A/77/10 (n 24) para (3) of the Commentary to Principle 1 versus the version during the Seventy-first session. See UN Doc. A/74/10, Commentary to Draft Principle 1, 216.

120 UN Doc. A/77/10 (n 24) para (3) of the Commentary to Principle 1, 100. See, for example, Principles 5, 8, 9(3) and 22.
121 Vhumbunu (n 12); Bekoe and others (n 9).
122 UN Doc. A/77/10 (n 24) 154–158.
123 Ibid, 140–144.
124 Mukpo (n 29); UNESCO (n 56).
125 See Chapter 4 for the discussion on internal displacement consequent on armed conflict and climate change.
126 Mozambique: Factsheet (n 26).
127 UN Doc. A/77/10 (n 24) 116.
128 Ibid, para (1) of the Commentary to Principle 8, 116–117.
129 Ibid, para (7) of the Commentary to Principle 8, 119.
130 UN Doc. A/CN.4/749, 53.
131 UN Doc. A/77/10 (n 24) para (7) of the Commentary to Principle 8, 119.
132 Weir (n 45); Stavros Pantazopoulos, 'UN Lawyers Approve 28 Legal Principles to Reduce the Environmental Impact of War' *CEOBS* (16 July 2019) <https://ceobs.org/un-lawyers-approve-28-legal-principles-to-reduce-the-environmental-impact-of-war/>.
133 UN Doc. A/77/10 (n 24) para (7) of the Commentary to Principle 8, 119.
134 UN Doc. A/77/10 (n 24) para (1) of the Commentary to Principle 16, 149.
135 Updated Guidelines of the ICRC (n 32) 74.
136 UN Doc. A/77/10 (n 24) para (1) of the Commentary to Principle 16.
137 ISS Report (n 30).
138 UN Doc. A/77/10 (n 24) para (7) of the Commentary to Principle 16, 152.
139 Rome Statute of the International Criminal Court (adopted 17 July 1998, entered into force 1 July 2002) 2187 UNTS 90, articles 8(2)(b) (xvi) and (e)(v); Updated Guidelines of the ICRC (n 32) 74.
140 UN Doc. A/CN.4/750, 13. As noted in Ms Lehto's report, there are Draft Principles where existing international obligations are referred to.
141 UN Doc. A/77/10 (n 24) 116; Weir (n 45).
142 Ibid, 149–152.
143 Statute of the International Court of Justice (adopted 26 June 1945, entered into force 24 October 1945) XV UNCIO 355 (ICJ Statute) article 38(1)(b); see also UN Doc. A/70/10 and UN Doc. A/CN.4/717, 58–59.
144 Ibid.
145 Weir (n 45).
146 Jonathan Somer, 'Environmental Protection and Non-State Armed Groups: Setting a Place at the Table for the Elephant in the Room' *CEOBS* (4 December 2015) <https://ceobs.org/environmental-protection-and-non-state-armed-groups-setting-a-place-at-the-table-for-the-elephant-in-the-room/>. See, in general, Heba Aly, 'Can Islamic Law Be an Answer for Humanitarians' *The New Humanitarian* (24 April 2014); ICRC, 'Islamic Law and International Humanitarian Law' (4 September 2018).
147 ICRC (n 6); See, in general, the website of Geneva Call, 'Humanitarian Engagement with Armed Groups and De Facto Authorities' <www.genevacall.org/>
148 UNGA Res. 77/104 (7 December 2022), 1–2; Rule 29 of the Updated Guidelines of the ICRC (n 32), 111–112. See also Jairo Munive and Finn Stepputat, 'How Non-State Armed Groups Engage in Environmental Protection' DIIS (24 January 2023) <https://pure.diis.dk/ws/files/15339879/Brief_2_NSAG_environmental_protection.pdf>; Conflict and Environment Observatory, 'States Adopt New Legal Framework on the Environmental Impact of War: Time to Transition to PERAC Implementation' *CEOBS* (8 December 2022) <https://ceobs.org/states-adopt-new-legal-framework-on-the-environmental-impact-of-war/>; Weir and Pantazopoulos (n 44).
149 De La Bourdonnaye (n 22) 601–602.
150 Sassòli (n 95) 6.

151 See Ahmed Al-Dawoody and Sarah Gale, 'Protection of the Environment and Non-State Armed Groups: IHL and Islamic Law Perspectives' Armed Groups and International Law (6 November 2020); See specifically Faculty of Islamic Studies and the International Committee of the Red Cross, 'Islamic law and International Humanitarian Law: Proceedings' (25 November 2020) 11, 47, 73.

Bibliography

Action on Armed Violence, 'The Broken Land: The Environmental Consequences of Explosive Weapon Use' (2020) <https://aoav.org.uk/wp-content/uploads/2020/04/The-Broken-Land-v4.pdf>.

Ahmed Al-Dawoody and Sarah Gale, 'Protection of the Environment and Non-State Armed Groups: IHL and Islamic Law Perspectives' *Armed Groups and International Law* (6 November 2020) <www.armedgroups-internationallaw.org/2020/11/06/protection-of-the-environment-and-non-state-armed-groups-ihl-and-islamic-law-perspectives/?mc_phishing_protection_id=28048-burse5f0s0vc5t9mgot0>.

Amnesty International, 'Mozambique: "What I Saw is Death": War Crimes in Mozambique's Forgotten Cape' (2021) <www.amnesty.org/en/documents/afr41/3545/2021/en/>.

Annyssa Bellal, 'The War Report: Armed Conflicts in 2018' *Geneva Academy of International Humanitarian Law and Human Rights* (April 2019) <www.geneva-academy.ch/joomlatools-files/docman-files/The%20War%20Report%202018.pdf>.

Ashoka Mukpo, 'Gas Fields and Jihad: Mozambique's Cabo Delgado Becomes a Resource-Rich War Zone' *Mongabay: News and Inspiration from Nature's Frontline* (26 April 2021) <https://news.mongabay.com/2021/04/gas-fields-and-jihad-mozambiques-cabo-delgado-becomes-a-resource-rich-war-zone/>.

Cabo Ligado, 'Mozambique Conflict Observatory' <www.caboligado.com/>.

Carl E Bruch, 'All's Not Fair in (Civil) War: Criminal Liability for Environmental Damage in Internal Armed Conflict' (2001) 25 (3) *Vermont Law Review*.

Case Concerning Military and Paramilitary Activities in and Against Nicaragua (Nicaragua v United States of America) (Judgment) [1986] ICJ Rep 14.

Charter of the United Nations (1945) <https://treaties.un.org/Pages/showDetails.aspx?objid=080000028017ebb8&clang=_en>.

Clayton Hazvinei Vhumbunu, 'Insurgency in Mozambique: The Role of the Southern African Development Community' *ACCORD* (21 April 2021) <www.accord.org.za/conflict-trends/insurgency-in-mozambique-the-role-of-the-southern-african-development-community/>.

Conflict and Environment Observatory, 'States Adopt New Legal Framework on the Environmental Impact of War: Time to Transition to PERAC Implementation' *CEOBS* (8 December 2022) <https://ceobs.org/states-adopt-new-legal-framework-on-the-environmental-impact-of-war/>.

Daniëla Dam, 'International Law and Resource Plunder: The Protection of Natural Resources During Armed Conflict' (2009) 19 (1) *Yearbook of International Environmental Law*.

Dorina A Bekoe, Stephanie M Burchard and Sarah A Daly, 'Extremism in Mozambique: Interpreting Group Tactics and the Role of the Government's Response in the Crisis in Cabo Delgado' *Institute for Defense Analyses IDA* (March 2020) <www.ida.org/-/media/feature/publications/e/ex/extremism-in-mozambique-interpreting-group-tactics-and-the-role-of-the-governments-response/d-13156.ashx>.

Doug Weir, 'How Does War Damage the Environment?' *CEOBS* (4 June 2020) <https://ceobs.org/how-does-war-damage-the-environment/>.

Doug Weir, 'The PERAC Legal Framework, Frequently Asked Questions' *CEOBS* (September 2022) <https://ceobs.org/perac-principles-frequently-asked-questions/#1663073164735-f59acb18-3a80>.

Doug Weir and Stavros-Evdokimos Pantazopoulos, 'If Not Us, Who? How States – With the Help of Civil Society – Can Implement the Legal Framework Protecting the Environment from Armed Conflict' *ICRC Humanitarian Law and Policy* (10 June 2021) <https://blogs.icrc.org/law-and-policy/2021/06/10/states-civil-society-protecting-environment-armed-conflict/>.

Emily Estelle and Jessica Trisko Darden, 'Combating the Islamic State's Spread in Africa: Assessment and Recommendations for Mozambique' *American Enterprise Institute* (February 2021) <www.aei.org/wp-content/uploads/2021/02/Combating-the-Islamic-State%E2%80%99s-Spread-in-Africa.pdf?x91208>.

Eoghan Darbyshire, *Witnessing the Environmental Impacts of War* (PAX for Peace 2020).

Erika Gibson, 'SADC Forces Tread Dangerous Ground in Mozambique: Landmines and IEDs Are Now Being Used by Insurgents, "Changing the Course of the Conflict"' *Business Day* (19 September 2021).

'European Commission: European Civil Protection and Humanitarian Aid Operations, 'Mozambique: Factsheet' (7 March 2023) <https://civil-protection-humanitarian-aid.ec.europa.eu/where/africa/mozambique_en>.

Faculty of Islamic Studies and the International Committee of the Red Cross, 'Islamic law and International Humanitarian Law: Proceedings' (25 November 2020) 47 <www.icrc.org/en/document/islamic-law-international-humanitarian-law>.

Geneva Call, 'Humanitarian Engagement with Armed Groups and De Facto Authorities' <www.genevacall.org/>.

Geneva Convention (I) for the Amelioration of the Condition of the Wounded and Sick in Armed Forces in the Field (1949) <https://treaties.un.org/Pages/showDetails.aspx?objid=080000028015847c&clang=_en>.

Geneva Convention (II) for the Amelioration of the Condition of Wounded, Sick and Shipwrecked Members of Armed Forces at Sea (1949) <https://treaties.un.org/Pages/showDetails.aspx?objid=08000002801591b0&clang=_en>.

Geneva Convention (III) Relative to the Treatment of Prisoners of War (1949) <https://treaties.un.org/Pages/showDetails.aspx?objid=0800000280159839&clang=_en>.

Geneva Convention (IV) Relative to the Protection of Civilian Persons in Time of War (1949) <https://treaties.un.org/Pages/showDetails.aspx?objid=0800000280158b1a&clang=_en>.

Heba Aly, 'Can Islamic Law Be an Answer for Humanitarians' *The New Humanitarian* (24 April 2014).

ICRC, 'Customary Law' (June 2023) <www.icrc.org/en/war-and-law/treaties-customary-law/customary-law>.

ICRC, 'Guidelines on the Protection of the Natural Environment in Armed Conflict' (25 September 2020) <www.icrc.org/en/document/guidelines-protection-natural-environment-armed-conflict-rules-and-recommendations-relating>.

ICRC, 'How Does Law Protect War? Incendiary Weapons' <https://casebook.icrc.org/a_to_z/glossary/incendiary-weapons#:~:text=Weapons%20or%20munitions%20primarily%20designed,substance%20delivered%20on%20the%20target>.

ICRC, 'ICRC Report on IHL and the Challenges of Contemporary Armed Conflicts: Recommitting to the Protection in Armed Conflict on the 70th Anniversary of the Geneva Conventions' (22 November 2019) <www.icrc.org/en/document/icrc-report-ihl-and-challenges-contemporary-armed-conflicts>.

ICRC, 'Islamic Law and International Humanitarian Law' (4 September 2018) <www.icrc.org/en/document/islamic-law-and-international-humanitarian-law>.

ICRC, 'Mozambique: How Does Armed Conflict in Cabo Delgado Affect Access to Basic Services Like Water, Sanitation and Health?' (9 March 2023) <www.icrc.org/en/document/mozambique-how-armed-conflict-cabo-delgado-affect-access-basic-services-water>.

ICRC, 'Non-International Armed Conflict: VIII. Who Is Bound by the Law of Non-International Armed Conflicts?' <https://casebook.icrc.org/law/non-international-armed-conflict#chapter9>.

ICRC, 'Sources of IHL: Treaties and Customary Law' <https://blogs.icrc.org/ir/en/international-humanitarian-law/sources-ihl-treaties-customary-law/>.

ICRC, 'Twelve Issues for 2022: What States Can Do to Improve Respect for International Humanitarian Law' (21 March 2022) <www.icrc.org/en/document/twelve-issues-what-states-can-do-improve-respect-ihl-2022>.

ICRC, 'When Rain Turns to Dust: Understanding and Responding to the Combined Impact of Armed Conflicts and the Climate and Environment Crisis on People's Lives' (2020) <www.icrc.org/sites/default/files/topic/file_plus_list/rain_turns_to_dust_climate_change_conflict.pdf>.

ICRC, 'Why the ICRC Talks to Armed Groups' (1 March 2023) <www.icrc.org/en/document/why-icrc-talks-armed-groups>.

ILC, 'Analytical Guide to the Work of the International Law Commission, Protection of the Environment in Relation to Armed Conflicts' (9 June 2023) <https://legal.un.org/ilc/guide/8_7.shtml>.

ILC, 'Report of the International Law Commission on the Work of Its Seventy-third Session' (18 April–3 June and 4 July–5 August 2022) UN Doc A/77/10.

Indrė Lechtimiakytė, 'Preservation of Environment in Times of Non-International Armed Conflict. Legal Framework, Its Sufficiency and Suggestion' (2013) 20 (2) *Jurisprudence.*

'Insurgent Attacks Intensify in Ancuabe District of Cabo Delgado' *Zitmar News* (21 June 2022) <www.zitamar.com/insurgent-attacks-intensify-in-ancuabe-district-of-cabo-delgado/>.

'Islam' *History* (29 June 2023) <www.history.com/topics/religion/islam>.

Jairo Munive and Finn Stepputat, 'How Non-State Armed Groups Engage in Environmental Protection' *DIIS* (24 January 2023) <https://pure.diis.dk/ws/files/15339879/Brief_2_NSAG_environmental_protection.pdf>.

Jeanique A Pretorius, 'Enhancing Environmental Protection in Non-International Armed Conflict: The Way Forward' (2018) 78 *Zeitschrift Für Ausländisches Öffentliches Recht Und Völkerrecht.*

Jeanique A Pretorius, 'Protecting the Environment in Non-International Armed Conflicts Means Looking Beyond International Humanitarian Law Alone' *Conflict and Environment Observatory* (15 March 2019) <https://ceobs.org/environmental-protection-in-non-international-armed-conflicts-finding-the-way-forward/>.

Jeanique A Pretorius, 'The Protection of the Natural Environment in Non-International Armed Conflict under International Treaty Law' (LLD thesis, University of Pretoria 2018).

Jean-Marie Henckaerts and Cornelius Wiesener, 'Human Rights Obligations of Non-State Armed Groups: An Assessment Based on Recent Practice' in Ezequiel Heffes, Marcos D Kotlik and Manuel J Ventura (eds), *International Humanitarian Law and Non-State Actors: Debates, Law and Practice* (TMC Asser Press 2020).

Jean-Marie Henckaerts and Louise Doswald-Beck (eds), *International Committee of the Red Cross, Customary International Humanitarian Law: Volume 1: Rules* (CUP 2005).

Jean-Marie Henckaerts and Louise Doswald-Beck (eds), *International Committee of the Red Cross: Customary International Humanitarian Law: Volume II: Practice: Part 1* (CUP 2005).

Jelena Pejic, 'The Protective Scope of Common Article 3: More Than Meets the Eye' (2011) 93 *International Review of the Red Cross.*

Jokin Alberdi and others, 'Ayuda en Acción: War, Forced Displacement and Responses to the Crisis in Cabo Delgado: Mozambique' *Alliance 2015* (22 March 2023) <www.alliance2015.org/wp-content/uploads/2023/03/Informe-Guerra-en-Cabo-Delgado-en.pdf>.

Jonathan Somer, 'Environmental Protection and Non-State Armed Groups: Setting a Place at the Table for the Elephant in the Room' *CEOBS* (4 December 2015) <https://ceobs.org/environmental-protection-and-non-state-armed-groups-setting-a-place-at-the-table-for-the-elephant-in-the-room/>.

Jonathan Timberlake and others, 'Coastal Dry Forest in Northern Mozambique' (2011) 144 (2) *Plant Ecology and Evolution.*

Julia Stanyard and others, 'Insurgency, Illicit Markets and Corruption: The Cabo Delgado Conflict and Its Regional Implications' *Global Initiative Against Transnational Organised Crime* (February 2022) <https://globalinitiative.net/wp-content/uploads/2022/02/

GITOC-ESAObs-Insurgency-illicit-markets-and-corruption-The-Cabo-Delgado-conflict-and-its-regional-implications.pdf>.

Marco Sassòli, *International Humanitarian Law: Rules, Controversies, and Solutions to Problems Arising in Warfare* (Edward Elgar 2019).

Marco Sassóli, 'Taking Armed Groups Seriously: Ways to Improve Their Compliance with International Humanitarian Law' (2010) 1 *International Humanitarian Legal Studies*.

Martin Ewi and others, 'Violent Extremism in Mozambique: Drivers and Links to Transnational Organised Crime' *Institute for Security Studies* (5 September 2022).

Monique Bennett and Nnaemeka Ohamadike, 'How to Silence the Guns in Cabo Delgado' *Good Governance Africa* (12 April 2023) <https://gga.org/how-to-silence-the-guns-in-cabo-delgado/>.

'Mozambique Announces It Is Now Free of All Known Landmines, 2015 First Year in Decades Without Landmine Casualties' (1 December 2015) <https://reliefweb.int/report/mozambique/mozambique-announces-it-now-free-all-known-landmines-2015-first-year-decades>.

Mozambique Conflict Observatory 6–12 February 2023 <www.caboligado.com/reports/cabo-ligado-weekly-6-12-february-2023>.

Mozambique Conflict Observatory 22–28 March 2021 <www.caboligado.com/reports/cabo-ligado-weekly-22-28-march-2021#:~:text=26%20March%202021%3A%20Palma,trapped%20inside%20the%20Amarula%20hotel>.

Mozambique Conflict Observatory 25 April–8 May 2022 <www.caboligado.com/reports/cabo-ligado-weekly-25-apri-8-may-2022>.

Mozambique Conflict Observatory 24–30 May 2021 <www.caboligado.com/reports/cabo-ligado-weekly-24-30-may-2021>.

Mozambique Conflict Observatory 4–10 July 2022 <www.caboligado.com/reports/cabo-ligado-weekly-4-10-july-2022>.

Mozambique Conflict Observatory 6–12 September 2021 <www.caboligado.com/reports/cabo-ligado-weekly-6-12-september-2021>.

Nicolaas C Steenkamp, 'Cabo Delgado, the Dark Treasure Trove of Mozambique' *African Mining* (1 June 2022) <www.africanmining.co.za/2022/06/01/cabo-delgado-the-dark-treasure-trove-of-mozambique/>.

Protocol Additional to the Geneva Conventions of 12 August 1949 and Relating to the Protection of Victims of International Armed Conflicts (Protocol I) (1977) <https://treaties.un.org/Pages/showDetails.aspx?objid=08000002800f3586&clang=_en>.

Protocol Additional to the Geneva Conventions of 12 August 1949, and relating to the Protection of Victims of Non-International Armed Conflicts (Protocol II) (1977) <https://treaties.un.org/Pages/showDetails.aspx?objid=08000002800f3cb8&clang=_en>.

Richard Pearhouse, *Witnessing the Environmental Impacts of War* (PAX for Peace 2020).

Rome Statute of the International Criminal Court (1998) <https://treaties.un.org/Pages/showDetails.aspx?objid=0800000280025774&clang=_en>.

RULAC Geneva Academy, 'Non-international Armed Conflicts in Mozambique' (18 May 2023) <www.rulac.org/browse/conflicts/non-international-aarmed-conflicts-in-mozambique#collapse2accord>.

Saide Habibe, Salvador Forquilha and João Pereira, 'Islamic Radicalisation in Northern Mozambique: The Case of Mocímboa da Praia' *IESE Scientific Council* (September 2019) <www.iese.ac.mz/wp-content/uploads/2019/12/cadernos_17eng.pdf>.

Statute of the International Court of Justice (1945) <https://treaties.un.org/Pages/showDetails.aspx?objid=080000028004ca91&clang=_en>.

Stravos Pantazopoulos, 'Report: 2019's UN General Assembly Debate on the Protection of the Environment in Relation to Armed Conflicts' *CEOBS* (December 2019) <https://ceobs.org/report-2019s-un-general-assembly-debate-on-the-protection-of-the-environment-in-relation-to-armed-conflicts/>.

Stavros Pantazopoulos, 'UN Lawyers Approve 28 Legal Principles to Reduce the Environmental Impact of War' *CEOBS* (16 July 2019) <https://ceobs.org/un-lawyers-approve-28-legal-principles-to-reduce-the-environmental-impact-of-war/>.

Tara Smith, 'The Prohibition of Environmental Damage During the Conduct of Hostilities in Non-International Armed Conflict' (PhD thesis, National University of Ireland Galway, 2013).

Tara Smith, 'The Protection of the Environment and Natural Resources in Armed Conflict' in Sergey Sayapin and others (eds), *International Conflict and Security Law: A Research Handbook* (TMC Asser Press 2022).

Theodor Meron, 'Chapter XX Comment: Protection of the Environment During Non-International Armed Conflicts' in Richard Grunawalt, John King and Ronald McClain (eds), *Protection of the Environment in Armed Conflict and Other Military Operations* (Naval War College International Law Studies 1996).

Thibaud de la Bourdonnaye, 'Greener Insurgencies? Engaging Non-State Armed Groups for the Protection of the Natural Environment During Non-International Armed Conflicts' (2020) 102 (914) *International Review of the Red Cross*.

Thor Hanson and others, 'Warfare in Biodiversity Hotspots' (2009) 23 (3) *Conservation Biology*.

UN Doc. A/70/10.

UN Doc. A/74/10.

UN Doc. A/C.6/74/SR.29.

UN Doc. A/C.6/74/SR.30.

UN Doc. A/CN.4/717.

UN Doc. A/CN.4/749.

UN Doc. A/CN.4/750.

UNEP, 'From Conflict to Peacebuilding: The Role of Natural Resources and the Environment' (UNEP 2009) <https://wedocs.unep.org/bitstream/handle/20.500.11822/7867/pcdmb_policy_01.pdf?sequence=4&isAllowed=y>.

UNEP, 'Protecting the Environment During Armed Conflict: An Inventory and Analysis of International Law' (November 2009) <https://wedocs.unep.org/bitstream/handle/20.500.11822/7813/Protecting%20the%20Environment%20During%20Armed%20Conflict_An%20Inventory%20and%20Analysis%20of%20International%20Law-2009891.pdf?sequence=3&%3BisAllowed>.

UNESCO, 'Quirimbas Biosphere Reserve, Mozambique' (April 2019) <https://en.unesco.org/biosphere/africa/quirimbas>.

UNGA Res. 36/39 (8 November 1981).

UNGA Res. 77/104 (7 December 2022).

UNGA Res. 174 (II) (21 November 1947).

UNGA Res. 485 (V) (12 December 1950).

UNGA Res. 984 (X) (3 December 1955).

UNGA Res. 985 (X) (3 December 1955).

United Nations, 'International Day for Preventing the Exploitation of the Environment in War and Armed Conflict: 6 November' <www.un.org/en/observances/environment-in-war-protection-day#:~:text=Though%20humanity%20has%20always%20counted,the%20unpublicized%20victim%20of%20war>.

Vanessa Murphy and Helen Obregón Gieseken, 'Fighting without a Planet B: How IHL Protects the Natural Environment in Armed Conflict' *ICRC Humanitarian Law and Policy* (25 May 2021) <https://blogs.icrc.org/law-and-policy/2021/05/25/fighting-without-planet-b/>.

WCS, Government of Mozambique and USAID, 'Key Biodiversity Areas (KBAs) Identified in Mozambique: Factsheets VOL. II: Red List of Threatened Species and Ecosystems, Identification and Mapping of Key Biodiversity Areas (KBAs) in Mozambique' *Combo Program* (2021) <https://comboprogram.org/Portals/1/Documents/1622457927-2021_KBAs_Moz_vol_ii_Factsheets_EN.pdf?ver=F2plHBM5lZ2x3-c8UYcMoA%3D%3D>.

'Witnessing the Environmental Impacts of War: Environmental Case Studies from Conflict Zones Around the World' *Zoï Environment Network* (November 2020) <https://zoinet.org/wp-content/uploads/2018/01/Witnessing-the-environmental-impacts-of-war_EN.pdf>.

10 The conflict in Cabo Delgado and the relationship between international disaster response law and international humanitarian law treaties

Jeanique Serradinho

10.1 Introduction

Mozambique is exposed to extreme climatic conditions such as cyclones, storms and flash floods that have detrimental effects on food security and nutrition nationwide. Mozambique was struck by two consecutive tropical cyclones, Idai and Kenneth, in March and April 2019. These cyclones left over two million[1] people in need of urgent humanitarian assistance in addition to 815 000 people already in need of assistance as a result of drought.[2]

Cyclone Idai struck on 14 March 2019 near the city of Beira. Within one week of Cyclone Idai, the government of Mozambique formally requested international assistance for all elements of the humanitarian response including food, shelter, education and health, as well as logistical support, including air assets, boats and communications.[3] Then, on 24 April 2019, Cyclone Kenneth struck the Macomia district of Cabo Delgado.[4] While Cyclone Idai impacted the central region of Mozambique, damaging more than 240 000 houses, Cyclone Kenneth impacted the northern region, destroying more than 45 000 houses.[5] Other direct and indirect impacts of the cyclones included aggravated food insecurity, compromised access to safe water and damage to key infrastructure, which led to challenges in accessing services and basic supplies and displacement and protection issues.[6] Following these cyclones, Mozambique was affected by the COVID-19 pandemic and tropical storm Chalane, tropical cyclone Eloise and tropical storm Ana in 2020, 2021 and 2022, respectively. Compounding these disasters, since October 2017 an insurgency by the name of Ansar al-Sunna has been conducting armed attacks against both Mozambican armed forces and civilians in Cabo Delgado province.

The consequences of a disaster and armed conflict for affected populations are similar. For example, physical and psychological suffering, damage to and loss of infrastructure, displacement and loss of livelihoods; and both situations can trigger a need for international humanitarian assistance for those impacted. Similarly, the types of access barriers and quality issues faced with respect to humanitarian assistance are largely the same in both disasters and armed conflicts, although the different dynamics and heightened security threats at play in non-international armed conflicts (NIACs) compared to disasters can make delivering humanitarian aid in

DOI: 10.4324/9781003317647-12

conflict settings more challenging.[7] Indeed, disasters and armed conflicts are generally governed by separate bodies of law, with international humanitarian law (IHL) being the primary area of law governing NIACs and international disaster response law (IDRL) governing the facilitation of international humanitarian assistance in disasters. The question arising in this complex scenario for the purposes of this chapter is how these bodies relate to one another. Of course, international human rights law (IHRL) applies to both scenarios.

The aim of this chapter is not to examine the nature of the conflict in Cabo Delgado and its classification under IHL. However, given that IHL *could* apply, should the relevant thresholds be reached, it is worth examining the international law framework applicable in the context of disasters and NIACs occurring simultaneously. This chapter examines whether IHL treaty law rules are sufficient to facilitate international humanitarian assistance in mixed situations of disasters and armed conflict. It also examines whether IDRL may add to and complement IHL in mixed situations of disaster and NIACs, particularly regarding facilitating humanitarian assistance.

10.2 Mixed situations of disaster and armed conflict

Before delving into the meaning of mixed situations of disaster and armed conflict, it is important to define the terms 'disaster' and 'NIAC', respectively. 'NIAC' has been defined in Chapter 6.[8] 'Disaster' is defined in the Draft Articles on the Protection of Persons in the Event of Disasters, adopted by the International Law Commission (ILC) in 2016, as 'a calamitous event or series of events resulting in widespread loss of life, great human suffering and distress, mass displacement, or large-scale material or environmental damage, thereby seriously disrupting the functioning of society'.[9] This includes both natural and human-made disasters, slow-onset disasters that emerge gradually over time, such as drought, desertification and sea-level rise, as well as sudden-onset disasters which are triggered by hazardous events that emerge quickly, such as earthquakes, volcanic eruptions, flash floods, chemical explosions, critical infrastructure failures or transport accidents.[10] While the definition is broad, for the purposes of this chapter, the term 'disaster' does not include armed conflicts as disasters in and of themselves.[11]

NIACS and disasters may occur concurrently – resulting in mixed situations of disaster and conflict.[12] This chapter focuses on disasters occurring in the same region as an armed conflict. Such situations often compound the suffering of those affected. For example, the ICRC reported that the insurgency in Cabo Delgado has affected people's ability to feed their families, with farmers abandoning their fields outside larger towns such as Macomia for fear they will be attacked.[13] This came after having lost their previous harvest to cyclone Kenneth.[14] As a result, many families were left with little to eat and limited options to earn a living.[15] Mixed situations of disaster and NIAC can also be particularly difficult for international humanitarian assisting actors to navigate. The insurgency in Cabo Delgado province was cited as a factor that complicated the humanitarian response to Cyclone Kenneth in 2019, halting aid distributions in some instances and preventing aid from reaching those who need it most.[16] For example, it was reported that damaged roads and bridges impeded humanitarian actors from reaching thousands in need, and this was compounded by attacks in the region which interrupted aid deliveries.[17]

10.3 IHL treaty rules facilitating humanitarian aid during NIACs

The main IHL instruments regulating the conduct of parties to NIACs are Common Article 3 of the four Geneva Conventions of 1949[18] and Additional Protocol II of 1977.[19] Mozambique is a party to these instruments.[20] Common Article 3 applies to armed conflicts 'not of an international character occurring in the territory of one of the High Contracting Parties'[21] and provides minimum standards of protection required in NIACs.[22] Additional Protocol II provides comparatively far more rules regulating hostilities than Common Article 3 but has a more restrictive scope of application.[23] Classifying the insurgency in Mozambique under international law falls outside the scope of this chapter and has been examined in detail in Chapter 6. Should it be accepted that the insurgency in Mozambique has reached the threshold of a NIAC, at a minimum, Common Article 3 and customary law apply.

Common Article 3 does not reference humanitarian assistance directly but does provide that an impartial humanitarian body, such as the ICRC, may offer its services to the parties to the conflict. The Commentary on this aspect of Common Article 3 provides that an 'impartial humanitarian body' does not need to have its headquarters within the territory of the affected state, to qualify as such an entity.[24] Therefore, Common Article 3 recognises both domestic and international humanitarian actors, as long as the impartiality requirement is met and the body is sufficiently organised.[25] In principle, an impartial humanitarian organisation will only be able to carry out humanitarian activities if it has consent to do so, but that consent cannot be arbitrarily withheld.[26]

The provisions of Additional Protocol II may also apply, should the relevant thresholds be reached. With respect to humanitarian assistance, Additional Protocol II provides in article 18(1) that relief societies in the territory of the state may offer their services to the victims of the armed conflict.[27] Article 18(2) further provides that, subject to the consent of the state concerned, impartial humanitarian relief shall be undertaken if the civilian population is suffering undue hardship due to a lack of supplies essential for survival.[28]

Article 18 is aimed at permitting and facilitating humanitarian activities in NIACs for the purpose of assisting victims and assuring their protection and is understood to encompass both domestic and international relief actions.[29] Other elements of the provision have also been further explored.[30] For example, supplies essential for the survival of the civilian population include food, water, medical supplies and shelter.[31] Impartiality is understood to mean that no discrimination should be rendered in respect of the victims, for example, as to whom they are supporting.[32] Consent of the government in power is explicitly required by article 18 but cannot be arbitrarily refused.[33] In cases where it is not possible to determine the authorities concerned, consent is to be presumed in light of the humanitarian imperative.[34] Article 18 has also been interpreted to imply that once relief actions are accepted in principle, the authorities are obligated to cooperate by facilitating the rapid transit of relief consignments.[35]

This section has examined the IHL treaty rules governing humanitarian assistance in NIACs. Although both Common Article 3 and Additional Protocol II provide for humanitarian assistance to be rendered during NIACs, their provisions on this topic are limited and lack the detail and specificity required to facilitate effective and comprehensive relief operations.[36] The following section introduces IDRL and examines whether any treaties relevant to this area of law can facilitate humanitarian relief in mixed situations of disaster and armed conflict.

10.4 Overview of IDRL

The domestic capacity of any government can be overwhelmed by a large-scale disaster. While states bear the primary responsibility to respond to disasters and meet the needs of the affected population, support from the international community should complement national efforts when domestic capacity is exceeded.[37] While IHL regulates the conduct of hostilities and is triggered by the existence of an armed conflict, IDRL is the body of law regulating the facilitation of international disaster assistance in disasters, to meet the essential needs of persons affected. IDRL is grounded in the principles of state sovereignty, international cooperation and respect for human rights.[38] In contrast to IHL, there is no binding 'flagship' global agreement regulating international disaster relief and initial recovery assistance comprehensively. IDRL is instead regulated in a fragmented manner across various branches and instruments of international law.[39] The parts below identify a number of IDRL treaties and also indicate whether or not Mozambique is a party to these treaties.

The Framework Convention on Civil Defence Assistance[40] provides a framework to reduce obstacles to effective international cooperation between states in disaster settings. However, it is not extensively ratified.[41] There are, nevertheless, a number of treaties across various branches of international law regulating specific aspects of international disaster relief. With respect to telecommunications, the Tampere Convention on the Provision of Telecommunication Resources for Disaster Mitigation and Relief Operations (Tampere Convention) requires state parties to reduce regulatory barriers to the use of telecommunication resources for disaster relief.[42] With regard to transport, Annex 9 to the Convention on International Civil Aviation (Chicago Convention)[43] provides guidance for the facilitation of relief flights and clearance of aircraft containing humanitarian assistance in disasters. The Convention on the Facilitation of International Maritime Traffic mandates parties to facilitate the entry of vessels, persons and cargo engaged in disaster relief.[44] With regard to customs procedures, annex B3 and J5 to the International Convention on the Simplification and Harmonisation of Customs Procedures, as amended (Revised Kyoto Convention)[45] and annex B9 and D of the Convention on Temporary Admission (Istanbul Convention)[46] simplify customs clearance procedures for the importation of goods in disaster relief efforts.[47]

Instruments regulating the management of specific types of disasters also contain provisions for international assistance. For example, the International Convention on Oil Pollution Preparedness, Response and Cooperation (OPRC)[48] and its Protocol on Preparedness, Response and Cooperation to Pollution Incidents by Hazardous and Noxious Substances (OPRC-HNS)[49] require state parties to cooperate and provide technical support and equipment to respond to an oil pollution incident and for states requesting assistance to take measures to facilitate assistance,[50] such as measures to facilitate the arrival and utilisation of personnel, equipment and goods.[51]

While there is no internationally recognised right to humanitarian assistance in disasters, IHRL contains a number of provisions indirectly relevant to humanitarian assistance.[52] For example, the International Covenant on Civil and Political Rights (ICCPR)[53] and the Convention on the Rights of the Child (CRC)[54] protect the right to life[55] and to freedom from inhumane treatment.[56] CRC also includes an obligation on states to ensure the survival and development of the child to the maximum extent.[57] Several social and cultural rights can also be linked to humanitarian assistance. For example, the International Covenant on Economic, Social and Cultural Rights (ICESCR)[58] recognises the right to an adequate standard of living (including adequate food, clothing and housing), the right to freedom from hunger and the right to the highest attainable standard of physical and mental health.[59] ICESCR is noted as being a particularly strong human rights instrument to facilitate international humanitarian assistance as state parties are bound to use the maximum of their available resources, including international assistance, to progressively realise the rights contained therein.[60]

Of these global agreements, Mozambique is a party to the Chicago Convention;[61] the Nuclear Accident Assistance Convention;[62] OPRC;[63] CRC;[64] and ICCPR.[65] Mozambique is also a party to the Kyoto Convention but does not appear to have accepted any of the specific annexes thereto.[66]

At the regional level, the African Union (AU) Convention for the Protection and Assistance of Internally Displaced Persons in Africa[67] (Kampala Convention) includes persons who have been forced to flee as a result of disaster in its definition of 'internally displaced persons' and obligates state parties to facilitate international relief.[68] In addition, the African Charter on the Rights and Welfare of the Child (ACRWC)[69] provides that states must take all appropriate measures to ensure children internally displaced due to disasters receive humanitarian assistance.[70] More indirectly, the African Charter on Human and Peoples' Rights (African Charter) protects the right to life and the right to the highest attainable standard of health.[71] Mozambique is a party to the Kampala Convention,[72] the African Charter[73] and the ACRWC.[74]

In terms of the sub-regional framework, the SADC Protocol on Politics, Defence and Security Cooperation states one of the objectives of the SADC Organ on Politics, Defence and Security is to enhance regional coordination of international humanitarian assistance;[75] and the SADC Protocol on Health obliges parties to cooperate in the coordination and management of disasters and develop mechanisms for cooperation with emergency services.[76] Mozambique is a party to both protocols.[77]

10.5 Applicability of IDRL treaties during NIACs

The question that arises is whether these IDRL treaty provisions apply during NIACs. The first step in determining the effect of armed conflict on a treaty is to look at the provisions of the treaty itself. If the treaty makes provisions for its application during armed conflict, those provisions must be applied.[78] An examination of the IDRL-related treaties referenced earlier to which Mozambique is a party reveals that some treaties do address their applicability in armed conflict. The provisions of several IHRL treaties listed indicate that they apply in armed conflicts, at least to a certain extent. CRC and the ACRWC provide that states parties shall take all feasible measures to ensure the protection and care of children affected by armed conflict, in accordance with their obligations under IHL.[79] ACRWC also obliges state parties to provide humanitarian assistance to children internally displaced due to armed conflicts.[80] The Kampala Convention's definition of 'internally displaced persons' includes persons displaced by disasters and persons displaced by armed conflicts,[81] prohibits displacement as a method of warfare and prohibits armed groups from impeding humanitarian assistance or attacking humanitarian personnel and resources.[82] Several objectives of the SADC Organ on Politics, Defence and Security relate to armed conflict, such as protecting people in the region against instability arising from armed conflicts, indicating its continued applicability in armed conflicts.[83] The final treaty to which Mozambique is a party that addresses armed conflict is the Chicago Convention. Article 1 read with article 89 provides that states have complete and exclusive sovereignty over the airspace above their territory and that in situations of armed conflict, the provisions of the Convention will not affect the freedom of action of any affected state. Therefore, states may restrict or prohibit entry into their national airspace in armed conflicts.[84] However, many treaties, such as the Kyoto Convention, OPC, ICCPR, the African Charter, and the SADC Protocol on Health, are silent on their applicability in armed conflict.

Guidance from the ILC indicates that the mere existence of an armed conflict does not automatically suspend the operation of a treaty. The Draft Articles on the Effects of Armed Conflicts on Treaties take as their starting point that the existence of an armed conflict does not *ipso facto* terminate or suspend the operation of treaties.[85] The Draft Articles further provide factors to determine the effect of an armed conflict on a treaty where the treaty is silent on the matter and where the rules on treaty interpretation fail to provide the answer,[86] namely, the nature of the treaty and the nature of the armed conflict.[87] With respect to the nature of the treaty, the Draft Articles provide that one should look at the subject matter of the treaty, its object and purpose, its content and the number of parties to the treaty.[88] The ILC has developed a non-exhaustive list of categories of treaties, the subject matter of which implies they continue to operate during an armed conflict. Several categories of IDRL-related treaties are included in this list, such as IHRL treaties.[89] Indeed, a degree of acceptance of the continued applicability of IHRL treaties in NIACs has developed, and it has been argued that IHRL provides a more substantive protection of humanitarian assistance than IHL.[90] Other categories of treaties presumed to continue to apply in armed conflict which are relevant to this chapter include treaties of friendship, commerce and navigation, which could include the Kyoto Convention as a customs (and therefore commerce) agreement; and treaties relating to the international protection of the environment, arguably include the OPC and the Nuclear Accident Assistance Convention.

10.6 Relationship between IDRL and IHL treaties

The parts above have illustrated that several IDRL treaties continue to apply in NIACs or can be presumed to continue to apply by virtue of their nature. However, the substantive relationship between treaties in these bodies of law remains unclear. When two bodies of law deal with the same issue, they could apply harmoniously, or one or more of their norms could conflict.[91]

Several tools can help navigate the relationships between different branches of international law. The principle of *lex specialis*, for example, entails that if both a general rule and a more specific rule regulate a particular subject matter, then the more specific rule should take precedence over the more general one, and is often used to resolve conflicts between international law norms.[92] The use of the *lex specialis* principle to determine the relationship between IHL and IDRL appears to have been supported by the IFRC as early as 2007, as the study on law and legal issues in international disaster response states that 'IHL, as *lex specialis* in situations of armed conflict, should be considered to prevail in any potential conflict of provisions with other applicable law or instruments and serves as an interpretive guide for provisions of any applicable non-conflicting laws and instruments'.[93] The use of the *lex specialis* principle is also supported in the ILC's Draft Articles on the Protection of Persons in the Event of Disasters which provide in Article 18(2) that the draft articles do not apply to the extent that the disaster response is governed by IHL rules. However, the Draft Articles do not contain a blanket exclusion of their applicability due to the coexistence of an armed conflict.[94] The commentary states in such instances, IHL would apply as *lex specialis* and the Draft Articles would only apply to the extent that issues raised by a disaster are not covered by IHL and would therefore 'fill the gaps' in the protection of persons affected by disasters during an armed conflict.[95]

The use of the *lex specialis* principle to determine the relationship between IHL and IDRL, however, has been criticised on the basis that it is unclear which is the *lex specialis* regime between IHL and IDRL in mixed situations of disasters and armed conflict.[96] As IDRL instruments address various technical details relating to the facilitation of international assistance, their level of detail is often higher than IHL.[97] Complementarity, which is based on the 'assumption that the regimes whose application is at issue are on an equal footing and can thus mutually support one another', has been proposed as an alternative interpretive tool to determine the relationship between IHL and IDRL.[98] This approach has been proposed as being more suitable than *lex specialis* on the basis that both regimes have a common core objective, namely, the protection of humanity and, therefore, their rules 'have to be interpreted in a coherent way and inform the interpretation of each other'.[99] In other words, if a disaster occurs in peace time, IDRL is applicable, but in a mixed situation of disaster and armed conflict, IHL has to be applied, together with IDRL.

Regardless of the interpretive tool selected, determining the precise contours of the relationship between IDRL and IHL treaties would require an in-depth examination of each specific treaty provision. While this falls outside the scope of this chapter, this author asserts that, in general, IDRL treaties are particularly suitable to be applied harmoniously with IHL in mixed situations of disaster and armed conflict as the two bodies of law have complementary aims. Additionally, the nature of IDRL treaty provisions typically allows a level of discretion as to how they should be applied, and therefore the specific context being faced can be appropriately accounted for.

10.7 Conclusion

This chapter has examined whether IHL is sufficient to facilitate international humanitarian assistance in mixed situations of disasters and NIACs and whether IDRL may add to and complement IHL in these complex contexts, such as in Northern Mozambique, to fill any gaps identified. The core IHL treaties applicable in NIACs contain limited provisions facilitating international humanitarian assistance and lack detail. While no flagship IDRL treaty exists at the global, regional or subregional level in Africa, provisions exist across several branches of international law which can help facilitate international disaster assistance. Therefore, IDRL treaties may be useful to supplement the regulation of international humanitarian assistance in mixed situations of disaster and armed conflict. However, several IDRL treaties apply in limited contexts, such as the OPC to oil spills. While these treaties could support the facilitation of international humanitarian assistance in these specific contexts, other treaties could apply more generally. For example, the provisions of Annex J5 to the Kyoto Convention provide for relief consignments to be cleared as a matter of priority and free of customs duties, which can allow relief consignments to reach those who need it most, sooner.

The starting point to navigating the relationship between IHL and IDRL treaties in such situations is to examine if the wording of the relevant IDRL treaty provides for its application during armed conflict, in which case those provisions must be applied. If the treaty itself provides no guidance, the factors proposed by the ILC, namely, the nature of the treaty and the nature of the armed conflict, serve as a useful starting point to determine the effect of an armed conflict on a treaty. It was shown above that many IDRL treaties are silent on their applicability in armed conflict, but several fall within the categories of treaties presumed to continue to apply in armed conflict. Regarding the nature of the conflict, the territorial extent of the NIAC, its scale, intensity and duration, as well as the degree of outside involvement in the NIAC, need to be considered.

Even if it is determined that a specific IDRL treaty continues to apply in NIACs, it may not apply in the same way as in peace time. This chapter briefly explored two tools, the *lex specialis* principle and complementarity, which could be used to navigate the relationship between these two bodies of law and determine how the relevant IDRL treaty rules can be applied to 'fill in the gaps' in IHL on a case-by-case basis. While the *lex specialis* principle allows for the displacement of one rule in favour of another in the event of a conflict, complementarity may be a more appropriate approach to determining the relationship between the two bodies of law because. This is because in general, true conflicts between provisions would be unlikely due to the complementary aims of the two bodies of law and because the nature of IDRL treaty provisions typically allows a level of flexibility and discretion as to how they should be applied.

Notes

1 UNRCO and OCHA, '2018–2019 Humanitarian Response Plan, Revised following Cyclones Idai and Kenneth' (May 2019) 2.
2 Ibid, 5.
3 See OCHA, 'Mozambique: Cyclone Idai and Floods Flash Update No 6' (21 March 2019) 1.
4 UNRCO and OCHA (n 1) 5.
5 Ibid.
6 Ibid, 5–7.
7 See IFRC, *Law and Legal Issues in International Disaster Response: A Desk Study* (IFRC 2007) 156. See also Yves Sandoz, Christophe Swinarski and Bruno Zimmerman (eds), *Commentary on the Additional Protocols of 8 June 1977 to the Geneva Conventions of 12 August 1949* (Martinus Nijhoff 1987) 1476 available online as ICRC, 'Protocol Additional to the Geneva Conventions of 12 August 1949, and Relating to the Protection of Victims of Non-International Armed Conflicts (Protocol II), 8 June 1977. Commentary of 1987, Relief Societies and Relief Actions' <https://ihl-databases.icrc.org/applic/ihl/ihl.nsf/Comment.xsp?action= openDocument&documentId=086657E594BB4CC2C12563CD0043ADD0>. See also David Fisher, 'Domestic Regulation of International Humanitarian Relief in Disasters and Armed Conflict: A Comparative Analysis' (2007) 89 *International Review of the Red Cross* 345; Rebecca Barber, 'Facilitating Humanitarian Assistance in International Humanitarian and Human Rights Law' (2009) 91 *International Review of the Red Cross* 371; Felix Schwendimann, 'The Legal Framework of Humanitarian Access in Armed Conflict' (2011) 93 *International Review of the Red Cross* 993.
8 See also Martha Bradley, 'Determining the Intensity Threshold in a Mosaic of Non-International Armed Conflicts from *Lubanga* to *Ongwen*: The Contribution of the International Criminal Court to a Cumulative Assessment Approach' (2021) 84 *Journal of Contemporary Roman Dutch Law* 199, 201.
9 Draft Articles on the Protection of Persons in the Event of Disasters, with Commentaries (68th Session, 2016) II (2) *Yearbook of the International Law Commission* 25, draft article 3(a).
10 Ibid, commentary to draft article 3(a).
11 Ibid.
12 See Daniela Gavshon, 'The Applicability of IHL in Mixed Situations of Disaster and Conflict' (2009) 14 *Journal of Conflict and Security Law* 243.
13 See ICRC, 'Armed Violence in Northern Mozambique Exacerbates Post-Cyclone Suffering' (4 December 2019).

14 Ibid.
15 Ibid.
16 Simon Allison, 'Conflict and Cost Hamper Mozambique Cyclone Response' *Mail & Guardian* (10 May 2019).
17 Tendai Marima, 'Militant Attacks Complicate Cyclone Response in Mozambique's Cabo Delgado' *The New Humanitarian* (9 May 2019). See also ICRC (n 13).
18 Article 3 of Geneva Convention for the Amelioration of the Condition of the Wounded and Sick in Armed Forces in the Field (adopted 12 August 1949, entered into force 21 October 1950) 75 UNTS 31 (Geneva I); Geneva Convention for the Amelioration of the Condition of Wounded, Sick and Shipwrecked Members of Armed Forces (adopted 12 August 1949, entered into force 21 October 1950) 75 UNTS 85 (Geneva II); Geneva Convention Relative to the Treatment of Prisoners of War (adopted 12 August 1949, entered into force 21 October 1950) 75 UNTS 135 (Geneva III); Geneva Convention Relative to the Protection of Civilian Persons in Time of War (adopted 12 August 1949, entered into force 21 October 1950) 75 UNTS 287 (Geneva IV) (Common Article 3).
19 Protocol Additional to the Geneva Conventions of 12 August 1949, and Relating to the Protection of Victims of Non-International Armed Conflicts (adopted 12 December 1977, entered into force 7 December 1978) 1125 UNTS 609 (Additional Protocol II) article 1.
20 See ICRC, 'Treaties, States Parties and Commentaries'.
21 Common Article 3 (n 18).
22 Sandesh Sivakumaran, 'Re-Envisaging the International Law of Internal Armed Conflict' (2011) 22 *European Journal of International Law* 223.
23 Additional Protocol II (n 19) article 1.
24 See ICRC, 'Convention (III) Relative to the Treatment of Prisoners of War. Geneva, 12 August 1949: Commentary of 2020' para 834 <https://ihl-databases.icrc.org/applic/ihl/ihl.nsf/Comment.xsp?action= openDocument&documentId=31FCB9705FF00261C1258585002FB096> (ICRC Commentary GC III).
25 Ibid, paras 828, 831, 834.
26 Ibid, paras 866–878.
27 Additional Protocol II (n 19) article 18(1).
28 Ibid, article 18(2).
29 ICRC (n 7).
30 See Sandesh Sivakumaran, *The Law of Non-International Armed Conflict* (OUP 2013) 330.
31 Ibid, 330.
32 Ibid.
33 ICRC (n 7) para 4885.
34 Ibid, para 4884.
35 Ibid, para 4888.
36 Gavshon (n 12) 244.
37 IFRC, *Introduction to the Guidelines for the Domestic Facilitation and Regulation of International Disaster Relief and Initial Recovery Assistance* (2011) (IDRL Guidelines) para 3.
38 ILC (n 9) Preamble.
39 For a full review of binding and non-binding instruments relating to international disaster assistance, see IFRC (n 7) Part II. See also María Martínez, 'Public Policy and Disaster Management: The Role of Law in International Disaster Assistance in Africa' in Gedion Onyango (ed), *Routledge Handbook of Public Policy in Africa* (Routledge 2021) 563–573 and Jeanique de Sousa Serradinho, Stella Njeri Ngugi and Reece da Costa, 'Legal Preparedness for International Disaster Assistance in the SADC Region: An Analysis of the Incorporation of International Disaster Response Laws, Rules and Principles (IDRL) in Domestic Disaster Risk Management Legal and Policy Frameworks' (2023) *Yearbook of International Disaster Law* 93–122.

40 See Framework Convention on Civil Defence Assistance (adopted 22 May 2000, entered into force 23 September 2001) 2172 UNTS 213.
41 Ibid.
42 See article 9 of the Tampere Convention on the Provision of Telecommunication Resources for Disaster Mitigation and Relief Operations (adopted June 1998, entered into force 8 January 2005) 2296 UNTS 5 (Tampere Convention).
43 Convention on International Civil Aviation (adopted 7 December 1944, entered into force 7 December 1947) 15 UNTS 295.
44 See articles 5.11 and 5.12 of Annex 1 of the Convention on the Facilitation of International Maritime Traffic (adopted 9 April 1965, entered into force 5 March 1967) 591 UNTS 265.
45 See the International Convention on the Simplification and Harmonisation of Customs Procedures (adopted 18 May 1973, entered into force 25 September 1974) 950 UNTS 269 as amended by the Protocol of Amendment to the International Convention on the Simplification and Harmonisation of Customs Procedures (adopted on 26 June 1999, entered into force 3 February 2006) 2370 UNTS 27 (Revised Kyoto Convention).
46 Convention on Temporary Admission (adopted 26 June 1990, entered into force 27 November 1993) 1762 UNTS 121 (Istanbul Convention).
47 See Annexes B3 and J5 of the Revised Kyoto Convention; and Annex B9 and D of the Istanbul Convention.
48 International Convention on Oil Pollution Preparedness, Response and Cooperation (adopted 30 November 1990, entered into force 13 May 1995) 1891 UNTS 51.
49 Protocol on Preparedness, Response and Co-operation to Pollution Incidents by Hazardous and Noxious Substances (adopted 15 March 2000, entered into force 14 June 2007).
50 See article 7 of the OPRC and article 5 of the OPRC-HNS.
51 OPRC articles 7(3)(a) and (b).
52 See on this Barber (n 7). See also Fisher (n 7) 347–349 and Matthias Vanhullebusch, *The Law of International Humanitarian Relief in Non-International Armed Conflicts* (Brill Nijhoff 2022) 58.
53 International Covenant on Civil and Political Rights (adopted 16 December 1966, entered into force 23 March 1976) 999 UNTS 171 (ICCPR).
54 Convention on the Rights of the Child (adopted 20 November 1989, entered into force 2 September 1990) 1577 UNTS 3 (CRC).
55 ICCPR article 6; CRC article 6(1).
56 ICCPR article 7; CRC article 37(1).
57 CRC article 6(2).
58 International Covenant on Economic, Social and Cultural Rights (adopted 16 December 1966, entered into force 3 January 1976) 993 UNTS 3 (ICESCR).
59 Ibid, articles 11(1), 11(2), 16.
60 ICESCR article 2(1). See also Barber (n 7) 395.
61 See ICAO, 'Convention on International Civil Aviation signed at Chicago on 7 December 1944' <www.icao.int/publications/Documents/chicago.pdf>.
62 See International Atomic Energy Agency, 'Convention on Assistance in the Case of a Nuclear Accident or Radiological Emergency' <www.iaea.org/sites/default/files/22/06/cacnare_status.pdf>.
63 International Maritime Organisation, 'Status of IMO Treaties' (18 October 2022) <wwwcdn.imo.org/localresources/en/About/Conventions/StatusOfConventions/Status%20of%20IMO%20Treaties.pdf>.
64 United Nations Treaty Collection, 'Convention on the Rights of the Child' <https://treaties.un.org/pages/ViewDetails.aspx?src=IND&mtdsg_no=IV-11&chapter=4&clang=_en>.
65 United Nations Treaty Collection, 'International Covenant on Civil and Political Rights' <https://treaties.un.org/Pages/ViewDetails.aspx?chapter=4&clang=_en&mtdsg_no=IV-4&src=IND>.

66 World Customs Organisation, 'International Convention on the Simplification and Harmonisation of Customs Procedures (as amended): Notification by the Republic of Mozambique' <www.wcoomd.org/-/media/wco/public/global/pdf/about-us/legal-instruments/conventions-and-agreements/contracting-parties-and-instruments/mozambique/pg0214b1-notification.pdf?la=en>.
67 African Union Convention for the Protection and Assistance of Internally Displaced Persons in Africa (adopted 23 October 2009, entered into force 6 December 2012) 3014 UNTS 3 (Kampala Convention).
68 Kampala Convention article 5(7).
69 African Charter on the Rights and Welfare of the Child (adopted 11 July 1990, entered into force 29 November 1999) (ACRWC).
70 Ibid, article 23.
71 African Charter of Human and Peoples' Rights (adopted 27 June 1981, entered into force 21 October 1986) (African Charter) 1520 UNTS 217 articles 4, 16 (African Charter).
72 Kampala Convention.
73 ACHPR, 'African Charter on Human and Peoples' Rights' <www.achpr.org/legalinstruments/detail?id=49>.
74 AU, 'African Charter on the Rights and Welfare of the Child' <https://au.int/sites/default/files/treaties/36804-sl-AFRICAN%20CHARTER%20ON%20THE%20RIGHTS%20AND%20WELFARE%20OF%20THE%20CHILD.pdf>.
75 SADC, Protocol on Politics, Defence and Security Cooperation (adopted 14 August 2001, entered into force 2 March 2004) 3158 UNTS article 2(2)(l).
76 SADC, Protocol on Health in the Southern African Development Community (adopted 18 August 1999, entered into force 13 June 2004) 3159 UNTS article 25.
77 See notes 75 and 76.
78 Report of the ILC, Draft Articles on the Effects of Armed Conflicts on Treaties with Commentaries (63rd Session, 2011) II(2) *Yearbook of the International Law Commission* 173, draft article 4.
79 CRC article 38(4); ACRWC article 22(3).
80 ACRWC article 23(4).
81 Kampala Convention article 1(k).
82 Ibid, articles 7(a), (g) and (h).
83 SADC, Protocol on Politics, Defence and Security Cooperation, article 2(a).
84 See Yoram Dinstein and Arne Willy Dahl, *Oslo Manual on Select Topics of the Law of Armed Conflict* (Springer 2020) 81.
85 See Draft Articles on the Effects of Armed Conflicts on Treaties (n 78) draft article 5 and the commentary thereto.
86 Namely, articles 31 and 32 of the Vienna Convention on the Law of Treaties (adopted 23 May 1969, entered into force 27 January 1980) 1155 UNTS 331. See Draft Articles on the Effects of Armed Conflicts on Treaties (n 78) draft article 5 and the commentary thereto.
87 Draft Articles on the Effects of Armed Conflicts on Treaties (n 78) draft article 6 and the commentary thereto.
88 Ibid. See also Arnold Pronto, 'The Effect of War on Treaties – What Happens to Their Treaties When States Go to War?' (2013) 2 *Cambridge Journal of International and Comparative Law* 227, 236–237.
89 Draft Articles on the Effects of Armed Conflict on Treaties (n 78) annex.
90 Schwendimann (n 7) 1004.
91 See Erika de Wet and Jann Kleffner, 'Introduction' in Erika de Wet and Jann Kleffner (eds), *Convergence and Conflicts of Human Rights and International Humanitarian Law in Military Operations* (PULP 2014) 3.
92 See Flavia Zorzi Giustiniani, *International Law in Disaster Scenarios: Applicable Rules and Principles* (Springer 2021) 41.

93 IFRC (n 7) 157.
94 ILC (n 9) Commentary to Draft Article 18(2).
95 Ibid.
96 Giustiniani (n 92) 49.
97 Ibid.
98 Ibid, 44, 48.
99 Ibid, 44.

Bibliography

African Charter of Human and Peoples' Rights (1981) <https://treaties.un.org/Pages/showDetails.aspx?objid=08000002800cb09f&clang=_en>.

African Charter on the Rights and Welfare of the Child (1990) <https://au.int/sites/default/files/treaties/36804-treaty-african_charter_on_rights_welfare_of_the_child.pdf>.

African Commission on Human and Peoples' Rights, 'African Charter on Human and Peoples' Rights' <www.achpr.org/legalinstruments/detail?id=49>.

African Union Convention for the Protection and Assistance of Internally Displaced Persons in Africa (2009) <https://au.int/en/treaties/african-union-convention-protection-and-assistance-internally-displaced-persons-africa>.

Arnold Pronto, 'The Effect of War on Treaties – What Happens to Their Treaties When States Go to War?' (2013) 2 *Cambridge Journal of International and Comparative Law*.

Convention on Facilitation of International Maritime Traffic (1965) <https://treaties.un.org/Pages/showDetails.aspx?objid=0800000280129d04&clang=_en>.

Convention on International Civil Aviation (1944) <https://treaties.un.org/Pages/showDetails.aspx?objid=080000028016 3d69&clang=_en>.

Convention on the Rights of the Child (1989) <https://treaties.un.org/Pages/showDetails.aspx?objid=08000002800007fe&clang=_en>.

Convention on Temporary Admission (1990) <https://treaties.un.org/Pages/showDetails.aspx?objid=08000002800b2770&clang=_en>.

Daniela Gavshon, 'The Applicability of IHL in Mixed Situations of Disaster and Conflict' (2009) 14 *Journal of Conflict and Security Law*.

David Fisher, 'Domestic Regulation of International Humanitarian Relief in Disasters and Armed Conflict: A Comparative Analysis' (2007) 89 *International Review of the Red Cross*.

Draft Articles on the Protection of Persons in the Event of Disasters, with Commentaries (68th Session, 2016) II (2) *Yearbook of the International Law Commission*.

Erika de Wet and Jann Kleffner, 'Introduction' in Erika de Wet and Jann Kleffner (eds), *Convergence and Conflicts of Human Rights and International Humanitarian Law in Military Operations* (PULP 2014).

Felix Schwendimann, 'The Legal Framework of Humanitarian Access in Armed Conflict' (2011) 93 *International Review of the Red Cross*.

Flavia Zorzi Giustiniani, *International Law in Disaster Scenarios: Applicable Rules and Principles* (Springer 2021).

Framework Convention on Civil Defence Assistance (2000) <https://treaties.un.org/Pages/showDetails.aspx?objid=0800000280086ecb&clang=_en>.

Geneva Convention for the Amelioration of the Condition of the Wounded and Sick in Armed Forces in the Field (1949) <https://treaties.un.org/Pages/showDetails.aspx?objid=080000028015847c&clang=_en>.

Geneva Convention for the Amelioration of the Condition of Wounded, Sick and Shipwrecked Members of the Armed Forces at Sea (1949) <https://treaties.un.org/Pages/showDetails.aspx?objid=08000002801591b0&clang=_en>.

Geneva Convention Relative to the Protection of Civilian Persons in Time of War (1949) <https://treaties.un.org/Pages/showDetails.aspx?objid=08000002801 58b1a&clang=_en>.

Geneva Convention Relative to the Treatment of Prisoners of War (1949) <https://treaties.un.org/Pages/showDetails.aspx?objid=0800000280159839&clang=_en>.

ICAO, 'Convention on International Civil Aviation Signed at Chicago on 7 December 1944' <www.icao.int/publications/Documents/chicago.pdf>.

ICRC, 'Armed Violence in Northern Mozambique Exacerbates Post-Cyclone Suffering' *ICRC* (4 December 2019) <www.icrc.org/en/document/mozambique-armed-violence-exacerbates-suffering-cyclone-aftermath>.

ICRC, 'Convention (III) Relative to the Treatment of Prisoners of War. Geneva, 12 August 1949: Commentary of 2020' <https://ihl-databases.icrc.org/applic/ihl/ihl.nsf/Comment.xsp?action= openDocument&documentId=31FCB9705FF00261C1258585002FB096>.

ICRC, 'Treaties, States Parties and Commentaries' <https://ihl-databases.icrc.org/applic/ihl/ihl.nsf/vwTreaties1949.xsp>.

ICRC Database, 'Customary IHL, Rules – Customary IHL – ICRC' <https://ihl-databases.icrc.org/en/customary-ihl/v1>.

IFRC, *Introduction to the Guidelines for the Domestic Facilitation and Regulation of International Disaster Relief and Initial Recovery Assistance* (IFRC 2011).

IFRC, *Law and Legal Issues in International Disaster Response: A Desk Study* (IFRC 2007).

International Atomic Energy Agency, 'Convention on Assistance in the Case of a Nuclear Accident or Radiological Emergency' <www.iaea.org/sites/default/files/22/06/cacnare_status.pdf>.

International Covenant on Civil and Political Rights (1966) <https://treaties.un.org/Pages/showDetails.aspx?objid=0800000280004bf5&clang=_en>.

International Covenant on Economic, Social and Cultural Rights (1966) <https://treaties.un.org/Pages/showDetails.aspx?objid=080000028002b6ed&clang=_en>.

International Convention on Oil Pollution Preparedness, Response and Cooperation (1990) <https://treaties.un.org/Pages/showDetails.aspx?objid=08000002800aada6&clang=_en>.

International Convention on the Simplification and Harmonisation of Customs Procedures (1973) <https://treaties.un.org/Pages/showDetails.aspx?objid=080000028010b40c&clang=_en>.

International Maritime Organisation, 'Status of IMO Treaties' (18 October 2022) <wwwcdn.imo.org/localresources/en/About/Conventions/StatusOfConventions/Status%20of%20IMO%20Treaties.pdf>.

Jeanique de Sousa Serradinho, Stella Njeri Ngugi and Reece da Costa, 'Legal Preparedness for International Disaster Assistance in the SADC Region: An Analysis of the Incorporation of International Disaster Response Laws, Rules and Principles (IDRL) in Domestic Disaster Risk Management Legal and Policy Frameworks' (2023) *Yearbook of International Disaster Law*.

María Martínez, 'Public Policy and Disaster Management: The Role of Law in International Disaster Assistance in Africa' in Gedion Onyango (ed), *Routledge Handbook of Public Policy in Africa* (Routledge 2021).

Martha Bradley, 'Determining the Intensity Threshold in a Mosaic of Non-International Armed Conflicts from *Lubanga* to *Ongwen*: The Contribution of the International Criminal Court to a Cumulative Assessment Approach' (2021) 84 *Journal of Contemporary Roman Dutch Law*.

Matthias Vanhullebusch, *The Law of International Humanitarian Relief in Non-International Armed Conflicts* (Brill Nijhoff 2022).

OCHA, 'Mozambique: Cyclone Idai and Floods Flash Update No 6' (21 March 2019).

The Prosecutor v Dusko Tadic a/k/a 'Dule' Case No IT-94–1-AR72.

Protocol Additional to the Geneva Conventions of 12 August 1949, and Relating to the Protection of Victims of Non-International Armed Conflicts (Protocol II) (1977) <https://treaties.un.org/Pages/showDetails.aspx?objid=08000002800f3cb8&clang=_en>.

Protocol of Amendment to the International Convention on the Simplification and Harmonisation of Customs Procedures (1999) <https://treaties.un.org/Pages/showDetails.aspx?objid=080000028006826f&clang=_en>.

Protocol on Preparedness, Response and Co-operation to Pollution Incidents by Hazardous and Noxious Substances (2000) <https://treaties.un.org/Pages/showDetails.aspx?objid=080000028058995б&clang=_en>.

Rebecca Barber, 'Facilitating Humanitarian Assistance in International Humanitarian and Human Rights Law' (2009) 91 *International Review of the Red Cross*.

Report of the ILC, Draft Articles on the Effects of Armed Conflicts on Treaties with Commentaries (63rd Session, 2011) II(2) *Yearbook of the International Law Commission*.

Protocol on Health in the Southern African Development Community (1999) <https://treaties.un.org/Pages/showDetails.aspx?objid=0800000280495709&clang=_en>.

Protocol on Politics, Defence and Security Cooperation (2001) <https://treaties.un.org/Pages/showDetails.aspx?objid=0800000280495db2&clang=_en>.

Sandesh Sivakumaran, *The Law of Non-International Armed Conflict* (OUP 2013).

Sandesh Sivakumaran, 'Re-Envisaging the International Law of Internal Armed Conflict' (2011) 22 *European Journal of International Law*.

Simon Allison, 'Conflict and Cost Hamper Mozambique Cyclone Response' *Mail & Guardian* (10 May 2019).

'Tampere Convention on the Provision of Telecommunication Resources for Disaster Mitigation and Relief Operations' (1998).

Tendai Marima, 'Militant Attacks Complicate Cyclone Response in Mozambique's Cabo Delgado' *The New Humanitarian* (9 May 2019).

UNRCO and OCHA, '2018–2019 Humanitarian Response Plan, Revised following Cyclones Idai and Kenneth' (May 2019).

Vienna Convention on the Law of Treaties (1969) <https://treaties.un.org/Pages/showDetails.aspx?objid=080000028003902f&clang=_en>.

World Customs Organisation, 'International Convention on the Simplification and Harmonisation of Customs Procedures (as Amended): Notification by the Republic of Mozambique' <www.wcoomd.org/-/media/wco/public/global/pdf/about-us/legal-instruments/conventions-and-agreements/contracting-parties-and-instruments/mozambique/pg0214b1-notification.pdf?la=en>.

Yoram Dinstein and Arne Willy Dahl, *Oslo Manual on Select Topics of the Law of Armed Conflict* (Springer 2020).

Yves Sandoz, Christophe Swinarski and Bruno Zimmerman (eds), *Commentary on the Additional Protocols of 8 June 1977 to the Geneva Conventions of 12 August 1949* (Martinus Nijhoff Publishers 1987) available online as ICRC, 'Protocol Additional to the Geneva Conventions of 12 August 1949, and Relating to the Protection of Victims of Non-International Armed Conflicts (Protocol II), 8 June 1977. Commentary of 1987, Relief Societies and Relief Actions' <https://ihl-databases.icrc.org/applic/ihl/ihl.nsf/Comment.xsp?action= openDocument&documentId=086657E594BB4CC2C12563CD0043ADD0>.

11 COVID-19 and its implications for the law of non-international armed conflict

The case of Mozambique

Annelize McKay, Chazanne Grobler and Martha M. Bradley

11.1 Introduction

The outbreak of the COVID-19 pandemic had a worldwide effect on many everyday aspects of human life. Therefore, it is not surprising that it should also have a significant effect on the way in which wars are fought.[1] The focus here is on the considerable impact the pandemic has on the law of non-international armed conflict (LoNIAC) that governs internal conflicts between state armed forces and non-state armed groups.[2] Borders are not an impediment to the spread of disease, epidemics or pandemics,[3] which crosses easily into war-torn areas regardless of who exercises control over such territory – a state or a non-state actor.[4]

The ongoing conflict in the Cabo Delgado region of Mozambique has affected the way in which the Mozambican government responded to those infected with and affected by COVID-19. The situation poses a challenge to the existing legal framework of LoNIAC. The pandemic raises questions about the content of those rules of LoNIAC governing non-international armed conflict (NIAC) in the context of a public health crisis. Are the current rules a sufficient response in a pandemic of such magnitude or should other areas of law, such as international human rights law, be consulted? The pandemic raises a novel question in relation to the legal obligations owed by Ansar al-Sunna to individuals who, due to a COVID-19 diagnosis, are symptomatic and in need of treatment but are in areas of Cabo Delgado under Ansar al-Sunna control.

This chapter examines the implications the COVID-19 pandemic has for the LoNIAC and focuses on the conflict in the Cabo Delgado region of Mozambique. In addition to an examination of aspects of international humanitarian law (IHL) in the context of the conflict and COVID-19, reference is made to international human rights law (IHRL) as it applies in situations not covered by IHL. Lastly, recommendations are offered as to what can be done better in the future, specifically with respect to the combination of the COVID-19 pandemic and conflict as well as more generally.

11.2 The role of COVID-19 in the conflict in the Cabo Delgado region

The COVID-19 pandemic has affected virtually every country in the world. Together with other communicable diseases, COVID-19 has significant implications for

DOI: 10.4324/9781003317647-13

humanity during armed conflict. In the case of Mozambique, the COVID-19 pandemic has compounded the destructive effect of the ongoing conflict in the Cabo Delgado region, worsened existing humanitarian needs and added to the difficulty in providing assistance to those affected by the conflict.[5] Humanitarian actors, such as the International Committee of the Red Cross (ICRC), face problems in providing essential aid to those in need.[6] The ICRC reports that access to affected populations is restricted due to safety concerns, a lack of infrastructure and delivering medical supplies, food and water to those who need it most is challenging.[7]

Second, the COVID-19 pandemic adds a further layer of complexity to an already complicated situation. In March 2020 the Mozambican government declared a state of emergency and implemented lockdown measures to slow the spread of the virus.[8] The effect of these measures has impeded humanitarian access to affected populations, whereas the need for assistance is still more urgent.[9] The ICRC has adapted its operations to respond to the COVID-19 pandemic; it has implemented preventive measures, such as providing personal protective equipment to its staff and partners and increased its support to healthcare facilities to ensure that, despite the pandemic, they continue to function.[10]

Third, as a result of the conflict itself, the healthcare system in the region has been severely affected and many health facilities are damaged or destroyed and healthcare workers are forced to flee the violence.[11] These developments leave the population vulnerable to other health risks, including the spread of communicable diseases, which increases the impact of COVID-19.[12] The ICRC has been supporting the healthcare facilities in the region, including by providing medical supplies and training healthcare workers in response to the pandemic and other health risks.[13]

In conclusion, the ongoing conflict in the Cabo Delgado region of Mozambique presents humanitarian actors with a significant challenge in providing aid and assistance to populations affected by armed conflict and the COVID-19 pandemic. The ICRC and other humanitarian organisations have adapted their operations in response to the challenges presented in a complex situation but, due to unsafe conditions, a lack of infrastructure and the impact of COVID-19 on the region's healthcare system, access to affected populations remains a difficulty.

The following text focus on the protective measures embedded in IHL and IHRL with reference to healthcare and related rights.

11.3 Protective measures in international humanitarian law and international human rights during a pandemic

11.3.1 International humanitarian law and COVID-19

The international legal framework applicable to the regulation of the COVID-19 response in Cabo Delgado is determined by the existence and nature of the conflict.[14] The existence of an armed conflict triggers the application of IHL.[15] The type of conflict, whether it is international or non-international, establishes the category of rules that apply under IHL.[16] Lastly, the category of non-international armed conflict decides the applicable treaty rules that regulate the situation.[17] As is shown in Chapter 6 of this edited volume, the ongoing armed conflict in Cabo Delgado, Mozambique, to which Ansar al-Sunna and the Mozambican government are parties, is non-international in nature and, furthermore, in every likelihood it fulfils the requirements of article 1(1) which triggers the application of Additional Protocol II (APII) to the four Geneva Conventions.[18] The classification of this situation as satisfying the requirements of an APII-type non-international armed conflict activates the entire corpus of the law of non-international armed conflict, including Common Article 3 to the Geneva Conventions,[19] APII (to which Mozambique is a signatory) and the customary law of non-international armed conflict. Both parties to the conflict are bound by the law of non-international armed conflict. Under treaty and customary IHL Mozambique and Ansar al-Sunna both incur the same legal obligations.

11.3.2 The wounded and the sick

Common Article 3(2), as well as article 7 of APII, provides the wounded and the sick with protection during an APII-type non-international armed conflict. To determine the scope of protection offered to the wounded and sick, as well as whether such protection is an adequate response in a pandemic, COVID-19 specifically, one needs to ask various questions. The first question to be addressed is whether COVID-19 qualifies as a situation that triggers the 'protection' of the wounded and the sick, as well as those who are the beneficiaries of such protection.

11.3.2.1 Who are 'the wounded and the sick'?

With regard to the protection of the wounded and sick, paragraph 1(2) of Common Article 3 provides as follows: 'The wounded and sick shall be collected and cared for.' APII elaborates on this obligation.[20] As Bellal points out, 'who is wounded and sick' is a seminal question, as it is 'the wounded and sick' who are the beneficiaries of protections afforded by the relevant provisions of the Geneva Conventions and their Additional Protocols.[21] Bellal remarks that it is a matter of interest 'what' constitutes a 'wound' or what type of 'sickness' is legally protected under the Geneva Conventions'.[22] The lack of a treaty definition of this phrase is interpreted to leave its meaning to 'common sense' and 'general usage'.[23] the rules of treaty interpretation will be employed to assess whether a pandemic such as COVID-19 qualifies as a 'sickness' that initiates the protection of the wounded and the sick.[24] In other words, does a person who tests positive for COVID-19 qualify under the term 'the sick' as included in the construct 'the wounded and the sick' and, further, can the person be a civilian or must 'the sick' be members of the armed forces or of the fighting forces of the armed group?

Paragraph 2 of Common Article 3 is constructed to be interpreted broadly in that it is worded that '[t]he wounded, and sick shall be collected and cared for'.[25]

Article 7 of APII provides greater detail as to the nature of the protective obligation. Article 7 provides:

Protection and care

1 All the wounded, sick and shipwrecked, whether or not they have taken part in the armed conflict, shall be respected and protected.
2 In all circumstances they shall be treated humanely and shall receive, to the fullest extent practicable and with the least possible delay, the medical care and attention required by their condition. There shall be no distinction among them founded on any grounds other than medical ones.[26]

Although the phrase 'the wounded and sick' is not defined in APII, article 8 of Additional Protocol I to the Four Geneva Conventions (API) provides a definition. Article 31(1), read with article 31(2)(b) of the Vienna Convention on the Law of Treaties (VCLT), permits the use of the definition in article 8 to promote a better understanding of the phrase. Article 31 of the VCLT determines that the ordinary meaning of a term should be given in its context and in light of its object and purpose and, therefore, the meaning of the construct 'wounded and sick' must be determined in the context in which it is used.[27] Article 31(2)(b) of the VCLT provides that 'context' may be found in a related instrument that is accepted as such by all parties to the original treaty that is being interpreted. API, in its relationship to APII, qualifies as being the type of instrument envisioned in article 31(2)(b). The ICRC, in its 1987 Commentary to Article 7 of AP II, similarly employs the definition in article 8(a) of API of 'wounded and sick' as the appropriate and applicable definition for APII.[28] Article 8(a) defines the 'wounded and sick' as 'wounded' and 'sick' to mean persons, whether military or civilian, who, because of trauma, disease or other physical or mental disorder or disability, are in need of medical assistance or care and who refrain from any act of hostility.[29]

Persons who are protected, therefore, are the sick (in the ordinary understanding of the term),[30] those who require medical care and those who refrain from participating in an act of hostility.[31] The wounded and sick during NIAC include members of the armed forces, members of an organised armed group (as represented in APII) party to the conflict and civilians[32] if two criteria are met. The first is the need for medical treatment. If such a person is not participating in hostilities, then such a person is a beneficiary of the protection offered in article 7 of APII. Therefore, it is established in the context of COVID-19 that members of the Mozambican armed forces, members of Ansar al-Sunna (that refrain from acts of hostility) and civilians who are symptomatic to the extent that they require medical care, are entitled to the protections offered in article 7 of APII.

The examination now turns to the nature of 'care' that is owed to the wounded and sick by the parties to the conflict, in other words, the type of medical care people who are COVID positive and symptomatic are owed in the context of the conflict in Cabo Delgado. Article 7(2) of APII determines the nature of the obligation of parties to the conflict to protect and care for the wounded and sick.

Article 7(2) has two parts. First, an obligation to provide medical care and, second, a prohibition on discrimination. The wording 'in all circumstances' in article 7(2) of APII imposes an absolute duty that the 'sick' are to be treated humanely.[33] The wounded and sick, also, are to receive the medical care and attention their medical condition demands. We interpret the wording 'to the fullest extent practicable' and 'with the least possible delay' to reflect on the part of the drafters a recognition of reality regarding the capacity, especially of the non-state party, as well as the battlefield reality and the resultant delay of treatment during the battle, and a lack of infrastructure or an overburdened healthcare system.

The nature or scope of 'medical care and attention' is an obligation of means.[34] Giacca explains that the nature and extent of medical care demanded of an organised armed group depends on the capability of the group as well as the situation at the time medical care is needed.[35] Giacca considers that the nature of care an armed group can deliver is 'context dependent' and 'capacity related'.[36] With respect to the treatment of patients symptomatic of COVID-19, the ability test inherent to article 7(2) entails that the Mozambican government as well as Ansar al-Sunna provide the medical care within their means and as timeously as possible. The type of medical care is understood as ranging from basic first-aid treatment to comprehensive medical care.[37] Similarly, Müller explains that the inclusive definition of 'wounded and sick' indicates that the form of medical care goes further than first-aid and emergency medical treatment in response to a battlefield injury.[38] Müller argues that the term 'adequate care' covers short and long-term medical, mental and rehabilitative care for those with conflict-related physical and psychological health issues.[39] Müller specifically considers the obligation of parties to the conflict to care for the sick who, in times of conflict, fall victim to deadly infectious diseases.[40] Armed conflicts are conducive to the creation of conditions that exacerbate the transmission, progression and lethal nature of deadly infectious diseases.[41] Overcrowding in detention centres, insufficient vaccination coverage, a lack of access to water and sanitation and hygiene conditions are catalysts for the spread of diseases transmitted by air droplets, such as COVID-19.[42] A NIAC is a situation that is ripe for the spread of COVID-19,[43] and within their capability the parties must provide medical care. Realistically, article 7(2) of APII is interpreted as encouraging organised armed groups, if they lack the capacity, to allow humanitarian assistance agencies into the areas under their territorial control to provide medical care.[44]

The focus now is on the final sentence in article 7(2) as being of seminal importance in an armed conflict where enemy combatants, civilians and own forces need healthcare in a resource-scarce setting. Article 7(2) determines that the only distinction that can be made is for medical reasons. There is to be no distinction based on 'race, colour, sex, language, religion, belief, political or other opinion, national or social origin, wealth, birth or other status, or any other similar criteria'.[45] The priority in providing medical care depends on urgency and is subject to medical ethics.[46] In the context of COVID-19 and the specific need for ventilators, a healthcare worker enlisted in the state armed forces may not show favour to a soldier in the provision of treatment in a situation of shortage of ventilators. The only factor in decision making should be medical:[47] If the condition of an enemy combatant is more severe, they should be put on a ventilator. All patients are guaranteed not to be subjected to an adverse distinction under article 7(2) of APII.

The content of the provisions in article 7(2) is sufficiently broad and flexible to correspond to reality. Under IHL, however, the description of medical care does not detail how the spread of disease, for example, COVID-19, should be addressed and, therefore, the prescripts of IHRL must be examined.

11.3.3 International human rights law and COVID-19

During armed conflict, IHL provides a detailed set of rules that acknowledges the realities of war, including protecting the wounded and sick. Mehring, correctly so, argues that (in theory) due to the detail and specificity of the rules in IHL, the rights of protected persons to receive necessary medical care are better protected under IHL than under IHRL.[48] However, IHL does not fully address healthcare provision during an armed conflict,[49] and it is argued that IHRL may provide valuable additional protection. As Footer and Rubenstein state, IHL is crucial but IHRL acts 'as a powerful complement to it'.[50] However, it is noted IHRL binds only the state and it is controversial to argue that IHRL also binds organised armed groups, such as Ansar al-Sunna.[51]

IHL and IHRL initially represented two separate and mutually exclusive branches of public international law, but the possibility of a concurrent application of the two branches is now recognised by the International Court of Justice (ICJ).[52] APII, adopted in 1977, explicitly referred to human rights instruments in the Preamble, already establishing a link between the two branches of international law.[53] The concurrent application of IHL and IHRL subsequently was confirmed in the Advisory Opinion regarding the construction of a wall in the Occupied Palestinian Territory, where the International Court of Justice (ICJ) held that[54]

> [m]ore generally, the Court considers that the protection offered by human rights conventions does not cease in case of armed conflict, save through the effect of provisions for derogation of the kind to be found in Article 4 of the International Covenant on Civil and Political Rights. As regards the relationship between international humanitarian law and human rights law, there are thus three possible situations: Some rights may be exclusively matters of international humanitarian law; others may be exclusively matters of human rights law; yet others may be matters of both these branches of international law.

To demonstrate that the intertwined areas of IHL and IHRL may provide the necessary normative framework for healthcare provision during the NIAC coupled with the COVID-19 pandemic in Mozambique, an analysis of specific human rights, namely, the right to life and the right to health, will be conducted later. The analysis concentrates on the International Covenant on Civil and Political Rights (ICCPR)[55] and the African Charter on Human and Peoples' Rights (African Charter).[56]

However, it is mentioned that in general the most authoritative provisions on the right to health are considered to be found in article 12 of the International Covenant on Economic, Social and Cultural Rights (ICESCR).[57] Given that Mozambique is not a party to and, therefore, is not bound by ICESCR,[58] the applicable regional treaty provisions from the African Charter will be examined.

11.3.3.1 The right to life

The right to life is universally recognised as a fundamental and foundational human right, a 'pre-requisite' to all other human rights.[59] The non-binding Universal Declaration of Human Rights (UDHR) states that 'everyone has the right to life, liberty, and security of person'.[60]

The right to life is entrenched in ICCPR[61] and the African Charter.[62] Article 6(1) of ICCPR provides that '[e]very human being has the inherent right to life. This right shall be protected by law. No one shall be arbitrarily deprived of his life.'[63]

The African Charter states that '[h]umans are inviolable. Every human being shall be entitled to respect for his life and the integrity of his person. No one may be arbitrarily deprived of this right.'[64]

ICCPR[65] and the African Charter[66] explicitly determine that the right to life is an absolute right that cannot be derogated from. Therefore, the right to life applies also during armed conflict[67] and must be respected by the state party. To determine the nature of the right and the obligations of the state with respect to the right to life, the African Commission on Human and Peoples' Rights (African Commission), in line with the reasoning of the UN Human Rights Commission,[68] indicated that the right to life must be interpreted broadly.[69]

General Comment 36 to article 6 of ICCPR notes that this broad interpretation means that state parties must take appropriate action to address 'general conditions in society that may give rise to direct threats to life or prevent individuals from enjoying their right to life with dignity', which includes 'the prevalence of life-threatening diseases'.[70] General Comment 3 on article 4 of the African Charter also explains that the right to life places an obligation on states to take preventive actions to stop outbreaks of infectious diseases.[71]

As discussed earlier, IHL already places an obligation on the Mozambican government and Ansar al-Sunna to provide life-saving medical care to protected persons in need. IHL, therefore, provides the *lex specialis* norm to supply medical care to the wounded and sick but, given the broad interpretation of the right to life, IHRL provides better protection with respect to addressing the prevention of the spread of diseases such as COVID-19. Should the Mozambican government not take the minimum steps to protect its population from the spread of COVID-19, it would be in violation of the right to life as contained in ICCPR and the African Charter.

Hathaway and others argue that the precise scope of the obligation in relation to life-threatening or infectious diseases is not clear, but in the context of COVID-19 a state should not 'knowingly contribute to the spread of the virus'.[72] This requirement, for example, can include the state ensuring that healthcare workers have access to personal protective equipment and that access to essential healthcare services for the treatment of those dying from COVID-19 should not be denied.[73]

The broad interpretation of the right to life also entails that the progressive realisation of various other rights, including the right to health, is further interpreted as being necessary to ensure a 'full and dignified life'.[74] The right to health will be discussed in more detail below.

11.3.3.2 The right to health

In 1946 the World Health Organization (WHO) defined 'health' in the Preamble to its constitution as '[a] state of complete physical, mental and social well-being and not merely the absence of disease or infirmity'.[75] Subsequently, in the UDHR of 1948, the right to health was recognised. The Declaration provides for the 'right to a standard of living adequate for the health and well-being of himself and of his family, including food, clothing, housing and medical care and necessary social services'.[76]

The UDHR is a non-binding international human rights instrument but was, and still is, influential in the drafting of other treaties and constitutions. In African countries, including Mozambique, the normative framework for the right to health is anchored in the African Charter.[77] Article 16 of the African Charter states:[78]

1 Every individual shall have the right to enjoy the best attainable state of physical and mental health.
2 State parties to the present Charter shall take the necessary measures to protect the health of their people and to ensure that they receive medical attention when they are sick.

The constitution of the WHO, the UDHR and the African Charter all go beyond merely addressing the presence of disease to addressing the protection of health. Health protection is of the utmost importance in preventing and mitigating the impact of infectious diseases such as COVID-19.

In November 2010 the African Commission adopted the Principles and Guidelines on the Interpretation of Economic, Social and Cultural Rights in the African Charter on Human and Peoples' Rights (Nairobi Guidelines) to assist state parties to the African Charter in complying with their obligations.[79] The Nairobi Guidelines indicate that a useful framework to understand the nature of the obligations is to appreciate that there are four layers of obligations on states: the duties to respect, protect, promote and fulfil.[80] In certain aspects the rules in IHL address the duties to respect and to protect the right to health but, as argued by Lubell, the duty to fulfil is not as clear in IHL.[81]

Along with the duties to respect, protect, promote and fulfil, state parties also must ensure that the following key elements of the right to health are guaranteed, namely, availability, adequacy, accessibility and acceptability.[82] 'Accessibility' in the context of the right to health requires that everyone has the right to access healthcare facilities, goods and services without discrimination,[83] echoing the principle of medical neutrality contained in article 7(2) of APII. IHL, however, focuses on the medical neutrality or impartiality of access in response to the *immediate* needs of the wounded and sick, whereas IHRL covers more of the dimensions of healthcare services, including the *continuous* availability and accessibility thereof.[84] For example, the day-to-day difficulties of a person with physical disabilities to access health facilities are not addressed by IHL but rather by IHRL.

Nevertheless, not all obligations with respect to the various rights are immediate. Rather, the African Charter recognises the obligation of progressive realisation,[85] which entails that to achieve the full realisation of the right to health, and all other economic, social and cultural rights, states must implement reasonable and measurable plans taking into consideration the available resources.[86] However, there are minimum core obligations that ensure minimum essential levels.[87] The following are some of the pertinent minimum core obligations of the right to health in the African Charter[88] that are essential in combating the spread of COVID-19 and ensuring the necessary humanitarian relief:

a ensure the right of access to health facilities, goods and services on a non-discriminatory basis, especially for vulnerable or marginalised groups;
b . . .
c ensure universal immunisation against major infectious diseases;
d take measures to prevent, treat and control epidemic and endemic diseases;
e provide education and access to information concerning the main health problems in the community, including methods of preventing and controlling them.

The African Commission included a section in the Nairobi Guidelines that addresses disease-specific obligations. According to the guidelines, the state must establish a national mechanism for the response to epidemic, endemic and other infectious diseases.[89] In adopting and implementing national plans, policies and systems, the guidelines specifically list that the state has a duty to educate and provide communities with access to information about the prevention and control of health problems.[90]

Considering minimum core obligations, the Mozambican government has a duty to ensure access to vaccinations, personal protective equipment and oxygen concentrators and to ensure that other protective measures are implemented, including adherence to social distancing measures to help control the spread of and treat COVID-19.

Mozambique's health infrastructure is fragile and, together with a lack of sufficient resources and trained health professionals,[91] outside support from humanitarian aid organisations is needed to deal with the outbreak of communicable diseases. The Mozambican government may not interfere with an individual's right to health by preventing safe access to humanitarian assistance, especially during an armed conflict. Given the duty to protect and fulfil the right to health, it is submitted that it includes a positive duty on the Mozambican government to negotiate safe passage agreements with all parties to the conflict.

Under IHL humanitarian assistance is a contentious issue and the rules of IHL do not provide legal certainty with regard to arbitrarily denying consent.[92] IHRL, to an extent, fills the gap, as the state, in this instance, the Mozambican government, would violate the right to health by denying or preventing access to humanitarian assistance and by not taking reasonable steps to ensure the safe delivery of humanitarian aid. IHRL, however, does not fully protect individuals as there is no obligation, whether a negative or a positive duty, on non-state actors such as Ansar al-Sunna to protect, fulfil, promote or respect the right to health.[93]

11.4 Reflections and recommendations

11.4.1 Reflections

The COVID-19 pandemic laid bare vulnerabilities in the healthcare system in Mozambique, but the picture is not entirely bleak and there have been efforts that were successful. With the support of the World Health Organization (WHO) and various other organisations, the Mozambican government rolled out an effective COVID-19 vaccination campaign.[94] By May 2022 more than 40 per cent of the total population had been vaccinated.[95] Dr Benigna Maia, Deputy National Director of Public Health at the Ministry of Health of Mozambique, attributes the success in part to ensuring that the communities were educated and well-informed.[96] A further contributory factor to the effectiveness of the rollout was training health workers in data management.[97] The aim was not only a focus on managing COVID-19 but also to develop transferable skills.[98] Also, the WHO assisted the government by establishing four temporary clinics in three districts of Cabo Delgado in 2020.[99]

A further positive step the government took is establishing an Inter-Ministerial Commission on Human Rights and International Humanitarian Law on 28 April 2022.[100] The purpose of the Commission is 'coordinating and monitoring the implementation of human rights and IHL in Mozambique through reports, statements and the drafting of recommendations'.[101] The Commission will assist in ensuring that progress is made in implementing the action plans on human rights and IHL issues and it is pivotal in addressing the unique challenge identified earlier that faces IHL and IHRL.[102]

The last section of the chapter provides a set of recommendations by taking into consideration the above reflections and challenges to IHRL and IHL.

11.4.2 Recommendations

11.4.2.1 Signing of the 2018 Deed of Commitment

Armed groups often attack healthcare providers.[103] These attacks are considered one of the 'greatest humanitarian problems of contemporary armed conflict'.[104] Often, it has proved difficult to improve compliance with international law norms, such as those that relate to the status and protection of healthcare personnel.[105]

In 2000 a non-governmental organisation (NGO) called the Geneva Call was set up.[106] In 2018 the Geneva Call issued the Deed of Commitment under the Geneva Call for the Protection of Health Care in Armed Conflict (2018 Deed of Commitment).[107] The 2018 Deed of Commitment offers armed groups an opportunity to pledge to respect humanitarian norms specifically the protection of healthcare.[108] It is further recommended that the deed of commitment deals exhaustively with pandemic and epidemic management in the context of the NIAC in Mozambique and in the context of NIACs more generally. In this way, the deeds will be adapted to the specific conflict and the specific groups that are taking part in the conflict.

The first recommendation is that Ansar al-Sunna signs and commits itself to the Geneva Call's 2018 Deed. This recommendation is made relying on the recognition that, generally, compliance by armed groups that engage with the Geneva Call has been good.[109]

11.4.2.2 Access to healthcare supplies

In keeping with obligations undertaken in terms of the 2018 Deed, Ansar al-Sunna and the Mozambican government should agree to assure access to essential medicines and medical supplies in the Cabo Delgado region. In the context of COVID-19, supplies include personal protective equipment (PPE) and life-support systems for those who are seriously ill. Vaccination programmes delivered to the general civilian population and to the combatants must be boosted, not only in respect of COVID-19 but also by vaccination directed at halting the spread of communicable diseases.

11.4.2.3 Monitoring by the ICRC (compliance with IHL) and the African Union (compliance with IHRL)

Further, it is recommended that the ICRC remains active in the region, monitoring compliance with IHL by both sides in the conflict and providing humanitarian assistance. The African Union (AU) must establish a Committee of Experts to monitor the situation, to provide feedback about developments to the regional organisation and, importantly, to monitor compliance with international human rights law. A monitoring role matches the mandate of the African Commission.[110]

11.4.2.4 Mozambique should ratify the International Covenant on Economic, Social and Cultural Rights

Further, it is recommended that the Mozambican government sets in motion the process of ratifying ICESCR. ICESCR and the General Comments set out a roadmap for the better realisation of economic, social and cultural rights.[111] This should be done so that the country may benefit from the constructive dialogue that state parties have with the Committee on Economic, Social and Cultural Rights (ESCR Committee) on their implementation of ICESCR. The Committee will be able to determine whether the Covenant's norms are being applied in Mozambique, specifically during the armed conflict, and assess how the implementation and enforcement of ICESCR could be improved so that all Mozambicans will be able to enjoy the rights in the Covenant in full.[112] Further, it is important that the Mozambican government grasps that ratification of ICESCR is not the endpoint, but the start of giving effect to the rights enshrined in ICESCR.

11.4.2.5 Health infrastructure

In the context of COVID-19, the situation has revealed the urgent need for the Mozambican government, and other governments in the region, to develop the health infrastructure, to provide much-needed care for the wounded and the sick, including those infected with COVID-19. More field hospitals and mobile health clinics are needed, giving greater access to emergency COVID care but also to the treatment of other diseases, as exemplified by a recent outbreak of cholera.

11.4.2.6 Health surveillance systems

It is recommended that in conflict-affected regions, generally, and not only in Mozambique, it is a priority for governments to strengthen public health surveillance systems so that the emergence of new variants of the COVID-19 virus and other infectious diseases are identified and acted upon timeously.

11.4.2.7 Community engagement

Humanitarian organisations must work alongside community leaders and members of the community to strengthen educational efforts relating to infectious diseases such as COVID-19, preventive measures and promoting vaccine uptake.

11.5 Conclusion

Disease flourishes in areas where there is strife. The COVID-19 pandemic brought greater challenges in combating infectious diseases in the context of armed conflict. This chapter illustrates that IHL on its own is insufficient to regulate a response to a pandemic during a NIAC and that different areas of the law must be accessed to provide guidance, including human rights law. The recommendations presented are offered in the hope of providing guidance in combating COVID-19 in the Cabo Delgado region, specifically, but also to serve as a roadmap in a fight against an outbreak of infectious disease in areas of armed conflict. The recommendations relate to specific problems identified in the COVID-19 pandemic but are adaptable and can be applied to circumstances of other infectious diseases and conflict-affected regions.

Notes

1 UNHCR, 'COVID-19 pandemic' (November 2022); Human Rights Watch, 'Africa: Conflicts, Violence Threaten Rights' (12 January 2023).

2 ICRC, 'What Is the Humanitarian Impact of the COVID-19 Pandemic?' (15 September 2020).

3 The chapter focuses on the effects of the COVID-19 pandemic. Nevertheless, the observations are equally relevant to an examination of epidemic outbreaks of disease. An epidemic, is limited in scope, possibly covering an extensive area, but generally is confined to a geographical region. A pandemic describes the spread of an epidemic outbreak of disease to several countries or even continents and affecting large numbers of people. The distinguishing feature of a pandemic such as COVID-19 is the extensive geographical reach; see CDC, 'Section 11: Epidemic Disease Occurrence Level of Disease' <www.cdc.gov/csels/dsepd/ss1978/lesson1/section11.html>.

4 ICRC (n 2).

5 Ibid.

6 Ibid.

7 Ibid; ICRC, 'As If the War Was Not Enough – Stories of Hardship and Resilience in Times of COVID-19: A Report on the Pandemic's Impact on the Protection of People Caught Up in Conflict' (7 April 2021).

8 Anne-Sophie Jung and others, 'COVID-19 Preparedness and Response: Implications for Future Pandemics National Responses to COVID-19: Drivers, Complexities, and Uncertainties in the First Year of the Pandemic' (2021) 375 *BMJ* e068954.

9 ICRC (n 7).

10 ICRC, 'Mozambique: 1 Million People in Conflict-Affected Regions Receive Two Doses of the COVID-19 Vaccine' (28 June 2022) <www.icrc.org/en/document/mozambique-1-million-people-conflict-affected-regions-receive-two-doses-covid-19-vaccine>; ICRC, 'Columbia: Living in the Shadow of Armed Conflict' (23 March 2022).

11 ICRC, 'Humanitarian Response to COVID-19 in Mozambique' (19 June 2022).

12 Ibid.

13 Ibid.

14 Marco Sassòli, *International Humanitarian Law: Rules, Controversies, and Solutions to Problems Arising in Warfare* (Edward Elgar 2019) 168 para 6.01.

15 Martha M Bradley, 'Revisiting the Notion of "Organised Armed Group" in Accordance with Common Article 3: Exploring the Inherent Minimum Threshold Requirements' (2018) *African Yearbook on International Humanitarian Law* 57, 61.

16 Ibid.

17 Martha M Bradley, 'Additional Protocol II: Elevating the Minimum Threshold of Intensity' (2021) 102 (915) *International Review of the Red Cross* 1131.

18 Article 1(1) of Additional Protocol II (Protocol Additional to the Geneva Conventions of 12 August 1949, and Relating to the Protection of Victims of Non-International Armed Conflicts (adopted 8 June 1977, entered into force 7 December 1978) 1125 UNTS 609) determines its scope of application. That Ansar al-Sunna controls strongholds on Mozambican territory, in turn, enables this organised armed group to fulfil the other criteria listed in article 1(1) of APII. Information as to the exact situation on the ground is limited but the factual situation does suggest that some territory is under the control of Ansar al-Sunna. See 'Mozambique Conflict Observatory' (Cabo Ligado) <www.caboligado.com/>.

19 Common Article 3 is common to all four Geneva Conventions: Geneva Convention (I) for the Amelioration of the Condition of the Wounded and Sick in Armed Forces in the Field (adopted 12 August 1949, entered into force 21 October 1950) 75 UNTS 31; Geneva Convention (II) for the Amelioration of the Condition of Wounded, Sick and Shipwrecked Members of Armed Forces at Sea (adopted 12 August 1949, entered into force 21 October 1950) 75 UNTS 85; Geneva Convention (III) relative to the Treatment of Prisoners of War (adopted 12 August 1949, entered into force 21 October 1950) 75 UNTS 135; Geneva Convention (IV) relative to the Protection of Civilian Persons in Time of War (adopted 12 August 1949, entered into force 21 October 1950) 75 UNTS 287.

20 Article 7(2) Additional Protocol II (n18).

21 Anyssa Bellal, 'Who Is Wounded and Sick?' in Andrew Clapham, Paola Gaeta and Marco Sassòli (eds), *The 1949 Geneva Conventions: A Commentary* (OUP 2018) 758–759.
22 Ibid, 759.
23 Ibid.
24 The rules of treaty interpretation are codified in articles 31–33 of the Vienna Convention on the Law of Treaties (adopted 23 May 1969, entered into force 27 January 1980)1155 UNTS 331 (VCLT).
25 Common Article 3 to the Geneva Conventions (n 19).
26 Additional Protocol II (n18).
27 Article 31(1) VCLT (n 24).
28 ICRC, 'Protocol Additional to the Geneva Conventions of 12 August 1949, and Relating to the Protection of Victims of Non-International Armed Conflicts (Protocol II), 8 June 1977, Commentary of 1.01.1987, Article 13 – Protection of the Civilian Population' para 4637 <https://ihl-databases.icrc.org/en/ihl-treaties/apii-1977/article-13/commentary/1987?activeTab=undefined> (ICRC 1987 Commentaries to APII).
29 Article 8(a) of Protocol Additional to the Geneva Conventions of 12 August 1949, and relating to the Protection of Victims of International Armed Conflicts (Protocol I) (adopted 8 June 1977, entered into force 7 December 1978) 1125 UNTS 3 (Additional Protocol I).
30 ICRC, 'Protocol Additional to the Geneva Conventions of 12 August 1949, and Relating to the Protection of Victims of International Armed Conflicts (Protocol I), 8 June 1977, Commentary of 01.01.1987, Article 8 – Terminology' para 302 <https://ihl-databases.icrc.org/en/ihl-treaties/api-1977/article-8/commentary/1987?activeTab=undefined>.
31 ICRC 1987 Commentaries to APII (n 34) para 4638.
32 Article 7(1) of Additional Protocol II (n 18): '*All* the wounded, sick and shipwrecked, *whether or not they have taken part in the armed conflict, shall be respected and protected'* (emphasis added).
33 Humane treatment is underscored by the principle of humanity. This foundational principle of humanity informs the rules contained in the Geneva Conventions and its Protocols. For an overview of the principle of humanity, see Larissa Fast, 'Unpacking the Principle of Humanity: Tensions and Implications' (2015) 97 *International Review of the Red Cross* 111–131.
34 ICRC, 'Rule 110: Civilian Objects' Loss of Protection from Attack' <https://ihl-databases.icrc.org/en/customary-ihl/v1/rule10>.
35 Gilles Giacca, 'The Obligations to Respect, Protect, Collect and Care for the Wounded, Sick and Shipwrecked' in Clapham and others (n 27) 802.
36 Ibid, 803.
37 Ibid.
38 Amrei Müller, 'States' Obligations to Mitigate the Direct and Indirect Consequences of Non-International Armed Conflicts: Complementarity of IHL and the Right to Health' (2013) 95 (889) *International Review of the Red Cross* 129–165, 143.
39 Ibid, 143–144.
40 Ibid, 152.
41 Ibid.
42 Ibid.
43 ICRC, 'IHL Rules on Humanitarian Access and COVID-19' (8 April 2020).
44 ICRC 1987 Commentaries to AP II (n 34) para 4645.
45 Article 7(2) Additional Protocol II (n 18).
46 ICRC 1987 Commentaries to AP II (n 34) para 4647. Whether the medical ethics of a system of triage on the battlefield differ from the ethics of triage in a civilian setting has been the topic of much scholarly debate; see, for example, Eric R Frykberg, 'Triage: Principles and Practice' (2005) 94 *Scandinavian Journal of Surgery* 272–278; Michael

L Gross, *Bioethics and Armed Conflict* (MIT Press 2006) 137; Kenneth G Swan, MC Usar and Swan Jr BS, 'Triage, the Past Revisited' (1996) 161 *Military Medicine* 448; Kenneth V Iserson and John C Moskop, 'Triage in Medicine (Part 1): Concept, History and Types' (2007) 49 *Annals of Emergency Medicine* 275–281; ICRC, 'First Aid in Armed Conflicts and Other Situations of Violence (2010)' 116.

47 ICRC 1987 Commentaries to APII (n 34) para 4646.

48 Sigrid Mehring, *First Do No Harm: Medical Ethics in International Humanitarian Law* (Brill Nijhoff 2015) 274.

49 Katherine HA Footer and Leonard S Rubenstein, 'A Human Rights Approach to Health Care in Conflict' (2013) 95 *International Review of the Red Cross* 168.

50 Ibid, 187.

51 See ICRC, 'Detention by Non-State Armed Groups Obligations Under International Humanitarian Law and Examples of How to Implement Them' (4 April 2023) 9.

52 Cordula Droege, 'The Interplay Between International Humanitarian Law and International Human Rights Law in Situations of Armed Conflict' (2007) 40 (2) *Israel Law Review* 310–355, 310–311. Many believe that the close relationship between these two areas existed and was perceived "from the outset". That is not at all the case. Formerly assigned to separate legal categories, it was only under the persistent scrutiny of modern analysts that they revealed the common attributes which would seem to promise many fruitful exchanges in the future.' Robert Kolb, 'The Relationship Between International Humanitarian Law and Human Rights Law: A Brief History of the 1948 Universal Declaration of Human Rights and the 1949 Geneva Conventions' (1998) 38 (324) *International Review of the Red Cross* (1961–1997) 409.

53 ICRC 1987 Commentaries to APII (n 34) para 4427.

54 *Legal Consequences of the Construction of a Wall in the Occupied Palestinian Territory*, Advisory Opinion, ICJ Reports (2004) 136 para 106.

55 Mozambique has been a party to ICCPR since 21 July 1993; see United Nations Treaty Collection, 'International Covenant on Civil and Political Rights' <https://treaties.un.org/Pages/ViewDetails.aspx?chapter=4&clang=_en&mtdsg_no=IV-4&src=IND>.

56 Mozambique ratified the African Charter on 22 February 1989; see African Union 'Status List' (2017) <https://au.int/sites/default/files/treaties/36390-sl-african_charter_on_human_and_peoples_rights_2.pdf>.

57 This must be read together with OHCHR, 'General Comment 14 on the Right to the Highest Attainable Standard of Health' (11 August 2000) UN Doc E/C.12/2000/4 which clarifies the implications of the right. See also Brigit Toebes, 'Healthcare on the Battlefield: In Search of a Legal and Ethical Framework' (2013) 4 *Journal of International Humanitarian Legal Studies* 210.

58 United Nations Treaty Collection, 'International Covenant on Economic, Social and Cultural Rights' <https://treaties.un.org/pages/ViewDetails.aspx?src=IND&mtdsg_no=IV-3&chapter=4&clang=_en>.

59 Hathaway and others (n 48) 173.

60 Article 3 of the Universal Declaration of Human Rights (adopted 10 December 1948 UNGA Res 217 A(III).

61 Article 6(1) of the International Covenant on Civil and Political Rights (adopted 16 December 1966, entered into force 23 March 1976) 999 UNTS 171 (ICCPR).

62 Article 4 of the African Charter on Human and Peoples' Rights (adopted 27 June 1981, entered into force 21 October 1986) 1520 UNTS 217 (African Charter).

63 Article 6(1) ICCPR (n 61).

64 Article 4 African Charter (n 62).

65 Article 6(1) ICCPR (n 61).

66 Article 4 African Charter (n 62).

67 However, it must be interpreted with reference to the rules of IHL; see African Commission on Human and Peoples' Rights 'General Comment No 3 on the African Charter on Human and Peoples' Rights: The Right to Life (Article 4)' (18 November 2015) para 13.

68 United Nations Human Rights Committee 'General Comment No 36 (Article 6: Right to Life)' (3 September 2019) para 3.
69 General Comment 3 on the African Charter (n 67) para 41.
70 General Comment 36 (n 68) para 26.
71 General Comment 3 on the African Charter (n 67) para 41.
72 Hathaway and others (n 48) 176.
73 Ibid.
74 General Comment 3 on the African Charter (n 67) para 43.
75 Constitution of the World Health Organization (adopted 22 July 1946, entered into force 7 April 1948).
76 Article 25 of the Universal Declaration of Human Rights (adopted 10 December 1948 UNGA Res, 217 A(III)).
77 African Charter (n 62).
78 Ibid, article 16.
79 African Commission on Human and Peoples' Rights, 'Principles and Guidelines on the Implementation of Economic, Social and Cultural Rights in the African Charter on Human and Peoples' Rights' (November 2010).
80 Ibid, para 4.
81 Noam Lubell, 'Challenges in Applying Human Rights Law to Armed Conflict' (2005) 87 (860) *International Review of the Red Cross* 752.
82 Principles and Guidelines on Implementation of the ACHPR (n 79) para 3.
83 Ibid.
84 Footer and Rubenstein (n 69) 182.
85 The Nairobi Guidelines indicate that the African Charter does not expressly use the words 'progressive realisation', but that it is implied in accordance with articles 61 and 61. See Principles and Guidelines (n 79) para 13.
86 Ibid, para 14.
87 Ibid, para 17.
88 Ibid, para 67.
89 Ibid, para 1(l).
90 Ibid.
91 WHO, 'Health Topics (Mozambique)'.
92 See Section 11.4.3.
93 Generally, human rights treaties refer to and bind the state party and not non-state actors. Bellal and others, however, argue that non-state actors could be bound by IHRL. See Annyssa Bellal, Gilles Giacca and Stuart Casey-Maslen, 'International Law and Armed Non-State Actors in Afghanistan' (2011) 93 (881) *International Review of the Red Cross* 1.
94 WHO, 'Mozambique Vaccinates Nearly All Adults Against COVID-19' (29 June 2022) <www.afro.who.int/countries/mozambique/news/mozambique-vaccinates-nearly-all-adults-against-covid-19>.
95 Ibid.
96 Ibid.
97 WHO, 'Data Management Reinforces COVID-19 Vaccination in Mozambique' (13 September 2022) <www.afro.who.int/photo-story/data-management-reinforces-covid-19-vaccination-mozambique>.
98 Ibid.
99 WHO, 'Providing Critical Health and Hygiene Services to Mozambique's Conflict-Affected Communities' (5 December 2022) <www.afro.who.int/countries/mozambique/news/providing-critical-health-and-hygiene-services-mozambiques-conflict-affected-communities?country=44&name=Mozambique>.
100 ICRC, 'Mozambique National IHL Committee Officially Established' (24 May 2022).
101 Ibid.
102 Ibid.

103 ICRC, 'Safeguarding the Provision of Health Care: Operational Practices and Relevant International Humanitarian Law Concerning Armed Groups' (June 2020).
104 Ezequiel Heffes, 'Armed Groups and the Protection of Health Care' (2019) 95 *International Law Studies* 277.
105 Ibid.
106 Ibid, 237.
107 Geneva Call, 'Deed of Commitment for the Protection of Health Care in Armed Conflict (2018)' <https://genevacall.org/wp-content/uploads/dlm_uploads/2018/11/Deed-of-Commitment-for-the-protection-of-health-care-in-armed-conflict-final-version.pdf>. Also see Heffes's (n 127) discussion on 239 ff. Heffes points out that armed groups may sign each deed only after they meet four specific conditions.
108 Ibid.
109 Ibid, 241.
110 One of the main functions of the African Commission is to monitor states parties' implementation of their human rights obligations as set out in the African Charter; see article 62 of the African Charter (n 82).
111 Especially, General Comment 15: The right to water; General Comment 14: The right to the highest attainable standard of health. The General Comments can be found on OCHRC, 'UN Treaty Body Database' <https://tbinternet.ohchr.org/_layouts/15/treatybodyexternal/TBSearch.aspx?Lang=en&TreatyID=9&DocTypeID=11>.
112 See OHCHR, 'Committee on Economic, Social and Cultural Rights' <www.ohchr.org/en/treaty-bodies/cescr>.

Bibliography

African Charter on Human and Peoples' Rights (1981) <https://treaties.un.org/Pages/showDetails.aspx?objid=08000002800cb09f&clang=_en>.

African Commission on Human and Peoples' Rights, 'General Comment No 3 on the African Charter on Human and Peoples' Rights: The Right to Life (Article 4)' (18 November 2015).

African Commission on Human and Peoples' Rights, 'Principles and Guidelines on the Implementation of Economic, Social and Cultural Rights in the African Charter on Human and Peoples' Rights' (November 2010).

African Union, 'Status List' (2017) <https://au.int/sites/default/files/treaties/36390-sl-african_charter_on_human_and_peoples_rights_2.pdf>.

Amrei Müller, 'States' Obligations to Mitigate the Direct and Indirect Consequences of Non-International Armed Conflicts: Complementarity of IHL and the Right to Health' (2013) 95 (889) *International Review of the Red Cross*.

Anne-Sophie Jung and others, 'COVID-19 Preparedness and Response: Implications for Future Pandemics National Responses to COVID-19: Drivers, Complexities, and Uncertainties in the First Year of the Pandemic' (2021) 375 *BMJ*.

Annyssa Bellal, Gilles Giacca and Stuart Casey-Maslen, 'International Law and Armed Non-State Actors in Afghanistan' (2011) 93 (881) *International Review of the Red Cross*.

Anyssa Bellal, 'Who Is Wounded and Sick?' in Andrew Clapham, Paola Gaeta and Marco Sassòli (eds), *The 1949 Geneva Conventions: A Commentary* (Oxford University Press 2018).

Brigit Toebes, 'Healthcare on the Battlefield: In Search of a Legal and Ethical Framework' (2013) 4 *Journal of International Humanitarian Legal Studies*.

CDC, 'Section 11: Epidemic Disease Occurrence Level of Disease' <www.cdc.gov/csels/dsepd/ss1978/lesson1/section11.html>.

CDDH, Official Records, Vol VII, CDDH/SR.51 (3 June 1977).

Chad R Wells and others, 'The Exacerbation of Ebola Outbreaks by Conflict in the Democratic Republic of the Congo' (2019) 116 (48) *Proceedings of the National Academy of Science USA*.

Constitution of the World Health Organization (1946) <https://treaties.un.org/Pages/ShowMTDSGDetails.aspx?src=UNTSONLINE&tabid=2&mtdsg_no=IX-1&chapter=9&lang=en>.

Cordula Droege, 'The Interplay Between International Humanitarian Law and International Human Rights Law in Situations of Armed Conflict' (2007) 40 (2) *Israel Law Review.*

D McQuoid-Mason, 'The Medical Profession and Medical Practice' in Willem Adolf Joubert and JA Faris (eds) (2008) 17 *The Law of South Africa.*

Eric R Frykberg, 'Triage: Principles and Practice' (2005) 94 *Scandinavian Journal of Surgery.*

Ezequiel Heffes, 'Armed Groups and the Protection of Health Care' (2019) 95 *International Law Studies.*

Felix Makonye, 'The Cabo Delgado Insurgency in Mozambique: Origin, Ideology, Recruitment Strategies, and Social, Political and Economic Implications for Natural Gas and Oil Exploration' (2020) 1 (3) *African Journal of Terrorism and Insurgency Research.*

Geneva Call, 'Deed of Commitment for the Protection of Health Care in Armed Conflict (2018)' <https://genevacall.org/wp-content/uploads/dlm_uploads/2018/11/Deed-of-Commitment-for-the-protection-of-health-care-in-armed-conflict-final-version.pdf>.

Geneva Convention (I) for the Amelioration of the Condition of the Wounded and Sick in Armed Forces in the Field (1949) <https://treaties.un.org/Pages/showDetails.aspx?objid=080000028015847c&clang=_en>.

Geneva Convention (II) for the Amelioration of the Condition of Wounded, Sick and Shipwrecked Members of Armed Forces at Sea (1949) <https://treaties.un.org/Pages/showDetails.aspx?objid=08000002801591b0&clang=_en>.

Geneva Convention (III) relative to the Treatment of Prisoners of War (1949) <https://treaties.un.org/Pages/showDetails.aspx?objid=0800000280159839&clang=_en>.

Geneva Convention (IV) relative to the Protection of Civilian Persons in Time of War (1949) <https://treaties.un.org/Pages/showDetails.aspx?objid=080000028015 8b1a&clang=_en>.

Gilles Giacca, 'The Obligations to Respect, Protect, Collect and Care for the Wounded, Sick and Shipwrecked' in Andrew Clapham, Paola Gaeta and Marco Sassòli (eds) *The 1949 Geneva Conventions: A Commentary* (OUP 2015).

Human Rights Watch, 'Africa: Conflicts, Violence Threaten Rights' (12 January 2023) <www.hrw.org/news/2023/01/12/africa-conflicts-violence-threaten-rights>.

ICRC, 'Advisory Service on International Humanitarian Law: Humanity after Life: Respecting and Protecting the Dead' (3 April 2020) <www.icrc.org/en/document/humanity-after-life-respect-and-protection-dead>.

ICRC, 'As If the War Was Not Enough – Stories of Hardship and Resilience in Times of COVID-19: A Report on the Pandemic's Impact on the Protection of People Caught Up in Conflict' (7 April 2021) <www.icrc.org/en/publication/4531-if-war-was-not-enough-stories-hardship-and-resilience-times-covid-19-report>.

ICRC, 'Columbia: Living in the Shadow of Armed Conflict' (23 March 2022) <www.icrc.org/en/document/colombia-humanitarian-challenges-2022-ihl>.

ICRC, 'Detention by Non-State Armed Groups Obligations Under International Humanitarian Law and Examples of How to Implement Them' (4 April 2023) 9 <www.icrc.org/en/document/detention-non-state-armed-groups>.

ICRC, 'First Aid in Armed Conflicts and Other Situations of Violence (2010)' 116 <www.icrc.org/en/doc/assets/files/other/icrc_002_0870.pdf>.

ICRC, 'Forensic Unit: COVID-19: General Guidance for the Management of the Dead' <www.icrc.org/sites/default/files/wysiwyg/Activities/covid-19_general_guidance.pdf>.

ICRC, 'Guiding Principles for Dignified Management of the Dead in Humanitarian Emergencies and to Prevent Them Becoming Missing Persons' (ICRC, 23 November 2021) <www.icrc.org/en/publication/4586-guiding-principles-dignified-management-dead-humanitarian-emergencies-and-prevent#:~:text=The%20Guiding%20Principles%20for%20Dignified%20Management%20of%20the,for%20their%20families%2C%20and%20complying%20with%20applicable%20law>.

ICRC, 'Humanitarian Response to COVID-19 in Mozambique' (19 June 2022) <www.icrc.org/en/document/humanitarian-response-covid-19-mozambique>.

ICRC, 'IHL and Islamic Law in Contemporary Armed Conflicts' Experts Workshop, Geneva 29–30 October 2018, Report Prepared and edited by Ahmed Al-Dawoody Legal Advisor (Islamic Law and Jurisprudence)' <https://library.icrc.org/library/docs/DOC/icrc-4386-002.pdf>.

ICRC, 'IHL Rules on Humanitarian Access and COVID-19' (8 April 2020).

ICRC, 'Mozambique: 1 Million People in Conflict-Affected Regions Receive Two Doses of the COVID-19 Vaccine' (28 June 2022) <www.icrc.org/en/document/mozambique-1-million-people-conflict-affected-regions-receive-two-doses-covid-19-vaccine>.

ICRC, 'Mozambique National IHL Committee Officially Established' (24 May 2022) <www.icrc.org/en/document/mozambique-national-ihl-committee-officially-established>.

ICRC, 'Outbreak: Fighting Ebola in a Conflict Zone' (14 August 2018) <www.icrc.org/en/document/outbreak-fighting-ebola-conflict-zone>.

ICRC, 'Protocol Additional to the Geneva Conventions of 12 August 1949, and Relating to the Protection of Victims of International Armed Conflicts (Protocol I), 8 June 1977, Commentary of 01.01.1987, Article 8 – Terminology' <https://ihl-databases.icrc.org/en/ihl-treaties/api-1977/article-8/commentary/1987?activeTab=undefined>.

ICRC, 'Protocol Additional to the Geneva Conventions of 12 August 1949, and Relating to the Protection of Victims of Non-International Armed Conflicts (Protocol II), 8 June 1977, Commentary of 1.01.1987, Article 13 – Protection of the Civilian Population' <https://ihl-databases.icrc.org/en/ihl-treaties/apii-1977/article-13/commentary/1987?activeTab=undefined>.

ICRC, 'Rule 110: Civilian Objects' Loss of Protection from Attack' <https://ihl-databases.icrc.org/en/customary-ihl/v1/rule10>.

ICRC, 'Rule 115: Disposal of the Dead' <https://ihl-databases.icrc.org/en/customary-ihl/v1/rule115>.

ICRC, 'Rule 116: Accounting for the Dead' <https://ihl-databases.icrc.org/en/customary-ihl/v1/rule116>.

ICRC, 'Safeguarding the Provision of Health Care: Operational Practices and Relevant International Humanitarian Law Concerning Armed Groups' (June 2020) <www.icrc.org/en/publication/4243-safeguarding-provision-health-care-operational-practices-and-relevant-international>.

ICRC, 'Tool on African Traditions and the Preservation of Humanity During War' (24 May 2021) <www.icrc.org/en/document/african-customs-tool-traditional-customs-and-ihl>.

ICRC, 'What Is the Humanitarian Impact of the COVID-19 Pandemic?' (15 September 2020) <www.icrc.org/en/document/what-humanitarian-impact-covid-19-pandemic#:~:text=%22It%20will%20have%20a%20devastating,devastation%20brought%20about%20by%20conflict>.

International Covenant on Civil and Political Rights (1966) <https://treaties.un.org/Pages/showDetails.aspx?objid=0800000280004bf5&clang=_en>.

International Covenant on Economic, Social and Cultural Rights (1966) <https://treaties.un.org/Pages/showDetails.aspx?objid=080000028002b6ed&clang=_en>.

Katherine HA Footer and Leonard S Rubenstein, 'A Human Rights Approach to Health Care in Conflict' (2013) 95 *International Review of the Red Cross*.

Kenneth G Swan, MC Usar and Swan Jr BS, 'Triage, the Past Revisited' (1996) 161 *Military Medicine*.

Kenneth V Iserson and John C Moskop, 'Triage in Medicine (Part 1): Concept, History and Types' (2007) 49 *Annals of Emergency Medicine*.

Larissa Fast, 'Unpacking the Principle of Humanity: Tensions and Implications' (2015) 97 *International Review of the Red Cross*.

Lawrence O Gostin, 'The Great Coronavirus Pandemic of 2020–7 Critical Lessons' (2020) 324 *Journal of the American Medical Association*.

Legal Consequences of the Construction of a Wall in the Occupied Palestinian Territory, Advisory Opinion, ICJ Reports (2004) 136.

Marco Sassòli *International Humanitarian Law: Rules, Controversies, and Solutions to Problems Arising in Warfare* (Edward Elgar 2019).

Martha M. Bradley, 'Additional Protocol II: Elevating the Minimum Threshold of Intensity' (2021) 102 (915) *International Review of the Red Cross*.

Martha M. Bradley, 'Revisiting the Notion of "Organised Armed Group" in Accordance with Common Article 3: Exploring the Inherent Minimum Threshold Requirements' (2018) *African Yearbook on International Humanitarian Law*.

MC van Hout and JSG Wells, 'The Right to Health, Public Health and COVID-19: A Discourse on the Importance of the Enforcement of Humanitarian and Human Rights Law in Conflict Settings for the Future Management of Zoonotic Pandemic Diseases' (2021) 192 *Public Health*.

Michael L Gross, *Bioethics and Armed Conflict* (MIT Press 2006).

Mozambique Conflict Observatory (Cabo Ligado) <www.caboligado.com/>.

Noam Lubell, 'Challenges in Applying Human Rights Law to Armed Conflict' (2005) 87 (860) *International Review of the Red Cross*.

OCHRC, 'UN Treaty Body Database' <https://tbinternet.ohchr.org/_layouts/15/treatybody-external/TBSearch.aspx?Lang=en&TreatyID=9&DocTypeID=11>.

OHCHR, 'General Comment 14 on the Right to the Highest Attainable Standard of Health' (11 August 2000) UN Doc E/C.12/2000/4.

Oona A Hathaway and others, 'The COVID-19 Pandemic and International Law' (2021) 54 *Cornell International Law Journal*.

Protocol Additional to the Geneva Conventions of 12 August 1949, and Relating to the Protection of Victims of International Armed Conflicts (Protocol I) (1977) <https://treaties.un.org/Pages/showDetails.aspx?objid=08000002800f3586&clang=_en>.

Protocol Additional to the Geneva Conventions of 12 August 1949, and Relating to the Protection of Victims of Non-International Armed Conflicts (Protocol II) (1977) <https://treaties.un.org/Pages/showDetails.aspx?objid=08000002800f3cb8&clang=_en>.

Robert Kolb, 'The Relationship Between International Humanitarian Law and Human Rights Law: A Brief History of the 1948 Universal Declaration of Human Rights and the 1949 Geneva Conventions' (1998) 38 (324) *International Review of the Red Cross*.

Roshini Haar and others, 'Violence Against Healthcare in Conflict: A Systematic Review of the Literature and Agenda for Future Research' (2021) 15 *Conflict Health*.

Sarah Jean Mabeza and Tamalin Bolus, 'Changing the Narrative: A Tool on African Traditions and the Preservation of Humanity During War' (2022) 104 (920–921) *International Review of the Red Cross*.

Sigrid Mehring, *First Do No Harm: Medical Ethics in International Humanitarian Law* (Brill Nijhoff 2015).

Simone E Carter and others, 'How to Improve Outbreak Response: A Case Study of Integrated Outbreak Analytics from Ebola in Eastern Democratic Republic of the Congo' (2021) 6 *Global Health*.

UNHCR, 'COVID-19 Pandemic' (November 2022) <www.unhcr.org/uk/coronavirus-covid-19.html>.

United Nations, 'Committee on Economic, Social and Cultural Rights' <www.ohchr.org/en/treaty-bodies/cescr>.

United Nations, 'Joint Statement by Independent United Nations Human Rights Experts on Human Rights Responsibilities of Armed Non-State Actors' (25 February 2021) <www.ohchr.org/en/press-releases/2021/02/joint-statement-independent-united-nations-human-rights-experts-human-rights#_ftn3>.

United Nations Human Rights Committee, 'General Comment No 36 (Article 6: Right to Life)' (3 September 2019).

Universal Declaration of Human Rights (1948) <https://www.refworld.org/docid/3ae6b3712c.html>.

UN News, 'Mozambique: Thousands Continue to Flee Violence in Cabo Delgado' (22 March 2022) <https://news.un.org/en/story/2022/03/1114412>.

Vienna Convention on the Law of Treaties (1969) <https://treaties.un.org/Pages/showDetails.aspx?objid=080000028003902f&clang=_en>.

WHO, 'Data Management Reinforces COVID-19 Vaccination in Mozambique' (13 September 2022) <www.afro.who.int/photo-story/data-management-reinforces-covid-19-vaccination-mozambique>.

WHO, 'Ebola Virus Disease – Democratic Republic of the Congo' (29 September 2022) <www.who.int/emergencies/disease-outbreak-news/item/2022-DON411>.

WHO, 'Ebola Virus Disease – Key Facts' (23 February 2021) <www.who.int/news-room/fact-sheets/detail/ebola-virus-disease?gclid=Cj0KCQjwk7ugBhDIARIsAGuvgPa0vNbX6s4FToLPvxkFjW4vXmvw7UzFHSfyybvMPEEMunY3HK95wOAaAjM4EALw_wcB>.

WHO, 'Health Topics (Mozambique)' <www.afro.who.int/health-topics/health-topics-mozambique>.

WHO, 'Mozambique Vaccinates Nearly All Adults Against COVID-19' (29 June 2022) <www.afro.who.int/countries/mozambique/news/mozambique-vaccinates-nearly-all-adults-against-covid-19>.

WHO, 'Providing Critical Health and Hygiene Services to Mozambique's Conflict-Affected Communities' (5 December 2022) <www.afro.who.int/countries/mozambique/news/providing-critical-health-and-hygiene-services-mozambiques-conflict-affected-communities?country=44&name=Mozambique>.

Part III

Regional and continental responses to the conflict

12 The potential for rights-based third-generation disarmament, demobilisation and reintegration programmes in Cabo Delgado

Josephat M. Kilonzo

12.1 Introduction

Since 2017, Mozambique's northern province of Cabo Delgado has faced violence perpetrated by Ansar al-Sunna. Over time, the attacks by the violent extremist group have become more frequent and brutal and have claimed an increasing number of lives.[1] The group targets security forces, local communities, transport systems, oil installations and other critical infrastructure.[2] The effect in local communities of the group's *modus operandi* is severe; their practice is to kill men, sometimes beheading them, and to abduct children and women.[3] In response to the violence perpetrated by Ansar al-Sunna in Cabo Delgado, Mozambique adopted a predominantly military approach.[4] The government deployed the security forces to secure towns and villages in the north of the country and to counter the activities of Ansar al-Sunna. The military efforts have been bolstered by the Wagner Group, Dyck Advisory Group, Rwandan troops and the SADC Mission in Mozambique.[5]

Despite an intensified military response, Ansar al-Sunna has continued conducting attacks on the local population and government installations. Many members of Ansar al-Sunna have been killed and the security forces have regained lost territory, but the group remains resilient.[6] The challenge to Mozambique is not unique. Other African states have grappled with violent extremist groups, such as Al Shabaab and Boko Haram.[7] In Cameroon, Chad, Niger, Nigeria and Somalia the initial state response to violent extremist groups was largely a combination of military and criminalisation approaches.[8] However, the resilience of the response by Boko Haram and Al Shabaab despite the forces ranged against them underscores the limits of a military approach to violent extremism.

The limited success of a military approach in tackling violent extremist groups has led to a broad agreement among states, scholars, practitioners and development partners that violent extremism cannot be effectively addressed solely through military and criminalisation approaches. The practice of disarmament, demobilisation and reintegration (DDR) has been adopted as a measure that complements and advances the goals in the military and criminalisation approaches.[9] As is discussed later, the nature of DDR that is adopted in the context of violent extremism differs significantly from traditional DDR, a discipline employed in post-conflict

DOI: 10.4324/9781003317647-15

situations where a peace agreement is in place. Clearly, that is not the situation in Cabo Delgado.

This chapter proposes a rights-based approach to third-generation DDR to aid in the effort to address the challenge posed by Ansar al-Sunna. A rights-based approach to DDR may prove an incentive to members and associates of the group to disengage and be rehabilitated and reintegrated into normal civilian life. The remainder of the chapter comprises the following parts: a brief overview of the distinction between traditional DDR and third-generation DDR (see Section 12.2); a discussion of a rights-based approach to DDR (see Section 12.3); and a conclusion (see Section 12.4).

12.2 Brief overview of the distinction between traditional DDR and third-generation DDR

Since the late 1980s, DDR programmes have evolved in response to shifts in conflict dynamics. Scholars and practitioners have found it important to distinguish between different generations of DDR based on contextual circumstances and their key objectives.[10] To date, three categories of DDR approaches exist: first-generation DDR, second-generation DDR and third-generation DDR. First- and second-generation DDR, termed 'traditional' DDR, are implemented in post-conflict societies.[11] They are underpinned by preconditions, such as (a) the presence of a peace agreement that forms a legal basis for DDR operations; (b) agreed eligibility criteria for DDR; (c) the political will of the warring parties; and (d) security guarantees.[12]

Unlike traditional DDR, third-generation DDR programming – increasingly referred to in UN circles as 'screening, prosecution, rehabilitation, and reintegration' or SPRR – is implemented during an armed conflict.[13] Third-generation DDR is designed and implemented in 'non-permissive' environments characterised by distorted and ongoing conflict, the absence of security guarantees and a lack of peace agreements because the violent extremist groups are opposed to political negotiations.[14]

Third-generation DDR comprises four key phases.[15] The first is when associates of a violent extremist group disengage, either voluntarily or involuntarily (through arrest or capture). Following the formal registration of the associates of a violent extremist group that has disengaged, the second phase begins with a screening process conducted by national authorities.[16] The third phase includes transitional rehabilitation that focuses on released former associates and former associates categorised as low risk. The low-risk former associates are not suspected of committing an international crime that would require prosecution but also are not deemed eligible for immediate release.[17] They may undergo community-based reintegration, but their release is conditional on participation in transitional rehabilitation. The fourth phase entails reintegration into society, which addresses the socio-economic needs of those going through a DDR process and enhancement of community welfare.[18]

In Africa, third-generation DDR programmes are being implemented in states such as Cameroon, Niger, Nigeria and Somalia, each of which is confronting violent extremist groups.[19] Facing a similar security threat, the situation in Mozambique is ripe for the adoption of a third-generation DDR programme. As discussed below, Mozambique should design its programme to follow a rights-based approach that respects fundamental human rights as well as draw on lessons and best practices learned from its traditional DDR experience and DDR programming in other affected states.

12.3 What should a rights-based approach to third-generation DDR in Cabo Delgado entail?

At present, third-generation DDR in Africa is implemented in complex environments in which multiple actors are involved and where peace deals are largely unfeasible. Unlike the case for traditional DDR, where guidance is offered by the UN Integrated Disarmament, Demobilisation, and Reintegration Standards (IDDRS), there is a lack of legal and policy frameworks to provide sufficient guidance on planning and implementing DDR in the context of ongoing violent extremist activity.[20] As noted by Muggah and O'Donnell, 'frameworks and models advocated in the IDDRS, although offering useful reference, are inadequate to guide practitioners in contexts where DDR is prescribed'.[21]

There is evidence that the execution of third-generation DDR programmes in Africa has been fragmentary and is shrouded by human rights challenges at different stages of implementation.[22] These programmes are implemented in environments characterised by human rights violations, including extra-judicial and summary executions, arbitrary detentions, fair-trial rights violations and inadequate justice and reparations for victims.[23] Without specific and comprehensive guiding frameworks, third-generation DDR programmes often fall short of the goal of advancing stability and instead negatively impact human rights.

With the benefit of being able to draw lessons from the experience of other African states, Mozambique has an opportunity to design and implement a rights-based third-generation DDR programme that will encourage Ansar al-Sunna members to defect and will degrade the capacity of Ansar al-Sunna. Such a process needs to adopt the principles and standards set out in international and regional human rights law. Although there is no specific treaty on the provision of DDR, the framework of international and regional law provides a solid basis for Mozambique to develop and implement a strong rights-based third-generation DDR programme.

The parts below discuss the human rights considerations Mozambique should follow to ensure human rights compliance in each phase of a third-generation DDR.

12.3.1 Disengagement phase

The experience of African states in facing the challenge of violent extremism shows that men, women and children leave violent extremist groups either voluntarily or involuntarily (by capture or arrest).[24] The factors that led to voluntary disengagement from violent extremist groups such as Boko Haram and Al Shabaab can be broken down into three categories: enabling factors, individual incentives and structural factors. Enabling factors include family intervention, amnesties and military pressure. Individual incentives include disillusionment and frustration over pay, a sense of guilt and a fear of being disowned by one's family. Structural factors include disillusionment with the group's ideology, objectives and strategy.[25] Taking cognisance of these drivers, Mozambique should design its DDR programme to leverage the factors that will make associates of Ansar al-Sunna abandon the group or work to undermine its activities.

As associates of Ansar al-Sunna leave the group, either voluntarily or involuntarily, the government of Mozambique and its development partners should design and implement a legal and policy framework that supports a rights-based approach to disengagement. This entails respect for fundamental human rights, in particular the rights to life, to freedom from ill-treatment, to liberty, to security and to health. The DDR programme should be established on a basis of transparency, accountability and non-discrimination and should respect and protect the rights of specific vulnerable groups such as women, children and PWDs. The following sections discuss in more detail the rights that Mozambique should follow during the disengagement phase to ensure its DDR programme is rights compliant.

12.3.1.1 Freedom from arbitrary detention

The experience of African states dealing with violent extremism shows that, upon defection or arrest, former associates of violent extremist groups often are subjected to prolonged detention by the military before their legal status and eligibility to take part in a DDR process is determined.[26] This practice by states constitutes a deprivation of liberty; a DDR programme may involve the arbitrary deprivation of liberty if international and regional human rights standards are not respected.

In line with article 9(1) of the International Covenant on Civil and Political Rights (ICCPR) and article 6 of the African Charter on Human and Peoples' Rights (African Charter), Mozambique must ensure any deprivation of liberty is predicated on conditions that are outlined in law.[27] The deprivation of liberty during the disengagement phase may not be arbitrary; thus it should be just, reasonable, predictable and proportionate.[28] A means of avoiding the arbitrary deprivation of liberty is to adopt without delay legal, policy and administrative measures that facilitate the non-coercive screening of former associates of Ansar al-Sunna. After screening, they should be processed for release, for prosecution or for participation in a rehabilitation programme.

12.3.1.2 Right to health in custody facilities

During the detention of former associates of Ansar al-Sunna, an individual's right to health may be affected negatively, especially if held in custody facilities that are overcrowded, have poor sanitation and lack adequate personal hygiene supplies. Some former associates may require medical attention due to illness, injury or disability. Mozambique has an obligation to promote the health of its citizens; it has a heightened obligation to respect and protect the right to health of anyone in its custody, including former associates of Ansar al-Sunna held in a custodial facility during the disengagement phase. Article 10 of ICCPR requires that 'all persons deprived of their liberty shall be treated with humanity and with respect for their inherent dignity of the human person'. Many associates of an extremist group fear mistreatment at the hands of the authorities but the practice followed must demonstrate that this fear is groundless.

Article 16 of the African Charter protects the rights of individuals to 'enjoy the best attainable state of physical and mental health'. A state obligation that stems from these provisions requires that Mozambique ensures access to health care services by former associates of Ansar al-Sunna.

12.3.1.3 Prohibition against arbitrary deprivation of life

Article 6(1) of ICCPR and article 4 of the African Charter guarantee the right to life of every individual. Former associates of Ansar al-Sunna are entitled to the protection of their right to life, especially when in custody and under the control of the Mozambican government. As underscored by the UN Human Rights Committee in General Comment 36, states have 'a heightened duty of care to take any necessary measures to protect the lives of individuals deprived of their liberty by the state'; 'by arresting, detaining, imprisoning, or otherwise depriving individuals of their liberty, [states] assume responsibility for their lives and bodily integrity'.[29]

Mozambique must take adequate steps to protect detained former associates of Ansar al-Sunna against arbitrary deprivation of life. The deprivation of life of a former associate of Ansar al-Sunna is considered arbitrary if not in accordance with domestic or international law. In this case, the notion of 'arbitrariness' is fully equated with being 'against the law' and is interpreted broadly to include the elements of inappropriateness, injustice, lack of predictability and due process, absence of reasonableness and a lack of proportionality.[30]

12.3.1.4 Protection of rights of vulnerable groups during disengagement

A rights-based approach during the disengagement phase requires Mozambique to respect and protect the rights of groups deemed to be vulnerable; t including women, children and PWDs. Often these groups are marginalised as a result of which they fail to enjoy a broad range of human rights.[31]

In the recent past, most third-generation DDR initiatives have been designed mainly for men and there has been little effort to create a DDR initiative that specifically addresses the needs of women associated with violent extremist groups[32] despite women associated with these groups eventually disengaging from their own individual reasons and benefitting from assistance in successfully reintegrating.[33]

The research on the extent of women and girls' association with Ansar al-Sunna is limited,[34] but some level of participation is to be expected based on experience in the Lake Chad basin and Somalia. Mozambique should start planning for a women's rights-compliant disengagement phase. Mozambique's design should be informed by further research into the nature of the association of women and girls in Ansar al-Sunna. The Convention on the Elimination of all Forms of Discrimination Against Women (CEDAW), the Protocol to the African Charter on Human and Peoples' Rights on the Rights of Women in Africa (Maputo Protocol) and UN Security Council Resolution 1325 (2000) must inform the actions of Mozambique to ensure that women and girls are included and actively participate in the disengagement phase.

The UN Convention on the Rights of the Child (CRC) and the African Charter on the Rights and Welfare of the Child (African Children's Charter) place an obligation on states to take 'all feasible measures to ensure protection and care of children who are affected by armed conflicts'.[35] For Mozambique to meet its obligation, it must consider the rights and needs of children in the disengagement phase. The Paris Principles and Guidelines on Children Associated with Armed Forces or Armed Groups (2007) (Paris Principles) underline that 'children who are accused of crimes under international law allegedly committed while they were associated with armed forces or armed groups should be considered primarily as victims' and not as perpetrators.[36]

The African Committee of Experts on the Rights and Welfare of the Child (ACERWC) in its General Comment 22 pertaining to the African Children's Charter asserts that 'detention is contrary to the best interests of the child and often associated with ill-treatment and torture'.[37] To avoid the detention of children, Mozambique can follow the example of Chad, Mali, Niger and Sudan that have signed such handover protocols.

In accordance with the Convention on the Rights of Persons with Disabilities (CRPD),[38] ICCPR[39] and the African Charter,[40] during the disengagement phase, Mozambique has an obligation to ensure the full realisation of the rights of persons with disabilities (PWDs) associated with Ansar al-Sunna. As a state party to the CRPD, Mozambique has an obligation to take the necessary measures to ensure the protection of PWDs in situations of risk, including an armed conflict.[41] This obligation requires Mozambique to adopt all necessary measures of protection and safety of PWDs, including those associated with Ansar al-Sunna, during the disengagement phase.

12.3.2 Screening phase

After associates of Ansar al-Sunna defect or have been arrested, Mozambique needs to draw a distinction between associates who can be reintegrated safely into local communities as civilians and those likely to pose an ongoing risk to the community. This effort calls for the establishment of a screening process. The term 'screening' can be defined as 'the initial process of determining the profile of an individual under the responsibility of authorities, in order to recommend the next course of action: either rehabilitation or prosecution'.[42] The screening process is important because there is an obligation on states, including Mozambique, to hold accountable those who have committed certain designated crimes such as war crimes, genocide, crimes against humanity and gross human rights violations.[43] States must provide the victims of serious crimes with remedies.[44] Therefore, Mozambique has an obligation to determine whether those who defect from Ansar al-Sunna should be rehabilitated and reintegrated into local communities or be prosecuted if they are suspected of committing an international crime.

In Somalia and Nigeria, former associates of violent extremist groups are admitted into DDR programmes subject to a screening by which they are categorised as either low risk or high risk. Those categorised as low risk have committed crimes that do not meet the standard of serious crimes requiring prosecution but whose release is pegged to participation in transitional rehabilitation.[45] Those categorised as high risk are suspected of having committed serious crimes that require prosecution in line with international standards.[46]

In Somalia and Nigeria the practice of screening former associates of violent extremism has experienced human rights challenges.[47] At the beginning the processes lacked transparency and independent oversight in that there was no public specification of the criteria followed.[48] The screening of women has been inconsistently applied, particularly in Somalia, where women are screened using tools designed for men.[49] Somalia and Nigeria, with the assistance of development partners, have made an effort to improve their screening processes by increasing predictability and enhancing respect for human rights.[50]

Mozambique has the opportunity to learn lessons from Somalia and Nigeria to ensure that its screening phase respects international and regional human rights standards. If the screening process for Ansar al-Sunna associates is to satisfy a rights-based approach, it must consider the issues outlined in the following sections.

12.3.2.1 Elimination of arbitrariness in the screening process

To ensure compliance with international obligations to prosecute those who commit serious crimes, the screening process adopted by Mozambique should not be arbitrary; it should not be characterised by capriciousness, injustice, a lack of reasonableness and proportionality and an absence of predictability. Coercion or the threat of violence should not be employed in the process. Being able to benefit from the experience of Somalia and Nigeria, Mozambique from the beginning should develop standard operating procedures that guarantee a degree of accuracy to identify and isolate associates of Ansar al-Sunna that have committed war crimes, gross human rights violations or crimes against humanity. This process is vital because associates of Ansar al-Sunna who commit these crimes should be prosecuted in a fair trial and should not immediately benefit under a DDR process.

12.3.2.2 Prohibition against torture during screening

During the screening process, Mozambique must respect the norm prohibiting torture and ensure accountability and redress in case of a violation. Under article 7 of ICCPR and article 5 of the African Charter, the prohibition of torture is absolute. The prohibition of torture is a peremptory norm, a norm of *jus cogens* nature that is non-derogable even when states face an emergency that threatens the life of the nation.[51] Because of its *jus cogens* character, Mozambique must adopt effective legislative, policy, judicial and other measures to prohibit, prevent and promptly address all acts of torture.

12.3.2.3 Respect for the rights to privacy during screening phase

During the screening process, the government of Mozambique will collect, synthesise and analyse a lot of sensitive data. The collection of data is essential for the determination of low or high risk. The collection and holding of data raise privacy concerns and the government is required to respect international human rights standards on the protection of privacy.

Although the right to privacy is not absolute, ICCPR under article 17 places an obligation on states not to subject individuals to arbitrary or unlawful interference with their privacy. Mozambique has an obligation to ensure that data on former associates of Ansar al-Sunna is collected and held in a manner that respects the right to privacy and data protection laws and standards. Therefore, the government must adopt legislative and administrative measures, as well as standard operating procedures that offer guidance for handling data during the screening phase.

12.3.2.4 Respect for and protection of the rights of vulnerable groups during screening phase

A key attribute of a rights-based approach to screening in Mozambique is the prioritisation of an inclusion of vulnerable groups, women, children and PWDs. Article 2 of CEDAW and article 2 of the Maputo Protocol provide an obligation to address the needs of women and protect their rights during screening. Mozambique must gain an understanding of the ways women and girls associate with Ansar al-Sunna to inform the development of proper screening tools. The current research on the conflict in Cabo Delgado ignores women or depicts them as victims[52] and calls for further research to fashion a screening process in a manner that addresses the needs of women and protects their rights.

Mozambique must develop child-sensitive procedures to meet the obligations under article 38 of CRC and article 22 of the African Children's Charter to protect and care for children affected by armed conflict. The development and implementation of screening processes for children must be based on the four cardinal principles of CRC and the African Children's Charter, namely, the best interests of the child; non-discrimination; child participation; and life, survival and development.

A nexus between extremist violence and disability means that Mozambique must design and implement a disability-inclusive screening process. Adopting such a process is critical for the fulfilment of Mozambique's obligation under article 11 of CRPD to take the necessary steps to ensure the protection of PWDs in situations of risk such as armed conflict. In addition, the development of a disability-sensitive screening process will align with Mozambique's obligations under ICCPR,[53] the African Charter[54] and CRPD[55] to address discrimination against PWDs.

12.3.3 Rehabilitation phase

Former associates of Ansar al-Sunna classified as low risk should be delivered to rehabilitation programmes that address radical beliefs and extremist behaviour. As stated by Veldhuis, rehabilitation is seen as 'a purposeful, planned intervention, which aims to change characteristics of the offender (attitudes, cognitive skills and processes, personality or mental health, and social, educational or vocational skills)' that are deemed to contribute to a person's criminal behaviour, with the objective of reducing their chances of re-offending.[56] Rehabilitation is prioritised as being an important springboard to the successful reintegration of former associates of Ansar al-Sunna.

In Africa, states dealing with violent extremist groups have adopted different approaches to rehabilitation. For instance, in Nigeria, the Operation Safe Corridor (OPSC) seeks to correct the world view of former associates of Boko Haram by providing an alternative religious interpretation and alternative sources of income such as tailoring and carpentry.[57] In Niger, the Goudoumaria reception centre includes rehabilitation centres in re-socialisation, re-education and vocational training in various fields.[58] In the circumstances in Cabo Delgado, Mozambique can use different modes of rehabilitation that focus on the religious, ideological, social, educational, vocational and psychological factors that lead individuals to join Ansar al-Sunna.

Under international and regional human rights law, Mozambique must adopt a rights-based approach to rehabilitation. During the rehabilitation process, the government must take into consideration the rights discussed in the following sections.

12.3.3.1 Freedom from arbitrary detention during rehabilitation phase

During the rehabilitation phase Mozambique must adopt a model that minimises restrictions on the liberty of former Ansar al-Sunna associates. It is a complicated undertaking to determine the correct balance between freedom and restriction during the rehabilitation phase. Most individuals who participate in a process of rehabilitation have been deemed a low risk, but they are undergoing rehabilitation because they still are deemed to need de-radicalisation. The continued deprivation of liberty of these individuals may undermine their faith in the process. The custodial-setting model has been adopted in Nigeria, Somalia and Niger.[59] Mozambique can learn a lesson of best practices from these states.

Article 9(1) of ICCPR and article 6 of the African Charter regulate that Mozambique ensures that the deprivation of liberty during the rehabilitation stage is not arbitrary. To avoid arbitrary detention during the rehabilitation phase, the government must ensure that the deprivation of liberty is for reasons and conditions outlined in law and is not characterised by inappropriateness, a lack of predictability and due process, injustice and the absence of reasonableness, necessity and proportionality.

12.3.3.2 Right to health during rehabilitation phase

The rehabilitation of former Ansar al-Sunna associates affects the right to health, because (i) some of them may require medical attention due to illness or injury sustained during the conflict; and (ii) some may require medical attention because of health conditions that arise during the disengagement, screening and rehabilitation phases.

Under article 12 of the International Covenant on Economic, Social and Cultural Rights (ICESCR) and article 16 of the African Charter, Mozambique has an obligation to respect and protect the right to health of former associates of Ansar al-Sunna during the rehabilitation phase, foremost, because they may have had a limited or no access to health care during the duration of their association with Ansar al-Sunna. The government must provide the underlying determinants of health, including access to safe water, an adequate supply of food and housing, and access to health-related education and information.

12.3.3.3 Respect for and protection of freedom of thought, conscience and religion during rehabilitation phase

Religion is cited as a contributing factor to violent extremism in Cabo Delgado.[60] There is an indication Ansar al-Sunna encompasses an ideological inclination that it shares with other Islamist groups such as Boko Haram and Al Shabaab.[61] To counter violent ideologies, Mozambique is likely to incorporate de-radicalisation into its rehabilitation phase. While doing so, it must respect freedom of thought, of conscience and religion.

Under article 18 of ICCPR and article 8 of the African Charter, Mozambique has an obligation to respect freedom of thought, conscience and religion. The government can limit the manifestation of religion during the rehabilitation phase,[62] but not freedom of thought and conscience because it is absolute.[63] Further, in accordance with article 18(2) of ICCPR, during rehabilitation the government should not coerce Ansar al-Sunna associates to adopt or abandon their religious beliefs. To uphold freedom of thought, conscience and religion, the government may rely on religious counsellors to offer the former associates of Ansar al-Sunna an alternative to a radical religious ideology.

12.3.3.4 Respect for and protection of the rights of vulnerable groups during rehabilitation phase

A rights-based approach to rehabilitation prioritises the rights and needs of vulnerable groups such as women, children and PWDs. In line with article 2 of CEDAW and article 2 of the Maputo Protocol, during the design and implementation of a rehabilitation programme, Mozambique and development partners must consider the needs and protect the rights of women associated with violent extremist groups. The government should avoid the mistake made in other African states such as Nigeria and Somalia where women and girls associated with violent extremist groups were not prioritised for participation in the DDR programmes.[64]

Mozambique and development partners should pay special attention to children's involvement with Ansar al-Sunna. As underscored by the ACERWC in General Comment 22 of the African Children's Charter, children associated with armed groups should be considered a special group and be rehabilitated through DDR programmes that provide psychosocial support, civic education and vocational skills.[65] The rehabilitation programme for children associated with Ansar al-Sunna must be in accordance with the four cardinal principles of CRC and the African Children's Charter, namely, the best interests of the child; non-discrimination; child participation; and life, survival and development.

Mozambique has a legal obligation to ensure the protection and enjoyment of the rights of associates of Ansar al-Sunna with disabilities during the rehabilitation phase. PWDs are likely to face discrimination, thus, in accordance with ICCPR,[66] the African Charter[67] and CRPD,[68] special attention must be paid to their needs in the planning and implementation of rehabilitation programmes.

12.3.4 Reintegration phase

After rehabilitation, Mozambique, with the assistance of development partners and civil society organisations, needs to reintegrate the former associates of Ansar al-Sunna into society. As stated by Veldhuis, 'reintegration is understood as a safe transition to the community, by which the individual proceeds to live a law-abiding life following his or her release and acquires attitudes and behaviours that generally lead to a productive functioning in society'.[69]

The reintegration of Ansar al-Sunna associates is essential to prevent recidivism, the mitigation of developments leading to the further radicalisation of young people and the establishment of a general community-level resilience to violent extremism.[70] Despite its importance, the reintegration of Ansar al-Sunna associates, as in the case of the associates of other violent extremist groups, is likely to present challenges such as the risk of retribution and a fear that they keep their ties and an ideological connection to the group.

Despite the challenges, Mozambique should adopt a rights-based approach to reintegration that includes respect for Mozambique's obligations under international and regional human rights law. To ensure that the reintegration phase is rights-compliant, the Mozambican government must consider the following rights.

12.3.4.1 Right to safety and security during reintegration phase

At the reintegration phase Mozambique is required to ensure the safety and security of rehabilitated former associates of Ansar al-Sunna and of the communities in Cabo Delgado into which they will be reintegrated. An absence of safety and security will undermine the likelihood of successful reintegration of rehabilitated former associates of Ansar al-Sunna as it limits the opportunities available in the community.

The obligation to protect requires the government to provide safeguards against the violation of their rights by others. As stated by the Human Rights Committee in General Comment 31, the obligation to protect goes beyond a state protecting individuals against violations and abuses of their rights by state agents to protecting them against acts by private persons or entities.[71] This position has been adopted by the African Commission on Human and Peoples' Rights in *SERAC v*

Nigeria.[72] Therefore, Mozambique is obliged to take measures to prevent, investigate or redress violations of the rights of former associates of Ansar al-Sunna and the community by state agents or by private persons or entities.

12.3.4.2 Right to adequate standard of living during reintegration phase

The attainment of the right to an adequate standard of living for rehabilitated former associates of Ansar al-Sunna will contribute to their successful reintegration. Under article 11 of ICESCR, the right to an adequate standard of living includes adequate food, housing and clothing and a continuous improvement in living conditions. These rights are necessary for the subsistence of individuals and their families. The realisation of an adequate standard of living for all individuals in Cabo Delgado, including former associates, is critical to delivering a guarantee that they will enjoy the fulfilment of basic needs in conditions of dignity.

12.3.4.3 Right to work during reintegration phase

Under article 6 of ICESCR and article 15 of the African Charter, every individual, including former associates of violent extremist groups, is guaranteed the right to work, which entails the right to an opportunity to earn a living. Mozambique must respect and protect the right of former associates of Ansar al-Sunna to work. In line with article 7 of ICESCR and article 15 of the African Charter, Mozambique has an obligation to ensure that rehabilitated former associates of Ansar al-Sunna enjoy full and favourable conditions to find employment.

The realisation of the right to work is essential to a successful reintegration of former associates of Ansar al-Sunna. In a study conducted by the United States Agency for International Development (USAID) in Nigeria, rehabilitated former associates of Boko Haram indicated employment as a critical factor in the prevention of recidivism.[73] Considering the importance of the right to work in reintegration, Mozambique, in an inclusive process, must develop and implement policies that guarantee the right.

12.3.4.4 Protection of rights of vulnerable groups during reintegration phase

A rights-based approach to reintegration must prioritise the rights and needs of vulnerable groups, including women, children and PWDs. In line with article 2 of CEDAW and article 2 of the Maputo Protocol UN Security Council Resolution 1325 (2000), Mozambique should ensure that reintegration entails inclusion and participation of women. Mozambique and development partners should bear in mind that the women associated with Ansar al-Sunna constitute a heterogeneous group and thus must consider their varied experiences.

Mozambique must adopt a child-centred rights-based approach to reintegration to correspond to the obligation under CRC and the African Children's Charter to take 'all feasible measures to ensure protection and care of children who are affected by armed conflicts'.[74] This approach is aligned with article 39 of CRC and the Paris Principles, which require Mozambique to ensure the successful reintegration of children associated with Ansar al-Sunna.[75]

Further, Mozambique and its development partners must adopt a disability-inclusive reintegration process. In line with ICCPR,[76] the African Charter[77] and CRPD,[78] Mozambique is obliged to pay them special attention by providing, among other needs, reasonable accommodation.

12.4 Conclusion

The resilience of Ansar al-Sunna despite the military approach by Mozambique necessitates the adoption of a rights-based approach to DDR in Cabo Delgado. Thus, building from experiences in other African States, this chapter proposes the adoption of a rights-based approach to DDR by Mozambique and development partners. A rights-based to third-generation DDR would require Mozambique and development partners to ensure that human rights standards are upheld. Special attention must be paid to human rights and freedoms of special groups including women, children and PWDs. Importantly, Mozambique has a chance to draw lessons and best practices from its previous DDR experience and the ongoing third-generation DDR programmes in Africa.

Notes

1 Énio Viegas Filipe Chingotuane and others, 'Strategic Options for Managing Violent Extremism in Southern Africa: The Case of Mozambique' (2021) *Friedrich-Ebert-Stiftung* 3.
2 Ibid.
3 Ibid.
4 See Chingotuane and others (n 1).
5 See Dorina A Bekoe, Stephanie M Burchard and Sarah A Daly, 'Extremism in Mozambique: Interpreting Group Tactics and the Role of the Government's Response in the Crisis in Cabo Delgado' *Institute for Defense Analyses* (2020) & 'Rwanda Deploys 1 000 Soldiers to Mozambique's Cabo Delgado' *Al Jazeera* (10 July 2021).
6 International Crisis Group, 'Winning Peace in Mozambique's Embattled North' (10 February 2022).
7 See Cale Salih, Ron Slye and Mark Freeman, *The Limits of Punishment, Transitional Justice and Violent Extremism* (United Nations University 2018).
8 Ibid.
9 As noted in the text below, the terminology increasingly used in UN Security Council resolutions is 'screening', prosecution', 'rehabilitation' and 'reintegration'. See also International Organisation for Migration, *Disengagement, Disassociation, Reintegration and Reconciliation: Eligibility Conditions and Practices* (IOM 2021).
10 See International Organisation for Migration (IOM), *Disarmament, Demobilisation and Reintegration: Compendium of Projects 2010–2017* (IOM 2019).
11 See Robert Muggah and Chris O'Donnell, 'Next Generation Disarmament, Demobilisation and Reintegration' (2015) 4 (1) *Stability: International Journal of Security and Development*.
12 See IOM, *Disengagement, Disassociation, Reintegration and Reconciliation: Eligibility Conditions and Practices* (IOM 2021).
13 See SC Res. 2396 (2017).

14 Joanne Richards, 'Demobilising and Disengaging Violent Extremists: Towards a New UN Framework' (2017) 6 (1) *Stability: International Journal of Security and Development* 14.
15 See IOM (n 12) xi.
16 IOM refers to this as a 'disassociation' phase.
17 Although those categorised as low risk may not trigger a state obligation to prosecute, their engagement with a violent extremist group and the risk level makes them ineligible for immediate release.
18 See IOM (n 12).
19 See James Cockayne and Siobhan O'Neil (eds), 'UN DDR in an Era of Violent Extremism: Is It Fit for Purpose (2015) *United Nations University Centre for Policy Research*; Saïbou Issa and Nadine Machikou, 'Reintegrating Former Boko Haram Associates Perspectives: From Far North Region in Cameroon' (February 2019) *Global Centre on Cooperative Security*.
20 Ibid.
21 Muggah and O'Donnell (n 11) 4.
22 Cockayne and O'Neil (n 19).
23 For instance, see Vanda Felbab-Brown, 'DDR in the Context of Offensive Military Operations, Counterterrorism, CVE and Non-Permissive Environments' and 'A Bridge Not Too Far: A Field Report from Somalia' in Cockayne and O'Neil (n 29) 110–111.
24 For instance, International Crisis Group, 'Watchmen of Lake Chad: Vigilante Groups Fighting Boko Haram' (2017) Report No 244.
25 See UNSOM, 'Voices of Al-Shabaab: Understanding Former Combatants From the Baidoa Reintegration Centre' (2016) 11–12.
26 IOM (n 12) 14.
27 Mozambique is a party to the African Charter on Human and Peoples' Rights.
28 See Human Rights Committee General Comment 35 para 12. See also Human Rights Committee in *Mukong v Cameroon*, Communication No 458/1991, views adopted on 21 July 1994, para 9.8.
29 UN Doc. CCPR/C/GC/35 (3 September 2019) para 25.
30 Ibid, para 12.
31 Audrey R Chapman and Benjamin Carbonetti, 'Human Rights Protections for Vulnerable and Disadvantaged Groups: The Contributions of the UN Committee on Economic, Social and Cultural Rights' (2011) 33 (3) *Human Rights Quarterly* 682.
32 See Orly Mayas Stern, 'The Invisible Women of Al-Shabaab' (2019) *Adam Smith International* 4.
33 Ibid.
34 Carmeliza Rosario, 'The Rights of Women in the New Islamist Insurgency in Northern Mozambique' (2022) *EU Preventing and Countering Violent Extremism Workshop in Maputo* (22 March 2022).
35 Article 38(4) of the Convention on the Rights of the Child (adopted 20 November 1989, entered into force 2 September 1990) 1577 UNTS 3, and article 22(3) of the African Charter on the Rights and Welfare of the Child (adopted 1 July 1990, entered into force 29 November 1999) (African Charter).
36 Paris Principles para 3.6.
37 ACERWC, General Comment on article 22 of the African Children's Charter para 58.
38 Article 4 Convention on the Rights of Persons with Disabilities (adopted 13 December 2006, entered into force 3 May 2008) 252 UNTS 3 (CRPD).
39 Article 2 International Covenant on Civil and Political Rights (adopted 16 December 1966, entered into force 23 March 1976) 999 UNTS 171 (ICCPR).
40 Article 2 African Charter.
41 Article 11 CRPD.
42 Florian Morier, 'Programme Insight: The Screening Process of Disengaged Boko Haram Associates in Niger' (2019) *Journal for Deradicalisation* 131.

43 At times, a state may decide to have perpetrators of crimes prosecuted and rehabilitated and reintegrated afterwards.
44 See article 2(3) ICCPR.
45 IOM (n 12) 1–2.
46 Ibid.
47 Anjli Parrin, 'Creating a Legal Framework for Terrorism Defectors and Detainees in Somalia' (2016) 55 *Columbia Journal of Transnational Law* 258; Saskia Brechenmacher, 'Achieving Peace in Northeast Nigeria: The Reintegration Challenge' *Carnegie Endowment for International Peace* (2018) <https://carnegieendowment.org/2018/09/05/achieving-peace-in-northeast-nigeria-reintegration-challenge-pub-77177>.
48 Ibid.
49 Stern (n 32) 32–34.
50 Vanda Felbab-Brown, 'Somalia Case Study' in *The Limits of Punishment* (n 7) 19; Vanda Felbab-Brown, 'Nigeria Case Study' in Salih and others (above) 103.
51 UN Human Rights Committee, General Comment 20: Article 7 (Prohibition of Torture, or Other Cruel, Inhuman or Degrading Treatment or Punishment) (10 March 1992) para 3.
52 Rosario (n 34).
53 Article 2 ICCPR.
54 Article 2 African Charter.
55 Article 4 CRPD.
56 Tinka Veldhuis, 'Designing Rehabilitation and Reintegration Programmes for Violent Extremist Offenders: A Realist Approach' *International Centre for Counter-Terrorism Research Paper* (March 2012) 2.
57 Bulama Bukarti, 'Making Peace with Enemies: Nigeria's Reintegration of Boko Haram Fighters' War on the Rocks' *War on the Rocks* (27 March 2019).
58 Jeannine Ella Abatan and Remadji Hoinathy, 'Getting Goudoumaria Right: Are Boko Haram Defectors Reintegrating Safely?' *Institute for Security Studies* (2021).
59 See IOM, *Disengagement, Disassociation, Reintegration and Reconciliation: Transitional Rehabilitation* (IOM 2021).
60 Martini Ewi and others, 'Violent extremism in Mozambique: Drivers and Links to Transnational Organised Crime' *Institute for Security Studies* (August 2022).
61 Ibid.
62 See UN Doc. CCPR/C/21/Rev.1/Add.4 (30 July 1993) para 3.
63 Ibid.
64 See Fonteh Akum and Malik Samuel, 'Understanding the Dangerous Journey from Boko Haram to Rehabilitation' *Institute for Security Studies* (4 May 2020); Stern (n 44).
65 ACERWC, General Comment on article 22 of the African Children's Charter para 58.
66 Article 2 ICCPR.
67 Article 2 African Charter.
68 Article 4 CRPD.
69 Veldhuis (n 56) 2.
70 See similar argument by Georgia Holmer and Adrian Shtuni, 'Returning Foreign Fighters and the Reintegration Imperative' *United States Institute of Peace* (2017) 1.
71 UN Doc. CCPR/C/21/Rev.1/Add.13 (26 May 2004) para 8.
72 *SERAC and Another v Nigeria* Communication 155/96.
73 USAID, 'Demobilization, Disassociation, Reintegration, and Reconciliation (DDRR) in Northeast Nigeria' (2021) 6.
74 Article 38(4) CRC and article 22(3) African Children's Charter.
75 See the Paris Principles paras 7.0–7.84.
76 Article 2 ICCPR.
77 Article 2 African Charter.
78 Article 4 CRPD.

Bibliography

ACERWC, 'General Comment on Article 22 of the African Charter on the Rights and Welfare of the Child' <https://www.acerwc.africa/en/key-documents/general-comments>.

African Charter on the Rights and Welfare of the Child (1990) <https://au.int/en/treaties/african-charter-rights-and-welfare-child>.

Anjli Parrin, 'Creating a Legal Framework for Terrorism Defectors and Detainees in Somalia' (2016) 55 *Columbia Journal of Transnational Law*.

Audrey R Chapman and Benjamin Carbonetti, 'Human Rights Protections for Vulnerable and Disadvantaged Groups: The Contributions of the UN Committee on Economic, Social and Cultural Rights' (2011) 33 (3) *Human Rights Quarterly*.

Bulama Bukarti, 'Making Peace with Enemies: Nigeria's Reintegration of Boko Haram Fighters' War on the Rocks' *War on the Rocks* (27 March 2019).

Cale Salih, Ron Slye and Mark Freeman, *The Limits of Punishment, Transitional Justice and Violent Extremism* (United Nations University 2018).

Carmeliza Rosario, 'The Rights of Women in the New Islamist Insurgency in Northern Mozambique' (2022) EU Preventing and Countering Violent Extremism Workshop in Maputo (22 March 2022).

Convention on the Rights of the Child (1989) <https://treaties.un.org/Pages/showDetails.aspx?objid=08000002800007fe&clang=_en>.

Convention on the Rights of Persons with Disabilities (2006) <https://treaties.un.org/Pages/showDetails.aspx?objid=080000028017bf87&clang=_en>.

Dorina A Bekoe, Stephanie M Burchard and Sarah A Daly, 'Extremism in Mozambique: Interpreting Group Tactics and the Role of the Government's Response in the Crisis in Cabo Delgado' *Institute for Defense Analyses* (2020).

Énio Viegas Filipe Chingotuane and others, 'Strategic Options for Managing Violent Extremism in Southern Africa: The Case of Mozambique' (2021) *Friedrich-Ebert-Stiftung*.

Florian Morier, 'Programme Insight: The Screening Process of Disengaged Boko Haram Associates in Niger' (2019) 21 *Journal for Deradicalisation*.

Fonteh Akum and Malik Samuel, 'Understanding the Dangerous Journey from Boko Haram to Rehabilitation' *Institute for Security Studies* (4 May 2020).

Georgia Holmer and Adrian Shtuni, 'Returning Foreign Fighters and the Reintegration Imperative' *United States Institute of Peace* (2017).

Human Rights Committee, 'General Comment No. 35 on Article 9, Liberty and Security of Person' <https://www.ohchr.org/en/calls-for-input/general-comment-no-35-article-9-liberty-and-security-person>.

Human Rights Committee, 'General Comment 20: Article 7' (Prohibition of Torture, or Other Cruel, Inhuman or Degrading Treatment or Punishment) (10 March 1992).

Human Rights Committee in *Mukong v Cameroon*, Communication No 458/1991, Views adopted on 21 July 1994.

International Covenant on Civil and Political Rights (1966) <https://treaties.un.org/Pages/showDetails.aspx?objid=0800000280004bf5&clang=_en>.

International Crisis Group, 'Watchmen of Lake Chad: Vigilante Groups Fighting Boko Haram' (23 February 2017) <https://www.crisisgroup.org/africa/west-africa/nigeria/244-watchmen-lake-chad-vigilante-groups-fighting-boko-haram>.

International Crisis Group, 'Winning Peace in Mozambique's Embattled North' (10 February 2022) <https://www.crisisgroup.org/africa/southern-africa/mozambique/winning-peace-mozambiques-embattled-north>.

IOM, *Disarmament, Demobilisation and Reintegration: Compendium of Projects 2010–2017* (IOM 2019).

IOM, *Disengagement, Disassociation, Reintegration and Reconciliation: Eligibility Conditions and Practices* (IOM 2021).

IOM, *Disengagement, Disassociation, Reintegration and Reconciliation: Transitional Rehabilitation* (IOM 2021).

James Cockayne and Siobhan O'Neil (eds), 'UN DDR in an Era of Violent Extremism: Is It Fit for Purpose (2015) *United Nations University Centre for Policy Research* <https://peacekeeping.un.org/sites/default/files/un_ddr_in_an_era_of_violent_extremism.pdf>.

Jeannine Ella Abatan and Remadji Hoinathy, 'Getting Goudoumaria Right: Are Boko Haram Defectors Reintegrating Safely?' *Institute for Security Studies* (2021).

Joanne Richards, 'Demobilising and Disengaging Violent Extremists: Towards a New UN Framework' (2017) 6 (1) *Stability: International Journal of Security and Development.*

Louise Mallinder, *Amnesty, Human Rights and Political Transitions: Bridging the Peace and Justice Divide* (Hart Publishing 2008).

Martin Ewi and others, 'Violent Extremism in Mozambique: Drivers and Links to Transnational Organised Crime' *Institute for Security Studies* (August 2022).

Orly Maya Stern, 'The Invisible Women of Al-Shabaab' (2019) *Adam Smith International* <https://orlystern.com/wp-content/uploads/2023/06/The-Invisible-Women-of-al-Shabaab-.pdf>.

Robert Muggah and Chris O'Donnell, 'Next Generation Disarmament, Demobilisation and Reintegration' (2015) 4 (1) *Stability: International Journal of Security and Development.*

'Rwanda Deploys 1 000 Soldiers to Mozambique's Cabo Delgado' *Al Jazeera* (10 July 2021).

Saïbou Issa and Nadine Machikou, 'Reintegrating Former Boko Haram Associates Perspectives: From Far North Region in Cameroon' (February 2019) *Global Centre on Cooperative Security* <https://www.globalcenter.org/wp-content/uploads/GCCS-PB-Reintegrating-Former-Boko-Haram-Associates-2019.pdf>.

Saskia Brechenmacher, 'Achieving Peace in Northeast Nigeria: The Reintegration Challenge' *Carnegie Endowment for International Peace* (2018) <https://carnegieendowment.org/2018/09/05/achieving-peace-in-northeast-nigeria-reintegration-challenge-pub-77177>.

SERAC and Another v Nigeria, Communication 155/96.

Tinka Veldhuis, 'Designing Rehabilitation and Reintegration Programmes for Violent Extremist Offenders: A Realist Approach' *International Centre for Counter-Terrorism Research Paper* (March 2012).

UN Doc. CCPR/C/21/Rev.1/Add.4 (30 July 1993).

UN Doc. CCPR/C/21/Rev.1/Add.13 (26 May 2004).

UN Doc. CCPR/C/GC/35 (3 September 2019).

UNSOM, 'Voices of Al-Shabaab: Understanding Former Combatants from the Baidoa Reintegration Centre' (2016) <https://unsom.unmissions.org/sites/default/files/voices_of_al-shabaab_understanding_former_combatants_from_the_baidoa_reintegration_center.pdf>.

USAID, 'Demobilization, Disassociation, Reintegration, and Reconciliation (DDRR) in Northeast Nigeria' (2021) <https://www.usip.org/sites/default/files/DDRRpublicreport_5.13.21_Final.pdf>.

Vanda Felbab-Brown, 'DDR in the Context of Offensive Military Operations, Counterterrorism, CVE and Non-Permissive Environments' and 'A Bridge Not Too Far: A Field Report from Somalia' in James Cockayne and Siobhan O'Neil (eds), 'UN DDR in an Era of Violent Extremism: Is It Fit for Purpose (2015) *United Nations University Centre for Policy Research.*

Vanda Felbab-Brown, 'Somalia Case Study' in Cale Salih, Ron Slye and Mark Freeman (eds), *The Limits of Punishment, Transitional Justice and Violent Extremism* (United Nations University 2018).

13 The use of private military companies to counter the insurgency in Northern Mozambique

Hennie Strydom

13.1 Introduction

Prior to both the Southern African Development Community (SADC) and Rwandan deployments in Cabo Delgado following the Palma attack on 24 March 2021, resulting in grave atrocities committed against civilians,[1] the Mozambican government relied on bilateral security arrangements with private military and security companies (PMSCs) to counter the Islamic State-linked insurgency in Northern Mozambique. The Russian Wagner Group was deployed already in 2019 but failed to achieve results.[2] They were followed by Dyck Advisory Group (DAG), a South African PMSC, that was deployed from April 2020 until April 2021 and was credited with saving many lives during the Palma attack. According to media reports, DAG's contract was not renewed by the government and they shipped out shortly after the Palma incident. Since no reasons were given for the termination of their contract, there is media speculation that the Mozambican government had been influenced by an Amnesty International Report that DAG was involved in indiscriminate killings in their pursuit of the insurgents.[3]

Over the last three decades the use of PMSCs as service providers for states, non-state entities and even the United Nations (UN), has led to various initiatives for establishing a regulatory framework for PMSCs, often and erroneously equated with mercenary outfits. It is especially their involvement in armed conflicts that raised serious questions in international law and international humanitarian law depending on the functions they are transacted to perform coupled with human rights abuses they are from time to time accused of.

Of further concern is the inefficiency or absence of regulatory frameworks setting out the norms and standards for private military and security services that for a long time have been at the centre of debates on the privatisation of what used to be inherent state functions. It is this issue that forms the focus of this chapter, in particular in view of the renewed efforts by the UN Human Rights Council to arrive at a workable regulatory framework for PMSC activities and to ensure the effective enforcement of international and national law and accountability in case of transgressions.

The chapter starts with a brief overview of existing treaty-based and voluntary regulatory frameworks that, in response to sequential historical developments, are

DOI: 10.4324/9781003317647-16

aimed at regulating the activities of mercenaries and PMSCs, respectively. The main part of the chapter covers the work undertaken by certain UN bodies in creating a regulatory framework for the activities of PMSCs and their accountability for violations under international human rights and humanitarian law. Against this background, the chapter concludes with an assessment of the Mozambican government's responsibility for the conduct of PMSCs and the need for UN bodies to avoid treating PMSCs as just another manifestation of mercenarism, which requires the finalisation of a workable definition of PMSCs.

13.2 Existing treaty-based and other regulatory frameworks

In the African context, the phenomenon of soldiers for hire is distinctly associated with the fateful events in the 1960s and 1970s when mercenary-supported armed conflicts and secessionist movements in the Congo and Biafra, in particular, alarmed African states to the threat this posed to the territorial integrity and political independence of certain nascent post-colonial African states.[4] These events also led to the Organisation of African Unity (OAU) adopting in 1977 the Convention for the Elimination of Mercenarism in Africa[5] with the aim of criminalising mercenary activities. By 2023 the OAU Convention could only show 32 ratifications, which is a poor record given the historical condemnation by African states of the use of mercenaries in conflict situations after decolonisation. Mozambique has also not ratified the Convention. In 2004 the AU Protocol to the Convention on the Prevention and Combating of Terrorism[6] drew attention to the link between terrorism, mercenarism and international organised crime. In the same year as the OAU mercenary convention, Protocol I to the 1949 Geneva Conventions stripped mercenaries of combatant and prisoner of war status.[7]

However, despite these early attempts at outlawing or regulating the use of mercenaries and the general apprehension shown by African states towards their use, the enlistment of foreign military and security contractors in Africa has grown. Reportedly, the Kremlin-linked Wagner Group, partly made up of convicted criminals, is also actively involved in the Central African Republic, Mali, Sudan and Libya. Its international reach and involvement in illicit activities and human rights violations have drawn wide-spread condemnation, and in January 2023 the United States (US) designated the group as a 'significant transnational criminal organisation' putting it in the same category as the Italian mafia and Japanese and Russian organised crime groups. This designation could mean a wider application of sanctions against the group and its leaders.[8] Other military and/or security providers in parts of Africa include US companies CACI and Academi; French company Secopex; Britain's Aegis Defence Services and G4S; Ukraine's Omega Consulting Group; Germany's Xeless; and South Africa's DAG.[9] The services they provide are varied ranging from protecting state officials to training and logistical support, the guarding of extractive industries and border posts and active participation in hostilities.

Since the 1990s, following the end of the Cold War, the rise of different modes of enlisting the services of PMSCs for combat-related and other functions set in motion condemnatory responses from the international community and a scramble for a workable regulatory framework. The first attempt at a binding international instrument was the 1989 International Convention Against the Recruitment, Use, Financing and Training of Mercenaries that entered into force in 2001. The Convention interdicts states from recruiting, using, financing and training mercenaries and criminalises mercenary activities. Its ratification rate is unimpressive. By 2023 only 37 states have ratified it, which include a mere 14 African states with Mozambique still a non-ratifying African state.

The above treaty-based attempts to provide a normative framework for regulating mercenary activities do not stand alone. In 2008 a joint initiative by the Swiss government and the International Committee of the Red Cross (ICRC) led to the adoption of the Montreux Document on Private Military and Security Companies[10] which confirmed the existing obligations of states under international law and international humanitarian and human rights law for the activities of PMSCs during armed conflict. Not intended as a legally binding instrument, the Montreux Document is an invitation to participating states to adopt its principles for the domestic regulation of PMSC activities in accordance with their existing obligations under international law. Currently 58 states have recorded their support for the Montreux Document, which include only five African states, namely, Angola, South Africa, Uganda, Madagascar and Sierra Leone.[11] In 2022 the Montreux Document Forum claimed that according to independent research, the implementation of the Montreux Document can be linked to a decrease in violence against civilians during and after the end of hostilities.[12] Building on this example, the Swiss government in 2010 concluded a Code of Conduct for Private Security Service Providers applying to such providers the responsibility to respect human rights and render humanitarian assistance to persons affected by their activities.[13] The enforcement of the Code is overseen and monitored by the International Code of Conduct Association established in 2013 as a multi-stakeholder entity comprising representatives from government, private security companies and civil society organisations.

As will be noted in the next part, debates in international fora are characterised by divisions among supporters for a treaty-based regulatory framework, on the one hand, and a voluntary framework, on the other. A third view is that an either-or solution should be avoided and that different approaches to regulation should be allowed to co-exist. This division has long remained an obstacle in reaching consensus on the nature of the instrument that should be adopted for developing a normative framework within which PMSCs should conduct their business.

13.3 A passing message by the UN Commission on Human Rights

At the time when the UN Commission was replaced by the UN Human Rights Council in 2006, two reports on mercenaries and the regulation of their activities were of direct relevance for the work that would resume on this topic under the auspices of the Human Rights Council. The one was the report by the UN Special Rapporteur on Mercenaries,[14] and the other was the Commission's working group report of 2007.[15]

The Special Rapporteur's report emanated from a 2005 UN General Assembly resolution,[16] which in one part is unforgiving in its denunciation of the recruitment and use of mercenaries. For instance, the resolution makes it clear that the use, recruitment, financing and training of mercenaries violated the purposes and principles of the UN Charter,[17] and it requests all states to exercise the utmost vigilance against 'any kind of recruitment, training, hiring or financing of mercenaries by private companies offering international military consultancy and security services'.[18] In keeping with this approach the resolution

> *[c]ondemns* any form of impunity granted to perpetrators of mercenary activities and to those responsible for the use, recruitment, financing and training of mercenaries, and urges all states, in accordance with their obligations under international law, to bring them, without distinction, to justice.[19]

Elsewhere in the resolution the Assembly's condemnation seems to be reserved for the use of mercenaries for certain specific purposes only. This would be the case where mercenary activities are

> designed to impede the right of peoples to self-determination, to destabilise or overthrow the Government of any State or to dismember or impair, totally or in part, the territorial integrity or political unity of sovereign and independent States conducting themselves in compliance with the right of peoples to self-determination.[20]

These concerns are also reflected in the title of the resolution that refers to the '[u]se of mercenaries as a means of violating human rights and impeding the exercise of the right of peoples to self-determination'. This differentiated approach applies in equal measure to mercenary interventions in armed conflicts or actions to destabilise constitutional regimes for which the resolution wants states to impose a special ban.[21]

That the General Assembly's approach to the matter, as an expression of member states' views, is removed from contemporary realities is clear from the Special Rapporteur's mandated report in terms of the resolution. In concluding her report[22] she alluded to the 'need for a fundamental reconsideration of issues concerning mercenaries' and to a 'paradigm shift' that needs to occur in respect of the mandate.[23] A core issue identified in the report is the ambiguity that exists with regard to the status of private military and security companies in relation to the definition of a mercenary in international law and the legal issues associated therewith. That such companies are employed by UN member states, non-governmental organisations and the UN itself to perform a range of duties further underscores the need for a rethink of the status of such companies.[24]

In the context of the current political and security climate, characterised by globalisation, military downsizing, privatisation and outsourcing, the Special Rapporteur introduced critical issues. Pertinent is the 'fundamental question of whether states wish to continue to be solely 'responsible for the use of force, for declaring war and for sanctioning the use of force within certain internationally acceptable rules of engagement'.[25] The wider context in which this must be deliberated is made up of numerous examples of UN member states being unwilling or unable to protect their citizens against gross human rights violations and of the UN's unreliability and outright failures to take action as a result of its own incapacitating and outdated procedures. Here, we could also add the poor record of the African Union (AU) Peace and Security Council and of sub-regional agencies in effectively and timeously responding to threats against peace and security on the continent. In this environment it is common cause that a long-standing lack of clarity on the application of the subsidiarity principle under the AU's peace and security architecture is a major obstacle in implementing effective and timely interventions to prevent or counter security threats in member states.[26] The peace and security dilemmas that could confront the AU and the sub-regional agencies in the absence of a clear division of labour according to the subsidiarity principle are illustrated by the Cabo Delgado insurgency on 24 March 2021. While the AU's response was trapped in the usual paralysis, the SADC was in no hurry and approved military assistance only on 23 June 2021 at an Extraordinary Summit.[27] Prior to this, Mozambique put its trust in PMSCs.

The Special Rapporteur is correct in concluding that in such circumstances the lack of an appropriate definition of a mercenary 'is likely to result in quite serious problems for the international community, including ones concerning security'.[28] However, she perhaps is over-ambitious where she requires that a policy decision at the UN level must first be reached on who is entitled to the lawful and legitimate use of force before a legal definition can be developed.[29] Currently, there is little, if any, chance that UN members would reach consensus on such a policy. However, what could emerge from a UN round-table discussion, as suggested by the Special Rapporteur,[30] is that member state responses to the guidelines for such a discussion may indicate which of the three options is most likely to underpin future developments and determine the elements of a legal definition of a mercenary. At the extreme ends the options are (i) a situation where states reclaim full responsibility for their armed forces without any possibility of outsourcing functions to private entities or (ii) that states should consider privatising and outsourcing all their military functions. The third option contemplates a hybrid scenario where states retain small military contingents and outsource additional functions as required.[31]

What the work of the Special Rapporteur also made clear is the fact that the attraction of the UN Convention, a relic of the decolonisation era and Cold War politics, has waned, which explains, even today, the low rate of ratifications by UN member states. Its conceptual framework simply is no longer relevant and the same can be said of the OAU Convention.

Notwithstanding, the UN Commission's Working Group on mercenaries which, as mentioned earlier, succeeded the Special Rapporteur, continued the campaign for the universal ratification of the UN Convention.[32] Even so, within its mandate to develop proposals for possible new standards on the regulation of mercenary activities, the Working Group endorsed the Special Rapporteur's proposal for a UN round-table policy discussion to address fundamental questions concerning core actors in the monopoly of the use of force.[33] However, it then pre-empted the outcome of such a process by stating, in the same breath:

> States must make a clear distinction between those private companies which offer security services in strict compliance with imperative norms, regulations and accountability, such as respect for the principle of the State's monopoly on the use of force, and those recruiting, training, hiring or financing mercenaries to operate in zones of armed conflict, whose activities should be criminalised.[34]

The issue of the regulation of mercenary activities and the licensing of private military and security companies is a major subject in the Working Group's recommendations.[35] This is informed by the lack or inadequacy of domestic legislative and other measures ensuring compliance and preventing impunity for violations of domestic laws as well as international human rights and humanitarian law. This has been a long-standing issue despite the fact that in the debates in the UN fora on mercenaries, domestic regulation and enforcement as a primary state responsibility enjoys strong support among the options that include self-regulation by the industry and the adoption of a binding international instrument.

After 2006, the Working Group continued its work under the UN Human Rights Council and concluded its work in 2010 with the submission of a Draft Convention on Private Military and Security Companies.[36] Since the Draft Convention features in the follow-up work undertaken by the Human Rights Council, some salient aspects thereof warrant attention.

Several opening paragraphs in the Preamble invoke aspects of the law on state responsibility, which clearly illustrate the importance of domestic action for the enforcement of national as well as international measures applicable to mercenary activities and their consequences. Underpinning this approach, member states are reminded of their duties under the general principles of the UN Charter, international human rights and humanitarian law, the International Law Commission's Draft Articles on State Responsibility and the principles of the Rome Statute of the International Criminal Court (ICC).

As regards its scope of application,[37] both states and international organisations can be signatories to the Draft Convention and it will apply to all situations, whether or not the situation is defined as an armed conflict. Cases not covered by the Draft Convention or other international agreements will remain bound 'by virtue of the principles of international law derived from established custom, from the principles of humanity and from the dictates of public conscience'. Here, the Draft Convention invokes the Martens Clause, the wording of which also appears, inter alia, in article 63 of the First Geneva Convention of 1949 and article 1(2) of the First Protocol (1977) to the Geneva Conventions. It is also a rule of customary international law.[38]

Further substance is given to the above preambular references to state responsibilities in Part II of the Draft Convention. This part contains general principles on a range of compliance and enforcement issues. Once registered or operating in their jurisdiction, state parties will be responsible for the activities of security and military companies, regardless of whether they are contracted by the state. If contracted, the contracting state must ensure that such companies not only are trained in but also respect international human rights and humanitarian law.[39] Procedures for contracting, the import and export of military and security personnel and services and customs controls must be determined by legislative and other measures.[40]

The Draft Convention prohibits the delegation or outsourcing to PMSCs of inherently state functions.[41] Such functions include[42]

> direct participation in hostilities, waging war and/or combat operations, taking prisoners, law-making, espionage, intelligence, knowledge transfer with military, security and policing application, use of and other activities related to weapons of mass destruction, police powers, especially the powers of arrest or detention including the interrogation of detainees, and other functions that a State Party considers to be inherently State functions.

What will constitute 'inherent state functions' is a matter that will be determined by a state's constitutional law, which may or may not fully coincide with the Draft Convention's determination. It is perhaps for this reason that the Draft Convention requires states to determine by law the full or partial prohibition of the delegation or outsourcing of military or security services.[43] In any event, this is a matter that is likely to become the subject of diverse views. The only guidance provided by the Draft Convention is the definition clause that defines 'inherent state functions' as 'functions which are consistent with the principle of the State monopoly on the legitimate use of force and that a State cannot outsource or delegate to PMSCs under any circumstances'.[44] However, the question arises as to whether an executive decision to outsource or delegate, at least to a certain extent, may be a competency ancillary to the exclusive competence on the legitimate use of force in the absence of a constitutional provision to the contrary.

State duties in respect of the enactment of legislative and other measures and their enforcement received the necessary attention in the Draft Convention. The aim is to provide for an official rule of law-based system at the domestic level that will be consistent with international human rights and humanitarian law and with the laws of the home state, the contracting state, the state of operations and third states of which the nationals are employed by a PMSC under contract.[45]

Also invoked are UN Charter obligations to the effect that states must ensure that no mercenary activities are carried out that will undermine the sovereignty, political independence and territorial integrity of states, the right to self-determination and the duty not to intervene in the internal affairs of a state.[46] In view of the above, it seems over-cautious of the Draft Convention to require states to prohibit and criminalise direct participation of PMSCs in hostilities, terrorist acts and military actions aimed at, or which states have grounds for suspecting would result in the overthrow of a government, coercive change of internationally recognised borders, the violation of sovereignty and the explicit targeting of civilians.[47] The same is true of the prohibition on the use or outsourcing of certain types of arms in article 10.

An important part of ensuring compliance with international and domestic norms and standards is the institutionalisation of an efficient authorisation, licensing and monitoring system. Several provisions in the Draft Convention spell out detailed state obligations in this regard.[48] Supplementing domestic measures, international oversight and monitoring under the Draft Convention is assigned to a Committee of Experts that shall keep and maintain an international register of PMSCs operating on the international market, based on information provided by state parties.[49]

Following the established practice in international human rights treaties in particular, the Draft Convention provides for a reporting duty member states owe to the Committee detailing the legislative and other measures states have undertaken in compliance with the Draft Convention.[50] Apart from considering state reports and engaging with states on their compliance performance,[51] the Committee is also empowered to inquire into grave or systematic violations of the Draft Convention by a member state for which certain procedures are prescribed.[52] A failure to resolve the issue to the satisfaction of the parties in this manner would entitle the Committee to submit it to a Conciliation Commission appointed by the Committee with the consent of the parties to the dispute.[53]

An inter-state complaints procedure is also provided. This mechanism is subject to a declaration by the state parties concerned recognising the competence of the Committee to receive and admit inter-state complaints.[54] It is general knowledge that inter-state complaints did not find support as an enforcement mechanism in international human rights treaties and it is unlikely that it will be different under the Draft Convention's proposal. As with inter-state complaints, the Draft Convention borrows from international human rights treaties in respect of the individual petition procedures. Complaints via this mechanism are subject to a declaration, submitted by the complainant's state party at the time of ratification of the Convention or at any time afterwards, declaring that it recognises the competence of the Committee to receive and consider communications from or on behalf of individuals.[55]

13.4 The work of the UN Human Rights Council on an international regulatory framework

Since 2010 the search for a regulatory framework for PMSC activities has been assigned to an open-ended intergovernmental working group (OEWG) by the Human Rights Council. The mandate given to the working group is to investigate the possibility of elaborating an international regulatory framework on the regulation, monitoring and oversight of the activities of PMSCs. This included the option of a legally binding instrument.[56] The Council's explanation for establishing an open-ended inter-governmental working group for this purpose was to ensure transparency and inclusivity.

By 2012 the OEWG reported that while there is agreement among the delegates on the common goal of protecting human rights in the context of PMSC activities and to ensure accountability for abuses, differences in the means to achieve the common goal persist.[57] What is clear from the report's account of discussions and comments by delegates[58] – representing member states, non-governmental organisations (NGOs) and research institutions[59] – was that the whole range of current regulatory attempts could suffice as a framework if the general enforcement deficit and defects in, for instance, the Montreux Document, the International Code of Conduct for Private Security Providers and the former Working Group's Draft Convention could be remedied. At the time of the 2012 report, the general sentiment seemed to be that 'one size doesn't fit all' and that each of the above instruments or approaches to regulation may have a role to play.

In the years following the 2012 report, the debate within the OEWG became stuck between consensus in respect of the objective and disunity in respect of the method of regulation. This is clear from the 2014 report[60] as well as the 2015 report[61] that contained nothing of substance to indicate a change in direction. An interesting aspect of the 2015 report is the positions taken by the European Union (EU) and the Group of African States, respectively. In its concluding remarks, the proposals put forward by the EU make no specific mention of a binding international agreement among the options to be considered. In fact, the sentiment clearly is in favour of building on the Montreux Document and the International Code of Conduct on Private Security Providers and on investigating other ways of setting international standards and guidelines.[62] By contrast, the African Group made clear its support for a legally binding international agreement.[63]

At the time of the 2017 OEWG Report, the above divisions between delegations favouring measures that would complement the existing framework contained in the Montreux Document, the International Code of Conduct and other non-binding instruments and those favouring a binding legal instrument remained unchanged.[64] The only difference was a new 'emerging consensus' to move forward on the basis of a discussion document submitted by the Chair-Rapporteur[65] containing essential elements for developing an international regulatory framework.[66] The elements contain nothing new; they are already covered by the provisions of the Draft Convention dealt with earlier.

Nonetheless, the discussion document on elements found new relevance when the Human Rights Council appointed a new OEWG in 2017.[67] The mandate given to the new Working Group was to elaborate the *content* of an international regulatory framework that was to be informed by the discussion document on elements.[68] As is clear from the 2019 report,[69] the introduction of the document on elements to guide the work of the OEWG achieved nothing more than a re-opening of familiar debates on semantics and terminology. If the purpose of the 2017 mandate was to build consensus on substantive issues and to press ahead in finalising the work on a regulatory framework, it made no contribution towards this goal by 2019.

The OEWG sessions between 2019 and the 2021 report[70] supplemented the previous debates with more of the same. The impasse on the nature of a regulatory framework also remained unsolved and consensus remained restricted to the obvious, namely, the need for a regulatory framework that would ensure accountability for human rights violations and that would provide for effective remedies for victims. After all, no one would dispute such an objective in the twenty-first century.

Nonetheless, by 2021 the time was considered ripe for taking a step forward. This was announced by the Chair-Rapporteur to the effect that the recommendations and inputs to date would enable him to update and expand on the elements document with a view to preparing a zero draft of a regulatory framework 'without prejudging the nature thereof'.[71] The working method, as explained in the same paragraph, was to circulate a zero draft of a regulatory framework followed by informal intersessional consultations on the basis of the zero draft and to then circulate a revised zero draft (RZD) for further discussion and inputs. It is to the latter that the discussion now turns.

13.5 The revised zero draft instrument

The RZD served as a basis for further discussion and for providing further impetus to the development of an international regulatory framework during the third session of the OEWG in May 2022.[72] In the general remarks to the RZD,[73] it is explained that the approach, based on the possibility that it may evolve into a legally binding document, is that states as subjects of international law would assume certain obligations. These will take the form of state obligations under the general principles of the law on state responsibility and obligations to enact the necessary legislative and other measures to implement the RZD in their domestic legal systems in accordance with their own laws and traditions.

In the substantive part of the RZD the obligations in question cover general obligations under international human rights and humanitarian law, and law-making obligations with respect to the registration, licensing and recruitment of PMSCs, criminalisation of certain activities, jurisdiction and the use and acquisition of weapons.[74] Potentially problematic in terms of the general obligations is the duty to prohibit PMSCs from exercising state functions[75] and not to employ PMSCs in any function that would result in their direct participation in hostilities.[76] In the case of the former the RZD follows the Draft Convention's definition of state functions[77] which, as indicated earlier, is a matter on which consensus will be near impossible to achieve because of the diverse constitutional and political set-up in different states. Equally problematic is the prohibition on direct participation in hostilities. This goes against what is already happening on the ground where, for example, the territorial state on its own is incapable of countering a threat to peace and security, or where other circumstances in an evolving or changing armed conflict make it imperative for a PMSC to be enlisted for that purpose, or to become directly involved in hostilities for reasons of self-defence, the protection of civilians, or another compelling reason.

As indicated earlier, the issue of accountability for human rights violations and other transgressions received much attention in the sessions of the different working groups. The concern with the lack of accountability is justified and relates to the enforcement gaps in the current frameworks and the ineffective legal measures, or the lack of such measures, at the domestic level. This is a subject that has been debated *ad nauseam* in international fora, and the remedies provided for in the RZD, such as access to justice, investigations and prosecutions, mutual legal assistance and extradition,[78] will, for their effectiveness, remain dependent on the political will of states to enforce the instrument at the domestic level. Even if the instrument evolves into a binding legal instrument, there is no guarantee that it will attract enough ratifications to turn it into an efficient enforcement mechanism. The history of the UN and OAU conventions on mercenaries provides food for thought.

Unlike the Draft Convention discussed earlier, the RZD makes no provision for a reporting obligation and monitoring by, for instance, a conference of state parties. According to the General Remarks to the RZD, delegations will have to provide guidance on the inclusion of a central authority responsible for monitoring and enforcement by such an authority and whether such an authority must be established as a treaty body or by a state as a domestic mechanism. Arguably, the latter may be possible under article 16(1) that provides for the establishment of national contact points for analysis and sharing of information on PMSCs and possible violations of national and international law.

In October 2022 an amended version (Second Draft) of the RZD[79] was released for consideration by the Working Group. Some of the amendments are of a substantive nature and deserve mention here. In respect of the monitoring and oversight issue mentioned in the previous paragraph, the Second Draft provides for a state duty to establish independent competent authorities to provide for monitoring, accountability and oversight of the PMSC industry. This is a significantly stronger mechanism than the contact point mechanism foreseen in article 16(1) of the RZD. The existing article 11 provision on the regulation of the use and acquisition of weapons is supplemented as follows. First, by prohibiting PMSCs:

> from using weapons and/or engaging in any activities related to certain types of weapons, such as weapons of mass destruction, weapons which cause superfluous injury or unnecessary suffering, or which are to cause widespread, long-term and severe damage to the environment, as well as from trafficking in firearms, their parts, components or ammunition and other related accessories.[80]

And second, by compelling states to adopt legislation clarifying that 'the use of force by Private Military and Security Companies must be guided by the personal right to self-defence unless explicitly authorised by law to perform wider tasks'.[81] This sensible addition to article 11 relates to my earlier observation in respect of the issue concerning direct participation in hostilities by PMSCs.

Finally, in a clumsily formulated addendum to the existing article 16, the Second Draft attempts to provide for a reporting duty by states. The amendment determines that states shall 'establish a monitoring and reporting mechanism to which they will report on their implementation of the International Regulatory Framework on Private Military and Security Companies'. However, in the very next sentence, the provision states that '[m]onitoring and reporting [is to be][shall] be undertaken by their respective National Contact Points'.[82] If the idea is that an independent monitoring body must be set up, whether nationally or internationally, is not clear, the national contact points, that will be responsible for the reporting according to the second sentence, cannot also be the monitoring entity.

Some comments recorded in the OEWG's Report of July 2022[83] should be mentioned at this juncture. This report preceded the release of the Second Draft and contains the proceedings of its third session during which the Second Draft was debated and commented upon. The first response is that of the Chair of the 2005 Working Group on the use of mercenaries who advised that a decision must be taken soon on the form/nature of the instrument and added that the Working Group was in favour of a binding instrument. In support of this outcome, the Chair mentioned that an insufficient number of states had committed to existing frameworks such as the Montreux Document and the International Code of Conduct and that national laws failed to deal adequately with the main concerns in respect of the activities of PMSCs.[84]

The second comment is that of the representative of the Working Group on the issue of human rights and transnational corporations and other business enterprises.[85] In this instance, the proposal was for a closer alignment between the Second Draft and the UN Guiding Principles on Business and Human Rights[86] while agreeing that binding initiatives 'were important and critical at the present stage'.[87] These are not lone voices and they share a common concern about the lack of enforceable hard law frameworks. Comments such as these from bodies within the UN system coupled with the general direction of the development of an international regulatory framework may indicate that sentiments are gradually shifting towards a binding multilateral treaty-based framework to replace the self-regulatory and other voluntary frameworks. Such an outcome may hold the potential of a more efficient regulatory framework, but it is by no means self-evident; states fail to implement and enforce in respect of binding as well as non-binding international standards.

13.6 Conclusion

In revisiting the Cabo Delgado episode in the context of the above developments, the following conclusions can be drawn. First, since Mozambique is not a member of either the OAU Convention or UN Convention on mercenaries, the Mozambican government's responsibility for preventing, investigating and ensuring accountability for human rights violations by PMSCs can only derive from the country's general obligations under national law as well as international human rights and humanitarian law. In the case of international human rights law, Mozambique ratified the 1966 International Covenant on Civil and Political Rights (ICCPR) in 1993 but is yet to ratify the first Optional Protocol providing for individual complaints. This leaves Mozambican citizens without a remedy under ICCPR if they are unsuccessful in finding a remedy under national law. Access to the African Court of Justice and Human Rights also is not permitted since Mozambique has signed but not ratified the Court's Statute. Hence, under the African Charter on Human and Peoples' Rights (African Charter) there only remains the option of petitioning the African Commission on Human and Peoples' Rights (African Commission) to investigate breaches of the African Charter and other international human rights instruments under articles 45, 46 and 60 of the Charter and to report on its findings. Another significant international instrument is the Rome Statute of the International Criminal Court. This Mozambique also has not ratified, which eliminates its use as a potential avenue for a remedy should the Mozambican government be unwilling or unable to prosecute Rome Statute crimes at the national level.

The above situation is cause for taking note of the outcome of the country's Universal Periodic Review (UPR) in terms of the Human Rights Council's mandate.[88] Following the third cycle of the UPR of Mozambique in 2021, the High Commissioner for Human Rights addressed a letter to the Minister of Foreign Affairs expressing concern about the human rights situation in the north. The peer comments annexed to the letter[89] are to the effect that the government must ratify the main international human rights treaties to which it is not yet a party,[90] ensure accountability and due process through independent and transparent investigations into cases of alleged human rights violations in Cabo Delgado and to ensure the protection of civilians, in particular in the context of the conflict in the area.[91] Other comments have specifically mentioned investigations into alleged human rights abuses by non-state armed groups, government security forces and private security forces and to bring the perpetrators to justice.[92] Notable is also the intervention of the African Commission that, in a resolution of 2021, called on the Mozambican government to ensure respect for its international obligations in terms of humanitarian law, particularly with regard to the protection of civilians during armed conflicts and to grant special protection to children and women affected by the armed conflict, to cease mass killings, extrajudicial and arbitrary executions, to grant protection to civilians and to investigate and prosecute the perpetrators of the violations.[93]

The question that remains is whether Mozambique has the capacity and resources to conduct investigations and bring perpetrators to justice. In the relevant UN reports there is little of substance indicating what the real situation is. For instance, a UN country team report of February 2021 cursorily mentions weaknesses in the functioning of the National Human Rights Commission, low per capita ratios in respect of the number of magistrates and prosecutors and regional disparities, and the need for improvement in the training of security and justice officials.[94]

Whatever the situation, there is justifiable criticism about the general lack of protection for the victims of human rights violations in the form of bringing the perpetrators to justice, including members of the government forces. According to a 2022 Human Rights Watch report, the Mozambican government has ignored calls by rights groups to investigate and appropriately punish the perpetrators of the violations except for a few successful prosecutions against members of the insurgency.[95] Given these circumstances, ensuring accountability for unlawful conduct by members of PMSCs is an even more remote dream.

This applies equally to the prospect of accountability in the home countries, in this instance Russia (Wagner) and South Africa (DAG), assuming the participation of these organisations in the commission of atrocities against civilians. It is preposterous to think that Russian authorities would even consider investigations into such atrocities and the prosecution of Wagner soldiers for unlawful conduct in Mozambique while large-scale breaches of international humanitarian and human rights law in Ukraine are ignored. As far as South Africa is concerned, there is no indication that the authorities are interested in DAG's conduct in Mozambique. It also is questionable whether the state has the investigative and prosecutorial ability to undertake this task. Furthermore, in assessing the prospect of home country enforcement in the case of South Africa, one cannot overlook the January 2023 incident in a social media video clip showing South African soldiers apparently burning bodies in Mozambique. Media reports at the time informed that the force commander of the SADC Mission, which included a South African contingent, had vowed to investigate the incident.[96] By June 2023, no evidence had emerged from the alleged investigation.

At the international level the approach by the General Assembly and the Human Rights Council's Working Group on mercenaries sometimes is misaligned with the work undertaken by the Council's OEWG on a regulatory framework for the activities of PMSCs. In their resolutions and reports both the General Assembly and the Working Group make no clear distinction between mercenaries and PMSCs and often treat the two groups of actors as one and call for the criminalisation of their activities in an indistinct manner. Over the years, both organs tried to sell the message in a register that no longer made any sense because of changes in the global security environment and the outsourcing practice of states affecting even functions that traditionally were considered inherently state functions.

At a time when progress on a regulatory framework for the activities of PMSCs has gained some traction in the work of the OEWG, one would expect the General Assembly and the Working Group to align themselves more meaningfully with the new trajectory instead of repeating the same message in the same hackneyed and repetitive style. In the General Assembly's latest resolution on the issue,[97] the Assembly is still *convinced* that 'notwithstanding the way in which mercenaries or mercenary-related activities are used or the form that they take to acquire some semblance of legitimacy, they are a threat to peace, security and the self-determination of peoples and an obstacle to the enjoyment of all human rights by peoples'.

This final preambular statement is preceded by an acknowledgement of the work done by the OEWG of the Human Rights Council elaborating an international regulatory framework on the regulation, monitoring and oversight of the activities of private military and security companies. Yet, the distinction made between mercenaries and PMSCs in the work on a regulatory framework seemed to have no effect on the Assembly's approach to the matter as is clear from the contents of the resolution that substantially is no different from the many previous resolutions. Perhaps the best way to make sense of this is to resign oneself to the fact that the historical objections to mercenarism and its denouncement live on as a project of the Assembly and that the work of the OEWG is an entirely separate project. Yet, treating mercenary activities and those of PMSCs as one and the same thing seems to be also well-ingrained in the work of the Human Rights Council's Working Group on 'the use of mercenaries as a means of violating human rights and impeding the exercise of the right of peoples to self-determination' as it is officially known. In its 2022 report on the activities of mercenaries and PMSCs in the maritime context,[98] the Working Group seems to treat PMSCs as just another manifestation of mercenarism. There could be two reasons for this undifferentiated approach by the General Assembly and the Working Group whose mandate is derived from the Assembly. One is an ideological leftover from the early post-colonial experience with mercenary activities, and the other is the unsuccessful attempts thus far to arrive at an acceptable and workable definition of a mercenary in contradistinction with that of a private military or security company. Settling this issue is integral to the work of the OEWG that should realise the urgency of bringing this project to a sensible close.

In this regard, hopeful signs have emerged in the process of formulating a regulatory framework. For instance, in the case of the Draft Convention on Private Military and Security Companies[99] proposals for the adoption of a new international regulatory instrument acknowledged the misalignment between the staff of PMSCs and the definition of a mercenary in article 47 of the 1977 Additional Protocol I to the Geneva Conventions and in article 1 of the UN Convention on Mercenaries by concluding that the definitions in these conventions do 'not generally apply to the personnel of PMSCs legally operating in foreign countries'.[100] After all, as the proposals made clear, the aim of the new binding legal instrument is not the outright banning of PMSCs but the establishment of minimum international standards for their operation.

This paradigm shift impacts the definition of a PMSC to the effect that such entities are defined in accordance with a description of the services they provide lawfully on a compensatory basis. Accordingly, article 2 of the Draft Convention defines a private military company as a corporate entity providing 'specialised military services related to military actions'. This core element of the definition is supplemented by a non-exhaustive list of related services.

Security services in article 2 refer to armed guarding or protection of building, installations, property and people and any kind of knowledge transfer with security and policing application and the development and implementation of informational security measures or services related thereto.

In the RZD Instrument the definition of military services was slightly amended by article 1(c) in specifying that the definition applies irrespective of whether the services in question are rendered on land, in the air or at sea, or in cyberspace or space.

The approach followed in these definitions constitutes a clear break with the criminalisation and banning objectives of the outdated earlier conventions referred to. It illustrates an acknowledgement of the contemporary security situation and the need for legal regulation of an industry that has the potential to cause great harm to civilians apart from being exploitable in furthering the interests of rogue governments or political factions in conflict-ridden societies.

Notes

1 See SADC Communiqué of 23 June 2021; Amnesty International, 'Mozambique: "What I Saw Is Death": War Crimes in Mozambique's Forgotten Cape' (2021). See also ACHPR/Res 477 (LXVIII) 2021.

2 Daniel Sixto, 'Russian Mercenaries: A String of Failures in Africa' *Geopolitical Monitor* (24 August 2020) <www.geopoliticalmonitor.com/russian-mercenaries-a-string-of-failures-in-africa/>.

3 Peter Fabricius, 'SA Military Company in Insurgent Zone, the Dyck Advisory Group, Will Not Extend Contract with Mozambique' *Daily Maverick* (31 March 2021).

4 On this episode in post-colonial statehood in Africa, see Martin Meredith, *The State of Africa: A History of Fifty Years of Independence* (Free Press 2006).

5 AU, Convention for the Elimination of Mercenarism in Africa (adopted 3 July 1977, entered into force 22 April 1985) 1490 UNTS 89.

6 AU, Protocol to the OAU Convention on the Prevention and Combating of Terrorism (adopted 8 July 2004, entered into force 26 February 2014) 3269 UNTS 1.

7 Protocol Additional to the Geneva Conventions of 12 August 1949 and Relating to the Protection of Victims of International Armed Conflicts (Protocol I) (adopted 8 June 1977, entered into force 7 December 1978) 1125 UNTS 3, article 47(1).

8 'US to Designate Russia's Wagner Group as "Transnational Criminal Organisation"' *The Guardian* (20 January 2023). There is also evidence that the Wagner Group pays for its military operations by plundering mineral resources in Africa, especially in the Central African Republic. See Debora Patta and Sarah Carter, 'How Russia's Wagner Group Funds Its Role in Putin's Ukraine War by Plundering Africa's Resources' *CBS News* (16 May 2023).

9 Antonio Cascais and Reliou Koubakin, 'Mercenary Armies in Africa' *Deutche Welle* (15 April 2022). See also Alan Doss, 'Africa and the Soldiers of Misfortune' *Africa Arguments* (10 May 2022); Mucahid Durmaz and Murtala Abdullahi, '"White Hands": The Rise of Private Armies in African Conflicts' *Al Jazeera* (28 April 2022).

10 The Montreux Document on Pertinent International Legal Obligations and Good Practices for States Related to Operations of Private Military and Security Companies During Armed Conflict (2008).

11 'Participating States of the Montreux Document' *Federal Department of Foreign Affairs* <www.eda.admin.ch/eda/en/fdfa/foreign-policy/international-law/international-humanitarian-law/private-military-security-companies/participating-states.html>.

12 'Independent Research Confirms the Positive Impact of the Montreux Document on the Reduction of PMSC's Violence Against Civilians' *Montreux Document Forum* (27 April 2022) <www.montreuxdocument.org/news/impactoncivilians.html>.

13 'The International Code of Conduct for Private Security Service Providers' *The Responsible Security Association.*

14 UN Doc. A/60/263 (17 August 2005).

15 UN Doc. A/62/301 (24 August 2007).

16 UNGA Res. 59/178 (3 March 2005).

17 Ibid, para 3.

18 Ibid, para 6.

19 Ibid, para 11.

20 Ibid, para 5.

21 Ibid, para 6.

22 UN Doc. A/60/263 (n 14).

23 Ibid, para 45.

24 Ibid, paras 47, 48.

25 Ibid, para 51.

26 See inter alia Hennie Strydom, 'The Evolution of the UN-AU Peace and Security Partnership' in Frans Viljoen and others (eds), *A Life Interrupted: Essays in Honour of the Lives and Legacies of Christ of Heyns* (PULP 2022) 222, 231.

27 SADC Communique of 23 June 2021 para 7.
28 UN Doc. A/60/263 (n 14) para 51.
29 Ibid.
30 Ibid, para 52.
31 Ibid.
32 UN Doc. A/62/301 (n 15) paras 71, 73.
33 Ibid, paras 66, 67, 73(i).
34 Ibid, para 66.
35 Ibid, paras 69, 72, 73.
36 UN Doc. A/HRC/15/25, Annex (2 July 2010).
37 Ibid, article 3.
38 On this and the history of the Martens Clause, see ICRC, *Commentary on the First Geneva Convention* (2016) 1184–1186.
39 UN Doc. A/HRC/15/25 (n 36) articles 4(1), (2).
40 Ibid, article 4(4).
41 Ibid, article 4(3).
42 Ibid, article 9.
43 Ibid, article 4(5).
44 Ibid, article 2(i).
45 Ibid articles 5, 7.
46 Ibid, article 6.
47 Ibid, article 8.
48 Ibid, articles 12–17.
49 Ibid, articles 29, 30.
50 Ibid, article 31.
51 Ibid, article 32.
52 Ibid, article 33.
53 Ibid, article 35.
54 Ibid, article 34.
55 Ibid, article 37.
56 HRC Res 15/26 (7 October 2010) para 4.
57 UN Doc. A/HRC/22/41 (24 December 2012) paras 44, 75.
58 Ibid, Part III A, C 1–3.
59 Ibid, paras 7–9.
60 A/HRC/WG.10/3/2 (2 September 2014) paras 45–51, 52.
61 A/HRC/30/47 (9 July 2015) paras 77, 78, 80.
62 Ibid, Annex II.
63 Ibid, Annex III.
64 A/HRC/36/36 (4 August 2017) paras 13–15.
65 Ibid, para 16.
66 Ibid, sec III.
67 HRC Res 36/11 (9 October 2017).
68 Ibid, para 1.
69 A/HRC/42/36 (16 July 2019) sec IV.
70 A/HRC/48/65 (6 July 2021).
71 Ibid, para 80.
72 A/HRC/51/40 (12 July 2022).
73 OCHCR, 'Revised Zero Draft Instrument on an International Regulatory Framework on the Regulation, Monitoring of and Oversight Over the Activities of Private Military and Security Companies' (14 April 2022).
74 Ibid, articles 4–12.
75 Ibid, article 4(3).
76 Ibid, article 4(4).
77 Ibid, article 1(g).

78 Ibid, articles 13–16.
79 OCHCR, 'Second Draft Instrument on an International Regulatory Framework on the Regulation, Monitoring of and Oversight Over the Activities of Private Military and Security Companies' (10 October 2022).
80 Ibid, article 11(1)(a *bis*).
81 Ibid, article 11(1)(a *ter*).
82 Ibid, article 16(2)*bis*.
83 A/HRC/51/40 (12 July 2022).
84 Ibid, para 27.
85 Established by HRC Res. 17/4 (2011).
86 OHCHR, 'Guiding Principles on Business and Human Rights' (2011).
87 A/HRC/51/40 (n 83) para 28.
88 See UNGA Res. 60/251 (3 April 2006) para 5(e).
89 A/HRC/48/6 (25 June 2021).
90 Ibid, para 149.2.
91 Ibid, paras 149.76–149.85.
92 Ibid, paras 149.96, 149.98.
93 ACHPR/Res. 477 (LXVIII) 2021 paras 2, 3.
94 A/HRC/WG.6/38/MOZ/2 (12 February 2021) sec III, paras 9–11; sec IV B para 27.
95 Zenaida Machado, 'Five Years On, Justice Still a Dream for Cabo Delgado Victims' *Human Rights Watch* (24 November 2022).
96 Eunice Masson, 'Southern Africa Military Force Investigates Video Showing Soldiers Apparently Burning Bodies in Mozambique' *Mail & Guardian* (12 January 2023).
97 UNGA Res. 77/206 (3 January 2023).
98 UN Doc. A/77/268 (4 August 2022).
99 UN Doc. A/HRC/15/25 (n 36).
100 Ibid, para 38.

Bibliography

A/HRC/30/47 (9 July 2015).
A/HRC/36/36 (4 August 2017).
A/HRC/42/36 (16 July 2019).
A/HRC/48/6 (25 June 2021).
A/HRC/48/65 (6 July 2021).
A/HRC/51/40 (12 July 2022).
A/HRC/WG.6/38/MOZ/2 (12 February 2021).
A/HRC/WG.10/3/2 (2 September 2014).
ACHPR/Res. 477 (LXVIII) 2021.
Alan Doss, 'Africa and the Soldiers of Misfortune' *Africa Arguments* (10 May 2022).
Amnesty International, 'Mozambique: "What I Saw Is Death": War Crimes in Mozambique's Forgotten Cape' (2021) <https://www.amnesty.org/en/documents/afr41/3545/2021/en/>.
Antonio Cascais and Reliou Koubakin, 'Mercenary Armies in Africa' *Deutche Welle* (15 April 2022).
Daniel Sixto, 'Russian Mercenaries: A String of Failures in Africa' *Geopolitical Monitor* (24 August 2020) <www.geopoliticalmonitor.com/russian-mercenaries-a-string-of-failures-in-africa/>.
Debora Patta and Sarah Carter, 'How Russia's Wagner Group Funds Its Role in Putin's Ukraine War by Plundering Africa's Resources' *CBS News* (16 May 2023).
Eunice Masson, 'Southern Africa Military Force Investigates Video Showing Soldiers Apparently Burning Bodies in Mozambique' *Mail & Guardian* (12 January 2023).
'Guiding Principles on Business and Human Rights' *Office of the High Commissioner for Human Rights* (2011).

Hennie Strydom, 'The Evolution of the UN-AU Peace and Security Partnership' in Frans Viljoen and others (eds), *A Life Interrupted: Essays in Honour of the Lives and Legacies of Christof Heyns* (PULP 2022).

HRC Res. 15/26 (7 October 2010).

HRC Res. 17/4 (6 July 2011).

HRC Res. 36/11 (9 October 2017).

ICRC, *Commentary on the First Geneva Convention* (2016) <https://www.cambridge.org/core/books/commentary-on-the-first-geneva-convention/4C3F3D571C1F6DB5E88004AF7540665C>.

'Independent Research Confirms the Positive Impact of the Montreux Document on the Reduction of PMSC's Violence Against Civilians' *Montreux Document Forum* (27 April 2022) <www.montreuxdocument.org/news/impactoncivilians.html>.

'The International Code of Conduct for Private Security Service Providers' *The Responsible Security Association* <https://icoca.ch/the-code/>.

Martin Meredith, *The State of Africa: A History of Fifty Years of Independence* (Free Press 2006).

Montreux Document on Private Military and Security Companies (2008) <https://www.montreuxdocument.org/pdf/document/en.pdf>.

Mucahid Durmaz and Murtala Abdullahi, '"White Hands": The Rise of Private Armies in African Conflicts' *Al Jazeera* (28 April 2022).

OAU Convention for the Elimination of Mercenarism in Africa (1977) <https://au.int/sites/default/files/treaties/37287-treaty-0009_-_oau_convention_for_the_elimination_of_mercenarism_in_africa_e.pdf>.

OCHCR, 'Revised Zero Draft Instrument on an International Regulatory Framework on the Regulation, Monitoring of and Oversight Over the Activities of Private Military and Security Companies' (14 April 2022) <www.ohchr.org/sites/default/files/2022-04/revised-zero-draft-instrument.pdf>.

OCHCR, 'Second Draft Instrument on an International Regulatory Framework on the Regulation, Monitoring of and Oversight Over the Activities of Private Military and Security Companies' (10 October 2022) <www.ohchr.org/sites/default/files/documents/hrbodies/hrcouncil/wgmilitary/2022-11-03/PMSCs-Second-Draft%20-Instrument-Track-Changes.pdf>.

'Participating States of the Montreux Document' *Federal Department of Foreign Affairs* <www.eda.admin.ch/eda/en/fdfa/foreign-policy/international-law/international-humanitarian-law/private-military-security-companies/participating-states.html>.

Peter Fabricius, 'SA Military Company in Insurgent Zone, the Dyck Advisory Group, Will Not Extend Contract with Mozambique' *Daily Maverick* (31 March 2021).

Protocol Additional to the Geneva Conventions of 12 August 1949 and Relating to the Protection of Victims of International Armed Conflicts (Protocol I) (1977) <https://treaties.un.org/Pages/showDetails.aspx?objid=08000002800f3586&clang=_en>.

Protocol to the OAU Convention on the Prevention and Combatting of Terrorism (2004) <https://au.int/en/treaties/protocol-oau-convention-prevention-and-combating-terrorism>.

SADC Communique of 23 June 2021.

UN Doc. A/60/263 (17 August 2005).

UN Doc. A/62/301 (24 August 2007).

UN Doc. A/77/268 (4 August 2022).

UN Doc. A/HRC/15/25, Annex (2 July 2010).

UN Doc. A/HRC/22/41 (24 December 2012).

UNGA Res. 59/178 (3 March 2005).

UNGA Res. 60/251 (3 April 2006).

UNGA Res. 77/206 (3 January 2023).

'US to Designate Russia's Wagner Group as "Transnational Criminal Organisation"' *The Guardian* (20 January 2023).

Zenaida Machado, 'Five Years on, Justice Still a Dream for Cabo Delgado Victims' *Human Rights Watch* (24 November 2022).

14 The SADC mission in Mozambique

Contextualising the historical role of SADC military operations under international law

Marko Svicevic

14.1 Introduction

The deployment by the Southern African Development Community (SADC) of its Mission in Mozambique (SAMIM) was approved on 23 June 2021 by the SADC Extraordinary Heads of State and Government.[1] The deployment was undertaken some four years after violence broke out in Cabo Delgado and the rise of the Islamist insurgency Ansar al-Sunna. Despite what was perceived as a delayed response by the regional bloc, the mobilisation of the SADC deployment was considered quick and well-resourced compared to previous deployments.[2] However, although the deployment has now been present in Mozambique's northern-most province for nearly two years and has notably reduced the scale and intensity of the ongoing violence, it has as yet been unable to extinguish it entirely.

The SADC's reliance on a military response to the situation in Mozambique is not a new phenomenon, representing its fourth military deployment in sub-Saharan Africa to date. Its resort to military means also is not uncommon, at least considering the region's sometimes turbulent history. Following its predecessor, the Southern African Development Coordination Conference (SADCC), SADC primarily aimed at uniting and harmonising international relations among the independent states in the sub-region.[3] With the independence of Namibia in 1990 and the formal end of apartheid in South Africa in 1994, SADC became increasingly involved in matters of regional peace and security. Chief among these included, in addition to the transformation of SADCC to SADC, the creation of the Organ on Politics, Defence and Security in 2001 and the adoption of several instruments strengthening its approach to regional security.[4]

This chapter examines the SADC security framework under international law in light of its previous military operations (the Democratic Republic of the Congo (DRC) (1998) and its two interventions in Lesotho (1999, 2017)) and then considers the SAMIM intervention against SADC historical practice. It departs with an examination of the SADC security framework and its qualification as a regional organisation under international law, thereby giving it competence over matters of regional peace and security. It then considers the role and relationship between SADC, the African Union (AU) and the United Nations Security Council (UN

DOI: 10.4324/9781003317647-17

Security Council) in so far as determining when SADC may legally intervene in its member states independent of the former two organisations. Thereafter, the chapter details the three previous military operations of SADC, including that of SAMIM, as well as their legal bases under both SADC treaty law and international law. Finally, it concludes by outlining some trends and characteristics among SADC's role in matters of regional peace and security.

14.2 SADC as an international organisation regulating matters of peace and security

The signing of the Treaty of SADC in 1992 effectively established the SADC of today: a multi-faceted regional organisation representing one of eight regional economic communities (RECs) of the AU. Article 9 of the founding treaty created six principal institutions: the Summit of Heads of State and Government; the Council of Ministers; commissions; the Standing Committee of Officials; the Secretariat; and the Tribunal.[5] However, the greatest effort towards regional peace and security came when in 2001 the treaty was amended to incorporate, among others, the Organ on Politics, Defence and Cooperation (Organ) and the Troika.[6]

On a continental level, SADC and its involvement in regional military operations is neither new nor unique. For its part, the AU has intervened militarily in a number of its member states.[7] Similarly, the Economic Community of West African States (ECOWAS) has intervened in no less than six of its member states.[8] Almost all of the AU's RECs, including the AU itself, have carved out greater roles and more intricate structures dealing with continental and regional peace and security matters. Today there is little dispute, if at all, that these institutions represent international organisations under international law. The same may be said of SADC.

As a regional organisation, SADC is primarily focused on regional issues and is composed of member states from the same region. Owing to its establishment under its constituent treaty, its existence as a separate legal entity (legal personality), and its competence over matters within the region, it suffices to say that the bloc maintains a certain degree of autonomy over its own matters. One question that arises is whether SADC represents the kind of organisation contemplated under article 52(1) of the UN Charter – an organisation that may deal expressly with matters of peace and security.[9]

There is no reason why SADC does not qualify as such an organisation. In fact, SADC itself recognises this role and explicitly binds itself under the authority of the UN Security Council. For example, the Preamble to the Protocol on Politics, Defence and Security Cooperation *bears in mind* that the provisions of Chapter VIII, under which article 52 and article 53 are found, provide for regional military action. In fact, the SADC security framework explicitly provides for the authority of the UN Security Council before SADC could ordinarily intervene. Article 11(3)(d) of the Protocol, detailing the methods of the Organ's conflict prevention, management and resolution, confirms that SADC may resort to enforcement action (military action) only as a last resort and only in accordance with the authorisation of the UN Security Council under article 53 of the UN Charter.[10]

14.3 The role of SADC in regional peace and security and its relationship with the African Union and United Nations Security Council

14.3.1 Independent action and the UN Security Council

Such provisions underlying the SADC security framework are significant for a number of reasons. First, they confirm that SADC considers itself a regional organisation for purposes of article 53 of the UN Charter. Second, they confirm article 53's corresponding limitations and the requirement of UN Security Council authorisation to intervene militarily in member states. The former is particularly noteworthy when considering the international law framework pertaining to the use of military force. There remains debate today as to whether regional organisations can at all intervene in their member states without UN Security Council authorisation.[11] In contrast to SADC, neither the relevant AU nor ECOWAS legal frameworks and instruments indicate whether they require such authorisation. For example, article 4(h) of the AU Constitutive Act allows it to intervene in member states in situations of crimes against humanity, genocide and war crimes.[12] Notably, the AU security framework is silent on the need for UN Security Council authorisation. In a similar fashion, article 25 of the ECOWAS Protocol Mechanism of 1999 permits the organisation to intervene militarily in member states on a number of bases, including internal conflict that threatens to trigger a humanitarian disaster or poses a serious threat to subregional peace and security.[13]

From an international law perspective on the use of force, the SADC security framework, therefore, is clearer in so far as it does not provide SADC with a basis for forcible military intervention independent of the UN Security Council.[14] In the absence of this authorisation, ultimately, SADC military action would be reliant on other established exceptions to the prohibition on the use of force found in article 2(4) of the UN Charter. These could be either individual or collective self-defence, as contemplated under the SADC Mutual Defence Pact, or deployments to member states with the consent of those states.[15]

14.3.2 SADC as a regional economic community and the role of AU authorisation

Beyond the fact that SADC explicitly requires UN Security Council authorisation for forcible intervention, another question that arises is the precise role of the AU. Although when initially established the AU firmly set within its sights the goal of maintaining continental peace and security, it was only in 2003 that its Peace and Security Council (PSC) came into being.[16] Created as a standing decision-making organ preventing, managing and resolving conflicts, the primary objectives of the PSC included the promotion of peace, security and stability across the continent; anticipating and preventing conflicts; and promoting and implementing peace building and post-conflict reconstruction activities.

Alongside the PSC, its founding protocol also established the African Standby Force (ASF).[17] The ASF in turn ensures the operationalisation of PSC decisions over deployments, observation, and monitoring missions, as well as intervention pursuant to article 4(h) of the AU Constitutive Act. Combined with the PSC, the ASF alongside a number of other organs, in particular the RECs, constitutes what has become known as the AU Peace and Security architecture.

Further, the ASF's Policy Framework of 2003 essentially envisages six scenarios under which the ASF could deploy. These are (i) AU/regional military advice to a political mission; (ii) AU/regional observer mission co-deployed with a UN mission; (iii) stand-alone AU regional observer mission; (iv) AU/regional peacekeeping force for Chapter VI and preventative deployment; (v) AU peacekeeping force for complex multi-dimensional peacekeeping mission low-level spoilers; and (vi) AU intervention on, for example, grounds of genocide situations where the international community fails to act promptly.[18] The first two of these scenarios concern political and observer missions; likely deployed at the request or with the consent of the state in question. The third to fifth scenarios concern peacekeeping – a key trait regarding such peacekeeping missions is that they require the consent of all parties involved. In essence, therefore, the first five scenarios are deployments likely contemplated following ceasefire or peace agreements or are requested by a party to the conflict. Only under the sixth scenario is forcible intervention per se contemplated; that is, intervention into a member state without that state's consent. On this basis, any SADC intervention into a member state without such a state's consent would likely need, within the AU security framework, AU authorisation pursuant to article 4(h) if such grounds exist, or under the UN Charter, the authorisation of the UN Security Council.

In addition to the six scenarios forwarded by the ASF Policy Framework, it is worth noting that the ASF in essence is composed of several regional arrangements that in fact comprise the corresponding RECs: the ECOWAS Standby Force; the Economic Community of Central African States Standby Force; the North African Regional Capability; the Eastern Africa Standby Force; and the SADC Standby Force (formerly Brigade).

Although some questions remain as to who may initiate action by the different standby forces or brigades and under which circumstances, the RECs, including SADC, work on the principle of subsidiarity. This is confirmed by the 2008 Memorandum of Agreement between the AU and the RECs, in so far as it concerns the 'adherence to the principles of subsidiarity, complementarity and comparative advantage'.[19] That is, RECs may deploy military operations within their regions and at their own initiatives, or at the initiative of the AU. This holds true for most of the military operations undertaken by both ECOWAS and SADC, having more often than not acted independently of the AU (and of the UN Security Council).

It is worth noting that the 2003 ASF Policy Framework itself envisaged that, although 'the AU should provide overall political direction of peace operations in Africa that are not commanded by the UN, it is clear that some missions could be managed at the strategic level by Regions, but with AU and UN sanction as appropriate'.[20] Appropriate sanction in such cases would likely be where the UN Security

Council has authorised regional enforcement action in line with article 53 of the UN Charter or where the AU has decided on intervention under articles 4(h) or 4(j) of the Constitutive Act.

Political wisdom, however, would suggest that even though the AU need not legally initiate or authorise a military operation by one of the RECs, its coordination and consultation, including diplomatic, financial and logistical support, prove immeasurable when tackling various conflicts.[21]

As one of the brigades of the ASF, the SADC Standby Force, established in 2007 by the SADC Summit of the Heads of State and Government, operates under the direction of the SADC Organ.[22] It is worth noting at this juncture that the SADC Standby Force is not a fixed composition, in other words, SADC has no standing army. Rather, the Force is composed of contributions from member states upon the decision of the Organ, including the size of any deployment. When authorised by the Organ, SADC also then appoints the relevant authorities under the deployment, including a Force Commander, Commissioner of Police and Head of the Civilian Component.[23] As will be seen further below, this certainly is how the SADC mission to Mozambique was undertaken.

14.4 Historical SADC military operations

It has already been mentioned above that the SAMIM deployment to Mozambique represents SADC's fourth military operation since its establishment. While the SAMIM deployment is the first of its kind concerning an operation aimed at targeting acts of terrorism in the region, it also is only the second operation deployed directly under the decision of the SADC Organ. In contrast, the first two SADC operations in the DRC (1998) and Lesotho (1999) were both undertaken prior to the formal incorporation of the Organ in 2001. As such, it is prudent to turn to an examination of the precise manner in which SAMIM and previous operations were deployed, and their exact legal basis under both international law and the SADC security framework.

14.4.1 Intervention in the Democratic Republic of the Congo (1998)

In the same year in which the DRC was formally admitted as a member state of SADC, the bloc undertook a military operation in the country. Codenamed Operation Sovereign Legitimacy, the mission is regularly branded as SADC's first-ever military operation. In 1996, aided by the invasion of Rwanda and Uganda, opposition leader Laurent Kabila assumed power in the DRC with the ousting of Mobutu Sese Seko. In the following two years, President Kabila requested the withdrawal of these troops from the DRC's territory. Tensions between both internal parties and neighbouring states in the region continued, however. Kabila's rise to power with assistance from Rwanda and Uganda turned over and his request for the departure of these states had them turned against him. Rwandan-supported rebels engulfed large areas and strategic installations within DRC territory. Kabila's subsequent plea for assistance to stabilise the situation went neither unheard nor unanswered.

In August 1998 and following a meeting of some six SADC states in Harare, although not without contestation, former President Robert Mugabe announced that SADC would be sending troops to aid Kabila. Angola, Namibia and Zimbabwe were the only three SADC member states that intervened in the DRC. Although the deployment only lasted several months and was followed by the signing of the Lusaka Ceasefire Agreement in July 1999,[24] the intervention in the DRC persistently raised serious questions as to its legal basis under the SADC security framework.[25]

Principal among these questions was whether the decision to intervene was made collectively by SADC and under SADC treaty law, or whether the intervening states were simply acting of their own accord pursuant to the request for assistance by Kabila; in addition, whether the intervention in the DRC was based only on a request for assistance or whether it had formed part of the three's states exercising the right of collective self-defence.

In so far as the question of SADC involvement is concerned, it is worth noting that during the intervention in the DRC the SADC Organ had not formally been incorporated into the SADC structure. Instead, it existed at the level of the SADC Summit. Interestingly, there also was major disagreement as to the structure and functioning of the Organ from the very beginning.[26] While South Africa wanted the Organ to be incorporated into the existing SADC structure and function under its authority, Zimbabwe preferred the Organ as a separate and independent institution operating alongside SADC.[27] Despite these differences and the fact that the Organ had been established in 1996, its structure and functioning had only been ironed out in the Protocol on Politics, Defence and Security Cooperation in 2001, and had only entered into force in 2004.[28]

For this reason, it has been well observed that a legal basis under the then (limited) security framework of SADC would be unlikely, if not entirely non-existent.[29] This conclusion holds despite the statement by the Organ Chairperson at the time, President Mugabe, that the decision to intervene was unanimous among SADC member states, or despite the fact that reports had emerged that South Africa, the SADC Chair at the time, was deliberately excluded from the August 1998 meeting in Harare.[30] Additionally, the fact that almost a month later South African President Nelson Mandela announced that SADC had supported the intervention is little more than a political statement, and cannot be regarded as giving rise to any legal basis under the then SADC security framework.[31]

A further indication that may point to the fact that the intervening states foresaw future problems of SADC-authorised intervention came shortly after the tensions among SADC members. Even before the three SADC states' troops had withdrawn from the DRC, they, along with the DRC, had signed a mutual defence pact.[32] Such an action could be perceived as a formalisation of collective security between the four states in each other's favour and outside the sphere and the need for SADC approval of future operations. Indeed, the signing of the mutual defence pact between the four states came some four years before SADC adopted its own Mutual Defence Pact.

From an SADC institutional perspective, it is factually and legally difficult to suggest that SADC authorised the operation itself since the meeting of August

1998 was undertaken by the SADC Interstate Defence and Security Committee (IDSC), and only nine of the 14 member states were present.[33] In the absence of the institutional mechanism to authorise such operations, the IDSC's decision on intervention is questionable at best, since it would presumably only be the SADC Summit that could take such a decision.[34]

From an international law perspective, the intervention by Angola, Namibia and Zimbabwe in the DRC could also not have been legally based on article 53 of the UN Charter, since no UN Security Council authorisation was forthcoming. Consequently, this also meant that even if SADC did authorise such a mission, it would not have been lawful under the UN Charter.[35]

Arguments of the illegality of the intervention, however, are overcome if one considers their legal basis under the right of individual or collective self-defence, found in article 51 of the UN Charter.[36] As is well known, a state that is the victim of an armed attack may respond in self-defence or request collective self-defence from other states. It is true that whether the DRC actually experienced an armed attack by virtue of a Rwandan/Ugandan invasion or whether the conflict was driven by internal issues is sometimes contested.[37] Nevertheless, an alternative legal basis for the operation could have rested with military assistance on request if one considered it an internal disturbance, since it was undertaken with the consent (in fact at the request) of the then-legitimate government.

It suffices to say, therefore, that the intervention in the DRC certainly was not unlawful under international law, as it was based either on collective self-defence or on military assistance on request.[38] What should be re-affirmed, however, is that its legality under the SADC security framework not only is highly contested but entirely improbable, given SADC's lack of a security framework for the Organ at the time and the fact that the decision to intervene was evidently undertaken at the level of the IDSC (without a decision of the SADC Summit).[39]

14.4.2 Interventions in Lesotho

14.4.2.1 Operation Boleas (1998)

Whereas Operation Sovereign Legitimacy was spearheaded by three SADC states and initially opposed by South Africa, the tables quickly turned just one month later when South Africa spearheaded Operation Boleas in Lesotho. Following parliamentary elections in May 1998 in which the Lesotho Congress for Democracy party claimed an overwhelming victory, widespread protests erupted. Then Prime Minister Pakalitha Mosisili, requesting intervention from four SADC states, claimed that a *coup* was taking place in Lesotho.[40] On 22 September 1998 the South African National Defence Force entered Lesotho, followed swiftly thereafter by the forces from Botswana. Although somewhat of a chaotic start to operations, the intervention ultimately was a success and resulted in the establishment of the Independent Political Authority in Lesotho.

South Africa's interests in Lesotho, particularly owing to its water supply to the country, were well noted. The question that, however, has been raised is whether the intervention was undertaken by SADC or simply by two SADC states: Botswana and South Africa. Moreover, the precise legal basis under international needs consideration.

In so far as the latter is concerned, the intervention arguably was lawful given that it was undertaken at the request of the then-legitimate government. Despite the protests and contestation of the preceding elections, the violence in Lesotho had not deteriorated into a non-international armed conflict potentially prohibiting a request for military assistance.[41] Given the consensual nature of the operation, it also was unnecessary at the time to seek UN Security Council authorisation in accordance with article 53 of the UN Charter, since the operation was not a regional enforcement action ordinarily taken without or against the consent of the target state.[42] From an international law perspective, therefore, Operation Boleas was lawful.

As for whether the operation truly was an SADC operation, there is similar doubt and contestation as was the case with Operation Sovereign Legitimacy. Operation Boleas received no SADC authorisation for deployment, despite its labelling as an operation under 'SADC auspices'. It is well documented that the SADC Organ was inoperative since 1997 before either of the interventions in the DRC and Lesotho. In addition, no formal decision nor process was ever taken in any of the SADC meetings held prior to the deployment of Operation Boleas.[43]

A post-deployment approval of the SADC operation in August 1999, however, did attempt to legitimise the intervention. An 18 August Summit of Heads of State and Government Communiqué stated that a *coup* attempted in Lesotho had failed 'as a result of SADC military intervention in the form of Botswana and South African forces, in response to a request by the Government of Lesotho'.[44] That Communiqué, other than confirming the request for assistance made by Lesotho, served little more than a political statement than an *ex post facto* authorisation of Operation Boleas.[45]

14.4.2.2 SADC Preventive Mission in the Kingdom of Lesotho (2017)

Nearly two decades after Operation Boleas, the assassination of Lesotho's commander of the defence force, Lieutenant General Khoantle Motsomotso, prompted alarm at further instability in the country. SADC was swift to act, sending a fact-finding mission to Lesotho within days. On 15 September 2017 the Double Troika Summit of Heads of State and Government, noting 'the volatile security situation and its implications for the political stability' requiring the 'urgent need' to 'restoring law and order, and a peaceful environment', approved the deployment of the SADC Preventive Mission in the Kingdom of Lesotho (SAPMIL).[46] The deployment consisted of military, security, intelligence and civilian experts.

Although a legal basis for the deployment was never provided, it was likely based on a request by the Lesotho government following the assassination of Lieutenant General Motsomotso.

What is clear is that in contrast to Operation Sovereign Legitimacy and Operation Boleas, the SAPMIL deployment was not only founded under international law (based on the request for assistance) but was clearly authorised and undertaken by SADC on an institutional level. SAPMIL's approval was undertaken with full compliance with the SADC institutional framework and was authorised by the Summit, the highest decision-making body and the only body that may legally authorise such an operation. Despite its two previous operations, however, which represent more of individual SADC member state interventions,[47] SAPMIL is a clear case of a collective SADC response duly authorised and deployed by the organisation. Consequently, the SADC decision to intervene is consistent and in harmony with the separate legal basis under international law (military assistance on request) for the deployment.

14.5 The SADC Mission in Mozambique

Whereas the first two SADC *claimed* operations were controversial given that they were neither formally nor properly institutionally authorised under SADC, they were both undertaken (including SAPMIL) at the request of the legitimate government. In contrast, SADC's ambitions of deployment to Mozambique were initially met with resistance.[48] It was in part its reliance on private military companies that saw Mozambique over a time span of some three years seemingly avoid requesting or consenting to an SADC deployment. Additionally, in the build-up to SAMIM's deployment, regional leaders, analysts and commentators seemed to continuously suggest that the SADC Mutual Defence Pact was a potential legal basis for such a deployment.[49]

It is worth noting that the reliance on the Mutual Defence Pact most likely was misplaced.[50] Article 6(1) of the pact provides the standard self-defence clause in international law, where 'an armed attack against a State Party shall be considered a threat to regional peace and security and such an attack shall be met with immediate collective action'.[51] Moreover, article 6(2) states that collective action shall be mandated by the SADC Summit, and under article 6(4), any armed attack and measures taken in response shall be reported to the AU PSC and the UN Security Council.[52] *In casu*, the Mutual Defence Pact could not be the legal basis for two reasons.[53] First, Mozambique had not been the victim of an armed attack and could not rely on self-defence. By extension, SADC could not invoke the pact to intervene in what had predominantly been an internal conflict. Second, even if it had invoked the pact, collective self-defence requires either the consent of or request by the victim state. In the absence of Mozambique's consent, a deployment would be unlawful under collective self-defence.[54]

Instead, SAMIM was undertaken on a consensual basis when, on 23 June 2021, the SADC Extraordinary Summit of Heads of State and Government, Mozambique participating, approved the deployment.[55] The SAMIM deployment followed a fact-finding mission composed of military, intelligence, communications and logistics experts from several SADC member states. The report of the mission proposed a deployment of nearly 3 000 troops to assist Mozambique in its fight against Ansar al-Sunna.[56] This report was subsequently adopted, and a mandate authorised by the extraordinary Summit – composed of the SADC troika and Organ troika at the

23 June meeting, which itself took place in Maputo. Eight SADC states currently provide troops to SAMIM, namely, Angola, Botswana, the DRC, Lesotho, Malawi, South Africa, Tanzania and Zambia.[57]

Although it is unclear whether a vote was taken on the decision to deploy, SADC Communiqués represent the collective decision making of the organisation. Considering that no member state nor Mozambique has since objected to the deployment and that, in practice, cooperation between the troop-contributing states and Mozambique is evident, it is clear that Mozambique agrees with the decision. Since its deployment, the SADC Summit, including both troikas of SADC and the Organ, has renewed the SAMIM mandate on a number of occasions and the operation continues to date.

At the same time, what cannot be ignored with SAMIM's deployment is the absence of the AU. Indeed, as with the three previous deployments discussed earlier, it would seem that the AU played no role in, and had no response to, the situation in Mozambique; it was at the least not involved in the decision making of the SAMIM deployment.[58] Nevertheless, according to an SADC letter directed to the Secretary-General of the UN, SAMIM was deployed under scenario six of the ASF Policy Framework.[59] Moreover, the letter also outlined that the deployment was '[c]onsistent with the SADC Protocol on Politics, Defence and Security Cooperation, and in recognition of the principle of subsidiarity as espoused in the Charter of the United Nations (Chapter VIII, regional arrangements, Article 52)'.

Scenario six of the ASF Policy Framework provides for enforcement in situations such as genocide, where urgent intervention is required, and where one or more of the parties to the conflict have not consented to such intervention.[60] Given that Ansar al-Sunna no doubt would have rejected SADC intervention, scenario six as the legal basis under the ASF Policy Framework is sound. In so far as the reference to article 52 of the UN Charter is concerned, it would in principle confirm that the SAMIM deployment falls outside the scope of article 53 of the UN Charter. Article 52 states that nothing under the UN Charter prohibits regional organisations from dealing with matters of peace and security provided their activities are consistent with the principles and purposes of the UN Charter. Further, given this basis and that SAMIM falls beyond the scope of article 53, this would confirm Mozambican consent to the deployment and the fact that UN Security Council authorisation, therefore, would be unnecessary.[61] The extent to which either the AU or the UN Security Council was consulted remains debatable. This notwithstanding, the SAMIM deployment under the current situation did not legally require approval from either organisation.

Since then, the AU has taken some note of the ongoing situation. At its 1119th meeting of the AU PSC at the ministerial level, the PSC endorsed a subsequent SADC decision to transform the SAMIM mandate from scenario six to five (and thereafter to scenario four).[62] Scenario five concerns peacekeeping forces for complex multi-dimensional peacekeeping missions, 'including those involving low-level spoilers'.[63] The AU has, albeit retroactively at the level of the PSC, endorsed SADC's ongoing mission, including calling for logistical assistance to the mission.[64]

It therefore suffices to say that the SAMIM deployment was firmly undertaken within the SADC security framework as a collective response to a situation in a member state. The consent of the Mozambican government ultimately proved the decisive point in ensuring that the deployment could legally proceed without authorisation by either the AU or UN Security Council. In principle, therefore, SAMIM represents only the second true instance under which SADC has intervened collectively and under its own security framework, with SAMPIL being the only previous situation undertaken collectively by the organisation.

14.6 Conclusion

While the SADC security framework by no means is the most comprehensive among the AU's RECs, its development certainly is the most aligned with the existing international legal order regulating military deployments. That international legal order provides that when engaging in forcible interventions without the consent of a target state, UN Security Council authorisation is required. Additionally, within the AU's Peace and Security architecture, the SADC security framework and its subsequent practice at least in part provide a strong argument as to why regional conflicts ought to be tackled by regional actors.

The intervention by SADC states in the DRC represents one of the earliest conflicts with which the organisation had to grapple, despite it ultimately leaving a response to individual member states. Similarly, when its member states deployed into Lesotho in the same year, the organisation again abrogated its responsibility to South Africa and Botswana. These interventions were not without controversy. The lack of a functioning Organ and the insufficient development of the SADC's security framework at the time gave rise to disputes about the precise reasons individual member states intervened on the side of the requesting governments. Nevertheless, when SADC intervened in Lesotho again some two decades later, it no doubt had the security framework in place and the hindsight to position a collective response over individual actions.

Even so, the three SADC or SADC states' interventions prior to Mozambique were all undertaken when the governments of the target states were threatened. In contrast, when domestic issues arose in a number of other member states, particularly allegations levelled against the governments of these states, SADC took a far more laxed approach. It is no wonder that the organisation at times has been called a 'club of presidents' rather than a dedicated intergovernmental organisation aimed at fostering peace, security and prosperity within the region.

SADC's intervention in Mozambique, however, may well represent its coming of age. Considering that the organisation's history of intervention has strongly revolved around upholding governments in place or at the least preventing their overthrowal, the SAMIM deployment is a first of its kind. Not only is it the first instance in which SADC has engaged against terrorism, but it is the first time it has deployed in a member state where that state was not at risk of a forceful change in government. While the SADC security framework has now been in place for some time, it remains to be seen how SADC will take up lessons learned in Mozambique when dealing with future conflicts.

Notes

1 SADC Communiqué of 23 June 2021, para 7.
2 PSC Report, 'Top-Level Discussions Were Needed Before Troops Marched Into Mozambique' *Institute for Security Studies* (20 August 2021).
3 SADC, Treaty of the Southern African Development Community (adopted 17 August 1992, entered into force September 1993) reproduced in Marko Svicevic, *Compendium of Documents Relating to Regional and Sub-Regional Peace and Security in Africa* (PULP 2021) 412–415.
4 See SADC, Protocol on Politics, Defence and Security Cooperation (adopted 14 August 2001, entered into force 2 March 2004) and SADC, Mutual Defence Pact (adopted 27 August 2003, entered into force 17 August 2008) in Svicevic (n 3) 416–423, 432–436.
5 Article 9 SADC Protocol on Politics.
6 Articles 9 and 10 SADC Agreement Amending the Treaty of the Southern African Development Community (14 August 2001). The organ was initially launched in June 1996 with the Gaborone Declaration but was only formally incorporated into the SADC structure in 2001. See Maxi van Aardt, 'The SADC Organ for Politics, Defence and Security: Challenges for Regional Community Building' (1996) 4 (2) *South African Journal of International Affairs* 144.
7 Svicevic (n 3) 58–60. These include, among others, operations in Burundi (2003–2004); Sudan (2004–2008); Somalia (2007–); Darfur (2007–); and The Comoros (2008).
8 Svicevic (n 3) 286–288. These include Liberia (1989–1996); Sierra Leone (1997–2000); Guinea-Bissau (1998); Côte d'Ivoire (2003, 2011); Mali (2013); and The Gambia (2017).
9 Article 52(1) Charter of the United Nations (adopted 26 June 1945, entered into force 24 October 1945) 1 UNTS XVI.
10 Mark Malan, 'Regional Power Politics Under Cover of SADC – Running Amok with Mythical Organ' *Africa Portal/Institute for Security Studies* (October 1998) 7; Suyasha Paliwal, 'The Primacy of Regional Organisations in International Peacekeeping: The African Example' (2010) 51 (1) *Virginia Journal of International Law* 215.
11 See broadly Paliwal (n 10) 185–230, Erika de Wet, 'Regional Organisations and Arrangements: Authorisation, Ratification, or Independent Action' in Marc Weller (ed), *The Oxford Handbook of the Use of Force in International Law* (OUP 2015) 314–327.
12 Article 4(h) Constitutive Act of the African Union (adopted 11 July 2000, entered into force 26 May 2001) 2158 UNTS 3.
13 Article 25 ECOWAS Protocol Relating to the Mechanism for Conflict Prevention, Management, Resolution, Peacekeeping and Security' (adopted and entered into force 10 December 1999).
14 Regarding the requirement of Security Council authorisation, see Marko Svicevic, 'Re-Assessing the (Continued) Need for UN Security Council Authorisation of Regional Enforcement Action: The African Union Twenty Years On' (2020) 45 *South African Yearbook of International Law* 45.
15 For collective self-defence, see article 6 of the SADC Mutual Defence Pact.
16 Article 2(1) AU Protocol Relating to the Establishment of the Peace and Security Council of the African Union (adopted 9 July 2002, entered into force 26 December 2003) 3264 UNTS (PSC Protocol).
17 Ibid, article 13.
18 Para 1.6 ASF Policy Framework.
19 Article IV(iv) Memorandum of Understanding on Cooperation in the Area of Peace and Security Between the AU, the RECs and the Coordinating Mechanisms of the Regional Standby Brigades of Eastern Africa and Northern Africa (2008). See Svicevic (n 3) 237–244.
20 Para 3.6 ASF Policy Framework.
21 Para 3.7 ASF Policy Framework. See also PSC Report (n 2).
22 SADC Communiqué of 17 August 2007; article 3 SADC Memorandum of Understanding Amongst the SADC Member States on the Establishment of a SADC Standby Brigade (16 August 2007).

23 Kizito Sikuka, 'Understanding the SADC Standby Force' *Southern African Research and Documentation Centre* (22 April 2021) <www.sardc.net/en/southern-african-news-features/understanding-the-sadc-standby-force/>.

24 See United Nations Peacemaker, Lusaka Agreement (10 July 1999).

25 Katharina Coleman, *International Organisations and Peace Enforcement: The Politics of International Legitimacy* (CUP 2007) 122 who questions why Zimbabwe decided to launch the intervention under SADC auspices.

26 Coleman (n 25) 117–119.

27 Nina Wilén, *Justifying Interventions in Africa: (De)Stabilizing Sovereignty in Liberia, Burundi and the Congo* (Palgrave Macmillan 2012) 100.

28 Ibid.

29 Ibid; Malan (n 10) 8; Coleman (n 25) 122; Kyu Deug Hwang, The Mechanisms of Politico-Security Regionalism in Southeast Asia and Southern Africa: A Comparative Case Study of ASEAN and SADC' (DPhil thesis, University of Pretoria 2006) 171–172.

30 Malan (n 10) 5; Wilén (n 27) 101. On South Africa's absence, see 'DRC: Regional Mediation Efforts Intensify' *The New Humanitarian* (18 August 1998).

31 Malan (n 10) 5; see also Robert Block, 'Mandela Backs Armed Support for Congo Government War' (4 September 1998); Hwang (n 29) 178.

32 Gwinyayi Dzinesa and Joyce Laker, 'Post-Conflict Reconstruction in the Democratic Republic of the Congo (DRC)' (2011) *Centre for Conflict Resolution* 20.

33 Coleman (n 25) 124; Wilén (n 27) 101.

34 Coleman (n 25) 125; Wilén (n 27) 101.

35 Coleman (n 25) 122. Such an intervention would remain lawful if it fell outside the scope of article 53, which it likely did given the consent of the DRC government at the time.

36 Coleman (n 25) 122. See also article 51, UN Charter.

37 Coleman (n 25) 123. Nevertheless, in a letter to the UN Security Council, the Zimbabwean delegation maintained article 51 as a legal basis. See UN Doc. S/1998/891 (25 September 1998).

38 Coleman (n 25) 156; De Wet (n 11) 84. See also Wilén (n 27) 102.

39 Coleman (n 25) 124–125, but see also 146. This holds despite the fact that SADC in September 1998 'commended' the states for their involvement in assisting the DRC. See SADC Communiqué of 14 September 1998.

40 Coleman (n 25) 162. See also TJ Vhangani and Richard R Molapo, 'The Role of the SADC in a Peacekeeping Mission: A Case Study of South Africa in the Lesotho Conflict' (2017) 15 (2) *Commonwealth Youth and Development* 2.

41 De Wet (n 11) 85. However, see arguments against military assistance on request in the case of Lesotho in Coleman (n 25) 164–165.

42 See again Coleman (n 25) 167 and Cedric de Coning, 'Lesotho Intervention: Implications for SADC. Military Interventions, Peacekeeping and the African Renaissance' (2000) 1 (1) *Africa Dialogue Monograph Series* 43–44.

43 De Coning (n 42) 42–43; Coleman (n 25) 167, 179, 182–183; Moeketsi Kali, 'Democratic Reversals: Examining the Role of the Armed Forces and Southern African Development Community in Lesotho' (2019) 3 (11) *International Journal of Research and Innovation in Social Science* 144. See also Roger Southall, 'SADC's Intervention in Lesotho: An Illegal Defence of Democracy?' in Oliver Furley and Roy May (eds), *African Interventionist States* (Routledge 2001) 194–195, who indicates that despite reliance on article 5 of the Protocol on Politics, it had not been ratified.

44 SADC Communiqué of 18 August 1999.

45 The request for assistance was made on 12 September 1998. See PMG, Joint Meeting of the Joint Standing Committee on Defence; Foreign Affairs Portfolio Committee; Security and Justice Select Committee, 'Report on Situation in Lesotho' (2 November 1998).

46 Para 7 SADC Communiqué of 15 September 2017.

47 Coleman (n 25) 191; Cedric de Coning, 'Preparing for the Third Millennium: Towards a Policy Framework for the OAU Conflict Management Mechanism' *The African Centre for the Constructive Resolution of Disputes Occasional Paper 4/99* (1999) 2.

48 See Chapter 13, which explores Mozambique's reliance on private military and security companies.
49 Article 6(1)'s invocation was discussed on at least one occasion by South Africa's Parliamentary Committee on International Relations. See PMG, 'DIRCO on Security Situation in Cabo Delgado and Impact on Region; with Minister' (2 September 2020) <https://pmg.org.za/committee-meeting/31026/>. Several regional leaders have also raised the question of invoking article 6(1). See SADC, 'SADC Has Responsibility to Help Member States Under Terrorist Threat' (29 April 2021); Ray Ndlovu, 'Zimbabwe Urges Southern Africa to Fight Islamists in Mozambique' *Bloomberg* (28 October 2020).
50 On the question of the legality of invoking article 6(1), see, generally, Marko Svicevic, 'Collective Self-Defence or Regional Enforcement Action: The Legality of a SADC Intervention in Cabo Delgado and the Question of Mozambican Consent' (2022) 9 (1) *Journal on the Use of Force and International Law* 138–170.
51 Article 6(1) SADC Mutual Defence Pact.
52 Articles 6(2), 6(4) SADC Mutual Defence Pact.
53 Svicevic (n 50) 147–156.
54 Instead, SADC would need to rely on its Protocol on Politics which, subject to UN Security Council authorisation under article 11(3)(d), could forcibly intervene where a target state was unwilling to consent to a SADC deployment.
55 SADC Communiqué (n 1).
56 Peter Fabricius, 'SADC Military Officials to Propose a 3000-Strong Rapid Response to Take on Mozambique Jihadists' *Daily Maverick* (27 April 2021). For the report itself, see 'SADC Mulls 3 000-Strong Deployment to Cabo Delgado' (27 April 2021) <https://zitamar.com/sadc-mulls-3000-strong-military-deployment-cabo-delgado/>.
57 SADC, 'SADC Mission in Mozambique (SAMIM) in Brief' (10 November 2021).
58 While criticism may be levelled at the AU for its lack of response, it is worth noting that RECs play an integral part of the African Peace and Security architecture, which itself is designed to ensure action from the relevant RECs.
59 See UN Doc. S/2021/658 (21 July 2021), annex.
60 Marko Svicevic, 'The Legal Status of SADC's Mission in Cabo Delgado' *ACCORD* (27 October 2021).
61 Ibid. See also Andrew E Yaw Tchie, 'How Do Ad-Hoc Security Initiatives Fit in Africa's Security Landscape' *IPI Global Observatory* (14 June 2023) <https://theglobalobservatory.org/2023/06/how-do-ad-hoc-security-initiatives-fit-in-africas-evolving-security-landscape/>.
62 Para 5 AU PSC Communiqué of 7 November 2022. The formal decision to move SAMIM from scenario six to five does not, however, explicitly appear in the SADC Communiqué. See SADC Communiqué of 17 August 2022.
63 Para 1.6 ASF Policy Framework.
64 Para 7 10–12, AU PSC Communiqué (n 62).

Bibliography

Andrew E Yaw Tchie, 'How Do Ad-Hoc Security Initiatives Fit in Africa's Security Landscape' *IPI Global Observatory* (14 June 2023) <https://theglobalobservatory.org/2023/06/how-do-ad-hoc-security-initiatives-fit-in-africas-evolving-security-landscape/>.

AU PSC Communiqué of 7 November 2022.

Cedric de Coning, 'Lesotho Intervention: Implications for SADC. Military Interventions, Peacekeeping and the African Renaissance' (2000) 1 (1) *Africa Dialogue Monograph Series*.

Cedric de Coning, 'Preparing for the Third Millennium: Towards a Policy Framework for the OAU Conflict Management Mechanism' *ACCORD 4/99* (1999).

Charter of the United Nations (1945) <https://treaties.un.org/Pages/showDetails.aspx?objid=080000028017ebb8&clang=_en>.

Constitutive Act of the African Union (2000) <https://treaties.un.org/Pages/showDetails.aspx?objid=0800000280089269&clang=_en>.

'DRC: Regional Mediation Efforts Intensify' *The New Humanitarian* (18 August 1998).

Erika de Wet, 'Regional Organisations and Arrangements: Authorisation, Ratification, or Independent Action' in Marc Weller (ed), *The Oxford Handbook of the Use of Force in International Law* (Oxford University Press, OUP, 2015).

Gwinyayi Dzinesa and Joyce Laker, 'Post-Conflict Reconstruction in the Democratic Republic of the Congo (DRC)' (2011) *Centre for Conflict Resolution* <https://www.asclibrary.nl/docs/333967755.pdf>.

Katharina Coleman, *International Organisations and Peace Enforcement: The Politics of International Legitimacy* (CUP 2007).

Kizito Sikuka, 'Understanding the SADC Standby Force' *Southern African Research and Documentation Centre* (22 April 2021) <www.sardc.net/en/southern-african-news-features/understanding-the-sadc-standby-force/>.

Kyu Deug Hwang, 'The Mechanisms of Politico-Security Regionalism in Southeast Asia and Southern Africa: A Comparative Case Study of ASEAN and SADC' (DPhil thesis, University of Pretoria 2006) <https://repository.up.ac.za/bitstream/handle/2263/28223/Complete.pdf?sequence=12&isAllowed=y>.

Mark Malan, 'Regional Power Politics Under Cover of SADC – Running Amok with Mythical Organ' *Africa Portal/Institute for Security Studies* (October 1998).

Marko Svicevic, 'Collective Self-Defence or Regional Enforcement Action: The Legality of a SADC Intervention in Cabo Delgado and the Question of Mozambican Consent' (2022) 9 (1) *Journal on the Use of Force and International Law*.

Marko Svicevic (ed), *Compendium of Documents Relating to Regional and Sub-Regional Peace and Security in Africa* (2nd edn, PULP 2021).

Marko Svicevic, 'The Legal Status of SADC's Mission in Cabo Delgado' *ACCORD* (27 October 2021).

Marko Svicevic, 'Re-Assessing the (Continued) Need for UN Security Council Authorisation of Regional Enforcement Action: The African Union Twenty Years On' (2020) 45 *South African Yearbook of International Law*.

Maxi van Aardt, 'The SADC Organ for Politics, Defence and Security: Challenges for Regional Community Building' (1996) 4 (2) *South African Journal of International Affairs*.

Memorandum of Understanding on Cooperation in the Area of Peace and Security Between the AU, the RECs and the Coordinating Mechanisms of the Regional Standby Brigades of Eastern Africa and Northern Africa (2008) <https://www.pulp.up.ac.za/component/edocman/compendium-of-documents-relating-to-regional-and-sub-regional-peace-and-security-in-africa-second-edition-2021>.

Moeketsi Kali, 'Democratic Reversals: Examining the Role of the Armed Forces and Southern African Development Community in Lesotho' (2019) 3 (11) *International Journal of Research and Innovation in Social Science*.

Nina Wilén, *Justifying Interventions in Africa: (De)Stabilizing Sovereignty in Liberia, Burundi and the Congo* (Palgrave Macmillan 2012).

Parliamentary Monitoring Group, 'DIRCO on Security Situation in Cabo Delgado and Impact on Region; with Minister' (2 September 2020) <https://pmg.org.za/committee-meeting/31026/>.

Parliamentary Monitoring Group, Joint Meeting of the Joint Standing Committee on Defence; Foreign Affairs Portfolio Committee; Security and Justice Select Committee, 'Report on Situation in Lesotho' (2 November 1998).

Peter Fabricius, 'SADC Military Officials to Propose a 3000-Strong Rapid Response to Take on Mozambique Jihadists' *Daily Maverick* (27 April 2021).

Protocol Relating to the Establishment of the Peace and Security Council of the African Union (2002) <https://treaties.un.org/Pages/showDetails.aspx?objid=0800000280337f32&clang=_en>.

Protocol Relating to the Mechanism for Conflict Prevention, Management, Resolution, Peacekeeping and Security' (1999) <https://www.pulp.up.ac.za/component/edocman/

compendium-of-documents-relating-to-regional-and-sub-regional-peace-and-security-in-africa-second-edition-2021>.
PSC Report, 'Top-Level Discussions Were Needed Before Troops Marched into Mozambique' *Institute for Security Studies* (20 August 2021).
Ray Ndlovu, 'Zimbabwe Urges Southern Africa to Fight Islamists in Mozambique' *Bloomberg* (28 October 2020).
Robert Block, 'Mandela Backs Armed Support for Congo Government War' (4 September 1998).
Roger Southall, 'SADC's Intervention in Lesotho: An Illegal Defence of Democracy?' in Oliver Furley and Roy May (eds), *African Interventionist States* (Routledge 2001).
Agreement Amending the Treaty of the Southern African Development Community' (2001) <https://www.sadc.int/sites/default/files/2021-08/Agreement_Amending_the_Treaty_-_2001.pdf>.
SADC Communiqué of 14 September 1998.
SADC Communiqué of 18 August 1999.
SADC Communiqué of 17 August 2007.
SADC Communiqué of 15 September 2017.
SADC Communiqué of 23 June 2021.
SADC Communiqué of 17 August 2022.
SADC, 'Memorandum of Understanding Amongst the SADC Member States on the Establishment of a SADC Standby Brigade' (16 August 2007).
'SADC Mulls 3 000-Strong Deployment to Cabo Delgado' (27 April 2021) <https://zitamar.com/sadc-mulls-3000-strong-military-deployment-cabo-delgado/>.
SADC Mutual Defence Pact (2003) <https://www.sadc.int/document/sadc-mutual-defence-pact-2003#:~:text=In%20compliance%20with%20the%20provisions,in%20defense%20and%20security%20matters.>.
SADC Protocol on Politics, Defence and Security Cooperation (2001) <https://www.sadc.int/sites/default/files/2021-08/Protocol_on_Politics_Defence_and_Security20001.pdf>.
SADC, 'SADC Has Responsibility to Help Member States Under Terrorist Threat' (29 April 2021) <www.sadc.int/news-events/news/sadc-has-responsibility-help-member-state-underterrorist-threat/>.
SADC, 'SADC Mission in Mozambique (SAMIM) in Brief' (10 November 2021) <www.sadc.int/latest-news/sadc-mission-mozambique-samim-brief>.
Treaty of the Southern African Development Community (1992) <https://www.sadc.int/sites/default/files/2021-11/Declaration__Treaty_of_SADC_0.pdf>.
Suyasha Paliwal, 'The Primacy of Regional Organisations in International Peacekeeping: The African Example' (2010) 51 (1) *Virginia Journal of International Law*.
TJ Vhangani and Richard R Molapo, 'The Role of the SADC in a Peacekeeping Mission: A Case Study of South Africa in the Lesotho Conflict' (2017) 15 (2) *Commonwealth Youth and Development*.
UN Doc. S/1998/891.
UN Doc. S/2021/658 (21 July 2021).
United Nations Peacemaker, 'Lusaka Agreement' (10 July 1999) <https://peacemaker.un.org/drc-lusaka-agreement99>.
'What Exactly Are We Waiting For?' *The Southern Times* (16 April 2021).

15 The military intervention against Ansar al-Sunna in Cabo Delgado

A primer on the law on the prohibition on the use of force and applicable exceptions

Dire Tladi

15.1 Introduction

The prohibition on the use of force remains one of the fundamental rules of the international system and by all accounts a peremptory norm of general international law.[1] Yet its contours remain highly contested.[2] While there never is any question about what constitutes the use of force, it is the various exceptions to the prohibitions on the use of force that are at the root of the contestations and uncertainty.

The arguments put forward by the Russian Federation in support of its patently unlawful use of force in Ukraine are an example of how the exceptions to the use of force can be interpreted so elastically as to undermine the prohibition.[3] Yet, the case of the Russian use of force in Ukraine is a classic case of inter-state use of force, for which the basic rules were designed.[4] The rules on the use of force, and the exceptions to that rule, in particular, become even more complex when the use of force is against non-state actors. For this reason, there has been a growth in the literature assessing the content of the legal rules on the use of force against non-state actors.[5] While much of the literature has focused on the use of force in self-defence, the uncertainty applies in other areas as well.

It is against this background that the situation in Cabo Delgado and the military intervention by third states against Ansar al-Sunna is discussed in this chapter. That situation raises many of the same questions arising in the context of the use of force against non-state actors. More specifically, this chapter will seek to provide some clarity on the legal basis for the third-party intervention.

The next section will set out the background necessary to evaluate the legal basis for the intervention in Cabo Delgado. This background consists of a brief description of the third-party intervention in Cabo Delgado. Section 15.3 will then provide an analysis of possible bases of the third-party intervention along with an evaluation of each of those bases in international law. The basis considered in Section 15.3 will be enforcement measures under the collective security framework, the use of force in self-defence, humanitarian intervention and intervention by invitation. Finally, some concluding observations are given.

DOI: 10.4324/9781003317647-18

15.2 Background: deployment of intervention forces

As described in Chapter 1, Ansar al-Sunna, a non-state actor loosely affiliated with the Islamic State (IS), has been engaged in terrorist activities in Cabo Delgado in Mozambique since around 2017.[6] Initially Mozambique was reluctant to accept outside assistance.[7] Mozambique is said to have 'invoked the principle of national sovereignty' and regarded the activities of Ansar al-Sunna as a problem of criminality.[8] Indeed, earlier discussions of the use of force implications for intervention against Ansar A-Sunna were predicated on this reluctance.[9] However, that reluctance eventually waned.

With Mozambique now open to external intervention, in June 2021 the Southern African Development Community (SADC) Summit decided to deploy a SADC Standby Force to intervene against terrorism in Cabo Delgado.[10] Incidentally, that decision was made in Maputo, Mozambique, with the President of Mozambique, Filipe Jacinto Nyusi, as Chairperson of SADC. The mandate of the SADC Standby Force was most recently renewed during a virtual Extraordinary Meeting of the SADC Troika Summit Plus the Chairperson of the Organ on Politics, Defence and Security Cooperation. It is on this basis that an SADC Standby Force is currently operating in Cabo Delgado in Mozambique.

Even earlier, the Rwandan military had deployed a force of around 1 000 military personnel, also with the agreement of the Mozambican government. The objective of the Rwandan deployment, as in the case of the SADC deployment, was to combat the terrorist activities of Ansar al-Sunna. While the two deployments share a common objective, there are differences. The first difference concerns the reported attitude of the government of Mozambique towards the respective deployments. There have been insinuations that the government of Mozambique preferred to have the Rwandan military rather than a SADC force.[11] The truth of this assertion and, if true, the reasons for the attitude of the Mozambican government are irrelevant for these purposes.

Another difference, which *may* be more relevant for the purposes of the current analysis, is the fact that the SADC is an international organisation to which Mozambique belongs and was acting in response to terrorist activities that potentially pose a threat not only to Mozambique but to the region as a whole. In this sense, the SADC intervention may be seen as a collective enforcement action. The next section will consider, in turn, the possible bases for third-party interventions.

15.2.1 An evaluation of the possible bases of the interventions

15.2.1.1 General

The prohibition on the use of force is a fundamental principle of international law and a norm of *jus cogens*.[12] The rule, reflected in article 2(4) of the United Nations (UN) Charter, provides that states 'shall refrain in their international relations from the threat or use of force against the territorial integrity or political independence of any state'. The Charter recognises only two exceptions to this basic rule. In addition to these, other exceptions have been put forward.[13]

Whether the deployment of forces by SADC or Rwanda is consistent with international law will fall to be determined by whether the deployments can be categorised under meeting one or more of the legal tests set out below. In addition to the generally recognised exceptions to the prohibition on the use of force, namely, the collective security framework and self-defence, the section will also consider other circumstances that have been put forward as exceptions in the literature.

15.2.1.2 Collective security framework

The main exception is the collective security framework provided for under chapter VII of the UN Charter. Under the Charter, the principal way to address threats to peace and security, including in the cases of breach of article 2(4), is through collective measures. This is because the first and most important of the purposes of the UN is to 'maintain international peace and security'. As Cohen states, the motto of the system is 'peace through collective security'.[14] The powers of collective enforcement action under the Charter are reserved for the UN Security Council. In particular, article 42 provides for the Charter to authorise 'such action by air, sea, or land forces as may be necessary to maintain or restore international peace and security', if the Security Council makes a determination under article 39 that there is a threat to international peace and security, aggression or breach of the peace.

Clearly, the Rwandan intervention cannot be justified under this ground since there is nothing collective about that intervention – that is to say, it was not undertaken on the basis of any collective security measure. The SADC intervention, however, was undertaken as an exercise of regional collective measure for the maintenance of international peace and security. Yet, to fall under the Charter exception, the intervention has to be authorised by the UN Security Council. There is no decision by the UN Security Council authorising the intervention in Mozambique by SADC or any other state, making questionable the reliance on the collective security framework as a possible basis for the intervention.

There has been some debate about whether the right to intervene under article 42 can be exercised by regional organisations.[15] There are different positions, on a spectrum, about the legality of the use of force as a collective enforcement measure by entities other than the Security Council.[16] At one end of the spectrum is the approach that is that any authorisation by a regional organisation that is not endorsed or approved by the Security Council is unlawful and falls foul of article 2(4) without the benefit of legitimation by the collective security framework. This perspective is based on a strict reading of the law of the Charter on the prohibition of the use of force, which foresees only two exceptions to the prohibition, namely, self-defence and authorisation of the UN Security Council. At the other end of the spectrum, action by a regional organisation, such as intervention by the African Union (AU) under article 4(h) of its Constitutive Act, may be seen as a new exception to the prohibition on the use of force or even an evolution of existing exceptions, whether through evolutive interpretation of the Charter or evolution of state practice and *opinio juris*.

There is a third, and middle, option, that enforcement action by a regional organisation is permissible under the framework of the Charter on the basis of Council endorsement of such intervention but that, in the absence of an affirmative decision to the contrary, the Council is deemed to have authorised the regional action. This view would be based on a permissive interpretation of article 53 of the Charter, which provides that 'no enforcement action shall be taken under regional arrangements or by regional agencies without the authorisation of the Security Council'.[17]

Under the first option, the one requiring express authorisation by the Security Council, the SADC intervention could not be justified on the basis of the collective security framework. The second option, under which there has been practice leading to the evolution of the rules to permit regional organisations to authorise the use of force under the collective security framework without any authorisation of the Security Council, is problematic from a number of perspectives. The problem here is that, as has been pointed out, not even AU decision makers put forward an interpretation of the Constitutive Act permitting the use of force without UN Security Council authorisation.[18]

The third option is more promise, namely, where the Council is deemed to have authorised an intervention unless and until evidence to the contrary emerges. Here, however, it would be important to adopt a restrictive interpretation. Under such a restrictive interpretation, only regional organisations with a track record of cooperation with the Security Council, such as the AU, can be deemed to enjoy the privilege of a presumption of acting on the implicit authorisation of the Security Council.[19] SADC does not have such a track record and, thus, without explicit UN, or potentially AU authorisation, the intervention could not be justified under the collective security framework.

In light of the above, the Rwandan and SADC deployments could not be justified as regional collective enforcement actions. The lawfulness of the interventions will thus have to be sought elsewhere.

15.2.1.3 Self-defence

The second exception to the prohibition on the use of force is self-defence. Under self-defence, a state has a right to use force in the territory of another state in response to an armed attack.[20] The right to the use of force in self-defence applies to collective self-defence. Thus, in cases of an attack against a state (or a group of states), the attacked states (or states) can enlist the assistance of other states in warding off the attack. Thus, the enlisted states do not, themselves, have to be under attack. The key element here is that the state under attack should have enlisted the assistance of the third states.

There are two ways that the right of self-defence might operate in the context of the interventions. First, self-defence might apply in the sense that the intervening states from SADC and Rwanda are responding to armed attacks by Ansar al-Sunna against their own territories. Second, the interventions may be seen as collective self-defence with the aid of Mozambique to repel an armed attack from Ansar al-Sunna. For the time being, I set out the broad principles relating to self-defence and, for that purpose, I treat both possibilities as similar. However, distinctions will be drawn in the latter parts of the section.

Traditionally, the right to use force has been reserved for inter-state use of force. In other words, the words 'an armed attack' have been understood as an armed attack from another state.[21] This traditional reading of article 51 means that self-defence is not available for the extraterritorial use of force directed against non-state actors. Its implication for the current analysis is that neither the SADC nor the Rwandese deployment could be seen as an exercise in self-defence.

Yet, in recent years, in particular, since the terrorist attacks on 11 September 2001, there has been an increase in literature, suggesting that an armed attack under the Charter (and customary international law) includes an armed attack from a non-state actor.[22] In other words, under this expanded interpretation of the law on self-defence, a state can use force in the territory of another state in response to an armed attack against itself. There are several arguments in support of this theory. First, it has been argued that article 51 does not refer to 'an armed attack *from a state*' but rather, article 51 refers only to an 'armed attack' without specifying the source of the armed attack. The second argument is that, whatever the content of the rule at the beginning, through practice, international law has evolved to the point where the rules now permit the use of force against non-state actors in the territory of third states. Whether the evolution is based on the evolution of customary international law or due to subsequent practice in the interpretation of treaties, the evaluation of these arguments ought to be assessed on the basis of the rules of international law.

Yet, convincing though these arguments are, they are deeply flawed and problematic. As to the first argument, while it is the case that article 51 does not state 'an armed attack from another state', treaties are not interpreted only through a purely literal meaning. Rather, under the customary rules of interpretation, words are to be given their ordinary meaning, in context and in light of the object and purpose of the treaties. The context, in this case, is that the Charter is an inter-state instrument and the rules on the use of force were to be understood as operating in that context. Even authors who now propose the expansive reading of the right to self-defence accept that the Charter, when adopted, operated in an inter-state context and that article 51 was to be understood in that context.[23] Moreover, this understanding has been consistently put forward by the International Court of Justice (ICJ).[24]

In the *Military and Paramilitary Activities* case, the Court accepted that an armed attack against a non-state actor was possible, but only if the non-state was sent by or is acting on behalf of the state. This line of reasoning has been accepted in subsequent decisions of the ICJ.[25] The significance of this understanding by the Court of the law on self-defence, which buttresses the common understanding that traditionally, the use of force in self-defence was available only against an armed attack from a state, is that any argument that the law now permits self-defence against non-state actors requires evidence of an evolution of law, which evidence would ordinarily be based on state practice.

The second argument, that is, that there has been practice resulting in the evolution of the rule on self-defence, though slightly more convincing, is also flawed. While practice can result in the evolution of the content of rules, the responses of other states are relevant in determining the value of any practice. The literature supporting an expansive understanding of self-defence generally puts forward three categories of practice. First, what one might call pre-9/11 acts by a state using force, purportedly in self-defence, in the territory of third states against non-state actors whose acts of violence against the state using force are not attributable to the territorial state. Second, a second category of practice consists of Security Council resolutions adopted in the aftermath of 9/11 and the US invasion of Afghanistan in response to 9/11, all directed at a non-state actor, Al-Qaeda. Third, the use of force by the United States and its allies against IS, the entity to which Ansar al-Sunna is affiliated, in the territory of Syria without the consent of the latter.

With respect to the first category of practice, while there certainly are a high number of examples of states using force, it is equally true that in each of the cases often cited, there also is enough objection or criticism from other states and international actors, to cast doubt on the value of the example as law producing or affecting. Although it is possible to provide more examples, due to limitations of time and space, I provide only one example, namely, the Turkish incursion in Iraq in response to attacks by the Kurdistan Workers Party, a non-state entity. In response to the Turkish incursion, the European Union (EU), through its then High Representative for Foreign Affairs, Javier Solana, expressed understanding of the concerns of Turkey but stated that its chosen course of action was 'not the best response'.[26] The statement continued that the 'territorial integrity of Iraq [was] very important for' the EU – a sentiment that suggested that the Turkish conduct was in breach of said territorial integrity.[27] Similarly, then UN Secretary-General, Ban Ki Moon, said that, while he was 'conscious of Turkey's concern', he appealed for the 'utmost restraint, and for respect of the border between Iraq and Turkey'.[28] Stephen Smith, then Australian Foreign Minister, also called on 'Turkey to respect Iraq's sovereignty and [to] retreat back over the border as soon as possible'.[29] A theme running through all of these statements is the acceptance of the seriousness of the attacks (by non-state actors) against Turkey, but a declaration that the attacks by the Kurdistan Workers Party cannot justify the violation of the territorial integrity of Iraq.

In respect of the second category practice, the proponents of an expansive interpretation put forward UN Security Council Resolutions 1368 and 1373. Yet, leaving aside that Security Council resolutions cannot on their own, without more, constitute subsequent practice for the purposes of treaty interpretation, those resolutions, on their own terms, say nothing about the right to use of force against non-state actors. They simply in preambular provisions reaffirm the right to self-defence. It is true that in response to an attack perpetrated by a non-state actor, Al-Qaeda, the United States launched an attack, purportedly in self-defence, against Afghanistan without the latter's consent. It is equally true that there is virtually no record of any state objecting to the United States' invasion at the time it occurred.[30] Yet, there are at least two problems with using the United States invasion of Afghanistan as the basis for an evolution of the rule. First, it is highly problematic to suggest that one incident, no matter how profile, is able to meet the strict requirements for state practice to result in the evolution of law. Second, and more importantly, it is not at all clear that in its conduct the United States saw itself as acting solely against Al-Qaeda. Rightly or wrongly (and probably wrongly), the United States seems to have attributed some responsibility to Afghanistan's governing entity, the Taliban, such that the launching of the war in Afghanistan could properly be seen as the use of force *against the state*. In the days leading up to the attacks, the President of the United States made several statements suggesting that it held the Taliban responsible for the attacks on 9/11.[31] The 9/11-related practice, therefore, does not take the argument for an expansive approach to the right to use force in self-defence much further.

It had been suggested that the use of force in Syria against IS by the United States and its allies, without the consent of Syria, produced the Grotian moment necessary to tilt into international law firmly to the position where non-state actors in third states were legitimate targets of self-defence.[32] Unlike the use of force by the United States, the intervention in Syria against IS clearly was not directed at Syria as it could hardly be argued that the acts of IS were attributable to Syria. Second, there certainly were a substantial number of states engaged in the acts. Yet, subsequent practice is only relevant as a means of interpretation if the practice establishes the agreement of the parties as to the meaning of the provision being interpreted.[33] The reasons put forward by the states for their use of force in Syria suggest a different interpretation of article 51. Some, for example, relied on a principle referred to as the 'unwilling or unable' principle – that is, the territorial state in question is either unwilling or unable to deal with the attacks by the non-state actors in question.[34] Yet other states used other theories to explain their interventions.[35] However, more importantly, the acts of intervention in question did not establish the agreement *of the parties* because not all UN members participated in the interventions or acquiesced as to their lawfulness. Quite the contrary, several states have, in light of these interventions, expressed their views that the Charter does not permit the extraterritorial use of force as a response to terrorism without the consent of the territorial state.[36]

The brief analysis above indicates that the traditional, inter-state understanding of the rules on self-defence remains in force. Here it might be necessary to draw a distinction between the two scenarios, that is, where the intervening states are intervening on account of an armed attack against their territories, or whether there is an intervention in aid of Mozambique and in response to an armed attack against it. With respect to the former, first of all, because there is no indication at all of an attack by Ansar al-Sunna against any of the intervening states, that ground is not available even if the expansive approach to self-defence was adopted. But second, assuming that there had been some kind of attack against the territories of the intervening states, the interventions could only be justified as self-defence in one of two circumstances: (a) if the acts of Ansar al-Sunna could be attributed to Mozambique (I leave outside the threshold of attribution) or (b) if Mozambique provides consent for the intervention.

The case of SADC and Rwanda interventions are not cases of the intervening states responding to attacks from Ansar al-Sunna. They are, rather, cases of third states responding to assistance from Mozambique against non-state entities acting within its own territory. In my view, however, the answer remains the same, that is, the right of self-defence is not the appropriate legal basis for the intervention. This is because self-defence operates as an exception in the event of armed attack, which is 'the most grave form of extraterritorial the use of force'.[37]

15.2.1.4 Humanitarian intervention

An argument may also be made that the intervention by Rwanda and SADC can be justified as humanitarian intervention. This is because it has been reported that Ansar al-Sunnah has committed atrocities in areas it has occupied. However, the doctrine of humanitarian intervention not only is controversial but is generally not accepted in international law. While there are some authors that defend the doctrine as consistent with international law,[38] there is very little support for it in international law. This discussion will therefore be relatively brief.[39] Yet there are two cases that have been put forward as practice leading to the evolution of the international law to recognise humanitarian intervention. The first of these is the famous intervention by the North Atlantic Treaty Organisation (NATO) in Yugoslavia in response to a genocide perpetrated against Kosovar Albanians.[40] A second example is the intervention by the United States and its allies in Syria in response to the alleged use of chemical weapons by the Syrian government against its people.[41]

The problem with both examples is that states generally have not accepted them as impacting on the law, even in cases where states have applauded, in political terms, the intervention.[42] In fact, only the United Kingdom has consistently made the explicit assertion that humanitarian intervention is lawful under international law.[43] Moreover, the Non-Aligned Movement, a group of more than 130 states, has a long-established position that humanitarian intervention is unlawful under international law.[44] In light of this, humanitarian intervention cannot serve as a legal basis for the intervention against Ansar al-Sunna in Cabo Delgado.

15.2.1.5 Intervention by invitation

The last possible ground for the lawfulness of the intervention in Cabo Delgado is intervention by invitation. In general, subject to the rules described later, international law permits intervention in the territory of another state with the consent of that state.[45] Since both the Rwanda and the SADC interventions have been consented to by the government of Mozambique, intervention by invitation thus provides a potential legal basis for the intervention.

There are potentially two different understandings of the intervention by invitation. The most common one is that the intervention, as a point of departure, is an unlawful breach of article 2(4) but that, as in the case of self-defence or authorisation of the UN Security Council, the consent renders it lawful.[46] Another view which, in my view, is more correct, is that as a point of departure, intervention by invitation is lawful and does not at all implicate article 2(4) since there is no breach of sovereignty or territorial integrity because the territorial state has given its consent.[47] Intervention by invitation thus is not an exception to the prohibition on the use of force since the prohibition is never disturbed. However, these differences of view are really cosmetic in that in the final analysis, whether the point is that the intervention is lawful, the outcome of any analysis will be the same. International law recognises the lawfulness of intervention by invitation.[48] Under the first approach, the interventions by SADC and Rwanda are in breach of article 2(4), but become lawful by virtue of the consent given by Mozambique. Under the second approach, article 2(4) is never breached to start off with and the interventions of SADC and Rwanda are lawful.

However, there are exceptions to the lawfulness of intervention by invitation. It is generally agreed in the doctrine that the right of the territorial state to invite third states to intervene ceases to exist in cases of civil war and in particular where the government has lost control over a significant portion of its territory.[49] Yet, in this case, Mozambique has not lost a sufficient amount of territory to qualify the situation as a civil war. Thus, the invitations and, thus, the interventions, remain untainted.

15.3 Conclusion

The interventions by SADC and Rwanda are lawful. While international law generally prohibits any military intervention in the territory of third states as a breach of article 2(4), there are two exceptions to the prohibition, namely, self-defence and collective security enforcement measures. In addition to these two recognised exceptions, other circumstances have been put forward as possible justifications. This chapter has served as a primer and explored the applicability of various legal bases for the interventions of SADC and Rwanda. In the end it concludes that the legal basis for the interventions simply is the consent given by Mozambique.

Notes

1 See generally Olivier Corten and Vaios Koutroulis, 'The *Jus Cogens* Status of the Prohibition on the Use of Force: What Is Its Scope and Why Does It Matter?' in Dire Tladi (ed), *Peremptory Norms of General International Law (Jus Cogens): Disquisitions and Disputations* (Brill 2021) 629.

2 Dire Tladi, 'The Nonconsenting Innocent State: The Problem with Bethlehem's Principle 12' (2013) 107 *American Journal of International Law* 570.

3 Marko Milanovic 'What Is Russia's Legal Justification for Using Force Against Ukraine?' *EJIL:Talk!* (24 February 2022).

4 See Christine Gray, *International Law and the Use of Force* (3rd edn, OUP 2008) 22; Hans Kelsen, 'Collective Security and Collective Self-Defence under the Charter of the United Nations' (1948) 42 *American Journal of International Law* 783, 791.

5 See, for example, Lindsay Moir, *Reappraising the Resort to Force: International Law,* Jus ad Bellum *and the War on Terror* (Hart Publishing 2010); Michael P Scharf, 'How the War against ISIS Changed International Law' (2016) 48 *Case Western Reserve Journal of International Law* 15; Christian Tams, 'The Use of Force against Terrorists' (2009) 20 *European Journal of International Law* 359; Michael Byers, 'Terrorism, the

Use of Force and Self-Defence after 11 September' (2002) 16 *International Relations* 155; Oscar Schachter, 'The Extraterritorial Use of Force against Terrorist Bases' (1989) 11 *Houston Journal of International Law* 309; Theresa Reinold, 'State Weakness, Irregular Warfare, and the Right to Self-Defence Post 9/11' (2011) 105 *American Journal of International Law* 244; Jordan Paust, 'Self-Defence Targeting of Non-State Actors and Permissibility of US Use of Drones in Pakistan' (2010) 19 *Journal of Transnational Law and Policy* 237; Mary Ellen O'Connell, Christian J Tams and Dire Tladi, *Max Planck Trialogues on the Law of Peace and War (Vol 1): Self-Defence against Non-State Actors* (CUP 2019).

6 Meryl Demunyck and Gijs Weijenberg, 'The Upcoming SADC Intervention: A New Way Ahead to Combat Terrorism in Mozambique?' <https://icct.nl/publication/the-upcoming-sadc-intervention-a-new-way-ahead-to-combat-terrorism-in-mozambique/>.

7 Ibid.

8 See Liesl Louw Vaudran, 'Coordination: Key to the Success of African Solutions for Mozambique' *Institute for Security Studies* (11 April 2022).

9 See Marko Svicevic, 'Collective Self-Defence or Regional Enforcement Action: The Legality of a SADC Intervention in Cabo Delgado and the Question of Mozambican Consent' (2022) 9 *Journal on the Use of Force in International Law* 138; Marko Svicevic, 'The Legality of a SADC Intervention in Cabo Delgado in the Absence of Mozambican Consent' *Opinio Juris Blog* (2 November 2020). See also Peter Fabricius, 'SADC Grapples with Response While Mercenaries, Energy Companies and Civilians Quit Mozambique's Islamic State Crisis' *Daily Maverick* (1 April 2021).

10 See para 7 of SADC Communiqué of 23 June 2021.

11 Darren Olivier, 'The Prospects for a Successful SADC Mission in Mozambique' *ACCORD* (21 September 2021). For a view that suggests a more mutually-supportive relationship between the two deployments, see Rich Mashimbye, 'Terrorism, Insurgency, and Regional Stability: The Case of Mozambique' (2022) 17 *International Journal of African Renaissance Studies* 60, 72.

12 See Corten and Koutroulis (n 1).

13 For a more comprehensive account of my view of these exceptions as applied to non-state actors, see Dire Tladi, 'The Extraterritorial Use of Force Against Non-State Actors' (2021) 418 *Recueil de Cours de l'Academie de Droit International de la Haye* 237.

14 Marcelo Cohen, 'The Use of Force by the United States after the End of the Cold War, and Its Implications on International Law' in Michael Byers and Georg Nolte (eds), *United States Hegemony and the Foundations of International Law* (CUP 2003) 197; see also Hans Kelsen, 'Collective Security and Collective Self-Defence under the Charter of the United Nations' (1948) 42 *American Journal of International Law* 783; see also Peter D Danchin, 'Things Fall Apart: The Concept of Collective Security in International Law' in Peter D Danchin and Horst Fischer (eds), *United Nations Reform and the New Collective Security* (CUP 2010) 53.

15 See, for example, Tiyanjana Maluwa, 'African State Practice and the Formation of Some Peremptory Norms of General International Law' in Tladi (n 1) 291–299; see Corten and Koutroulis (n 1).

16 For discussion, see Dire Tladi, 'The African Union's Right to Intervene and the Right to Life: Tension or Concordance' in Frans Viljoen and others (eds), *A Life Interrupted: Essays in Honour of Christof Heyns* (PULP 2022) 252; Ben Kioko, 'The Right of Intervention under the African Union's Constitutive Act: From Non-Interference and Non-Intervention' (2003) 85 *International Review of the Red Cross* 807; Jeremy Levitt, 'The Peace and Security Council of the African Union, the Use of Force and the United Nations Security Council: The Case of Sudan' in Niels Blokker and Nico Schrijver (eds), *The Security Council and the Use of Force: Theory and Practice* (Brill 2005) 213.

17 An analysis of this possibility is provided in Tladi (n 16).

18 Corten and Koutroulis (n 1) 649 ff.

19 See, generally, Evelyne Asaala and Dire Tladi, 'Assessing the Respective Mandates of the UN and AU in the Maintenance of International Peace and Security: Partnership and Cooperative Division of Labour or Competition' (2022) *Kazan Journal of International Law and International Relations* 17. For examples of this track record, see UN Docs SC/143/71 (4 December 2020); S/PRST/2020/11 (4 December 2020); S/PRST/2004/7 (25 March 2004) and S/PRST/2004/44 (19 November 2004); AU Doc. PSC/PR/2(DII) (29 April 2015); S/PRST/2007/7; UN, 'United Nations, African Union Launch Joint Task Force on Peace and Security' (25 September 2010); Joint United Nations-African Union Framework for Enhanced Partnership in Peace and Security <https://reliefweb.int/sites/reliefweb.int/files/resources/signed_joint_framework.pdf>.

20 Article 51 of the Charter of the United Nations (adopted 26 June 1945, entered into force 24 October 1945) 1 UNTS XVI. The rule in article in 51 is also part of customary international law. See *Case Concerning Military and Paramilitary Activities in and Around Nicaragua (Nicaragua v United States of America),* Merits, Judgment, ICJ Reports 1986 14, para 193.

21 See Gray (n 4) 7; André de Hoogh, 'Restrictivist Reasoning on the *Ratione Personae* Dimension of Armed Attacks in the Post 9/11 World' (2016) 29 *Leiden Journal of International Law* 19, 22.

22 Michael Wood, 'International Law and the Use of Force: What Happens in Practice?' (2013) 53 *Indian Journal of International Law* 345; Oscar Schachter, 'The Extraterritorial Use of Force against Terrorist Bases' (1989) 11 *Houston Journal of International Law* 309; Theresa Reinold, 'State Weakness, Irregular Warfare, and the Right to Self-Defence Post 9/11' (2011) 105 *American Journal of International Law* 244; Jordan Paust, 'Self-Defence Targeting of Non-State Actors and Permissibility of US Use of Drones in Pakistan' (2010) 19 *Journal of Transnational Law and Policy* 237; Daniel Bethlehem, 'Principles Relevant to the Scope of a State's Right of Self-Defence Against an Imminent or Actual Armed Attack by Nonstate Actors' (2012) 106 *American Journal of International Law* 769; Harold Hongju Koh, *The Trump Administration and International Law* (OUP 2019) 136. See also Principles of International Law on the Use of Force by States in Self-Defence (2005) <www.chathamhouse.org/sites/files/chathamhouse/public/Research/International%20Law/ilpforce.doc>; Leiden Policy Recommendations on Counter-Terrorism and International Law (2010) <www.grotiuscentre.org/resources/1/Leiden%20Policy%20Recommendations%201%20April%202010.pdf>.

23 Christian Tams, 'The Use of Force Against Terrorists' (2009) 20 *European Journal of International Law* 359, 363, stating that the restrictive approach to the use of force in self-defence 'represented the dominant approach to the *jus ad bellum*' and 'was reflected in many of the influential writings of the time'. See also Scharf (n 5) 15 ('Use of force in self-defence has traditionally not been viewed as lawful against non-state actors in a third state unless they are under the effective control of that state, but the United States argued that in the aftermath of the 9/11 attacks by al-Qaeda, such force can be justified where a government is unable or unwilling to suppress the threat posed by non-state actors operating within its borders'.)

24 *Military and Paramilitary Activities* case (n 20) para 195.

25 *Case Concerning Oil Platforms (Iran v United States)*, Judgment, ICJ Reports 2003, 161, para 51 ('The Court determined that for the United States to rely on self-defence, it would have had to show "that attacks had been made upon it *for which Iran was responsible*", which attacks would qualify as "armed attacks"'); *Legal Consequences of the Construction of the Wall in the Occupied Palestinian Territory*, Advisory Opinion, ICJ Reports 2004, 136, para 139 where the Court rejected Israel's claim of self-defence because the attacks in question did not constitute armed attacks as they were not from a state.

26 Mark John, 'EU's Solana: Turkey Incursion "Not Best Response"' *Reuters* (22 February 2008).

27 Ibid.

28 'EU Voices Concern Over Turkish Military Incursion into Iraq' *Deutsche Welle* (22 February 2008).
29 'Australia Urges Turkey to Pull Troops from Iraqi Kurdistan' *Ekurd Daily* (24 February 2008).
30 Griffin, for example, states that the question of the legality of the war in Afghanistan 'has been considered off-limits, not to be raised in polite company'. See David Ray Griffin, 'Did 9/11 Justify the War in Afghanistan? Using the McChrystal Moment to Raise a Forbidden Question' (25 June 2010) <www.globalresearch.ca/did-9-11-justify-thewar-in-afghanistan/19891>.
31 See address by President George W Bush to a Joint Sitting of Congress on 20 September 2011 <www.americanrhetoric.com/speeches/gwbush911jointsessionspeech.htm>; '9/11 Address to the Nation: A Great People has been Moved to Defend a Great Nation' Speech by President George W Bush on 11 September 2001 <www.americanrhetoric.com/speeches/gwbush911addresstothenation.htm>.
32 See generally Scharf (n 5) 15.
33 See article 31(3)(b) of the Vienna Convention on the Law of Treaties (adopted 23 May 1969, entered into force 27 January 1980) 1155 UNTS 331.
34 UN Docs S/2014/695 (23 September 2014); S/2015/693 (9 September 2015); S/2015/563 (24 July 2015); S/2015/221 (31 March 2015).
35 Germany, for example, seemed to suggest that Syria had lost control of its territory, such that it was not using force in Syria. See UN Doc. S/2015/946 (10 December 2015).
36 Final Document of the 17th Summit of Heads of State and Government of the Non-Aligned Movement, 17–18 September 2016, Island of Margarita, Venezuela, para 258.34; see, for example, Statement of the Permanent Mission of the Republic of El Salvador on behalf of the Community of Latin American and Caribbean States (CELAC) during the United Nations' Special Committee on the Charter of the United Nations and the Strengthening of the Role of Organisation, New York (20–28 February 2018) <https://celac.rree.gob.sv/wp-content/uploads/2018/02/Statement-CELAC-Charter-Committee-Feb-2018.pdf>.
37 *Military and Paramilitary Activities* case (n 20) para 191 ('As regards particular aspects of the principle in question, it will be necessary to distinguish the most grave forms of the use of force (those constituting an armed attack) from other less grave forms'.)
38 See, for example, Fernando R Tesón, 'The Liberal Case for Humanitarian Intervention' *Florida State University College of Law, Public Law Research Paper No 39* (November 2001); Michael Walzer, *Just and Unjust Wars: A Moral Argument with Historical Illustrations* (5th edn, Basic Books 1997) 107.
39 For a more extensive account of my view on the subject, see Aniel de Beer and Dire Tladi, 'The Use of Force Against Syria in Response to Alleged Use of Chemical Weapons by Syria: A Return to Humanitarian Intervention?' (2019) 79 *Heidelberg Journal of International Law* 205.
40 For discussion, see Daniel Franchini and Antonios Tzanakopoulos, 'The Kosovo Crisis – 1999' in Tom Ruys and Olivier Corten (eds), *The Use of Force in International Law: A Case Based Approach* (OUP 2018) 1.
41 See Milena Sterio, 'Humanitarian Intervention Post-Syria: A Grotian Moment?' (2014) 20 *ILSA Journal of International and Comparative Law* 343.
42 For discussion, see De Beer and Tladi (n 39) 218–222, addressing responses of states to the 1999 Kosovo intervention, and 227–235, discussing the response to Syria's chemical weapons.
43 UN Doc. S/PV.3988 (24 March 1999); Statement by the Secretary Defence in the UK House of Commons (25 March 1999).
44 See 17th Non-Aligned Movement Summit (n 36) para 258.
45 For discussion, see Laura Visser, 'May the Force Be with You: The Legal Classification of Intervention by Invitation' (2019) 66 *Netherlands International Law Review* 21; Max Byrne, 'Consent and the Use of Force: An Examination of "Intervention by Invitation"

as a Basis for US Drone Strikes in Pakistan, Somalia and Yemen' (2016) 3(1) *Journal on the Use of Force and International Law* 97.

46 Erika de Wet, 'The Modern Practice of Intervention by Invitation in Africa and Its Implications for the Prohibition of the Use of Force' (2016) 26 *European Journal of International Law* 979, 980 ('According to another (in this contribution, preferred) line of argument, the reference to force "against territorial integrity or political independence" also covers military intervention on request, unless it is certain that the request does not undermine the territorial integrity or political independence of the requesting State'); Christopher J le Mon, 'Unilateral Intervention by Invitation in Civil Wars: The Effective Control Test Tested' (2003) 35 *New York University Journal of International Law and Policy* 741, 742 ('Invited military intervention focuses on the consent of the inviting State to justify action that *would absent such a consent, constitute an illegal use of force by one State within the territory of another*') (emphasis added).

47 See Tladi (n 13) 334–335.

48 *Military and Paramilitary Activities* case (n 20) 246.

49 See, however, Karine Bannelier and Theodore Christakis, 'The Intervention of France and African Countries in Mali – 2013' in Ruys and Corten (n 40) 819, who state that 'international legal scholarship is profoundly divided on the issue of legality of intervention by invitation in the context of civil war'.

Bibliography

'9/11 Address to the Nation: A Great People has been Moved to Defend a Great Nation' Speech by President George W Bush on 11 September 2001 <www.americanrhetoric.com/speeches/gwbush911addresstothenation.htm>.

'Address by President George W Bush to a Joint Sitting of Congress on 20 September 2011' <www.americanrhetoric.com/speeches/gwbush911jointsessionspeech.htm>.

André de Hoogh, 'Restrictivist Reasoning on the *Ratione Personae* Dimension of Armed Attacks in the Post 9/11 World' (2016) 29 *Leiden Journal of International Law*.

Aniel de Beer and Dire Tladi, 'The Use of Force Against Syria in Response to Alleged Use of Chemical Weapons by Syria: A Return to Humanitarian Intervention?' (2019) 79 *Heidelberg Journal of International Law*.

AU Doc. PSC/PR/2(DII) (29 April 2015).

'Australia Urges Turkey to Pull Troops from Iraqi Kurdistan' *Ekurd Daily* (24 February 2008).

Ben Kioko, 'The Right of Intervention under the African Union's Constitutive Act: From Non-Interference and Non-Intervention' (2003) 85 *International Review of the Red Cross*.

Case Concerning Military and Paramilitary Activities in and Around Nicaragua (Nicaragua v United States of America), Merits, Judgment, ICJ Reports 1986.

Case Concerning Oil Platforms (Iran v United States), Judgment, ICJ Reports 2003, 161.

Charter of the United Nations (1945) <https://treaties.un.org/Pages/showDetails.aspx?objid=080000028017ebb8&clang=_en>.

Christian Tams, 'The Use of Force against Terrorists' (2009) 20 *European Journal of International Law*.

Christine Gray, *International Law and the Use of Force* (3rd edn, OUP 2008).

Christopher J le Mon, 'Unilateral Intervention by Invitation in Civil Wars: The Effective Control Test Tested' (2003) 35 *New York University Journal of International Law and Policy*.

Daniel Bethlehem, 'Principles Relevant to the Scope of a State's Right of Self-Defence against an Imminent or Actual Armed Attack by Nonstate Actors' (2012) 106 *American Journal of International Law*.

Daniel Franchini and Antonios Tzanakopoulos, 'The Kosovo Crisis – 1999' in Tom Ruys and Olivier Corten (eds), *The Use of Force in International Law: A Case Based Approach* (OUP 2018).

Darren Olivier, 'The Prospects for a Successful SADC Mission in Mozambique' *ACCORD* (21 September 2021).

David Ray Griffin, 'Did 9/11 Justify the War in Afghanistan? Using the McChrystal Moment to Raise a Forbidden Question' (25 June 2010) <www.globalresearch.ca/did-9-11-justify-thewar-in-afghanistan/19891>.

Dire Tladi, 'The African Union's Right to Intervene and the Right to Life: Tension or Concordance' in Frans Viljoen and others (eds), *A Life Interrupted: Essays in Honour of Christof Heyns* (PULP 2022).

Dire Tladi, 'The Extraterritorial Use of Force Against Non-State Actors' (2021) 418 *Recueil de Cours de l'Academie de Droit International de la Haye*.

Dire Tladi, 'The Nonconsenting Innocent State: The Problem with Bethlehem's Principle 12' (2013) 107 *American Journal of International Law*.

Erika de Wet, 'The Modern Practice of Intervention by Invitation in Africa and Its Implications for the Prohibition of the Use of Force' (2016) 26 *European Journal of International Law*.

'EU Voices Concern Over Turkish Military Incursion into Iraq' *Deutsche Welle* (22 February 2008).

Evelyne Asaala and Dire Tladi, 'Assessing the Respective Mandates of the UN and AU in the Maintenance of International Peace and Security: Partnership and Cooperative Division of Labour or Competition' (2022) *Kazan Journal of International Law and International Relations*.

Fernando R Tesón, 'The Liberal Case for Humanitarian Intervention' *Florida State University College of Law, Public Law Research Paper No 39* (November 2001) <https://papers.ssrn.com/sol3/papers.cfm?abstract_id=291661>.

Final Document of the 17th Summit of Heads of State and Government of the Non-Aligned Movement, 17–18 September 2016, Island of Margarita, Venezuela.

Hans Kelsen, 'Collective Security and Collective Self-Defence under the Charter of the United Nations' (1948) 42 *American Journal of International Law*.

Harold Hongju Koh, *The Trump Administration and International Law* (OUP 2019).

Jeremy Levitt, 'The Peace and Security Council of the African Union, the Use of Force and the United Nations Security Council: The Case of Sudan' in Niels Blokker and Nico Schrijver (eds), *The Security Council and the Use of Force: Theory and Practice* (Brill 2005).

'Joint United Nations-African Union Framework for Enhanced Partnership in Peace and Security' <https://reliefweb.int/sites/reliefweb.int/files/resources/signed_joint_framework.pdf>.

Jordan Paust, 'Self-Defence Targeting of Non-State Actors and Permissibility of US Use of Drones in Pakistan' (2010) 19 *Journal of Transnational Law and Policy*.

Karine Bannelier and Theodore Christakis, 'The Intervention of France and African Countries in Mali – 2013' in Tom Ruys and Olivier Corten (eds), *The Use of Force in International Law: A Case-Based Approach* (OUP 2018).

Laura Visser, 'May the Force Be with You: The Legal Classification of Intervention by Invitation' (2019) 66 *Netherlands International Law Review*.

Legal Consequences of the Construction of the Wall in the Occupied Palestinian Territory, Advisory Opinion, ICJ Reports 2004, 136.

'Leiden Policy Recommendations on Counter-Terrorism and International Law' *Grotius Centre for International Legal Studies* (2010) <www.grotiuscentre.org/resources/1/Leiden%20Policy%20Recommendations%201%20April%202010.pdf>.

Liesl Louw Vaudran, 'Coordination: Key to the Success of African Solutions for Mozambique' *Institute for Security Studies* (11 April 2022).

Lindsay Moir, *Reappraising the Resort to Force: International Law, Jus ad Bellum and the War on Terror* (Hart Publishing 2010).

Marcelo Cohen, 'The Use of Force by the United States after the End of the Cold War, and Its Implications on International Law' in Michael Byers and Georg Nolte (eds), *United States Hegemony and the Foundations of International Law* (Cambridge 2003).

Mark John, 'EU's Solana: Turkey Incursion "Not Best Response"' *Reuters* (22 February 2008).

Marko Milanovic 'What Is Russia's Legal Justification for Using Force against Ukraine?' *EJIL:Talk!* (24 February 2022).

Marko Svicevic, 'Collective Self-Defence or Regional Enforcement Action: The Legality of a SADC Intervention in Cabo Delgado and the Question of Mozambican Consent' (2022) 9 *Journal on the Use of Force in International Law*.

Marko Svicevic, 'The Legality of a SADC Intervention in Cabo Delgado in the Absence of Mozambican Consent' *Opinio Juris Blog* (2 November 2020).

Mary Ellen O'Connell, Christian J Tams and Dire Tladi, *Max Planck Trialogues on the Law of Peace and War (Vol 1): Self-Defence Against Non-State Actors* (CUP 2019).

Max Byrne, 'Consent and the Use of Force: An Examination of "Intervention by Invitation" as a Basis for US Drone Strikes in Pakistan, Somalia and Yemen' (2016) 3(1) *Journal on the Use of Force and International Law*.

Meryl Demunyck and Gijs Weijenberg, 'The Upcoming SADC Intervention: A New Way Ahead to Combat Terrorism in Mozambique?' <https://icct.nl/publication/the-upcoming-sadc-intervention-a-new-way-ahead-to-combat-terrorism-in-mozambique/>.

Michael Byers, 'Terrorism, the Use of Force and Self-Defence after 11 September' (2002) 16 *International Relations*.

Michael P Scharf, 'How the War against ISIS Changed International Law' (2016) 48 *Case Western Reserve Journal of International Law*.

Michael Walzer, *Just and Unjust Wars: A Moral Argument with Historical Illustrations* (5th edn, Basic Books 1997).

Michael Wood, 'International Law and the Use of Force: What Happens in Practice?' (2013) 53 *Indian Journal of International Law*.

Milena Sterio, 'Humanitarian Intervention Post-Syria: A Grotian Moment?' (2014) 20 *ILSA Journal of International and Comparative Law*.

Olivier Corten and Vaios Koutroulis, 'The *Jus Cogens* Status of the Prohibition on the Use of Force: What Is Its Scope and Why Does It Matter?' in Dire Tladi (ed), *Peremptory Norms of General International Law (Jus Cogens): Disquisitions and Disputations* (Brill 2021).

Oscar Schachter, 'The Extraterritorial Use of Force against Terrorist Bases' (1989) 11 *Houston Journal of International Law*.

Peter D Danchin, 'Things Fall Apart: The Concept of Collective Security in International Law' in Peter D Danchin and Horst Fischer (eds), *United Nations Reform and the New Collective Security* (CUP 2010).

Peter Fabricius, 'SADC Grapples with Response While Mercenaries, Energy Companies and Civilians Quit Mozambique's Islamic State Crisis' *Daily Maverick* (1 April 2021).

'Principles of International Law on the Use of Force by States in Self-Defence' *Chatham House* (2005) <www.chathamhouse.org/sites/files/chathamhouse/public/Research/International%20Law/ilpforce.doc>.

Rich Mashimbye, 'Terrorism, Insurgency, and Regional Stability: The Case of Mozambique' (2022) 17 *International Journal of African Renaissance Studies*.

SADC, 'Communiqué of the Extraordinary Summit of SADC Heads of State and Government' (23 June 2021).

Statement by the Secretary Defence in the UK House of Commons (25 March 1999).

Statement of the Permanent Mission of the Republic of El Salvador on behalf of the Community of Latin American and Caribbean States (CELAC) during the United Nations' Special Committee on the Charter of the United Nations and the Strengthening of the Role of Organisation, New York (20–28 February 2018) <https://celac.rree.gob.sv/wp-content/uploads/2018/02/Statement-CELAC-Charter-Committee-Feb-2018.pdf>.

Theresa Reinold, 'State Weakness, Irregular Warfare, and the Right to Self-Defence Post 9/11' (2011) 105 *American Journal of International Law*.

Tiyanjana Maluwa, 'African State Practice and the Formation of Some Peremptory Norms of General International Law' in Dire Tladi (ed), *Peremptory Norms of General International Law (Jus Cogens)* (Brill 2021).

UN Doc. S/2014/695 (23 September 2014).

UN Doc. S/2015/221 (31 March 2015).
UN Doc. S/2015/563 (24 July 2015).
UN Doc. S/2015/693 (9 September 2015).
UN Doc. S/2015/946 (10 December 2015).
UN Doc. S/PRST/2004/44 (19 November 2994).
UN Doc. S/PRST/2004/7 (25 March 2004).
UN Doc. S/PRST/2007/7 (28 March 2007).
UN Doc. S/PRST/2020/11 (4 December 2020).
UN Doc. S/PV.3988 (24 March 1999).
UN Doc. SC/143/71 (4 December 2020).
UN, 'United Nations, African Union Launch Joint Task Force on Peace and Security' (25 September 2010) <www.un.org/press/en/2010/sg2166.doc.htm>.
Vienna Convention on the Law of Treaties (1969) <https://treaties.un.org/Pages/showDetails.aspx?objid=080000028003902f&clang=_en>.

16 Revisiting the African Union's right to intervene (militarily) 20 years on and the conflict in Mozambique

A missed opportunity?

Ntombizozuko Dyani-Mhango

16.1 Introduction

The African Union (AU)[1] as a founding principle codifies the right to intervene in a member state's territorial affairs in cases of grave circumstances involving crimes against humanity, war crimes and genocide.[2] This chapter revisits the AU's right to intervention in light of the conflict in Cabo Delgado in Mozambique and the 20th anniversary of the existence of the AU. Reports suggest that the conflict in Cabo Delgado is a consequence of an Islamic militant group's violent attacks in that region since 2017.[3] The proposal is that the atrocities committed constitute war crimes and crimes against humanity.[4] The reports include incidents of torture;[5] the killing of civilians;[6] and the degrading and inhuman treatment of women.[7] This chapter explores the possibility of an intervention by the AU in the Cabo Delgado conflict in terms of article 4(h) of the AU Constitutive Act.

The Constitutive Act does not define what the right to intervene entails. Nevertheless, from the outset the discussion in this chapter proposes the right to intervene as manifested in the use of force – it is military intervention. Article 4(h) of the Constitutive Act read with article 13 of the AU Protocol Relating to the Establishment of the Peace and Security Council of the AU (PSC Protocol)[8] complements this understanding in that it establishes the African Standby Force to support the AU Peace and Security Council (PSC)[9] in the performance of its functions, which include the implementation of the right to intervene.[10] The African Standby Force is constituted of civilian and military components[11] and '[f]or each operation undertaken by the African Standby Force', a force commander is appointed.[12] The role of the PSC is discussed later in this chapter.

This chapter revisits the AU's right to intervene in the following ways. Firstly, it revisits the meaning of the right to intervene and clarifies the view that it constitutes a military intervention. In the same vein, it discusses the trigger mechanisms initiated to exercise the right to intervene in terms of article 4(h). Second, the chapter considers the applicability of the right to intervene by revisiting the role of the PSC in relation to its failed recommendation to the AU Assembly to intervene militarily in the Burundi conflict and its role in the Cabo Delgado conflict. Lastly, the chapter argues that, since the attacks in the Cabo Delgado conflict are not characterised as

DOI: 10.4324/9781003317647-19

international crimes, military intervention as contemplated in article 4(h) of the Constitutive Act likely is impossible. The chapter concludes that 20 years after its adoption the AU is yet to exercise the right to intervene in terms of article 4(h) of the Constitutive Act.

16.2 Unpacking the right to intervene in terms of article 4(h) of the Constitutive Act

A raft of scholarship discusses the AU's right to intervene in terms of article 4(h) of the Constitutive Act.[13] Article 4(h) of the Constitutive Act states that the AU 'shall function in accordance with . . . the right of the [AU] to intervene in a member state pursuant to a decision of the Assembly in respect of grave circumstances, namely: war crimes, genocide and crimes against humanity'. From this provision, one can ascertain that there are two triggers for the right to intervene to be exercised. First, there must exist grave circumstances that result in war crimes, genocide and crimes against humanity in the territory of a member state and, second, the AU must decide to intervene militarily. This second trigger, though not expressly stated in article 4(h), assumes that the AU Assembly is willing to take the decision and that the resources to enable the intervention will be readily available.[14] These triggers are discussed briefly below.

16.2.1 Grave circumstances to trigger the right to intervene in terms of article 4(h) of the AU Constitutive Act

The Constitutive Act does not define the grave circumstances mentioned in article 4(h), and the AU Assembly has neither defined nor interpreted these circumstances.[15] The assumption is that grave circumstances, such as crimes against humanity, war crimes and genocide, are international crimes as described in the Rome Statute and in other treaties.[16] Indeed, the PSC Protocol confirms that the right to intervene may be exercised in the event of grave circumstances such as crimes against humanity, war crimes and genocide 'as defined in relevant conventions and instruments'.[17] One scholar correctly explains that article 4(h) of the Constitutive Act 'is in line with current international law' as it limits the grave circumstances to international crimes found in the statutes of the *ad hoc* international criminal tribunals for Rwanda[18] and the former Yugoslavia,[19] as well as in the Rome Statute.[20]

International crimes such as war crimes, genocide and crimes against humanity often are referred to as 'core' crimes.[21] State parties to the Rome Statute consider these crimes to be 'unimaginable atrocities that deeply shock the conscience of humanity', as 'grave crimes [that] threaten the peace, security and well-being of the world', and 'the most serious crimes of concern to the international community as a whole [that] must not go unpunished'.[22] These crimes include acts committed 'with an intent to destroy, in whole or in part, a national, ethnical, racial or religious group';[23] acts 'as a part of a widespread or systematic attack directed against any civilian population'[24] and/or 'as part of a plan or policy or as part of a large-scale commission of such crimes'.[25] The seriousness of these crimes has been confirmed by the judgments of the International Criminal Court (ICC)[26] and by the *ad hoc* tribunals.[27] The prohibition of these international crimes is accepted generally as having acquired the status of peremptory norms (*jus cogens*)[28] that may trigger obligations *erga omnes* – that when a state breaches an obligation *erga omnes* it injures every state, including those not directly impacted.[29]

The AU also condemns the occurrence of these crimes in the African region and has called for an end to impunity in relation to the crimes.[30] These international crimes also have been condemned by the United Nations (UN) Security Council (SC), which deems them to constitute a threat to international peace and security.[31] The designation of a threat to international peace and security is significant since it triggers action by the Security Council, which has the primary responsibility to maintain international peace and security.[32] Article 39 of the UN Charter provides that '[t]he Security Council shall determine the existence of any threat to the peace, breach of peace, or act of aggression and shall make recommendations, or decide what measures shall be taken in accordance with articles 41 and 42, to maintain or restore international peace and security'.

Therefore, it is not surprising that the AU member states include a prohibition on these crimes in the legal instruments[33] and incorporate them in the trigger mechanisms for exercising the right to intervene.[34]

16.2.2 The decision of the AU Assembly to intervene in a member state

The AU Assembly constitutes the supreme organ of the AU[35] and represents all heads of state and/or heads of government of the AU member states.[36] The ultimate decision to exercise the right to intervene in the territory of an AU member state lies with the AU Assembly. The Constitutive Act does not stipulate how reaching this decision takes place; however, it confers on the AU the power to determine its own Rules of Procedure.[37] The Rules of Procedure have been adopted, but do not articulate a process for the AU Assembly to consider when making the decision to use force. Rule 4(1)(e) of the Rules of Procedure merely confirms that the AU Assembly has the power to 'decide on intervention in a member state in respect of grave circumstances, namely, war crimes, genocide and crimes against humanity'.[38]

The AU Assembly takes decisions by means of consensus or with a two-thirds majority vote if they fail to reach such a consensus in relation to substantive matters.[39] For procedural matters the AU Assembly votes by way of a simple majority.[40] The AU Assembly Rules of Procedure differentiate between binding and non-binding decisions.[41] The regulations and directives are binding,[42] whereas recommendations, declarations, resolutions and opinions are not binding.[43] An argument could be made that the decision for a military intervention in a member state in terms of article 4(h) of the Constitutive Act constitutes a directive that is binding.[44] The AU Assembly is yet to decide on the modalities regarding the exercise of the right to intervene pursuant to article 4(h) of the Constitutive Act.

A question that arises from studying article 4(h) is whether the right to intervene (militarily) in the Constitutive Act can be equated to the doctrine of humanitarian intervention and the concept of the responsibility to protect (R2P). The next section examines this question.

16.3 Making practical sense of the exercise of the right to intervene within the African Peace and Security Architecture

As explained earlier, the AU Assembly's decision to intervene depends on a PSC recommendation.[45] The PSC is the chief organ responsible for implementing and carrying out intervention in the region.[46] The PSC, therefore, forms part of the African Peace and Security Architecture (APSA) alongside other organs as regulated by the PSC Protocol. The other organs within the APSA are the Chairperson of the AU Commission;[47] the Panel of the Wise;[48] the Early Warning System;[49] the African Standby Force;[50] and the AU Peace Fund[51] established to support the PSC. The PSC Protocol requires the PSC to seek close cooperation with the African Commission on Human and Peoples' Rights (African Commission) in all matters relevant to its objectives and mandate, and the African Commission is to bring to the attention of the PSC any information relevant to the objectives and mandate of the PSC.[52] These organs are discussed in detail elsewhere.[53] This chapter focuses on the role of the PSC in light of recent developments on the right to intervene and in relation to the Cabo Delgado situation. The PSC is constituted by 15 AU member states, 10 of which are appointed for a term of two years and five are appointed for a term of three years.[54] The PSC acts on behalf of the state parties to the PSC Protocol.[55] Currently, the PSC Protocol is ratified by 53 of 55 AU members. The exceptions are the Cape Verde and South Sudan. Mozambique is a state party to the PSC Protocol.[56]

The PSC has only once recommended military intervention in terms of article 4(h).[57] The next section turns to that discussion.

16.4 The PSC and the recommendation to the AU Assembly of military intervention in Burundi

The Burundi situation concerned 'the use of violence in the pursuit of political objectives'.[58] The preliminary findings of the African Commission, after having conducted a fact-finding mission to Burundi during this period, reported 'arbitrary killings and targeted assassinations, arbitrary arrests and detentions, acts of torture, suspension and arbitrary closure of some civil society organisations and media'.[59] The PSC decided 'to authorise the deployment of an African Prevention and Protection Mission in Burundi (MAPROBU)'[60] with a proviso that should Burundi not accept the deployment of MAPROBU, it would recommend to the AU Assembly the exercise of the right to intervene in terms of article 4(h) of the Constitutive Act.[61] Burundi rejected the demand; it accepted the deployment of MAPROBU.[62]

It is reported that this issue was deliberated in a closed session during the AU Assembly's Ordinary Meeting in January 2016, where the AU Assembly rejected the PSC recommendation.[63] Instead, the AU Assembly expressed 'its deep concern about the continuing political impasse in Burundi, and the level of insecurity and violence which resulted in an acute humanitarian and economic crisis, including internal displacement of people and refugee flows into the neighbouring countries'.[64] The AU decided 'to dispatch a high-level delegation of Heads of State and Government of the Assembly to Burundi to consult with the government as well as other Burundian actors on the inclusive dialogue and the contribution of the AU to the stabilisation and resolution of the crisis in Burundi'.[65] It is not clear why the AU Assembly chose this form of intervention as opposed to following the PSC recommendation for military intervention in terms of article 4(h) of the Constitutive Act. However, this decision is not unusual; the AU is slow to decide, especially in relation to intrastate conflicts in the region.[66]

The AU Assembly's rejection of the PSC recommendation to invoke article 4(h) of the Constitutive Act is a cause for comment because of the subsequent election of Burundi as a member of the PSC for a two-year term despite the reported atrocities occurring in its territory at the time – and the subsequent decision by the PSC.[67] Certain considerations must be met by the AU Assembly before it elects a member state to the PSC.[68] These include '(a) the commitment to uphold the principles of the [AU];[69] (b) contribution to the promotion and maintenance of peace and security in Africa;[70] [and] (g) respect for constitutional governance . . . as well as the rule of law and human rights'.[71]

This move by the AU Assembly confirmed the previous observation that the AU Assembly lacks the will to act and to call its leaders to order.[72] A scrutiny of the AU Assembly's decisions and resolutions up to July 2012 leads to three observations: The AU Assembly strongly rejects an unconstitutional change of government on the continent; the AU Assembly is constrained by a fear of member states criticising one another;[73] and the AU Assembly is reluctant to accept external intervention by the international community, as is evidenced by the Libya situation in 2011.[74] Although the AU Assembly has taken a decision to become involved in a situation in the territory of some of its member states, this decision was not taken in the exercise of the right to intervene in terms of article 4(h) of the Constitutive Act.[75]

This next section considers the involvement of the AU in the Cabo Delgado conflict.

16.5 The Cabo Delgado conflict and the AU's right to exercise the right to intervene: an opportunity missed?

This chapter argues that the atrocities reported to have taken place in Cabo Delgado amount to international crimes as contemplated in article 4(h) of the Constitutive Act. It should be noted that the atrocities that are reported to have occurred in Cabo Delgado are the same as those reported to have occurred in Burundi in 2015, as discussed earlier. Notably, the PSC has not made a similar recommendation to the AU Assembly for military intervention as it did in the case of Burundi. Despite making no recommendation, the PSC has condemned the atrocities in Cabo Delgado.[76] A further aspect noted in respect of the Cabo Delgado situation is that neither the AU Assembly nor the PSC references the international crimes being committed in the region, although such crimes have been reported. Is this an opportunity missed to invoke article 4(h) intervention? A conclusion is difficult based on two factors. First, the PSC and the AU Assembly have characterised the attacks in Cabo Delgado as acts of terrorism;[77] a characterisation that makes impossible a PSC recommendation of military intervention to the AU Assembly. Second, the AU Assembly and the PSC leave it to the Southern African Development Community (SADC)[78] to deal with the conflict in Cabo Delgado. The Extraordinary SADC Summit of Heads of State and Government approved the SADC Mission in Mozambique (SAMIM) on 23 June 2021[79] to act as a 'regional response to Mozambique to combat terrorism and acts of violent extremism'.[80] SAMIM was deployed to Mozambique on 15 July 2021.[81] The Summit approved the extension of SAMIM in August 2022.[82] However, the legal basis upon which the SAMIM is acting does not reflect that it is acting on behalf of the AU under article 4(h).

When the PSC endorsed the SADC's deployment of SAMIM in Cabo Delgado, it referenced article 4(j) of the Constitutive Act which gives an AU member state an option 'to request intervention from the [AU] in order to restore peace and security' in its territory.[83] In addition, the decisions and statements by the PSC state that the SADC Summit deployed SAMIM as part of the AU's Peace and Security Architecture. Indeed, the PSC, acting under its *article 7 of the PSC Protocol* powers, endorsed SADC's intervention in Cabo Delgado and 'specifically commend[ed] the collective leadership demonstrated by SADC in committing resources and deploying SAMIM, *within the framework of [the African Standby Force]*'.[84] The AU Assembly decisions agree.[85]

However, it is difficult to ascertain from the available SADC Summit Communiqués or statements that the decision to establish the SAMIM was taken in line with article 4(j) of the Constitutive Act, even though the government of Mozambique consented to SAMIM assisting in its quest to counter the terrorism acts in Cabo Delgado.[86] In fact, the SADC statements are silent on the legal basis of deploying the SAMIM. It is also clear that SAMIM is not deployed in terms of article 4(h) of the Constitutive Act because no decision has been taken by the AU Assembly under this provision. It must be recalled that the endorsements from the PSC and the AU Assembly came only about six months after the deployment of SAMIM. A convincing argument, to which the discussion in this chapter is aligned, is that the SADC Summit did not need authorisation from either the UN Security Council or the AU Assembly as the SADC Summit acted in terms of article 52 of the UN Charter.[87]

16.6 Conclusion

This chapter has revisited the meaning of the right to intervene and clarified that the right is manifested through military intervention. In this regard, the chapter discussed the mechanisms that trigger an exercise of the right to intervene in terms of article 4(h). Second, the chapter considered the applicability of the right to intervene by revisiting the role of the PSC considering the failed recommendation to intervene militarily in the Burundi conflict and its role in the Cabo Delgado conflict. Lastly, the chapter argued that, since the attacks in Cabo Delgado were not characterised as international crimes, it was impossible to militarily intervene in terms of article 4(h) of the Constitutive Act. The chapter concluded that the AU is yet to exercise the right to intervene in terms of article 4(h) of the Constitutive Act 20 years after its adoption.

Further research is needed to clarify the relationship between the AU and the RECs, especially in relation to the issues of subsidiarity and conflict management in the region. Clarification will enable proper coordination and an avoidance of the contradictory statements by the AU Assembly, the PSC and the RECs.

Notes

1 The AU was established by article 2 of the Constitutive Act of the African Union (adopted 11 July 2000, entered into force 26 May 2001) 2158 UNTS 3 (Constitutive Act). The Constitutive Act was adopted at the 36th ordinary session of the Assembly of Heads of State and Government of the Organisation of African Unity (OAU) on 11 July 2000. See AU Doc. ASS/AU/Decl. 2 (I) (10 July 2002).

2 Article 4(h) of the Constitutive Act states that the AU 'shall function in accordance with . . . the right of the [AU] to intervene in a member state pursuant to a decision of the Assembly in respect of grave circumstances, namely: war crimes, genocide and crimes against humanity'.

3 See Peter Bofin, 'The Conflict in Cabo Delgado, Mozambique – A Five-Year Summary' *Daily Maverick* (20 December 2022); and Liesl Louw-Vaudran 'Coordination: Key to the Success of African Solutions for Mozambique' *Institute for Security Studies* (2022).

4 See, for example, articles 7(1) and 8(2) of the Rome Statute of the International Criminal Court (adopted 17 July 1998, entered into force 1 July 2002) 2187 UNTS 3 (Rome Statute), which deal with crimes against humanity and war crimes respectively: '7(1) (e) Other *serious violations of the laws and customs applicable in armed conflicts not of an international character*, within the established framework of international law, namely, any of the following acts: (i) *Intentionally directing attacks against the civilian population as such or against individual civilians* not taking direct part in hostilities; . . . (k) *Other inhumane acts of a similar character intentionally causing great suffering, or serious injury to body or to mental or physical health.*' See also articles 8(2)(c)–(e).

5 Amnesty international reports of torture perpetrated by all parties to the conflict. See Amnesty International, 'Mozambique: Civilians Killed as War Crimes Committed by Armed Group, Government Forces, and Private Military Contractors – New Report' (2 March 2021).

6 Ibid.

7 See ACHPR Res. ACHPR/Res 477 (LXVIII) 2021.

8 AU, Protocol Relating to the Establishment of the Peace and Security Council of the African Union (adopted 9 July 2002, entered into force on 26 December 2003) 3264 UNTS 1, after 27 ratifications (PSC Protocol).

9 Article 2(1) of the PSC Protocol established the PSC 'as a standing decision-making organ for the prevention, management, and resolutions of conflicts'.

10 Article 13(3)(c) read with article 6(d) of the PSC Protocol, which deals with the functions of the PSC including 'peace support operations and intervention, pursuant to article 4(h) and (j) of the Constitutive Act'.

11 Article 13(1) PSC Protocol.

12 Article 13(6) PSC Protocol.

13 See, for example, Tiyanjana Maluwa, 'Reassessing Aspects of the Contribution of African States to the Development of International Law through African Regional Multilateral Treaties' (2020) 41 *Michigan Journal of International Law* 327; Tiyanjana Maluwa, 'African State Practice and the Formation of Some Peremptory Norms of General International Law' in Dire Tladi (ed), *Peremptory Norms of General International Law (Jus*

Cogens): Disquisitions and Disputations (Brill 2021) 259; Tiyanjana Maluwa, 'The Constitutive Act of the African Union and Institution-Building in Postcolonial Africa' (2003) 16 *Leiden Journal of International Law* 157; Dan Kuwali, *The Responsibility to Protect: Implementation of Article 4(h) Intervention* (Martinus Nijhoff 2011); Dan Kuwali, 'Art 4(h) + R2p: Towards a Doctrine of Persuasive Prevention to End Mass Atrocity Crimes' (2008–2009) *Interdisciplinary Journal of Human Rights Law* 55; Dan Kuwali, 'The Architecture of AU Intervention: Institutions for Implementation of Article 4(h) of the AU Act' (2008) *African Yearbook of International Humanitarian Law* 100; Ntombizozuko Dyani-Mhango, 'Reflections on the African Union's Right to Intervene' (2012) 38 (1) *Brooklyn Journal of International Law* 1; Ben Kioko, 'The Right of Intervention Under the African Union's Constitutive Act: From Non-Interference to Non-Intervention' (2003) 85 (852) *International Review of the Red Cross* 807; Kithure Kindiki, 'The Normative and Institutional Framework of the African Union Relating to the Protection of Human Rights and the Maintenance of International Peace and Security: A Critical Appraisal' (2003) 3 *African Human Rights Law Journal* 97; Jeremy Sarkin, 'Humanitarian Intervention and the Responsibility to Protect in Africa' in John Akokpari and Daniel Shea Zibler (eds), *Africa's Human Rights Architecture* (Fanele 2008) 45; A Abass and M Baderin, 'Towards Effective Collective Security and Human Rights Protection in Africa: An Assessment of the Constitutive Act of the New African Union' (2002) 49 *Netherlands International Law Review* 1.

14 See Dyani-Mhango (n 13) 46, who reflects that '[l]ack of resources and unwillingness by member states to contribute finances and troops hamper the work of the AU [and render the AU's missions] failures'.

15 See, for example, AU Doc. Doc EX. CL/670 (XIX), and AU Doc. Assembly/AU/Dec.372 (XVII) para 2, reiterating 'its commitment to fight impunity in conformity with the provisions of *Article 4(h) of the Constitutive Act of the African Union*;' and AU Doc. EX. CL/640 (XVIII), AU Doc. Assembly/AU/Dec.341 (XVI) para 2, using the same wording (emphasis added).

16 Tiyanjana Maluwa, 'The OAU/African Union and International Law: Mapping New Boundaries or Revisiting Old Terrain?' (2004) 98 *ASIL Proceedings* 232, 236.

17 Article 7 PSC Protocol.

18 The International Criminal Tribunal for Rwanda (ICTR) was established for the 'Prosecution of Persons Responsible for Genocide and Other Serious Violations of International Humanitarian Law Committed in the Territory of Rwanda and Rwandan Citizens Responsible for Genocide and Other Violations in the Territory of Neighbouring States, between 1 Jan 1994 and 31 Dec 1994'; SC Res. 955 (1994), annex.

19 The International Criminal Tribunal for the former Yugoslavia (ICTY) was established to prosecute 'Persons Responsible for Serious Violations of International Humanitarian Law Committed in the Territory of the Former Yugoslavia since 1991'; SC Res. 827 (1993). The Statute of the ICTY is contained in UN Doc. S/25704, Annex (3 May 1993).

20 See Maluwa (n 16) 236.

21 Robert Cryer, Darryl Robinson and Sergey Vasiliev, *An Introduction to International Criminal Law and Procedure* (4th edn, CUP 2019) 4. It should be noted that the crime of aggression found in article 8*bis* of the Rome Statute is also considered a core crime.

22 See paras 2, 3 and 4 of the Preamble to the Rome Statute.

23 See article 6 of the Rome Statute, referring to the crime of genocide.

24 See article 7 of the Rome Statute, referring to crimes against humanity.

25 See article 8 of the Rome Statute, referring to war crimes.

26 *Prosecutor v Thomas Lubanga Dyilo*, ICC-01/04–01/06 (Trial Chamber Judgment) 14 March 2012; *Prosecutor v Bosco Ntaganda*, CC-01/04–02/06–2359 (Trial Chamber Judgment), 8 July 2019; and *Prosecutor v Dominic Ongwen,* ICC-02/04–01/15 (Trial Chamber Judgment), 4 February 2021.

27 For example, see *Prosecutor v Akayesu*, Case No ICTR-96–13-T, Judgment, 2 September 1998; *Prosecutor v Musema* (Judgment and Sentence), Case No ICTR-96–13-A, 27

January 2000; *Prosecutor v Rutaganda*, Case No ICTR-96–3-T, 6 December 1999; *Prosecutor v Nahimana and Others* (Appeal Judgment), Case No ICTR-99–52-A, 28 November 2007; and *Prosecutor v Nyiramasuhuko and Others*, Case No ICTR-98–42-T, 24 June 2011. Also see, for example, *Prosecutor v Tadic, Opinion and Judgment,* Case No IT-94–1, 7 May 1997; *Prosecutor v Delalic and Others* Judgment 16 November 1998, Case No IT-96–21; *Prosecutor v Kunarac and Others* Judgment, 22 February 2001, Case No IT-96–23; and *Prosecutor v Furundzija*, Case No IT-95–17/1, Judgment, 10 December 1998.

28 See, for example, *Prosecutor v Kupreškić and Others*, Judgment, Case No IT-95–16, 14 January 2000, para 520 confirming that 'most norms of international humanitarian law, especially those prohibiting war crimes, crimes against humanity and genocide, are also peremptory norms of international law or *jus cogens*'; and Draft conclusion 2 [3(1)], Annex, the Draft Conclusions on Peremptory Norms of General International Law (*Jus Cogens*) adopted on first reading, Report of the international Law Commission, 71st session, General Assembly Official Records (A/74/10) (2019), defining a peremptory norm as 'a norm [of general international law] accepted and recognised by the international community of states as a whole as a norm from which no derogation is permitted and which can be modified only by a subsequent norm of general international law having the same character'.

29 The obligations *erga omnes* doctrine, which was introduced in the *obiter dictum* of *Barcelona Traction Light and Power Co Ltd (Belgium v Spain)* 1970 ICJ Rep 1970 3, 32.

30 See, for example, AU Doc. Assembly/AU/14 (XI), AU Doc. Assembly/AU/Dec.199(XIII) para 3, which recognised the importance of the principle of universal jurisdiction 'to ensure that individuals who commit grave offences such as war crimes and crimes against humanity do not do so with impunity and are brought to justice, which is in line with Article 4(h) of the Constitutive Act'; AU Doc. EX. CL/670 (XIX), AU Doc. Assembly/AU/Dec.372 (XVII) para 2, reiterating 'its commitment to fight impunity in conformity with the provisions of *Article 4(h) of the Constitutive Act of the African Union*'; and AU Doc. EX. CL/640 (XVIII), AU Doc. Assembly/AU/Dec.341 (XVI) para 2, using the same wording (emphasis added).

31 See, for example, SC Res. 1325 (2000), para 11, emphasising 'the responsibility of all States to put an end to impunity and to prosecute those responsible for genocide, crimes against humanity, and war crimes including those relating to sexual and other violence against women and girls, and in this regard stresses the need to exclude these crimes, where feasible from amnesty provisions'; and SC Res. 1674 (2006), 'Reaffirms the provisions of paragraphs 138 and 139 of the 2005 World Summit Outcome Document regarding the responsibility to protect populations from genocide, war crimes, ethnic cleansing and crimes against humanity'.

32 Article 24(1) of the Charter of the United Nations (adopted 26 June 1945, entered into force 24 October 1945) 1 UNTS XVI (UN Charter) confers the primary responsibility to maintain international peace and security to the Security Council and acts on behalf of all UN member states.

33 The Protocol to the African Charter on Human and Peoples' Rights on the Rights of Women in Africa (adopted 1 July 2003, entered into force 25 November 2005) (Maputo Protocol). Article 11(3) considers 'all forms of violence, rape and other forms of sexual violence' committed against asylum seeking women, refugees, returnees, and internally displaced persons to constitute 'war crimes, genocide and/or crimes against humanity'.

34 See the AU Convention on the Protection and Assistance of the Internally Displaced Persons in Africa (adopted 22 October 2009, entered into force 6 December 2012). Article 8(1) confirms that '[t]he [AU] shall have the right to intervene in a Member State pursuant to a decision of the Assembly in accordance with Article 4(h) of the Constitutive Act'.

35 Article 6(2) AU Constitutive Act.

36 Article 6(1) AU Constitutive Act.

37 Article 8 Constitutive Act.

38 See Rule 4(1)(e) of the AU Assembly Rules of Procedure.

39 Article 7(1) of the AU Constitutive Act and Rule 18 of the AU Assembly Rules of Procedure.
40 Article 7(1) Constitutive Act.
41 See Rule 33(1) of the AU Assembly Rules of Procedure.
42 See Rules 33(1)(a) and (b) and 34(2) of the AU Assembly Rules of Procedure.
43 See Rule 33(1)(c) of the AU Assembly Rules of Procedure.
44 See Rule 33(2) of the AU Assembly Rules of Procedure that states that non-compliance with the AU Regulations and Directives attracts sanctions in terms of article 23(2) of the Constitutive Act.
45 Article 7(1)(e) PSC Protocol.
46 Article 6 PSC Protocol.
47 PSC Protocol.
48 Ibid.
49 Article 12 PSC Protocol.
50 Article 13 PSC Protocol.
51 Article 21 PSC Protocol.
52 Article 19 PSC Protocol.
53 See Dyani-Mhango (n 13) 24–28.
54 Article 5(1) PSC Protocol.
55 Article 7(2) PSC Protocol. Fifty-three out of 55 AU member states have ratified the PSC Protocol. See <https://au.int/en/treaties/protocol-relating-establishment-peace-and-security-council-african-union>.
56 Mozambique ratified the PSC Protocol on 20 May 2003.
57 AU PSC Communiqué of 17 December 2015, para 13(1)(c)(iv).
58 Ibid, para 4. See also AU PSC Press Statement of 6 August 2015, AU Doc. PSC/BR/PR.(DXXXI), where the PSC 'expressed deep concern over the deterioration of the security situation in Burundi marked by political assassinations and increased violence'.
59 Ibid, para 5.
60 Ibid, para 13(a)(ii).
61 Ibid, para 13(i)(c)(iv).
62 See 'Burundi: We Will Not Allow Foreign Troops to Enter' *Al Jazeera News* (21 December 2015); James Butty, 'Burundi Rejects AU Force Deployment' *VOA* (23 December 2015).
63 See Occasional Paper by Solomon Dersso, 'To Intervene or Not to Intervene? An Inside View of the AU's Decision-Making on Article 4(h) and Burundi' *World Peace Foundation* (16 February 2016), noting that '[w]hile the meeting was open for two agenda items on South Sudan and terrorism in Africa, the situation in Burundi was considered in closed session'. See also, generally, AU Assembly, 'Decisions, Declarations and Resolutions' 26th ordinary session, 30–31 January 2016, Addis Ababa, Ethiopia, Assembly/AU/Dec.588–604(XXVI); Assembly/AU/Decl.1–2(XXVI); Assembly/AU/Res.1(XXVI). See also Ty McCormick, 'The Burundi Intervention That Wasn't' *Foreign Policy* (2 February 2016).
64 AU Doc. Assembly/AU/2(XXVI), and AU Doc. Assembly/AU/Dec.598(XXVI), para 13.
65 Ibid. For further discussion on the situation in Burundi and the subsequent failure of the AU Assembly to exercise article 4(h) of the Constitutive Act, see, Nina Wilén, 'The African Union and Coercive Diplomacy: The Case of Burundi' (2018) 56 (4) *Journal of Modern African Studies* 673.
66 See Thabo Mbeki, 'How the West Won Control Over Africa' *The Herald* (5 April 2011), arguing that when dealing with the situations in Tunisia, Egypt and Libya, African leaders were 'unable to decide how [they] should respond [and] instinctively resolved that [they] had no choice but to stand back and wait'.
67 See AU Doc. Doc EX.CL/954(XXVIII), and AU Doc. Assembly/AU/Dec.594(XXVI), para 3.
68 See article 5(2) PSC Protocol.

69 Article 5(2)(a) PSC Protocol.
70 Article 5(2)(b) PSC Protocol.
71 Article 5(2)(g) PSC Protocol.
72 See Dyani-Mhango (n 13) 1, especially 28–48.
73 Dyani-Mhango (n 13) 30.
74 Dyani-Mhango (n 13) 44–46.
75 Ibid, 44.
76 See AU PSC Communiqué of 5 November 2020, para 7, where the PSC 'Expresses grave concerns on the growing threat to peace and security in Mozambique posed by the incessant terrorist attacks in the northern province of Cabo Delgado resulting in the loss of lives and dire humanitarian crisis; and AU PSC Communiqué of 31 January 2022, para 1.
77 See, for example, AU, Statement of HE Mr Moussa Faki Mahamat, Chairperson of the African Union Commission, on the terrorist attacks in Mozambique, 31 March 2021 (stating that the Chairperson of the AU Commission 'condemns in the strongest terms the *terrorist attacks* in Cabo Delgado region'); and AU Doc. Assembly/AU/Dec. 815(XXXV), para 19, ('[affirming] the AU solidarity with the people of Mozambique in their campaign against *terrorism* and *violent extremism* in the northern province of Cabo Delgado') (emphasis added).
78 SADC is one of the regional economic communities (RECs) recognised by the AU in terms of the OAU, Protocol to the Treaty Establishing the African Community (1991) 30 ILM 1241. It was established by the Declaration and Treaty Establishing SADC (SADC Treaty). See article 2(1) of the SADC Treaty.
79 SADC Communiqué of 23 June 2021, para 7.
80 SADC, 'SADC Mission in Mozambique (SAMIM) in Brief' (10 December 2021).
81 Ibid.
82 SADC Communiqué of 17 August 2022.
83 See AU PSC Communiqué of 31 January 2022 (n 140), Preamble, para 1, '[recalling] the relevant provisions of the Constitutive Act, *especially article 4 (j)* and the [PSC Protocol], particularly Article 13 (g) concerning the deployment of peace support missions and the establishment of the African Standby Force (ASF)'. However, there is no evidence that Mozambique invoked this provision when it requested SADC assistance.
84 AU PSC Communiqué of 31 January 2022, paras 2 and 5 (emphasis added); and AU PSC Communiqué of 7 November 2022, para 4 which 'Acknowledges the collective leadership demonstrated by SADC for its continued commitment towards the deployment of SAMIM, within the framework of the ASF, to neutralise the terrorist threat and restore state authority in Cabo Delgado' (emphasis added).
85 AU Doc. Assembly/AU/Dec. 815(XXXV) '[commends] the Southern African Development Community (SADC) for the prompt deployment of SADC Mission in Mozambique (SAMIM), within the framework of the African Standby Force (ASF)'; and AU Doc. Assembly/AU/Dec.842(XXXVI), where the AU Assembly '[commends] the Southern African Development Community (SADC) for its deployment of troops in Cabo Delgado Province in Mozambique; [and calls] for enhanced cooperation and coordination between the SADC and the AU Commission through regular information sharing, as well as joint engagements in support of the Southern African Development Community Mission in Mozambique (SAMIM) operations to further strengthen the effectiveness of the mission'.
86 See also 'Resolving the African Standby Force's identity crisis' *Institute for Security Studies* (22 June 2022), arguing that '[t]his does not conform with the PSC Protocol, which requires the AU to be in full command and control of ASF missions through a special representative, force commander and police commissioner appointed by the AU Commission chairperson. The absence of clarity on the type and scope of ASF missions has resulted in a crisis of identity for the ASF.'

87 See Marko Svicevic, 'The Legal Status of SADC's Mission in Cabo Delgado' *ACCORD* (27 October 2021), arguing that the SAMIM deployment neither falls under collective self-defence in terms of article 51 of the UN Charter nor collective enforcement under article 53 of the UN Charter and that, therefore, there is no need for authorisation. Article 52(1) of the UN Charter among others recognises the 'existence of regional arrangements or agencies for dealing with such matters relating to the maintenance of international peace and security'.

Bibliography

ACHPR, 'Press Statement on Reports of Acts of Brutality on the Dead Involving Troops of the Southern Africa Development Community' (15 January 2023) <https://achpr.au.int/en/news/press-releases/2023-01-15/press-statement-reports-acts-brutality-dead-involving-troops>.

Ademola Abass and Mashood A Baderin, 'Towards Effective Collective Security and Human Rights Protection in Africa: An Assessment of the Constitutive Act of the New African Union' (2002) 49 *Netherlands International Law Review*.

African Commission on Human and Peoples' Rights, 'Resolution on the Situation of Military Instability in Northern Mozambique', *ACHPR/Res 477* (LXVIII) 2021, <https://achpr.au.int/en/adopted-resolutions/477-resolution-situation-military-instability-northern-mozambique-ach>.

Amnesty International, 'Mozambique: Civilians Killed as War Crimes Committed by Armed Group, Government Forces, and Private Military Contractors – New Report' *Amnesty International News* (2 March 2021) <www.amnesty.org/en/latest/news/2021/03/mozambique-civilians-killed-as-war-crimes-committed-by-armed-group-government-forces-and-private-military-contractors-new-report/>.

Amrita Kapur, '"Humanity as the A and [Omega] of Sovereignty": Four Replies to Anne Peters' (2009) 20 *European Journal of International Law* 560.

African Union Convention on the Protection and Assistance of the Internally Displaced Persons in Africa (2009) <https://au.int/en/treaties/african-union-convention-protection-and-assistance-internally-displaced-persons-africa>.

AU, 'The Common African Position on the Proposed Reform of the United Nations' (Ezulwini Consensus), AU Doc. Ext./EX. CL/2 (VII).

AU, 'The Durban Declaration in Tribute to the Organisation of African Unity and on the Launching of the African Union' AU Doc. ASS/AU/Decl. 2 (I) (10 July 2002).

AU, 'List of Countries Which Have Signed, Ratified and Acceded to the Constitutive Act of the African Union' <https://au.int/sites/default/files/treaties/7758-sl-constitutive_act_of_the_african_union_2.pdf>.

AU, 'Rules of Procedure of the Assembly and the Executive Council, Statutes of the Commission and Rules of Procedure of the Permanent Representatives' Council' <https://archives.au.int/handle/123456789/6448>.

AU, 'Statement of HE Mr Moussa Faki Mahamat, Chairperson of the African Union Commission, on the Terrorist Attacks in Mozambique' (31 March 2021) <https://au.int/en/pressreleases/20210331/statement-chairperson-terrorist-attacks-mozambique>.

AU Doc. Assembly/AU/2(XXVI).

AU Doc. Assembly/AU/14 (XI).

AU Doc. Assembly/AU/Dec.199(XIII).

AU Doc. Assembly/AU/Dec.341 (XVI).

AU Doc. Assembly/AU/Dec.372 (XVII).

AU Doc. Assembly/AU/Dec.588–604(XXVI).

AU Doc. Assembly/AU/Dec.594(XXVI).

AU Doc. Assembly/AU/Dec.598(XXVI).

AU Doc. Assembly/AU/Dec.815(XXXV).

AU Doc. Assembly/AU/Dec.842(XXXVI).
AU Doc. Assembly/AU/Decl.1–2(XXVI).
AU Doc. Assembly/AU/Res.1(XXVI).
AU Doc. EX. CL/640 (XVIII).
AU Doc. EX. CL/670 (XIX).
AU Doc. EX.CL/954(XXVIII).
AU PSC Communiqué of 17 December 2015.
AU PSC Communiqué of 5 November 2020.
AU PSC Communiqué of 31 January 2022.
AU PSC Communiqué of 7 November 2022.
AU PSC Press Statement of 6 August 2015, AU Doc. PSC/BR/PR.(DXXXI).
Babatunde Fagbayibo, *Transcending Member States: Political and Legal Dynamics of Building Continental Supranationalism in Africa* (Springer 2022).
Barcelona Traction Light and Power Co Ltd (Belgium v Spain), 1970 ICJ Rep 1970.
Ben Kioko, 'The Right of Intervention Under the African Union's Constitutive Act: From Non-Interference to Non-Intervention' (2003) 85 (852) *International Review of the Red Cross.*
'Burundi: We Will Not Allow Foreign Troops to Enter' *Al Jazeera News* (21 December 2015).
Charter of the United Nations (1945) <https://treaties.un.org/Pages/showDetails.aspx?objid=08000002801 7ebb8&clang=_en>.
Constitutive Act of the African Union (2001) <https://treaties.un.org/Pages/showDetails.aspx?objid=0800000280089269&clang=_en>.
Dan Kuwali, 'The Architecture of AU Intervention: Institutions for Implementation of Article 4(h) of the AU Act' (2008) *African Yearbook of International Humanitarian Law* 100.
Dan Kuwali, 'Art 4(h) + R2p: Towards a Doctrine of Persuasive Prevention to End Mass Atrocity Crimes' (2008–2009) 3(1) *Interdisciplinary Journal of Human Rights Law.*
Dan Kuwali, *The Responsibility to Protect: Implementation of Article 4(h) Intervention* (Martinus Nijhoff 2011).
Draft Conclusions on Peremptory Norms of General International Law (*Jus Cogens*) Adopted on First Reading, Report of the international Law Commission, 71st session, General Assembly Official Records (A/74/10) (2019).
James Butty, 'Burundi Rejects AU Force Deployment' *VOA* (23 December 2015).
Jeremy Sarkin, 'Humanitarian Intervention and the Responsibility to Protect in Africa' in John Akokpari and Daniel Shea Zibler (eds), *Africa's Human Rights Architecture* (Fanele 2008).
Kithure Kindiki, 'The Normative and Institutional Framework of the African Union Relating to the Protection of Human Rights and the Maintenance of International Peace and Security: A Critical Appraisal' (2003) 3 *African Human Rights Law Journal.*
Liesl Louw-Vaudran 'Coordination: Key to the Success of African Solutions for Mozambique' *Institute for Security Studies* (2022).
Marko Svicevic, 'The Legal Status of SADC's Mission in Cabo Delgado' *ACCORD* (27 October 2021).
Nina Wilén, 'The African Union and Coercive Diplomacy: The Case of Burundi' (2018) 56 (4) *Journal of Modern African Studies.*
Nsongurua Udombana, 'When Neutrality Is a Sin: The Darfur Crisis and the Crisis of a Humanitarian Intervention in Sudan' (2005) 27 *Human Rights Quarterly.*
Ntombizozuko Dyani-Mhango, 'Reflections on the African Union's Right to Intervene' (2012) 38 (1) *Brooklyn Journal of International Law.*
Owiso Owiso, 'A Cosmopolitan International Law: The Authority of Regional Intergovernmental Organisations to Establish International Criminal Accountability Mechanisms' (PhD thesis, University of Luxembourg, 2022).
Peter Bofin, 'The Conflict in Cabo Delgado, Mozambique – A Five-Year Summary' *Daily Maverick* (20 December 2022).
Prosecutor v Akayesu, Case No ICTR-96–13-T, Judgment, 2 September 1998.
Prosecutor v Bosco Ntaganda, CC-01/04–02/06–2359 (Trial Chamber Judgment), 8 July 2019.

Prosecutor v Delalic and Others Judgment 16 November 1998, Case No IT-96–21.
Prosecutor v Dominic Ongwen, ICC-02/04–01/15 (Trial Chamber Judgment), 4 February 2021.
Prosecutor v Furundzija, Case No IT-95–17/1, Judgment, 10 December 1998.
Prosecutor v Kunarac and Others Judgment, 22 February 2001, Case No IT-96–23.
Prosecutor v Kupreškić and Others, Judgment, Case No IT-95–16, 14 January 2000.
Prosecutor v Musema (Judgment and Sentence), Case No ICTR-96–13-A, 27 January 2000.
Prosecutor v Nahimana and Others (Appeal Judgment), Case No ICTR-99–52-A, 28 November 2007.
Prosecutor v Nyiramasuhuko and Others, Case No ICTR-98–42-T, 24 June 2011.
Prosecutor v Rutaganda, Case No ICTR-96–3-T, 6 December 1999.
Prosecutor v Tadic, Opinion and Judgment, Case No IT-94–1, 7 May 1997.
Prosecutor v Thomas Lubanga Dyilo, ICC-01/04–01/06, (Trial Chamber Judgment) 14 March 2012.
Protocol Relating to the Establishment of the Peace and Security Council of the African Union' (2002) <https://au.int/en/treaties/protocol-relating-establishment-peace-and-security-council-african-union>.
Protocol to the African Charter on Human and Peoples' Rights on the Rights of Women in Africa (2003) <https://au.int/en/treaties/protocol-african-charter-human-and-peoples-rights-rights-women-africa>.
'Resolving the African Standby Force's Identity Crisis' *Institute for Security Studies* (22 June 2022).
Robert Cryer, Darryl Robinson and Sergey Vasiliev, *An Introduction to International Criminal Law and Procedure* (4th edn, CUP 2019).
Rome Statute of the International Criminal Court (1998) <https://treaties.un.org/Pages/showDetails.aspx?objid=0800000280025774&clang=_en >.
SADC Communiqué of 23 June 2021.
SADC Communiqué of 17 August 2022.
SADC, 'Declaration and Treaty Establishing SADC (SADC Treaty)' (1992) <https://www.sadc.int/document/declaration-treaty-sadc-1992#:~:text=On%2017%20August%201992%2C%20the,Development%20Community%2C%20officially%20creating%20SADC.>.
SADC, 'SADC Mission in Mozambique (SAMIM) in Brief' *SADC* (10 December 2021) <www.sadc.int/latest-news/sadc-mission-mozambique-samim-brief>.
SC Res. 1325 (2000).
SC Res. 1674 (2006).
Solomon Dersso, 'To Intervene or Not to Intervene? An Inside View of the AU's Decision-Making on Article 4(h) and Burundi' *World Peace Foundation* (16 February 2016).
Thabo Mbeki, 'How the West Won Control Over Africa' *The Herald* (5 April 2011).
Tiyanjana Maluwa, 'African State Practice and the Formation of Some Peremptory Norms of General International Law' in Dire Tladi (ed) *Peremptory Norms of General International Law (Jus Cogens): Disquisitions and Disputations* (Brill 2021).
Tiyanjana Maluwa, 'The Constitutive Act of the African Union and Institution-Building in Postcolonial Africa' (2003) 16 *Leiden Journal of International Law*.
Tiyanjana Maluwa, 'The OAU/African Union and International Law: Mapping New Boundaries or Revisiting Old Terrain?' (2004) 98 *ASIL Proceedings*.
Tiyanjana Maluwa, 'Reassessing Aspects of the Contribution of African States to the Development of International Law through African Regional Multilateral Treaties' (2020) 41 *Michigan Journal of International Law*.
Ty McCormick, 'The Burundi Intervention That Wasn't' *Foreign Policy* (2 February 2016).
UN Doc. A/CONF.183/9.
UN, 'Secretary-General Defends, Clarifies "Responsibility to Protect" at Berlin Event on "Responsible Sovereignty: International Cooperation for a Changed World"' SG/SM/11701, 15 July 2008 <https://press.un.org/en/2008/sgsm11701.doc.htm>.
UN, World Summit Outcome Document UN Docs SG/SM/10089 (13 September 2005).

Index

FSC
www.fsc.org
MIX
Papier | Fördert gute Waldnutzung
FSC® C083411

Kolibri 360 GmbH
Ferdinand-Jühlke-Straße 7
99095 Erfurt, Deutschland
produktsicherheit@kolibri360.de